W9-BCB-946

# The President Makers

# The President Makers

## From Mark Hanna to Joseph P. Kennedy

by Francis Russell

Little, Brown and Company
Boston/Toronto

*For my uncle*
*Charles Herbert Kent*



FIRST EDITION

T 04/76

**Library of Congress Cataloging in Publication Data**
Russell, Francis, 1910-
President makers of the twentieth century.

Bibliography: p.
Includes index.
1. United States—Politics and government—20th century. 2. President—United States—Election.
I. Title.
E743.R92 329'.00973 75-33631
ISBN 0-316-76297-0

*Published simultaneously in Canada*
*by Little, Brown & Company (Canada) Limited*

PRINTED IN THE UNITED STATES OF AMERICA

# Preface

Of the fourteen presidents of the United States in the twentieth century only five can be said to have won the office on their own. Hoover, Eisenhower and Nixon reached the White House through a kind of political determinism, Truman and Johnson by a process of elimination that more closely resembled chance. Ford attained by default the goal he never sought. The remaining eight — five Republicans and three Democrats — would never have become president if eight other men had not stood implacably behind them. Motives of these president makers were various, covering the spectrum from affection to hate. Mark Hanna and Frank Stearns developed an avuncular, almost paternal interest in McKinley and Coolidge for reasons they could not have explained to themselves, while wanting little or nothing in return. But if disinterested affection prompted Hanna and Stearns, interested affection for Franklin Roosevelt spurred on Louis Howe to attain a grey eminence, since nature had denied him a brighter color. Thomas Collier Platt was motivated by sheer malice. He would have preferred to hang Theodore Roosevelt or lock him up in a mental institution. Since he could manage neither, he arranged to neutralize that irritating overpresence by promoting him to the vacuity of the vice-presidency, unmindful of the syllogistic cliché that all men are mortal. Wilson was incidental to George Harvey's blueprint for reconstructing the Democratic party, a candidate who merely happened to fit Harvey's specifications. Personal vanity motivated Harry Daugherty and Joseph Kennedy, a vanity burned into them by their early struggles. As

Harding's obsessive backer, Daugherty — like Howe — sought the prestige he could not win alone. Personal gain was secondary, but it was still an important consideration. Kennedy's presidential ambition for his son Jack was merely an extension of his own passionate need to justify himself. He would have been equally content to see any one of his four sons president, or all four of them.

These eight makers of presidents, without giving much heed to the larger implications of their choice, changed the course of their country's history as much as any eight men of their age. However one may rate their protégés in the scale of achievement, America as we know it would be a very different place today if those presidents had been William Jennings Bryan, Alton B. Parker, Charles Evans Hughes, Leonard Wood, William Gibbs McAdoo, Al Smith, Wendell Willkie and the 1960 Richard Nixon, though whether the country would have been better or worse one can only conjecture according to one's bias.

# Contents

"No Wonder They Laugh"
*Hanna as Homer Davenport made the country see him.*

CHAPTER ONE

# The Red Boss of Cleveland: Marcus Alonzo Hanna

IF THE AMERICAN phrenologist Orson Squire Fowler had examined Mark Hanna's skull in the 1840s he would undoubtedly have felt the large twin bumps of acquisitiveness under that childish scalp. For Mark was born with the acquisitive instinct just as a bird is born with the instinct for building a nest, a blind unqualified impulse independent of consequences. His adult feeling for Ohio's Congressman William McKinley was almost as instinctive; fraternal, avuncular, paternal. "I love McKinley," he once remarked, in that innocent era when one man in public life could make such a remark about another. H. H. Kohlsaat, the Chicago multiple-lunchroom millionaire turned editor and politician, wrote that Hanna's attitude toward McKinley was "always that of a big, bashful boy toward the girl he loves," a remark Hanna liked to repeat.

Hanna is vaguely recalled from Homer Davenport's cartoons in Hearst's New York *Journal* as the capitalist arch-monster of the century's end for whom McKinley was no more than a monkey capering on the end of an organ-grinder's string. Until the spring of the 1896 election year Hanna had seemed merely an extraordinarily successful Cleveland merchant-industrialist. Only in the course of the presidential campaign that he organized and ran that year for McKinley's nomination and election did he become known nationally, transformed by Davenport's corrosive pen to Dollar Mark, a gross, bull-necked primitive in a suit covered with dollar signs and with his feet planted on a pile of money bags next to the skull of labor. Pig-eyed, rapacious, his face a blob of suet, he wore a lump of coal for a stickpin and wielded a huge cigar as if it were a club. Dollar signs were branded on his pendulous earlobes and on the ends of his thumbs. Davenport himself, after he had met Hanna, came to regret the grossness of his caricature. But the image remained. "That hurts," Hanna once told a colleague on the Republican National Committee, the tears running down his cheeks, as he showed him the latest cartoon: a gorilla-Mark trampling women and children underfoot until their eyes bulged in agony.

Despite the Hearst-Davenport image, Hanna was a personable man, portly, of medium height, with a kindly if heavy-jowled face, luminous eyes, and an almost equine way of twitching his nose and upper lip. For all his inflexible pursuit of wealth, he was in many of his social attitudes ahead of his times, and well regarded even by his adversaries. Even such an arch-reformer as Frederick Howe came to have an affection for him. The peppery progressive Harold Ickes considered him "a likable man — short and squat with a round friendly face."

For Hanna it was an often-repeated axiom that "some men must rule; the great mass of men must be ruled. Some men must own; the great mass of men must work for those who own." Yet behind this axiomatic grimness lay a warm paternalism, in flexible contrast to the laissez-faire rigidities of the Rockefellers and the Fricks and the Pullmans. Early in his business years he had found himself as a mine owner caught up in a strike at Massillon that had brought on violence, bloodshed and clashes with the militia. The lesson sank in. To win a strike with militia bayonets was to lose it. From then on Hanna chose cooperation rather than confrontation. He took pains to pay the highest wages. He was among the first capitalists to sit down at the bargaining table with labor leaders. The door to his office was always open to any man with a grievance. In a day when most employers disclaimed such responsibilities, he made provision for sick and injured workers, carrying them at half pay until they had recovered. After his first strike he was never faced with another.

Hanna was the first American politician fully to grasp the implications of the new industrialism. Before his emergence on the scene, the prevailing political image was still that of the lawyer-politician. Politics had seemed too dirty and dangerous a stream for any but a professional to swim in; businessmen had been content to angle from the banks with golden lines. Hanna took the plunge into the dubious waters. In place of the slippery spoilsmen of the Grant administration manipulated by bribes and flattery, he would substitute frank business control of the machinery of government, and in the process he would remake the old party of the abolitionists and free-soilers into the party of business — streamlined, efficient, relentless.

From the melioristic Republicanism of his political beginnings Hanna was to progress downward to the point where he became known as the Red Boss of Cleveland, whose blast furnaces cast a reddish smoke pall over the city he dominated. Yet the boss label was scarcely more accurate than Davenport's cartoons. For though Hanna had few scruples in reaching a political goal, he was never a boss in the traditional sense of organization, tribute, patronage and the lining up of voters living and dead. Once a campaign was over he tended to lose interest in the details of politics, most of which he turned over to his more assiduously political lieutenants. Within the Republican party he tolerated his enemies and tended to underestimate them. Even after he had made McKinley president and himself a United States senator, he could not always control his own northern lake city.

By the standards of his day Hanna's beginnings were easy. He was born in 1837, the second child of Leonard Hanna, an ailing country doctor, and Samantha Converse, a stern-minded schoolmistress from Vermont. Before his birth his grandfather Benjamin and six uncles had formed the firm of B. L. & T. Hanna, the leading wholesale and commission house in New Lisbon, one of the busiest trading towns in eastern Ohio. Dr. Leonard, as his health declined, gave up his rural rounds to join the family firm.

During Mark's boyhood the national canal boom that had followed the completion of the Erie Canal and that had spread across Ohio was cut short by the arrival of the railroads. Grandfather Benjamin had invested $200,000 in the ill-conceived Sandy & Beaver Canal, linking New Lisbon to the Ohio Canal thirty-five miles away. The Sandy & Beaver's completion in 1846 was also its end, bringing disaster to the countryside and ruin to the house of Hanna. Salvaging what they could from the financial collapse, the Hannas moved on to Cleveland, and Leonard and his brother

Robert, aided by a fellow townsman, Hiram Garretson, made a second start with a grocery and commission business.

In Cleveland Mark attended Central High School, where he numbered William and John D. Rockefeller among his classmates. After graduating, he was one of a freshman class of five to enter Western Reserve College. His college career ended abruptly in his sophomore year when he was suspended for helping to prepare and distribute a bawdy burlesque program for the Junior Oratoricals. In 1858 he entered the renewed family firm of Hanna, Garretson & Company. Starting near the bottom as an overalled warehouse clerk, he worked for a time as a dockhand, then a purser on a lake vessel belonging to the firm, and not long after that as one of the first traveling salesmen in the United States. Gay and sociable, deft at cards as at racing, Mark shared neither the Baptist pieties nor the cold eye for the main chance of his Rockefeller schoolmates, devoting as much time to entertaining and being entertained as he did to the family business.

The outbreak of the Civil War found the twenty-five-year-old Mark restlessly eager to join the army. But with his ailing father semiretired and his younger brother Howard less experienced in business, he felt he had to stay home and take charge of family affairs. Howard joined the Union Navy. Because the Hannas refused on principle to deal in liquor — even though the quickest and surest mercantile profits were to be made there — Garretson in 1862 withdrew from the firm. Hanna, Garretson & Company was then succeeded by Robert Hanna & Company, the new firm consisting of Dr. Leonard and his brother Robert, Mark and S. H. Baird, who remained only until Howard returned from the navy and bought him out. Two weeks after the firm was organized, Mark's father died.

In 1863 the hard-pressed Federal Government finally passed a conscription act, and early the following year Mark was drafted. Rather than buy himself an exemption, as he was allowed to do by law, he became a second lieutenant in the 29th Ohio National Guard, one of those skeletal hundred-day regiments sent to Washington for guard and garrison duty in order to release more seasoned troops for Grant's Wilderness campaign. Mark's hundred days proved less than heroic. He was mustered out in September. A few weeks later he married.

The young man with the shaved upper lip and the reddish chin whiskers covering his powerful jaw had long been one of Cleveland's most eligible bachelors. In the spring of 1862 he had met Charlotte Augusta Rhodes, the daughter of Cleveland's leading coal and iron merchant, the self-made Daniel Rhodes. A strong Democrat like his cousin, Lincoln's old debating opponent Stephen Douglas, and a not-so-strong Unionist, the testy Rhodes disapproved of his daughter's Republican ex-soldier suitor and did not mind saying so. He ordered Augusta to stop seeing the young man, an edict difficult to enforce since Mark was conspicuously ubiquitous on the Cleveland social scene and Augusta as stubborn as her father. Rhodes finally if grudgingly gave in to his wife's pleas and his daughter's tears.

Like most self-made men Rhodes was determined to control his associates and rule his family, and he insisted that Augusta and Mark after their honeymoon live in the Rhodes mansion on Franklin Avenue. His paternalism extended even to his son-in-law's business affairs, and he objected violently when Mark started up a petroleum refinery — at that time considered a most risky venture. Every time the fire bells rang the old man would remark: "There! I suppose Mark's damned oil refinery is burning down!" Mark put up with his cantankerous father-in-law for a year; then in spite of the latter's profane objections moved to a small house on Prospect Street.

In December of that same year, 1866, Mark came down with a severe attack of typhoid. His recovery was slow, and during his convalescence he grew increasingly depressed. While still under this cloud he learned that the Hanna firm's steamship, *Lac La Belle*, one of the first vessels on the lakes, had sunk after a collision, a total and uninsured loss. Then the oil refinery, as predicted by Rhodes, did burn to the ground.

The morning after the refinery's destruction, Rhodes appeared at the Prospect Street house to lay down the law to the young couple. "Now," he informed them, "I guess you two young fools will be good and come home." Mark had no alternative. With Augusta he returned to the Rhodes mansion that same day. "Your money is all gone, Mark, and I am damned glad of it," Rhodes told his ailing and penniless son-in-law by way of consolation, as he helped him unpack.

With thousands of dollars in debts, Mark was in no position to refuse when his father-in-law offered to take him into Rhodes &

Company. He knew little about coal and iron, and still felt he could make more money in oil. In spite of Rhodes's objurgations he rebuilt the refinery, later selling it to his brother Leonard who subsequently sold out at a vast profit to the Rockefellers.

By the time Mark joined the firm, Rhodes was feeling his age and ready to retire. As soon as his son-in-law was reestablished, the old man left with his wife for Europe, turning over the family mansion to his daughter. Mark rapidly demonstrated that he was the leading member of Rhodes & Company. Within six years he had built up the company to one of the largest coal and iron firms in the lake district. Coal and iron selling remained the foundation of the Rhodes business, but under his direction the firm branched out to acquire mines, smelting plants, fleets of lake steamers, docks and warehouses, shipbuilding yards, everything concerned with the iron trade but steel mills.

For all Mark's energy, shrewdness and imagination he also had the indispensable factor of luck. When he joined the Rhodes firm, the commercial and industrial expansion of the Middle West was just beginning to gather momentum. Demands for the basic ingredients of industrial life — iron, copper, steel — were clamorous and insatiable. His firm brought coal from interior Ohio and Pennsylvania to the lakeshore cities, and shipped iron ore and pig copper from the upper lake mines to foundries and factories south of Lake Erie. When scarcely out of his twenties, he became one of the leaders in coordinating such activities, in bringing system to the still haphazard industrial and commercial pattern. By the time the five-year depression of the seventies had withered the industrial bloom, his own position was unchallengeable. Prosperity, when it finally returned, made him one of the richest men in Ohio. Rhodes & Company came to be his in all but name, and it was merely a matter of form when in 1885 the firm became M. A. Hanna & Company.

For all the variety of his success, Hanna's restless nature drove him constantly into new ventures and new acquisitions. He became a director of several railroads. Almost by accident he entered the newspaper world, taking over the declining Cleveland *Herald*, once the most influential Republican paper in northern Ohio. One day out of curiosity he happened to stroll into an auction just as the Cleveland Opera House, the city's largest and handsomest theater, was being put on the block. Instinctively he began to bid, and to his surprise found himself the new owner. Almost as casually he became a banker. Sometime in 1884 he organized the Union National Bank, ostensibly to find a remunerative job for a friend, but mostly from a notion that he would like to own a bank.

The last of his miscellaneous ventures, as capricious as his purchase of the opera house but one that would in the end turn him to politics, was his taking over of the West Side Street Railway Company. Less imposing than its name, the line — consisting of several score battered wooden horsecars and a stable of decrepit nags — provided cheap but irregular service over fifteen miles of bumpy track from Cleveland's West Side to the Public Square. Years before, Rhodes had bought into the line jointly with his partner Elias Sims, a hard-fisted old steamboatman who acted as the line's president and manager. After Rhodes's death, Augusta inherited her father's West Side shares, which with the rest of her inheritance came under her husband's management. For Hanna the West Side line seemed a new toy. As a director working under Sims, he soon found himself drawn into conflict with a formidable street railway rival across the Cuyahoga River, Tom Johnson. When Johnson managed to wangle a particularly juicy franchise from the venal city council under the nose of the West Side management, Hanna, his chin whiskers bobbling with anger, confronted Sims and demanded that the old man either buy out or sell out. Sims chose to sell. With the West Side line at last under his control, Hanna proceeded to install his own superintendent, repair the tracks and the roadbed, buy new cars and horses, and bring regularity to the erratic schedule. Luck was again with him, for he started renovating his line just at a time when street railways were switching to electricity and pushing out into the suburbs. As his line prospered, he expanded it. Soon he bought up the adjoining Woodland Avenue line and began to replace his horsecars with trolleys. Expanding still further, he absorbed the Cleveland City Cable Company to form the Cleveland City Railway Company, popularly known as the Little Consolidated. As president of Little Consolidated he left the operating details to his superintendent, but he watched over the line with fatherly affection and made it into one of the most efficient in the country. Electrification brought him steady profits. His "savings banks," he came to call his street railways. Yet he had turned to public transportation rather from a superabundance of energy than from any urge to make money, and the time and effort that he put into his streetcar enterprises would far exceed any profits that they might bring him.

In Cleveland as elsewhere the franchises necessary to operate a street railway effectively required a regular greasing of the palms of local politicians. Hanna when faced with this practical necessity did not hesitate to apply the grease. Johnson across the river, nicer in his methods, preferred campaign contributions to outright bribery. Much like Hanna in drive and initiative, he had started out in life as a newsboy, then as a clerk in a street-railway company had invented a fare box that netted him thirty thousand dollars. With this money and his experience he moved confidently into public transportation. By the time he was twenty-two he owned his own street railway in Indianapolis. In 1879 he moved on to Cleveland, buying up the various small lines across the river to form the city's largest, the Big Consolidated.

Hanna saw the Big Consolidated as a direct challenge and responded with all the force of his combative nature. He and Johnson fought most of their battles in the City Council chamber. When Johnson sought an additional franchise from the council to unite his line with one on Hanna's side of the Cuyahoga in order to give a continuous crosstown ride for a nickel, he found his rival barring the way. Hanna's squat pugnacious figure now became volubly evident at each council session as he buttonholed councilmen, argued, expostulated, hammered the floor with his cane. Two days before the council's vote Councilor Elias Sims sent for Johnson and told his astonished former adversary that the two council votes he controlled were going to Johnson. "You beat me once," he explained gruffly. "I want you to beat Hanna. It takes more than a fool to beat Hanna. If you beat him, nobody can say any damned fool can beat Sims." Johnson did beat Hanna and won his franchise by a single vote.

After this defeat Hanna proposed a partnership with his formidable rival, but Johnson declined, saying that he and Hanna were too much alike and that they "would make good opponents but not good partners." Alike indeed they were, in energy, acquisitiveness, even in their solid aggressive physique. Yet there was a fundamental difference, for Hanna was and would remain the businessman in politics, whereas Johnson, for all the millions he had amassed in railways and steel and stock manipulations, would become the political reformer in business.

Johnson's journey to Damascus came on a train ride between Cleveland and Indianapolis when a news vendor persuaded him to buy a book, *Social Problems,* by an author he had never heard of, Henry George. Picking up the book, he soon found himself reading it almost without stopping, overwhelmed by George's lay religion. Within weeks he had read all of George's other books, including *Progress and Poverty.* Then from reading he turned to action. With a convert's zeal he sold his railway and steel holdings because "the requirements of my work didn't square with my principles," and resolved to apply the Georgian doctrines to his home city. "Single Tax" Johnson they now called him. Campaigning for municipal ownership and the three-cent fare, the forty-seven-year-old single-taxer Democrat was elected reform manager of Cleveland on the slogan of "people against privilege."

To Hanna, as spokesman of the iron, oil, gas, electric and transit interests, the new Johnson appeared "a radical, a socialist, a destroyer of society." As they rose in their political spheres each grew to hate the other. For such reformers as Johnson and Toledo's Bible-quoting mayor, "Golden Rule" Jones, Hanna had nothing but the practical man's contempt. Political and personal ethics he considered as impossible to combine as oil and water. In his greener years he had felt otherwise. He himself had started down the devious political road as an "innocent Republican," eager to persuade the "better elements," the taxpayers and businessmen of his own Ninth Ward, to oppose the entrenched bosses and their hangers-on. When Cleveland's Republican bosses nominated a notorious political hack for mayor, he had backed the successful Democratic candidate. Following President Garfield's assassination by a disgruntled office seeker, he had shared the general revulsion against venal politicians and bagmen. As a still-innocent Republican he had believed that city, state and country would be better served by competent nonpartisan civil servants than by dubious spoilsmen. Business itself, above all his business, would benefit.

In the election of 1880, when Garfield just managed to defeat the Democrats' pompous General Hancock, Hanna was still the innocent, but his innocence would not last long. During that campaign he organized Cleveland's industrialists into a Republican Business Men's Marching Club and led silk-hatted torchlight parades through the city. Using the personnel of his Little Consolidated as canvassers and persuaders, he elected his own councilmen and made himself undisputed boss of the West Side. His amateur efforts beyond the council he soon found frustrated. When he organized Republican rallies at his opera house, rank and file politicians attended, took his money, and went their ways. Hanna soon learned those ways and came to accept working with the professionals. They in turn found themselves forced to accept him as an unrivaled fund-raiser, the boss of the bosses. With the acquiescence, however reluctant, of the ward leaders, with the support of the city's commercial interests, with the backing of his old schoolmate Rockefeller, Hanna from his Cleveland bastion gradually moved into control of northern Ohio. The Red Boss, they began to call him, equating his political power with his power to pollute the atmosphere. "Up to the time when Mark became skipper of the good Republican ship 'Buckeye,' " a grateful Ohio politician wrote, "getting money from the National Committee for use downstate was difficult. But when Captain Hanna took command the lean days of local self-help suddenly ended and it seemed as if the funds came to us by the barrel. Did those of us who were running for office downstate feel kindly toward Uncle Mark? You know the answer!"

The Ohio of Hanna's emergent day was considered a key state by any would-be president. Indeed, politicians of both parties had come to believe that a presidential candidate who lost Ohio would lose the country. Within its borders the state reflected the conflicting regional interests and tensions of the country at large. Rural Protestants of a vengeful fundamentalism confronted an urban Catholic proletariat; the Ohio-born Anti-Saloon League flourished within sight and sound of German beer drinkers; while that most formidable of city bosses, George Barnstable Cox, ruled Cincinnati invisibly from the back room of his Mecca Saloon. Yankee farmers had given the northern regions an almost New England atmosphere, whereas in the southern sections the common speech took on the drawling tones of the Confederacy. Ohio had been on the main line of the Underground Railway spiriting slaves north to Canada; yet the state had also sent the copperhead Clement Vallandigham to Congress, the most redoubtable opponent of Lincoln and the Civil War.

If politics is in most places the art of the possible, in Ohio it became the art of the impossible, of walking a picket fence between Protestants and Catholics, Wets and Drys, farmers and workers, "gold" zealots and paper-money fanatics, Northerners and Southerners — a balancing act much aided by the thought-concealing baroque oratory then favored by most public figures. Nor, even in the face of potential electoral disaster, could Ohio's nominally majority Republicans muster a self-protective united front. No one state boss was ever able to impose his unity on the regional bosses as Platt had done in New York and Quay in Pennsylvania. Ohio Republican leaders fought one another with more vindictive zeal than they did the Democrats. "I think there is only one thing I cannot understand," the exasperated young Theodore Roosevelt wrote, "and that is Ohio politics."

The two most powerful rivals in Ohio's Republican party — Hanna would make a third — were John Sherman, perpetual United States senator and almost as perpetual presidential candidate, and the fiery-tongued Governor Joseph Benson Foraker, known from his incandescent spread-eagle oratory as "Fire Alarm Joe" and "Boomtara." Sherman, the brother of the general who had scorched the red Georgian earth from Atlanta to the sea, had his roots in the pre–Civil War era and seemed fashioned from the same lawyer-statesman mold as Clay and Webster. "Uncle Jawn" they called him in his home state, where he was respected and admired as an institution rather than loved as a man. The "Ohio Icicle" the outsiders called him.

Sherman had been elected to Congress in 1854 as a Whig, and shortly afterward was among the first to organize the new Republican party in Ohio. In 1860 the Ohio Assembly elected him to the United States Senate, and during the Civil War he served as the chairman of the Finance Committee, sponsoring the issue of paper greenbacks to finance the war. After the war he was responsible for the Refunding Act which insured specie payment to those sufficiently well-off during the war to have exchanged their greenbacks for government bonds.

As Hayes's secretary of the treasury from 1877 to 1881, Uncle Jawn made an end to the surviving greenbacks, leading his countrymen, reluctant or otherwise, out of the inflationary bog to the firm land of hard currency with a skill that placed him among the great treasury names of Hamilton, Gallatin and Chase. Indignant ex-soldiers, however, charged that he had paid them in paper and was now paying bondholders in gold, and called the Refunding Act "the crime of '73." Despite the ex-soldiers, he might in 1880 have been nominated for president over Garfield if he had been more accommodating in the use of patronage.

If Uncle Jawn was in the old mold of the lawyer-statesman, Fire Alarm Joe Foraker was in the new mold of the lawyer-politician. Though he would later ally himself with predatory corporations, in the immediate years after the Civil War the still-boyish orator with eyes that shot sparks above his drooping mustache seemed full of idealistic courage, a battler against corporate greed and corruption. Eloquent on the rights of the people, passionate in defense of the boys in blue, he sent his audiences into frenzies with his stock-in-trade bloody-shirt invective. While active in politics, he was equally active as counsel for railroads, public utilities and trusts. Untroubled by any thought of conflict of interests, he felt that the wealth he acquired from looking after the political needs of assorted corporations was his incidental due. His conscience, though elastic, was clear. "The difference between Foraker and me," Hanna once explained succinctly, "is that I buy and he sells."

At the outbreak of the Civil War Foraker had joined the Union Army as a sixteen-year-old private, surviving the great campaigns and marching through Georgia with Sherman's general-brother. In 1882 his political career began with his election as judge of the superior court at Cincinnati. The following year he was chosen Republican candidate for governor, but failed election by a few thousand votes. He was again nominated in 1885 and this time elected, without, however, carrying his home city. Faced with the necessity of securing his Cincinnati bastion, he cemented an alliance with Boss Cox that gave them both control of the southern section of the state. The solid thirty thousand votes, dead or living, that Cox could deliver in any election through his "Strangler" organization, were, when added to Foraker's own wider and more mercurial following, enough to carry most state elections. But for the rise of Hanna in the north, the Foraker-Cox organization might have succeeded in conquering Ohio.

The Red Boss did not at first appear as a challenger but as a Republican ally. His nomination as delegate-at-large to the Republican National Convention of 1884 marked his introduction to national politics; at this convention he came to know his fellow Ohio delegates, Foraker and William McKinley, Jr. It was a Blaine convention, with the galleries hysterically and most of the delegates boisterously for James G. Blaine, Ingersoll's Plumed Knight of the somewhat tarnished pinions, the magnetic man from Maine making his third bid for the Republican nomination. In spite of the efforts of the reform Republicans, the Plumed Knight was nominated on the fifth ballot. Hanna felt himself closer to Foraker than to McKinley at the convention, for he and Fire Alarm Joe were pledged to Sherman while the young McKinley — for all his youth already showing signs of rotundity — was for Blaine.

On returning to Ohio Hanna wrote to Foraker: "Among the few pleasures I found at the Convention was meeting and working with you. . . . It will not be my fault if our acquaintance does not ripen, . . . for I shall certainly *go for you* whenever you are within reach." A year later their acquaintance had so ripened that Hanna served on Fire Alarm Joe's campaign committee in his second, and this time successful, candidacy for governor. In 1887 Hanna again supported Foraker, backing him with much-needed funds. The governor's reelection found Hanna the most influential political figure in Cleveland. His friendship with Foraker, however, did not survive the governor's second inauguration. Hanna had managed and financed two Foraker campaigns, and like all politicians he expected a return; in his case the appointment of William Baynes — whom he had tried in vain to elect mayor of Cleveland — as state oil inspector. That incongruously named office was one of the juiciest plums a governor had at his disposal, for the oil inspector was paid fees by oil refineries throughout the state and controlled the appointment of deputies who did the actual inspecting. Without notifying Hanna, Foraker appointed his crony, Boss Cox, to the lush position, and Baynes was not even made a deputy. Hanna never felt the same about Foraker again. Yet strained though relations were between the two Ohio leaders, they were not broken until the national convention of 1888.

Following Blaine's narrow defeat for the presidency in 1884, Hanna became convinced that Sherman could and should be the Republican candidate in 1888. He had met Uncle Jawn shortly after the Philadelphia convention and was impressed by what he considered the firmness of his Republican principles. By 1887 the two had become close friends. Unlike Sherman and Foraker and even McKinley, Hanna himself had no great hunger for public office. But by now, with the elderly Sherman as his protégé, he developed an appetite for working behind the scenes and began to fancy himself in the role of a president maker. All the fervor and energy that he had put into his business enterprises, he now directed to pushing Sherman toward the White House. Early in 1888 he became the senator's campaign manager, and Sherman named him his personal representative at the convention. In 1888, after four years of Cleveland, the tide was again running Republican. The tariff was the chief issue of the campaign, with industrialists and manufacturers welded into a united front against the president's low-tariff policies; and it was in this campaign that the old party of the abolitionists, free soilers, reconstructionists and disaffected Whigs began to assume the solid outline of the party of Big Business.

If Sherman, astutely guided by Hanna, was the leading contender for the Republican nomination in 1888, rank-and-file Republicans still cherished the mesmeric image of the Plumed Knight. Blaine himself showed so little concern at the possibility of his nomination that late in 1887 he went abroad. In May he wrote to Whitelaw Reid, editor of the New York *Tribune*, that "if I should now by speech or silence, by omission or commission, permit my name in any event to come before the convention, I should incur the reproach of being incandid with those who have always been candid with me." Nevertheless, Sherman felt that Blaine was merely feigning reluctance in order to test his strength. "My theory is," he told Hanna, "that Blaine is a candidate, has been from the beginning and will be until defeated."

As the Republicans gathered in Chicago in June for their convention amidst the ritual flag-waving parades and blaring of bands, the name that was still whispered from delegate to delegate was that of Blaine. In spite of the refusal of the Republican independents to support him, in spite of his murky railroad dealings that had come to light with the publication of the Mulligan letters, Blaine was still the magnetic leader that could touch men's hearts. Chicago's streets echoed with

> Blaine, Blaine, James G. Blaine.
> We've had him once and we'll have him again!

Ohio's delegation was nevertheless solidly for Sherman — Hanna had taken care of that — and Hanna, Foraker and McKinley were again delegates. Yet though Foraker wore a Sherman badge and would indeed flutter the rafters with his nominating speech for Uncle Jawn, Hanna and Sherman had long ceased to trust him. As governor, Foraker had refused President Cleveland's conciliating request for Northern governors to return to the southern states Confederate battle flags captured in the Civil War. On meeting Foraker at the convention, Hanna, who respected Cleveland and liked southerners, told Fire Alarm Joe that his gesture was "stale" and might damage Sherman's candidacy. Foraker considered the remark an affront, and said so. Hanna saw the incident as the first step in breaking up their uneasy alliance. Foraker had his own version of the break as he wrote in his autobiography-apologia, *Notes of a Busy Life*.

> A great many colored delegates from the South, as is their custom, had tickets to the Convention which they desired to sell. They brought their tickets to our rooms at the hotel, and Mr. Hanna, in the presence of us all, bought them. I protested against such methods, saying that it would bring scandal on the entire delegation and hurt Sherman's cause. Mr. Hanna and I had a spirited discussion over the matter, and it resulted in my leaving the rooms and seeking an apartment on another floor.

The buying-up of delegates from the South's rotten boroughs through purchase of their gallery tickets was an old Republican custom that would continue into the days of William Howard Taft. To Hanna, the indignation of Ohio's slippery governor must have seemed grimly comic. For the Red Boss of Cleveland, even as he dealt out his money and stacked up his southern delegates, was aware that at some critical moment Foraker intended to maneuver the convention into a stampede for Blaine that would carry him in its swirling wake as the party's vice-presidential nominee.

The maneuvers of that convention, marked by furtive comings and goings in the sweaty hall and in neighboring hotels, are unrealistically simplified when outlined in print. At the start of the balloting Hanna, shepherding his southern votes plus the delegates from Ohio and Boss Quay's Pennsylvania, was convinced that the swing to Sherman would soon draw the state favorite-son votes like a magnet. But other candidates had been suborning Hanna's black sheep, reputedly at $50 a head. Although Sherman on the first ballot had double the votes of any of the favorite sons, he still lacked a majority and on the next three ballots his total fell away. By the time the convention adjourned for the weekend it was clear that he did not have enough strength to win, and the predicted stampede for Blaine seemed in the making.

Over the weekend there was a scurrying in dark places, meetings between bosses and favorite sons, a certain amount of sentiment for or at least talk of Congressman McKinley, the "young Napoleon" of protection — a sentiment quietly cultivated by New York's catlike Boss Platt, who saw McKinley as a means of undermining Sherman. The members of the Foraker Marching Club of Ohio, ready for the quick change, wore Blaine's name on the reverse side of their Sherman badges, and Foraker — who had been privately offered second place on the ticket by a Blaine lieutenant — told reporters that since Sherman was no longer a possibility he would now vote for Blaine. Blaine's two sons circulated persuasively among the delegates. Desperately Hanna telegraphed Sherman in Washington to withdraw in favor of McKinley and "save the party from the Blaine lunatics." Sherman considered that this would be unfair to his supporters. Meanwhile, frantic cables from Blaine lieutenants in Chicago to the leader in Scotland brought the flat order to "refrain from voting for me." That evening Elkins, Bosses Quay and Platt and other Republican leaders of the inner circle met at the Grand Pacific Hotel and in the midnight hours decided on a compromise candidate. Their choice was the undistinguished Benjamin Harrison, a longtime Blaine partisan, ex-senator from Indiana and grandson of the hero of Tippecanoe.

When the convention opened on Monday, the dalliant Foraker was back in the wavering Sherman camp, but Harrison with Blaine support at once took the lead and on the third ballot of the day gathered in almost two-thirds of the delegates. Foraker, with mercurial zeal, sprang to his feet to move that the nomination be made unanimous. And so it was. In their platform the Republicans, after condemning polygamy and Chinese immigration, adopted a high tariff platform, going so far as to declare for "the entire repeal of internal taxes rather than surrender any part of our protective system." The Democrats at their convention had renominated Cleveland by acclaim while taking his low tariff policy as their platform.

Cleveland's tariff-based campaign represented the first real challenge to the business world and its corporate privileges since the Civil War, and in accepting the challenge the Republicans aligned themselves irrevocably with big business. The campaign, for all its mildness — Cleveland considered it beneath the dignity of his office to take the stump — became known as the Boodle Campaign, from the amount of money poured out by the Republicans. No such sums had ever before been raised or spent in an American election. Instead of the customary assessments of officeholders, the Republican National Committee levied dues on interested industrialists and manufacturers. As if to emphasize the new look, Hanna, the "cheerful giver," had shaved off his chin whiskers. Harrison would be, in fact, the last major party candidate to wear a beard.

All in all the Republicans raised close to four million dollars, an astonishing sum for its day. Backed by the Protective Tariff League and "One Thousand Defenders of American Industry," John "One Price" Wanamaker, the Philadelphia merchant, formed a committee of high-tariff businessmen. Blaine returned from Scotland to take the stump for Harrison and Protection. Republican leaders so pounded home the message of a high tariff as a protector of the American workingman that even the Knights of Labor were induced to come out for Harrison, and the Republican message found its way into pay envelopes along with the admonition that a Cleveland victory would mean less work and lower wages. Even more persuasive than argument was the amplitude of Republican money. In the critical state of New York, Cleveland's enemy, Tammany Governor David Hill, accepted the backing of the Republican organization for his own reelection in return for his surreptitious support of Harrison. On election day Boss Quay rushed gangs of his Philadelphia ward boys to New York to vote. Harrison carried the state. In Indiana, some twenty to thirty thousand floaters were dragooned by Republican organizers into G.A.R. halls, each paid three five-dollar gold pieces, and marched to the polls to vote for Harrison who with such help won in his home state by 2,344 votes. Although Cleveland carried the country by over a hundred thousand popular votes, in the electoral college the votes of New York and Indiana gave Harrison 233 votes to his 168. "Providence," Presbyterian Deacon Harrison intoned on hearing the election news, "has given us the victory." "Think of the man!" was Boss Quay's sputtering reaction. "He ought to know that Providence hadn't a damned thing to do with it!"

Though Hanna had worked loyally and vigorously for Harrison, his heart was elsewhere. Uncle Jawn, as Hanna and everyone else except Sherman himself now knew, was through as a Republican presidential candidate. "I am going to stop riding the wrong horse," Hanna told his brother-in-law ruefully. Yet his urge to become a president maker persisted, and the void left by the elderly bearded Sherman he now saw filled by the square clean-shaven younger face of Congressman McKinley.

Hanna's first meeting with McKinley had taken place sometime in the seventies, when McKinley as a rising young lawyer undertook the unpopular defense of twenty-three Massillon miners charged with setting fire to the Hanna-Rhodes coal mines in the 1876 strike that had converted Hanna to collective bargaining. Each man made so little impression on the other that neither could remember the occasion in after years. Although the two were fellow-delegates to the 1884 convention, it was not until four years later that Congressman McKinley obtruded on Hanna's political consciousness. McKinley's stubbornly honest loyalty to Sherman, his refusal to allow himself even remotely to be considered a dark horse candidate, impressed Hanna.

By his forty-sixth year McKinley — the Major, they called him — had contrived a stately if sedentary presence that he had even come to believe in himself.

> He was a pious soul [wrote John T. Flynn] distinguished in appearance, an able speaker, and greatly admired for his domestic virtues. He staged himself elaborately, remained always in character. He was a man who looked learned, yet who possessed very limited information on history or economics or law. He was never a student or reader of books though he came to be looked upon as a model of wisdom. His range of ideas was, like that of Mark Hanna, limited. He took up the philosophy, the mood, the character of the generation in which he was born and held fast to it. As a politician he had almost no fixed or important political views which could not be easily altered to suit his party.*

* *Scribner's*, August, 1936.

The young Kansas journalist William Allen White saw in McKinley "a statesman's face, unwrinkled, unperturbed; a face without vision but without guile . . . the mask of a kindly dull gentleman . . . a cast not typical to represent American politics; on the whole dumb, and rarely reaching above the least common denominator of the popular intelligence. . . . He walked among men like a bronze statue . . . determinedly looking for his pedestal." It was this handsome politicians' politician, a man with less intelligence but more integrity than himself that Hanna now determined should by the grace of Mark be the next Republican President of the United States.

By the time McKinley had reached his forties he had indeed come to resemble a statue, his frock coat and stiff white shirt as much part of him as his own skin, his square face with its tufted eyebrows a solemn mask. During his years in Congress he had made himself a tariff expert and one of the leading advocates of protection, not from any sectional interest but from the larger view in which he saw a tariff wall as a rampart behind which American industries and workers could prosper, happily safe against cheap foreign labor and manufacturers. McKinley, a man without enemies, seemed to Hanna cast in the presidential mold both in his appearance and in his record. As an Ohio country boy of eighteen who had worked in a post office briefly and taught school, he had volunteered for the Union army following the fall of Fort Sumter and had seen four years of fighting. Made a second lieutenant in the field, he was described by his commanding officer — General and President-to-be Rutherford Hayes — as "one of the bravest officers in the army." At twenty-two he left the army a brevet major, entered law school and after a year passed his bar examination and set himself up as a lawyer in Canton, Ohio. The good-looking young lawyer with the pleasant manner, a teetotaler, a devout Methodist, a great joiner of fraternal organizations, soon found himself a local success. An elderly judge who was on the point of retiring took him into partnership, and McKinley did not have to wait the usual years to build up a practice. He was elected president of the Canton Y.M.C.A., and county prosecutor, and in 1871 he married a charming but fragile belle of Canton society, Ida Saxton. Eleven months afterward their first child, Katherine, was born. Two years later Ida gave birth to a second daughter who lived only a few months. Katherine died at the age of four. The loss of her children sent Ida into a neurasthenic melancholia from which she never recovered, and for the rest of her life she remained an invalid, subject to epileptic seizures, capricious, unreasonable, demanding. With quiet courage her husband devoted himself to her, consoled her, endured her whims.

McKinley's nature and impulses turned him to politics, but the bustling preoccupations of politics also grew to be an escape from the tragedy of his domestic life. Politics and the machinery of politics became the engrossing, almost the sole interest of his middle years. He was first elected to Congress in 1876 and defeated a Democratic attempt to gerrymander him out of his seat two years later. Elected for a third term, he just missed election in the Democratic sweep of 1882, but 1884 found him once more in Congress. Congressman Joe Cannon of Missouri, that testy and cynical observer of his fellow politicians, maintained that McKinley kept his ear so close to the ground that he got it full of grasshoppers.

Hanna's initial efforts to push his protégé forward foundered in November, 1889, when he went to Washington to lobby for McKinley's election as speaker of the newly Republican House of Representatives. Thomas B. Reed, the deft cynical parliamentarian from Maine, easily defeated the man he contemptuously referred to as "Napoleon." McKinley, typically, made no effort on his own behalf. As consolation for the missed speakership he was appointed chairman of the Ways and Means Committee and as such became responsible for Republican tariff policy. The bill that he prepared and that would bear his name was not an instrument for revenue or even for protection, but a means to exclude completely cheap foreign goods made by cheap foreign labor. McKinley hated the word "cheap." "It is not a word of hope," he said; "it is not a word of inspiration! It is the badge of poverty; it is the signal of distress." Not only would his bill shield infant industries from foreign competition, it would even nurture some — such as the steel-plate industry — that were yet to be born.

McKinley's attempt to put the United States behind a Chinese tariff wall was indeed successful, but success was followed by such a sharp rise in retail prices and such farm discontent that in the mid-term congressional elections the topheavy Republican majority was almost swept away and the Populists emerged as a protest third party. McKinley lost his seat, not so much as a reaction to his eponymous tariff as because of another and more successful gerrymandering of his district by Ohio's newly Democratic legislature. He accepted the defeat with a forced serenity, observing to Cannon — who had also been temporarily retired that year — that on the whole he was really glad it had happened. "That is what I am saying to everyone," Cannon admitted, "but, boys, don't let's lie to one another!" Hanna, unwavering in his determination, saw in the defeat the seeds of future victory. Protection, he was convinced, would triumph in the end. Meanwhile Bill McKinley and the McKinley bill had at least become household words.

Hanna's breach with Foraker had widened when in the state convention of 1889 he opposed Fire Alarm Joe's third-term candidacy for governor. In spite of Hanna's opposition Foraker was nominated, only to be defeated in the election — a defeat he blamed on the "treachery" of Hanna and McKinley. In revenge he released to a Cleveland newspaper a copy of a contract, signed by both Sherman and McKinley, in which a Democratic congressman, James Campbell, had attempted to use his official position to sell the government a patent ballot box. The document was a forgery, but even if it had been genuine, Foraker had shown himself willing to implicate leaders of his own party in a fraud without warning them or giving them a hearing.

With a Democratic governor installed in Columbus, with Foraker (he hoped) driven from public life, Hanna now set his sights on the 1891 state election. So deftly did he manage the Republican convention that McKinley was nominated for governor almost without opposition. Foraker, maneuvering to have the next legislature elect him to the United States Senate in place of the antiquated Sherman, even consented in the interests of party unity to make McKinley's nominating speech. But a Republican nomination in Ohio gave no assurance of election in that uncertain year. Harrison and his cabinet of businessmen had shown themselves aloofly indifferent to the distress of farmers harried by successive years of drought and workers whose wages remained stationary or fell while prices soared in the wake of the McKinley Tariff. "The Period of No Decision," Harrison's administration had come to be called. Yet in spite of the unpopularity of his party and of his tariff, McKinley had to demonstrate his hold on the people of Ohio by winning the election. Defeat, as Hanna well realized, would eliminate him as a presidential possibility. The Red Boss was equally concerned with defeating Foraker's attempt to oust Sherman from the Senate. In this campaign Hanna's efforts were devoted primarily to raising money, and this he managed with his usual flair, persuading industrialists even outside Ohio to contribute, on the grounds that a defeat for McKinley would be a defeat for protection. In such efforts Hanna was too deft, too knowing to fail. Not only was McKinley elected by a large majority in a year of Republican reverses but he carried along a Republican majority in the legislature. The election was Hanna's first real political triumph. Foraker, however, managed to sway so many legislators that for a time it looked as if he might succeed in ending Sherman's long tenure. When the situation appeared desperate for Uncle Jawn, Hanna went to Columbus purse in hand and took charge, saving the day for his friend while humiliating his enemy. Sherman admitted afterward that he owed his reelection to Hanna's "energy, enthusiasm and ability to bend men to his will"— and he might have added, "to his pocketbook."

Throughout McKinley's two-year term, Hanna carefully watched over the major's interests, bending circumstances toward the propitious moment when he could launch a full-fledged movement to make the governor a president. To further his long-range strategy he appointed his friend ex-Senator Charles Dick chairman of the Republican State Committee, instructing him to have McKinley speak wherever it would do the most good, and to run all local campaigns with the presidential year 1896 in mind. The realistic Hanna knew that the increasingly unpopular Harrison would undoubtedly be renominated in 1892 and almost as undoubtedly be defeated. All the Red Boss needed to do was to keep his man in the public eye for the ensuing four years.

As governor of Ohio McKinley eschewed national issues. Nothing he did was notable, everything he did was conscientious. He said little, and the effect was deceptively oracular. For all his starched dignity he was accessible to all, a sympathetic listener, with a politician's instinctive rapport with the people. Ever since he had defended the Massillon miners he remained popular with workingmen, and he managed to keep the goodwill of union leaders even after he felt obliged to call out the militia in a Mine Workers dispute. Reluctant as he must then have been to act, he tempered his action by strict orders to the militiamen to avoid conflict with the strikers. He was described as "colorlessly fair," but both sides trusted him, and his popularity grew with his months in office.

Although Hanna, for all his efforts for Harrison in 1888, had been snubbed by the White House in his patronage requests, he had no intention of contesting the president's 1892 renomination. Yet, a tactical move to keep his candidate in the public eye, he made the gesture of pushing McKinley's name forward as an alternate candidate. When the Republicans held their national convention in Minneapolis, Hanna had McKinley badges printed and opened a McKinley headquarters in the West House, closing it down, however, before the balloting began.

Unenthusiastically renominated, Harrison was defeated in the election — as Hanna had foreseen — by a revitalized Cleveland campaigning against the McKinley tariff and the Sherman Silver Purchase Act. For Cleveland his victory turned out to be a hollow one, since his return to the White House was followed within weeks by the Great Panic of 1893. By the end of the year 642 banks had closed, a quarter of the country's heavy industries had shut down, most railroads were in the hands of receivers, prosperous farmers saw themselves ruined and their farms foreclosed as corn dropped to 36¢ a bushel and cotton to 10¢ a pound, and the anonymous unemployed walked the city streets where grass grew between the cobbles.

Harrison's defeat had cleared the way for McKinley's nomination in 1896, and the 1893 panic with its inevitable reaction against the party in office seemed to be clearing the way for his election. Then, even as the political prospect grew pleasing, disaster struck. Some time earlier McKinley had endorsed the note of a boyhood friend, Robert Walker, for $17,000. McKinley had a trusting nature, but would have found it difficult in any case to have turned down the man who had once lent him $5,000 to go to law school — money that McKinley had never paid back. Walker, a respected banker and industrialist, had taken a flyer in manufacturing tin plate, and when he found that he had lost his own fortune in the new enterprise he tried to stave off collapse with other people's money. Several times he appeared at the governor's office to have his promissory notes renewed, and the guileless McKinley signed the notes "in blank." When other creditors finally caught up with Walker and bankruptcy followed, McKinley found that Walker had secretly raised the notes and that he himself was obligated to pay $130,000 — a sum far greater than he and his wife possessed. To a man of McKinley's integrity, retirement from public life seemed the only course, and he was preparing to resign as governor just as Hanna arrived to check him. In such a crisis Hanna was all action. Exuding confidence, he told McKinley to stay in office and leave the finances to him. Stressing McKinley's importance to the party, with irresistible persuasiveness he tapped such archcapitalists as Andrew Carnegie, Henry Frick, and H. H. Kohlsaat, and within a few days of McKinley's renomination had raised enough money to pay off the governor's debts. McKinley's financial difficulties when they became publicly known only increased his popularity. Here at least, it seemed, was a politician who had not profited from office. Over five thousand unsolicited small donations arrived in his mail, many of them from Democrats.

Hanna was triumphantly vindicated that November when McKinley was reelected governor by the greatest Ohio majority since the Civil War. Hundreds of telegrams and letters of congratulations poured into the major's Canton home, hailing him as the next president of the United States, and he with quiet imperturbability agreed privately while maintaining public silence. For McKinley was gradually coming to the belief that fate had destined him to be president. A few days after the election the Cleveland *Leader* published a cartoon showing Uncle Sam pointing to the rising sun of McKinley in 1896, the dawn of a new prosperity. It was a symbol that McKinley appreciated and that Hanna would exploit to its limits: the "Advance Agent of Prosperity."

As the Cleveland depression years succeeded each other in the wake of the panic, Hanna's slogan loomed larger. Distress increased the western and Populist clamor for silver. Cleveland, standing firm against such inflationary pressures, forced the repeal of the Sherman Silver Purchase Act, which he maintained was draining the treasury of gold and threatening to cut the value of the dollar in half. His efforts to alter the McKinley tariff were less successful, for a Democratic-sponsored Wilson-Gorman Bill arrived on his desk so riddled with amendments — some six hundred of them — that he refused to sign it, allowing it to become law without his signature. That butchered bill's failure to alleviate the depression seemed proof of McKinley's claim that any lowering of the barriers he had raised would injure the country. Silver Democrats, calling themselves the Wild Horses, broke with their "gold" president. In Ohio General Coxey was gathering the unemployed to march on Washington, while "Coin" Harvey held forth in his eloquent pamphlets on the gold standard as the villain of the times. Desperation gave way to strikes, and Cleveland's repute dimmed further in the violence that followed after he ordered troops to Chicago to protect the mails in the Pullman strike of 1894. That year the Republicans scored such gains in the mid-term elections that they outnumbered the Democrats in Congress by over two to one. The Democratic Party found itself fragmenting over the currency issue. State organizations one after the other were being taken over by the Silver Democrats, while the volubly rising Populists bid for an alliance with them and the western Republicans. As the year 1896 approached, Silver with a capital S had replaced the tariff as the country's leading political issue, and Cleveland in the gold-plated isolation of the White House seemed a repudiated president.

After the 1894 Republican sweep, Hanna decided to retire from the company that had been his chief concern for the last twenty-eight years and devote all his time and energy to making McKinley the next president. Despite McKinley's almost superstitious conviction that he was one day destined to become president of the United States, neither he nor Hanna was willing to trust wholly to destiny. Hanna busied himself in building up the country's first really streamlined political organization, papering the land with copies of McKinley's speeches, deluging the mails with McKinley posters, tracts, pamphlets, flyers, badges and buttons. The Republican party in the South might be no more than a skeleton without flesh and blood, but Hanna took care to have most of the skeletal southern delegates in his capacious pocket a year before the convention.

In May of 1895 Hanna received an unexpected setback when Foraker and Cox outsmarted him at the Ohio convention at Zanesville by nominating their own candidate for governor while persuading the delegates to endorse Foraker as the next United States senator. Foraker's private secretary, Charles Kurtz, was even made chairman of the state committee. To those outside Ohio, the so-called Zanesville Rout cast doubts not only on

McKinley's strength within his own state but on Hanna's long-term strategy. In swift retaliation Hanna moved the McKinley organization to Cleveland, where, with the help of Major Charles Dick and Ohio's Attorney General J. K. Richards, he felt he could better shape developments. He kept lavish open house, and with McKinley present entertained a sequence of influential Republicans in an almost permanent house party. His agents made confidential calls on Republican committeemen across the country. More and more McKinley, the Republican without enemies, the soothing presence whose very name had become a symbol of economic and political nationalism, seemed the most desirable candidate. Straw votes that Hanna had taken in selected states confirmed the rising tide of popular favor.

Against the tide stood the political dike controlled by the eastern bosses led by Platt and Quay. Unenthusiastic though they were about the Ohio governor, they were nevertheless willing to listen to McKinley if McKinley in turn would listen to reason. In the autumn of 1895 Hanna went east to talk terms. Platt and Quay were blunt. In exchange for their support they demanded two cabinet appointments and control of patronage within their states. Hanna would have been willing to pay the price for what seemed to him the last real obstacle to McKinley's success. But McKinley felt otherwise. "Mark, there are some things in this world that come too high," he told his friend. "If I cannot be president without promising to make Tom Platt secretary of the treasury, I will never be president."

The only other candidates of consequence were the discredited ex-President Harrison and New England's Speaker Reed, the "Czar" of the House of Representatives. When a friend remarked to the vitriolic Reed that he was the logical Republican presidential choice, he replied that "the convention could do worse and probably will." In January of 1896 Platt and Quay held a conference of leaders in New York to determine the best way of stopping McKinley. With Platt controlling New York, with Reed keeping his hold on New England, their plan was to split the convention by sponsoring favorite sons in the northern states and by buying up as many southern delegates as possible. But when Platt attempted to call "snap" southern conventions to line up delegates, he found that "Hanna had the South practically solid before some of us waked up."

After some indecision, Harrison announced in February that he was not a candidate. McKinley was now left with Reed who, though he detested the Ohio governor, refused to campaign actively for himself. Hard times were giving the candidate of Protection and Prosperity a glamour that no other Republican candidate could approach. John Hay noted that "the McKinley boom shows curious and increasing vitality." Much of the increase was due to Hanna. All over the country, even in Reed's New England, he organized his McKinley clubs. Before the nomination campaign was over he had spent over $100,000 of his own money — an enormous sum in those days — and he spent it with prudent effectiveness. Turning the Quay-Platt threat into a challenge, he and McKinley proclaimed "The Bosses Against the People!"

Hanna used his home state for a formal declaration of McKinley's candidacy, arranging to hold the Ohio convention early in March. Although Foraker controlled the state organization, when the McKinley machine — which looked like a bandwagon and moved like a steamroller — bore down on him, he deftly jumped aboard.

Ohio was a foregone conclusion. Hanna determined to demonstrate McKinley's inevitability in boss-ridden Illinois where the senior senator, Shelby Cullom, was a favorite son, chiefly from his fancied resemblance to Lincoln. Hanna was lucky in finding an Illinois leader in the young and dynamic former Congressman Charles Dawes, who was eager to challenge Cullom and bring the Illinois delegates into the McKinley camp. He would, he told Hanna, "make the machine sick before we get through with them." Against odds Dawes did just that, although the outcome was still in doubt when the state convention met in Chicago in April. On the decision day Hanna sat at his big roll-top desk in Cleveland for ten hours, telephone in hand, and did not quit until he learned that Cullom had withdrawn. "That settles it," a Reed manager said resignedly on hearing the news; "McKinley will be nominated."

At the June national Republican convention in St. Louis McKinley's nomination was assured on the first ballot, even though Reed's name as well as those of several favorite sons were placed before the convention as token gestures. It fell to Foraker to nominate the man he despised, in an oratorical shower of sparks phosphorescent even for him:

> On behalf of the dismantled chimney and the deserted factory at its base, that the furnaces may once more flame, the mighty wheels revolve, the whistles scream, the anvils ring, the spindles hum . . . that the firesides may again glow, the women sing, the children laugh, yes, and on behalf of the American flag and all it stands for and represents, for the honor of every stripe, for the glory of every star, that its power may fill the earth and its splendor fill the sky, I ask for the nomination of that loyal American, that Christian gentleman, soldier, statesman, patriot, William McKinley!*

On the increasingly prickly issue of the currency, McKinley had kept a discreet bimetallic silence. No one knew just where he stood. In Congress he had voted repeatedly for increased silver coinage and once even for a free silver bill. He would have preferred an ambiguous sound-money platform, and even Hanna with his heart of gold was not eager to alienate the Silver West by too obvious a commitment to the gold standard. Yet the Red Boss knew that the leaders and party paymasters of the East, though they were prepared to accept the inevitability of McKinley, were not prepared to tolerate financial heresy. Although Hanna himself was as sound as any easterner on the currency, he preferred to float the impression that only with reluctance had he yielded to eastern pressure.

While the bands blared outside and delegates reinforced themselves inside at the bars, a select committee prepared a currency platform that had been underlined by J. P. Morgan himself. Eight years before, the Republicans, in opposition to Cleveland's Gold Democrats, had declared themselves "in favor of the use of both gold and silver as money," and condemned the Democrats for their efforts to demonetize silver. In 1896 the platform had veered round to sound money and against the "free coinage of silver." The shift was received ominously by the western Republicans. Led by Colorado's Senator William Teller—one of the founders of the Republican party — thirty-four delegates from the Silver states marched down the aisle and out of the hall amidst the jeering howls of the majority with Hanna's bull voice bellowing "Go! Go!" In their absence the platform was voted in with jubilation, ten thousand delegates and spectators rising to their feet

* Minutes of the Republican National Convention, 1896.

to sing "America" while newspapermen tossed yellow telegraph blanks in the air.

After the applause and demonstrations following McKinley's overwhelming nomination on the first ballot there were cries of Hanna! Hanna! from all over the convention floor. Standing up with awkward pride the happily embarrassed Red Boss told the delegates that "what feeble efforts I may have contributed to the result, I am here to lay . . . at the feet of my party and upon the altar of my country." It was his moment of triumph. A huge crowd met him at the Cleveland railroad station on his return, drowned out his stammered thanks with their cheers, and escorted his carriage home. On the way he caught the eye of an old friend at the edge of the crowd, threw out his chest in mock pride, pointed to himself and called out genially: "Big Injun! Me big Injun!"

With Cleveland as committed to the gold standard as any eastern Republican, McKinley even after his nomination still refused to take the currency question seriously, falling back on vague phrases like "sound money" and "an honest dollar." "I am a tariff man standing on a tariff platform," he told his friend Judge William Day. "This money matter is too prominent. In thirty days you won't hear anything about it." "In thirty days," the judge warned him, "you won't hear of anything else!"

By the time the Democrats met in Chicago three weeks after the Republican convention, the Silver issue had indeed dimmed all others. Under its inflationary banner the anti-Cleveland Democrats at last made common cause with the Populists and Teller's western Republicans, rallying the bankrupt farmers and the unemployed, the rednecks, the Grangers, the followers of "General" Coxie and "Coin" Harvey, the disaffected of all groups and the anonymous casualties of the depression, while the mining magnates of the West dealt out dollars discreetly in the background. Even before the delegates assembled, it was clear that the Silverites would overthrow Cleveland's embattled Goldbugs. The quickly adopted platform repudiated the President, condemned the gold standard not only as un-American but anti-American, invoked "that spirit . . . which proclaimed our political independence in 1776 and won in the war of the Revolution" and called for the "free and unlimited coinage of both gold and silver at the present legal ratio of sixteen to one." "Pitchfork Ben" Tillman, the one-eyed senator from South Carolina, then leapt onto the rostrum to denounce Cleveland as a "tool of Wall Street" and demand his impeachment.

All that the Democratic party needed for its silver transformation was a unifying leader, and he arrived like a cyclone from the West in the person of Nebraska's thirty-six-year-old Boy Orator of the River Platte, William Jennings Bryan. The most dramatic moment of the convention, perhaps of any American convention, occurred when the Boy Orator stood before the delegates and made his Cross of Gold speech. Again and again he was interrupted by frenetic applause as he denounced the gold merchants of the East and championed the little man against the great. He concluded:

> Having behind us the producing masses of this nation and the world supported by the commercial interests, the laboring interests and the toilers everywhere, we will answer their demand for a gold standard by saying to them: "You shall not press down upon the brow of labor this crown of thorns, you shall not crucify mankind upon a cross of gold."*

When he had finished, his twenty thousand auditors were too hypnotized to respond. Only after he had left the rostrum and neared his seat did a surge of voices break the silence. Edgar Lee Masters, present as a reporter, recorded the moment: "The delegates arose and marched for an hour, shouting, weeping, rejoicing. They lifted this orator upon their shoulders and carried him as if he had been a god. At last a man!" Cries of "Bryan! Bryan!" echoed through the hall, and on the fourth ballot the relatively unknown Boy Orator was nominated for the presidency. The Populists in an anticlimactic convention of their own also adopted Bryan as their candidate, although they drew the line at the Democrats' vice-presidential nominee, the wealthy shipbuilder Arthur Sewall.

With Bryan's nomination Republican leaders, who had taken a Democratic defeat for granted, found themselves threatened by the most class-oriented challenge since that of Jackson's common-man challenge to Adams in 1828. A week after Bryan's nomination Hanna wrote to McKinley:

* Quoted in Wayne C. Williams, *William Jennings Bryan* (New York: 1936), p. 146.

> The Chicago convention has changed everything. It has knocked out my holiday and cruise along the New England coast. [The campaign will be] work and hard work. I consider the situation in the West quite alarming as business is all going to pieces and idle men will multiply rapidly. With this communistic spirit abroad the cry of "free silver" will be catching.*

The silver-crowned Bryan seemed to be riding an irresistible wave of dissidence and protest. Hanna admitted afterward that if the election had been held in August or September the Republicans would have lost. Businessmen grew panicky. The stock market fell. Many found in this outbreak of class war a prelude to revolution. *The Saturday Review* of London considered

> the presidential campaign of 1896 an event of profound historical significance from every point of view, political, social, ethical, international. There is no exaggeration in putting it among the great epoch-making occurrences like the gathering of the States General in 1789.

Though Bryan seemed unbeatable as he crisscrossed the country on his private train during the summer making variations on his Cross of Gold speech and drawing the multitudes to him like a second Savior, Hanna still had three vital months to demonstrate his political acumen. All subsequent American political campaigns have, for better or worse, followed the model established by the Red Boss in 1896.

Immediately following McKinley's nomination, Hanna was made chairman of the Republican National Committee, the field commander for the as yet unrealized struggle-to-come. "A born general in politics," John Hay observed admiringly. Like a general Hanna set up his staff, established twin headquarters in Chicago and New York, formed racial and religious subdivisions and gathered together skilled ghostwriters and publicity experts. Money, in Hanna's opinion, spoke louder than words, and the first task he set himself was to raise a campaign fund. He told corporation heads, shivering before the Bryan ogre, that they must "do the fair thing," and let them know just how much "fair" amounted to; he levied an assessment of a quarter of one per cent on the assets of every bank and insurance company; and, according to official figures, he raised and spent $3,562,325. Foraker esti-

* *The Politicos*, p. 680.

mated that the unofficial amount disposed of was almost double that.

There was no buying up of votes in the Quay-Platt manner. Hanna would not resort to that except in isolated extremities. But by election day Republican headquarters had sent out a quarter of a billion documents; five million families were on the Republican weekly mailing lists; two hundred and seventy-five different pamphlets had been published, mostly on the fallacy of Silver and what inflation would really mean to the common man; circulars proclaiming Hanna's slogan of the "Full Dinner-Pail" appeared in German, French, Spanish, Italian, Swedish, Danish, Dutch and Yiddish; fourteen hundred trained speakers covered the doubtful areas of the West, areas to which Hanna devoted his particular attention. Almost by instinct he developed the first political advertising campaign, selling McKinley to the public like soap or tobacco. In early alarm at Bryan's triumphant progress through the Corn Belt, he went to McKinley in Canton to map out a speech-making tour. McKinley refused to budge from his hometown. Not only was he reluctant to leave his invalid wife, but his politician's instinct warned him that he was no match for Bryan's spontaneous oratory. "I have to *think* when I speak," he told Hanna.

If McKinley would not visit the people, then the people must visit McKinley. That was Hanna's conclusion. What followed was a "Front-porch Campaign" in the manner of Harrison's campaign of 1888. Aided by railroad cut-rate excursions and free round-trip tickets that, in one Ohio paper's opinion, made it cheaper to travel than to stay home, Republican delegations from all over the country flocked to Canton where they were met at the station and shepherded along bunting-hung streets under arches of "protected" tin, past hot dog and lemonade stands to McKinley's angular gingerbread house with its wide front porch. Everything was done with clockwork regularity. Each delegation marched behind its band, with banners flying and brass blaring "The Honest Little Dollar's Come to Stay," into the yard before the Front Porch. Then, as if on an automatic signal, the McKinley front door would open and the grave frock-coated figure would appear, speak a few carefully prepared truisms, mention the delegation by name and shake hands with the leaders. "Good money never made times hard," he told his shifting audiences, and he condemned the "un-American attempt to array labor against capital." "For," he liked to conclude, "the prosperity of the one is the prosperity of the other."

Sometimes a dozen "dinner-pail brigades" would arrive at Canton in one day, and over three hundred delegations came there in the months before the election — farmers, workers, businessmen, college students, Civil War veterans north and south, with gifts ranging from watermelons and cheeses to cakes, clothing and live American eagles. The eager visitors trampled the grass in the front yard to dirt that turned to mud when it rained; they brought their picnic lunches and sprawled under the ruined grape arbor and in the geranium beds. So many souvenir hunters cut splinters from the slender porch columns that the Front Porch threatened to fall on McKinley's head.

By mid-summer Bryan's mesmeric organ voice was reduced to a hoarse whisper and his single theme of Silver began to sound a little shopworn. "He's talking silver all the time," Hanna noted with satisfaction, "and that's where we've got him." Hanna's private opinion polls showed a slow swing away from the Boy Orator as Republican propaganda began to take effect. Farmers were instructed in the perils of inflation. Workers found notices in their pay envelopes informing them that if Bryan won, their factory would close down. Respectable eastern clergymen used their pulpits to denounce Bryan as a fiend. Ten days before the election an exhausted Hanna felt that "there is no doubt of our success." Even the farmers of the West were hesitating. Bryan's voice of protest had divided his party, the Gold Democrats splitting off to name their own candidate while castigating Bryan as "a demagogue, a word juggler."

McKinley won easily, in the greatest Republican triumph since Grant's. When in the early morning hours enough returns had come in to show that victory was certain, Hanna telegraphed: "God's in his Heaven, all's right with the world!" McKinley on hearing the news went upstairs with his wife to his mother's room and knelt by her bed. "Oh, God, keep him humble," the old lady prayed, her arm around her son.

Six days after the election McKinley put aside his mask of imperturbability for once to write to Hanna from his heart:

> We are through with the election, and before turning to the future I want to express to you my great debt of gratitude for your generous life-long and devoted services to me. Was there ever such unselfish devotion before? Your unfaltering and increasing friendship through more than twenty years has been to me an encouragement and a source of strength which I am sure you have never realized, but which I have constantly felt and for which I thank you from the bottom of my heart. The recollection of all those years of uninterrupted loyalty and affection, of mutual confidences and growing regard fill me with emotions too deep for the pen to portray. I want you to know, but I cannot find the right words to tell you, how much I appreciate your friendship and faith. God bless and prosper you and yours is my constant prayer.*

"There are idiots who think that Mark Hanna will run him," said Hay of the President-elect, whose face he compared to that of an Italian ecclesiastic of the fifteenth century. McKinley was aware of such "idiots," sensitive to the Hearst-Davenport implications of his being a monkey on Hanna's string. Politically McKinley would keep Hanna at a discreet distance. After he became President, their friendship persisted but, as William Allen White noted, their relations remained stationary. "Hanna was always welcome," wrote White, who knew both men, "but he never headed for the White House to see McKinley in any other capacity than as a friend. . . . His affection for McKinley never wavered. Probably he always thought of him as 'William' though he was chary of that name in public. . . . Hanna had but one friendship, one master passion; that was for McKinley's fame and welfare. . . . He did what he did expecting no rewards and indeed asking few favors. And the President, whose outlook was always official and large, paid back the kindness Hanna gave him with such gentleness and manly gratitude as a man may bestow upon another, but little more."

It was assumed that McKinley would include Hanna in his cabinet, even though he carefully refrained from consulting Hanna on his other appointments. "What a glorious record Mark Hanna has made this year," John Hay wrote to a friend. "I never knew him intimately until we went into this fight together, but my esteem and admiration have grown every hour. . . . I do not know whether he will take a share in the government, but I hope he

* *William McKinley and His America,* p. 346.

will." Several times McKinley pressed him to accept the postmaster-generalship, the conventional reward for a successful national committee chairman. Each time Hanna refused. "Me in the cabinet?" Hanna told a friend. "All the newspapers would have cartoons of me selling the White House kitchen stove!"

There was, however, something that Hanna did want, something within the president's power to give. Four years earlier when Hanna was engaged in reelecting Uncle Jawn to the Senate he remarked offhandedly that he himself "would rather be senator in Congress than have any other office on earth. But," he added, "I could no more be elected senator than I could fly." After McKinley's election he confessed to a friend that he still wanted to go to the Senate, although he did not know how to do it.

McKinley in the White House did know how. With due consideration for his office and his presidential image, this was a gift that he could offer to his friend. Foraker had just been reelected to the Senate. Sherman had two years of his term still to serve. But by appointing the now-senile Uncle Jawn as figurehead secretary of state, the president made his senate seat available. Unrelenting White House pressure was brought on Ohio's reluctant Governor Asa Bushnell, who finally yielded, in spite of Foraker's objections, and appointed Hanna to the Senate for the remainder of Sherman's term.

The Senate that Hanna entered with self-conscious eagerness in the spring of 1897 had become an embodiment of corporate power and wealth. Known familiarly as the Millionaire's Club, it exuded a plush atmosphere the new Ohio senator was bound to find congenial. During his appointed term he was content to take a back desk, to watch and to observe, a cloakroom general sizing up each senator and each senator's master. When he spoke it was in private, but others grew aware of him as a silent force. Later he would speak easily, but the time had not yet come. Even as he sat quiescently in the Senate chamber, the sun of prosperity that he had predicted was climbing the sky. With more and more gold being mined in the Klondike, South Africa and Australia, with improved domestic methods of ore extraction, the gold scarcity was easing and the decades-long drop in prices beginning to reverse itself. Under its central banking system the Treasury was able to increase its supply of notes; and as wheels of industry picked up speed, the currency issue faded.

The Hearst-sponsored belief that Hanna was the power behind the president was one that died hard. McKinley, all too aware of this belief, felt he had fulfilled his obligations to Hanna by making him a senator. Though still regarding his old friend as a friend, he considered him one to be kept at presidential arm's length. "Hanna brought his valise to the White House," William Allen White wrote, "but he always left his trunk at the hotel." Nor did Hanna expect more than this restrained friendship.

What soon rose to trouble both Hanna and McKinley was the swirling war cloud over Cuba that threatened to blot the McKinley sun. That unhappy island's struggle by native insurgents against the loosened authority of Spain was compared by simplistic Americans to the resistance of the patriots of 1776 to British oppression. Despite the pacific intentions of McKinley, Hanna, and the established business world, the man in the street grew belligerent. Impelled by the heady winds of Manifest Destiny, stirred by manufactured Cuban atrocity stories, inflamed by the screaming headlines of Hearst and Pulitzer, the American public clamored for war even while forgetting its actuality. Theodore Roosevelt as McKinley's pugnacious young assistant secretary of the navy expressed the prevailing mood succinctly when he wrote that the country needed another war, "something to think about which isn't material gain." The blowing up of the American battleship *Maine* in Havana Harbor on February 15, 1898, though undoubtedly accidental, gave the country a pretence and a slogan, and made war with Spain inevitable. But before the country could "Remember the Maine," Hanna's term in the Senate expired.

Hanna took it for granted that the Ohio Republican convention of June, 1897, would nominate him for a regular term as senator and that the new Republican legislature would obediently elect him. At first things went as he had expected. The convention nominated him without opposition; then, as a placating gesture to Foraker, renominated Governor Bushnell. Before the November elections Hanna stumped the state campaigning for the Republican legislators who were the guarantee of his own reelection. The Republicans carried Ohio easily, and on the surface his return to the Senate seemed certain. But beneath the surface, the usual murky Ohio countercurrents were at work. As the time for the convocation of the legislature neared, he learned that Foraker's supporters were plotting to unite with the Democrats and replace Hanna by his enemy, "Curly Bob" McKisson, the mayor of Cleveland. While Foraker maneuvered deftly in the shadows, Bushnell manipulated all the levers of state patronage to garner votes for Curly Bob. Hanna, caught off guard by this palace revolt, hurried belatedly to Columbus a week before the legislature met and set up his headquarters at Neil House. It was a week of turmoil bordering on violence. Money flowed, and when its flow seemed to lose effect, force followed. One wavering assemblyman was even kidnapped by a McKisson flying squad, only to be recaptured by Hanna counterinsurgents. As Herbert Croly, Hanna's biographer, wrote:

> Columbus came to resemble a medieval city given over to an angry feud between armed partisans. . . . Blows were exchanged in the hotels and on the streets. There were threats of assassination. . . . Certain members of the Legislature were supplied with body-guards. Many of them never left their rooms. . . . Hanna legislators went to the State House under the protection of Mr. Hanna's friends. Armed guards were stationed at every important point. The State House was full of desperate and determined men. A system of signals was arranged and operated so that Mr. Hanna and his friends at the Neil House could be informed of the progress of the ballot. . . . A white handkerchief waved violently by a man on the steps of the State House gave notice to Mr. Hanna, who was watching anxiously at the window, that he was elected.*

For all the political and financial pressure that Hanna applied with such ruthless skill, he managed to retain his senate seat by only a single vote. During McKinley's presidency, Hanna in his silence remained one of the most conspicuous members of the Senate. Tourists and visitors to the senate gallery always asked to have the now wheezy and rheumatic senator pointed out to them. So besieged was he by place- and favor-seekers that he sometimes sought refuge in the anonymity of his dentist's chair. He took no part in the debates over the war with Spain, although once it broke out he, like McKinley, became a rapid convert to the new imperialism. Always he remained a friend in need for the president, ready at a call to tidy up McKinley's relations with the Sen-

* *Marcus Alonzo Hanna,* pp. 256–259.

ate. And long before 1900 his politician's sixth sense told him that McKinley's reelection would be a certainty.

A short and successful war, renewed prosperity, the Republican-sponsored Dingley Tariff, and the easing of the currency issue made Democratic chances in the first election of the new century seem slight. Still hypnotized by the Boy Orator, the Democrats again nominated Bryan by acclamation with a platform opposing the tariff, the gold standard and imperialism.

McKinley's concern for posterity increased with his popularity. Still sensitive to the old charges that the power behind him was the Red Boss, he hesitated for months in making Hanna manager of the 1900 campaign, even though he knew in the end that the choice was inevitable. As Hanna well understood, the delay was a public indication of the gap McKinley considered necessary between them. Hanna felt the slight. He felt further slighted when McKinley, following the death of Vice President Garret Hobart, sent a telegram not to him but to Charles Dawes announcing that he had no choice for a running mate. What really alarmed Hanna was the possible nomination of Theodore Roosevelt as vice-president, for he regarded the ebullient Rough Rider as a political irresponsible who might well sweep the Republican National Convention.

After the convention had realized Hanna's worst fears, he left for South Dakota on his own and in spite of his doctor's warnings, to conduct a personal campaign against Senator Richard Pettigrew, a former Republican who had left his party over the silver issue, and who had insulted Hanna on the floor of the Senate. The Red Boss's campaign of personal vengeance made the cautious McKinley uneasy as to its western repercussions, and he sent his postmaster general to South Dakota to suggest tactfully to Hanna that he desist. Hanna realized at once that the message was being relayed from the White House. "Go back to Washington," he told the postmaster general, his face flushed with anger, "and tell the president that God hates a coward!" Hanna is said to have spent up to half a million dollars of his own money in driving Pettigrew from public life. Late in the campaign summer of 1900 Hanna complained to McKinley that work in a number of navy yards was being held up, and that this would mean lost votes. McKinley replied, as if he were also sending a carbon copy to a future biographer, that "I do not want to feel that improper or questionable methods have been employed." Again Hanna received the snub in silence.

Yet for all McKinley's bronze-image diffidence, and for all Hanna's moments of bristling anger, the senator never wavered in his devotion to the president, *his* president. The election results were indeed the triumph that both men had anticipated, McKinley increasing his popular majority by almost half a million votes. "I can no longer be called the President of a party," McKinley wrote exultingly in his copy-book hand; "I am now President of the whole people."

The first inauguration of the twentieth century, on March 4, 1901, was held under lowering skies that gave way to heavy rain as McKinley for the second time took his oath of office. He was more than a president now; he was an era. There was muted talk of a third term. But even as McKinley stood on the East Portico platform in the rain with his hand on the Bible, time was running out for him and for his era, time measured in days and weeks rather than in months and years

McKinley started off his new term with a swing round the country, a political tour that had to be cut short because of the ailing Ida. The summer of 1901 he spent quietly in Canton, taking her on occasional drives, receiving a minimum of visitors. On September 5 he planned to break his extended vacation by making a policy speech at the Pan-American Exposition in Buffalo, New York, for — as he told his secretary — "expositions are the timekeepers of progress." Having moved toward a less isolationist tariff attitude as American exports expanded, he planned a major address in which he would call for mutual tariff reductions between nations.

McKinley was a man fatalistically indifferent to his personal safety. In May 1899 Hanna had watched tourists and sight-seers troop to the White House to shake the president's hand and had wondered then "what would happen if some crank got there with a revolver in his pants?" After the second inaugural he was haunted by the premonition that McKinley would not live out his term. He was even more concerned when he learned from a Secret Service agent that anarchists — who had already assassinated the Empress of Austria, President Carnot of France and

King Humbert of Italy — had drawn up plans to kill Queen Victoria, Kaiser William II and the President of the United States. The agent advised that steps should be taken to increase the president's protection. Little or nothing was done. McKinley's secretary, equally concerned, tried to persuade the president to cancel the open reception scheduled to be held after his Buffalo speech. "Why should I?" McKinley asked. "No one would wish to hurt me."

On September 5 the President made his speech at the exposition, stating flatly that "isolation is no longer possible or desirable." He had come a long way from the congressman who would have built a tariff wall round the United States. The next day he visited Niagara Falls, then rested briefly before an open reception at the Temple of Music. Hundreds had been standing for hours in the sun outside the building waiting to shake his hand. As he took his place in the ornate palm-fringed hall, the doors were flung back and the restive public flooded in. There, against a floral backdrop, while an invisible organ played a Bach sonata, nemesis in the shape of the half-mad half-anarchist Leon Czolgosz overtook McKinley. As the inconspicuous vapid-faced young man with the heavily bandaged hand reached the president, his hidden fingers twitched, two shots rang out, and smoke curled from a hole in the bandaging. In the shattering moment of silence, McKinley stared at his assailant with cold contempt before the others fell on him.

One shot had merely grazed McKinley's ribs; the other had passed through his stomach and buried itself in his back muscles. Doctors were unable to recover the bullet, but they were hopeful. Men like Andrew Jackson had lived out their lives with bullets in their bodies. For the first few days the president seemed to be recovering. "Is Mark there?" he had asked several times, in this crisis drawn back to his old friend. Hanna was not allowed to see him.

McKinley's body was strong, but not strong enough for the infection that showed itself toward the end of the week. By the afternoon of the 13th he knew that he was dying. "It is useless, gentlemen," he told his doctors. "I think we ought to have prayer." At the last Hanna was sent for. When he arrived in the evening, bent with rheumatism, to stand at McKinley's bedside, the president was moaning incoherently, his eyes glazed. "Mr. President, Mr. President," Hanna called out to him. "Don't you know me?" McKinley gave no answer. Then Hanna, in that final moment pushing aside all dividing formalities, cried out loudly: "William! Don't you know me?"

THE GLAD HAND

*Platt and Roosevelt meet*
*at the 1900 New York state Republican convention.*

CHAPTER TWO

# The Easy Boss: Thomas Collier Platt

---

ON A HOT Wednesday evening in June, 1881, the Half-Breed members of the New York Assembly's self-appointed "Committee of Inspection" gathered quietly in a corridor of Delavan House, Albany's political headquarters, in front of Room 113. Assemblyman Abram Disbecker gingerly placed a stepladder before the locked door, and one by one his legislative colleagues climbed it to peer through the transom of the darkened room. Though it was after midnight, enough light filtered in from the lamps of the portico just outside for them to see the emaciated figure of the stalwart family man and Stalwart political leader, Thomas Collier Platt, his nightshirt hoisted up to his shoulders, oscillating in the arms of an "unspeakable female." As each assemblyman stepped down from the ladder with smirking satisfaction, another scrambled up to take his place. Beneath them on the rumpled bed the oscillations quickened, and one or two of the committee sought a confirming second look. Then State Senator Woodin gave the Negro hall boy an enveloped addressed to:

> Ex-U.S. Senator Thomas C. Platt
> in care of Mrs. Baldwin
> Room 113, Delavan House

The hall boy knocked, and a woman called out in a querulous voice. When she refused to open the door, he slipped the envelope underneath. The letter read:

> You are caught. If within thirty minutes you are not in your room, No. 88, the door of 113 will be broken in.
>
> A Friend

Inside Room 113 the gaslight flared up, reflected in the transom. A few minutes later a rumpled Platt "furtively emerged and was pursued with jeers and salutations by some of those who had hived and unhived him."

Several weeks before this, the mousy Senator Platt had followed his Stalwart chief, New York's truculently elegant senior senator, Roscoe Conkling, in resigning his seat in protest against President Garfield's appointment of a Conkling enemy to the collectorship of the New York Custom House. That house of patronage supplied vital nutriment for Conkling's Stalwart machine, and the two Republican senators intended to teach a Republican president a lesson, certain that they would be vindicated through reelection by the Stalwart-dominated legislature. Platt had spent thousands of dollars "persuading" wavering legislators. Until that midnight tryst in Room 113, his reelection seemed assured. The next morning it had become impossible. On Saturday he announced that he was withdrawing his candidacy.

The Albany *Argus* saw Platt "dissolving into his original obscurity." He himself saw his public career as finished and was ready to turn to making money — something that always intrigued him, if not as much as politics and power. But politics are long and the public's memory is fleeting, and Platt was destined to rise from his bed and in his mousy way eventually find himself the political master of his state, maker of assemblymen, judges, congressmen, governors and senators, whose shadow would even fall across the White House.

A sixth-generation American, descendant of Revolutionary officers and the son of a respectable if preternaturally pious small-town lawyer, Thomas Collier Platt was brought up within the rural simplicities of upstate New York's Tioga County in Owego. He was born in 1833, and his sternly Presbyterian father determined to make the boy a clergyman. "I had such a surfeit of church going in my youth," Platt admitted later, "that if it could be averaged up and spread out, it would do for all my life." Sunday after Sunday clergymen were invited to dine cold with the Platts in hope of impressing young Tom. "I was not at all favorably impressed," Platt wrote, though he never went so far as to reject his father's piety.

He first took a job as a clerk in a local drugstore where he compounded pills, mixed elixirs and enlarged his acquaintanceship. At the age of nineteen, after saving up several hundred dollars, the young druggist married Ellen Lucy Barstow. "If ever man was blessed in a wife, it was I," he wrote half a century later with wistful regret. "To her I owe much of whatever has made for success and uplift during the subsequent years."

A wife did not impede Platt's thrifty nature. Two years after his marriage he and a young pharmaceutical friend, Frederic Hull, made a down payment on Platt & Hull's Corner Drug Store. Their store was as much an emporium as a purveyor of medicines. There one could buy writing paper, pens, slates; paints, varnishes and window glass; and (until Owego voted itself dry) Catawba wines, porter, brandy, gin and whiskey. Saloons were frowned on in rural New York, and men sought their kind at the drugstore, gathering on long summer evenings to stand in the garish reflection of the red and blue glass window urns or in winter squatting around the glowing pot-bellied stove. In a day when politics was America's prime diversion, Platt & Hull's became a social center for the town's footloose males. Tom Platt listened and absorbed the political atmosphere. Early in life he had become an abolitionist, the natural course to take in upstate New York. Behind the drug counter he read the speeches of Seward and Horace Greeley, and studied the Albany *Evening Journal* whose publisher, Thurlow Weed, had for a quarter of a century fashioned New York's state officials, controlled the state conventions, distributed patronage and supervised the legislature. Young Tom was soon as well-known as most older men in his small community, genial, discreet, confidential, his little office in the rear of the store always open to political friends and passing politicians.

The election year of 1856 and the national emergence of the Republican party brought him into active politics for the first time. Soon he developed into one of the most energetic Republican tub-thumpers of Tioga County. A member of the Presbyterian choir who could play the melodeon and several other instruments by ear, he enrolled his musical talents in the Republican cause, gathering his choirmates and friends into the Owego Campaign Glee Club. With Platt giving the pitch and beating time with a tuning fork, Republican choristers whirled about the county in hay-wagons and carry-alls, bellowing out the campaign ditties that Platt and a versifying associate had set to popular tunes.

Though President Buchanan was not beaten, the Republican John C. Frémont did manage to carry New York State, and the young druggist had the satisfaction of seeing his candidate sweep Tioga County with over a two-thirds majority. Two years later Platt revived his glee club to accompany Edwin Morgan, who was elected as New York's first Republican governor, and Tioga County Republicans rewarded their zealous musician the next year by nominating and electing him to a three-year term as county clerk. Platt viewed the office as merely a stepping-stone in his political path.

Meanwhile the young man on the make had become president of the Tioga County National Bank and was speculating with lumber acreage in Michigan. During the 1860 presidential campaign, from the back room of his drugstore he organized county torchlight parades for Lincoln, composed new Republican jingles, and even marched with the Wide-Awakes in a forage cap and oilcloth cape. The Republican triumph he saw as his own. A stomach ailment — which somehow disappeared after the war — kept him out of uniform from 1861 to 1865, but he satisfied his martial ardor as an auxiliary member of the State War Committee, raising money locally for the maintenance of the soldiers. Again in 1864 he campaigned zealously for Lincoln, as well as for the successful Republican candidate for governor, the rustic-mannered Reuben Fenton, known from his scraggly chin-whiskers as "Spinach."

In the months following Lincoln's death, Platt, after wetting a sensitive finger to the political winds, took the side of the Radical Republicans opposing President Johnson's policy of southern reconciliation, allying himself with Fenton and Horace Greeley against such New York administrative Republicans as Secretary of State Seward and the New York *Times* editor Congressman Henry Raymond, and even Thurlow Weed. Fenton, for all his bucolic manner and vegetal whiskers, was a deft political strategist and distributor of patronage where it would do the most good, the leader of the Radical Republicans in a Radical Republican state until his leadership was threatened by the election of Congressman Roscoe Conkling to the Senate in 1867.

Yet though Fenton would follow Conkling to the Senate, he

would never catch up with him. For Conkling was a presence. Hyperion — the sun-titan — his fellow Stalwarts called him, those entrenched supporters of President Grant and Grant-supported corruption. His enemies called him "my Lord Roscoe." No one took the senate floor more dramatically than this golden-haired, golden-bearded giant whose empurpled eloquence could hypnotize what he contemptuously referred to as the "spaniel element in human nature." Platt, destined to become Conkling's shadow, considered him one of the handsomest men he had ever known, "over six feet tall, of slender build, and straight as an arrow. . . . His noble figure, flashing eye and majestic voice made one forget that he was somewhat foppish in his dress." In cream-colored pantaloons and yellow satin waistcoat, the Stalwart orator of the Grant administration would elaborate his sonorities in the Senate. When President Grant at Conkling's urging made Thomas Murphy, a Stalwart political hack closely associated with Tammany's Boss Tweed, collector of customs at the New York Custom House, the largest source of federal patronage in the country came under Conkling's control. As Conkling explained, "a government is a machine, a political party is a machine." To run efficiently the machine required the fuel of patronage, fuel which in New York State the senior senator came to consider his to dispense by divine right. And with Grant in the White House, all was well with Conkling's world.

It was in 1870 that Platt, mousily emerging from the shadows, "really began to know Roscoe Conkling." They drew close at that year's Republican State Convention where Conkling, with Platt's help as a delegate, drove the Fenton supporters to the wall, making Conkling's lieutenant, Alonzo Cornell, chairman and seizing control of the State Republican Committee. "Conkling whipped Fenton to a finish," Platt wrote with satisfaction. "I helped him do it."

The histrionic Conkling loved the limelight. Platt instinctively sought the shadows. But the senior senator was willing to accept the tried and useful Platt as a member of the Republican inner circle that controlled conventions and made the party decisions. In 1872, with a nod from Conkling, Platt emerged as a candidate for Congress against the apostate Goodrich, who had embraced the heresy of Liberal Republicanism. Goodrich had even gone so far in that presidential election year as to support the Democrat-sponsored Horace Greeley against a second term for President Grant. Platt won as easily as did Grant himself.

The Congress that Platt entered at about the time of the Crédit Mobilier scandal had reached a low ebb, and the tidal odor was noxious. "Statesmanship," Thurlow Weed wrote in that year, "is now so low that it will take it many years to build it up to a higher tone." Under the impervious Grant, scandal seemed to follow scandal in an endless chain. Yet whatever the new congressman from Owego became aware of, he was untroubled by any reforming itch. Inconspicuous by choice, friendly to all — even to Conkling's archenemy Blaine — he remained the loyalest of administration Republicans and was rewarded by being made a member of the (later notorious) National Republican Campaign Committee.

In 1876 Platt became a delegate to his first national convention, in a year that saw the bitter nomination struggle between the Half-Breed Blaine — the formidable if slightly tarnished "Plumed Knight"— and the Stalwart Conkling who wore his own peacock plumes. Blaine as the leading candidate and the darling of the galleries might have won in the frenzy following the golden-voiced Robert Ingersoll's nominating speech, but before the balloting could take place, his enemies managed to cut the gas main and plunge the hall in darkness. In the cold light of the following morning Blaine could not muster a majority. Conkling never managed to reach more than a third of Blaine's vote total, but he held enough of the balance to combine with other Stalwart leaders and deny Blaine the nomination, which then went to the compromise candidate — a "third rate nonentity" in Henry Adams's opinion — Rutherford Hayes.

The election that followed was one of the most bizarre in the nation's history. Swept along by disgust with the blatancy of corruption under Grant, the Democratic candidate, New York's Governor Samuel Tilden, not only carried his own state but across the country received over a quarter of a million more popular votes than Hayes. At first it seemed that he had been elected. In Florida, Louisiana and South Carolina, the three southern states still under carpetbag rule, the voters themselves had been overwhelmingly for Tilden. But in each case the carpetbag returning boards had reversed the popular results, certifying their states for Hayes. If their reversal could be sustained, Hayes would have a one-vote majority in the Electoral College. Congress appointed an electoral commission to decide the issue that seemed in the weeks that followed to verge on revolution. The commission, made up of eight Republicans and seven Democrats and voting on the strictest party lines, reached its decision only the day before the new president was to be inaugurated. It awarded the votes of all three disputed states to Hayes who for some time after he occupied the White House was known as "His Fraudulency" and "Old Eight to Seven."

In President Hayes the country was given the paradox of a reform-minded president elected through corrupt means by a minority of the voters. Yet the new president's reformist attitude was sincere, as the disgusted Conkling soon discovered. One of Hayes's early acts was to appoint a committee to investigate the federal custom house establishment, the most constant source of political corruption in the country. "A scandalous system of robbery," Missouri's reformist-minded Republican Senator Carl Schurz called it, and New York's Custom House, the largest, was the most corrupt of all. So scandal-ridden had it become under Collector Murphy that even the insensitive Grant had finally felt obliged to ask for his resignation, replacing him with Chester Arthur, Conkling's suave and dapper lieutenant, who was assisted by New York's state committee chairman Alonzo Cornell bearing the odd title of Naval Officer of the Port of New York. Under Arthur the Custom House had become a clearing-house for Conkling. In June of 1877 Hayes issued an order for the reform of the custom service and demanded the resignation of Arthur and Cornell. Conkling, who regarded the New York Custom House as his fief, was outraged. And the Senate, jealous of its prerogatives and solicitous of its own, refused to confirm the president's new appointees. "We saw to it," Platt wrote in his autobiography, "that the President's plan was foiled." Hayes bided his time until Congress adjourned and then suspended Arthur and Cornell by executive order. As a measure of revenge, Conkling two years later forced through the nomination of Cornell for governor and made Platt New York's national Republican committeeman. Platt, Cornell, Arthur and Conkling were now, in Platt's words, the "Big Four" of New York State, though Conkling loomed bigger than the other three combined.

The year that Cornell was elected governor saw Platt made

general manager and secretary of the United States Express Company, an organization formed to do business with the Erie Railroad. A year later he became the company's president and as such the chief dispenser of railroad favors to small-town editors and politicians along the Erie routes. No longer the friendly druggist, he had grown so hesitant about committing himself that he could scarcely be brought to express an opinion about even the weather in front of strangers. Grown old before he had become truly middle-aged, frail but with a basilisk eye, he had achieved a provincially sinister air by allowing his sideburns to descend until they formed a scraggly beard. Men laughed at the beard, but they wilted before that cold look.

> He puts men under obligation to him and commands their friendship and services [the Syracuse *Journal* observed]. Why, he has secured places for not less than seventy-five persons in public offices. He has appointees in the New York Custom House, in the New York Post Office and in the New York City government. He has practically "run" Cornell's administration; and the canal officials, from Superintendent Dutcher down to the boat inspector at Syracuse are under obligation to him. . . . And so it is all along the canals and in the government offices. Platt men are plenty in all the state departments at Albany.

In the Republican National Convention of 1880 Conkling and Platt maneuvered their Stalwart best to secure a third term for former President Grant. Yet, though Grant led all the other convention candidates through twenty-five ballots, he came some seventy votes short of the necessary majority. On the thirty-sixth ballot the weary delegates turned to a compromise candidate, James Garfield, a man much like Hayes in birth, appearance, obscurity and concealed instinct for reform. As a friend of Blaine, Garfield became automatically Conkling's enemy, nor could Conkling find much satisfaction in the convention's stalwart-conciliating gesture of nominating Chester Arthur as vice-president.

In the end Garfield owed his victory over the Democrats' portly, undistinguished General Winfield Hancock to a reconciliation with the Stalwarts, who with zeal and boodle managed to carry the three doubtful states of Indiana, Ohio and New York. For such efforts in New York, Conkling expected the right to control federal appointments in his own state, particularly to that post most vital to his political well-being, the collectorship of the New York

Custom House. Yet there were indications that Garfield would not acquiesce. An indignant Conkling visited the president-elect, alternately upbraiding and cajoling him as he demanded complete control of New York patronage. Under such intrusive pressure Garfield's good intentions wavered. Fearing the worst, Secretary of State-designate Blaine rose from his sickbed to set the waverer straight. Safely removed from the New York senator's overbearing presence, and fortified by Blaine, Garfield — without even notifying Conkling or Platt — appointed Judge William Robertson as the New York Custom House's new collector. Stalwart Vice-President Arthur was heard to complain that "Garfield has not been square, nor honorable, nor truthful with Conkling."

The day before Garfield's inauguration, Platt was sworn in as New York's junior United States senator. "A dwarf on stilts," William Allen White called the new senator, "the political camp follower — but not even the creature, and certainly not the ally — of the great Roscoe Conkling." However grotesque Platt's metaphorical appearance in a toga, he had for some time cast a longing eye toward the Senate. Although there was a certain amount of ventriloquism involved, he maintained that in the byways of Albany he had heard himself "talked about for the United States Senate"; that "friends insisted he should be a candidate." Vice-President Arthur and other Conkling Stalwarts had not been among those insisting. They had their own candidate, as did the Half-Breeds who had picked Chauncey Depew, the suave courtier of the Vanderbilts and president of the Vanderbilt-owned New York Central Railroad. Depew had sought Platt out, offering to back him for senator if he, once elected, would agree to support Garfield instead of Conkling. Platt was willing. "I have done my best to elect a Republican president and I shall support him," he told Depew. And when Depew asked if he would even support Judge Robertson as collector, Platt assured him that he would. Without Depew's Half-Breed votes in the legislature, Platt would not have been elected. But his election placed him in a dilemma: either he must go back on his word to Depew or he must face Conkling's fury. Platt tried to temporize, even as Conkling attempted to make deals with Democratic senators to oppose Robertson. But the junior senator's two-month efforts to arrange matters between Garfield and Conkling came to nothing. Both men insisted on control of the New York Custom House. As a concession Garfield was willing to withdraw the other nominations he had made for New York offices in favor of Conkling appointees. Further than that he would not go. On Judge Robertson as the collector of the Custom House, he was adamant. When the president's message requesting Robertson's appointment was read in the Senate, Platt at his desk hung his head. The only way he could see out of his dilemma was for him to resign his seat This would technically relieve him of his promise to Depew. Then he could seek a "vindicating" reelection from the new Stalwart-dominated legislature. Deviously he suggested to Conkling that they both resign. Conkling agreed.

Conkling's resignation was from pique, Platt's from calculation. But neither pique nor calculation produced the expected result. The Half-Breeds considered that Platt had betrayed them, while the more cautious Stalwarts — among them Governor Cornell — had become dubious of Conkling's "rule or ruin" policy in opposing the president. Not even Vice-President Arthur's appearance as a lobbyist at Albany was sufficient to sway a majority of the legislature. For a month the members balloted on the two empty senate seats, with no candidate obtaining a majority until Platt's night-errancy forced his withdrawal.

The day after Platt's enforced announcement, Garfield was shot by a disappointed office-seeker, Charles Guitreau who, after firing two bullets almost point blank into the president, shouted, "I did it and will go to jail for it. I am a Stalwart and Arthur will be president." Garfield survived for seventy-nine days, fading away gradually in the summer heat. It seems unlikely that even without this event Conkling could have secured his vindication while Garfield and Blaine opposed him, but the attempt on the president cut the remaining ground from under his feet. His earlier attacks, with their savagely abusive language, were held to be at least partly responsible for Guitreau's act. Finally the Half-Breeds at Albany combined with the waverers —"Featherheads," the more intransigent Stalwarts called them — and elected Elbridge Lapham and Warner Miller to replace Conkling and Platt in the Senate. Conkling's political career had come to an abrupt end.

Following their twin repudiation, Platt seemed even more eclipsed than Conkling, a laughingstock to his enemies, an object of contempt to his old chief and friend. "Me Too Platt," the papers dubbed him, unaware of his real role in Conkling's resignation. Platt's career too seemed to have come to an end. In his autobiography he glossed over the dismal interlude with glib half-truths: "I served Conkling faithfully so long as he was willing to lead. When disheartened, and stung by the refusal of the Legislature to send him back to the Senate, Conkling voluntarily quit politics, all his old allies marshaled themselves about me and hailed me as his heir."

That marshaling of the allies was a slow process. For two years Platt stayed away from Albany, keeping his grievances to himself and his thoughts of revenge green. Those who had brought him down he was implacably determined to destroy. With the bait of his express company he could still set traps. Gradually his stooped, bearded figure became more familiar to Albany, and his lobbying and political influence grew.

Those were the years of the Republican party's disintegration in New York State. To the outraged astonishment of the Stalwarts, Arthur in the White House had shown himself more the president than the politician, more concerned with leaving a worthy name to history than with party and patronage. Conducting himself with newly acquired dignity, surrounding himself with able and upright associates, the former custom house collector now demonstrated an unsuspected inclination toward civil service reform. So far behind him had he left his past that he refused to remove Conkling's enemy, Judge Robertson from his New York collector's post. Even the cynical Mark Twain came to feel that "it would be hard to better President Arthur's administration."

In an attempt to take control of the fragmented New York Republicans, Arthur persuaded Secretary of the Treasury Charles Folger to oppose Governor Cornell's renomination. Yet Cornell, in a lesser post, had like Arthur grown in office, even to the point of breaking with Conkling after the senator had defied Garfield. Conkling, though out of politics, was willing as Jay Gould's "legal adviser" to help defeat Cornell. Platt, too, moved actively in Folger's shadow. Their help was scarcely needed, for Arthur summoned enough of his old skills to see that the state convention was well packed with federal office holders ready to vote as the White House directed. Folger was nominated, only to be abandoned by the Independents and a large segment of the Stalwarts.

He was overwhelmed in the election by the sturdy figure of the Democratic candidate, the reform mayor of Buffalo, Grover Cleveland.

Platt realized that vindictive infighting between New York's Stalwarts and Half-Breeds had made Cleveland's election inevitable. What his faction-riven party needed was "harmony." He grasped that the day of the flamboyant party dictator sustained by federal patronage was fading, eroded by the spread of civil service and the expansion of big business. No longer would the collectorship of the Port of New York provide the main sinews of party strength. No longer would a Lord Roscoe strut across the political stage with his Apollo lock and yellow satin waistcoat. He would be replaced by muter presences, inconspicuous behind-the-scenes mediators. Like Hanna in Ohio, Platt instinctively sensed the new trend. And just as Hanna was realizing the businessman in politics, so would Platt realize the politician in business.

The leading candidates for the Republican nomination in 1884 were President Arthur and the perennial Blaine. But the belatedly virtuous Arthur found himself at the end of his term a man without a party, deserted by most of the Stalwarts and unacceptable to the Half-Breeds. Platt could not forgive him his refusal to remove Judge Robertson even though Arthur maintained that as Garfield's heir he was morally obliged to continue the dead president's policies. For Platt, politics was a science unconnected with morality. But beyond his resentment toward Arthur, he was aware that Blaine was the idol of the rank-and-file Republicans no matter how clay-footed he might appear to reforming Independents like Carl Schurz. So bitter, however, was the feeling of the old-line New York Stalwarts against Blaine that Platt had to pull every string within reach to get himself elected a Blaine delegate from his own district.

As a delegate Platt sat in Chicago's Exposition Hall while the tides of the convention surged about him and the galleries stamped and chanted: "Blaine! Blaine! James G. Blaine!" Judge West's pyrotechnic nominating speech kindled no sparks in the New York boss. Yet it was the coldly logical Platt who seconded the Plumed Knight's nomination on the reasonable though scarcely inflammatory grounds that "the Republican people of the Republican states that must give the Republican majorities want him."

Seated with Platt among the New York delegates was the combative young assemblyman, Theodore Roosevelt, who boasted that he was neither Half-Breed nor Stalwart. Roosevelt felt that *Blaine from Maine* was "of all the men presented to the convention . . . by far the most objectionable," an opinion shared by the disgruntled Schurz who, after Blaine's tumultuous nomination, led his Independents* with ostentatious rectitude out of the Republican party to support the Democratic candidate, Grover Cleveland. But three terms in the assembly had taught Roosevelt much about politics as the art of the possible, and summer's end found him bending to the winds of popular choice, not because he thought so highly of the "decidedly mottled" Blaine but because he thought so little of the Democrats. "One cannot," he stated, "act both without and within the party." His place, he decided, was within.

Cleveland's margin of victory in November was so narrow that a change of a mere 575 votes in New York would have given the state and the presidency to Blaine. The Mugwumps had swung the election. Yet even without them Blaine might have squeezed through if a few days before the voting a Republican New York clergyman by the name of Burchard had not denounced the Democrats as the party of "rum, Romanism and rebellion." Tammany Democrats, long at odds with Cleveland, had been rallying to Blaine, but Burchard's diatribe stopped this heretical drift and — according to the estimate of one Catholic prelate — cost Blaine 50,000 votes. The gaffe was the more ironical in that Blaine's Irish-born mother was a Catholic and his cousin the superior of a convent.

Blaine's defeat left the New York Republicans even more fragmented than after Cleveland's election as governor. To the sorry task of piecing the party together, Platt applied his devious talents. This haggard, stoop-shouldered man, with skin like yellowed parchment and a caricature of a beard, drew no one to him by his magnetism. Even when he shook hands, he seemed limp and listless. What he did have in lieu of dynamic charm was energy, patience, an encyclopedic knowledge of New York politics, relentlessness and a mild manner. He had long observed Boss

* Derisively called Mugwumps — from the Algonquian word meaning "big chief" — the Independents included such ramrod Republicans as George Curtis of *Harper's* and Henry Ward Beecher. Even the Republican New York *Times* and that voice of Beacon Hill, the Boston *Transcript*, refused to support Blaine.

Croker's Tammany with envious admiration of its imposed hierarchy, the deftness with which it manipulated voters, its sleight-of-hand deals in contracts and franchises. Tammany's strength was in the urban immigrant, unskilled, semiliterate, pliable, with a mindless devotion to the Catholic Church and roots in a lost Ireland overseas. Platt saw his political sinews in the small cities and towns of upper New York, the rural areas, Protestant and nativist in attitudes. He realized that to control this heartland of the hard-back Yankee was to control the state.

During the eighties, with an unrivaled singlemindedness, he built up a Republican Tammany in upper New York through forty-six counties and hundreds of upstate towns, working through the state, county and city committees. He cultivated and nurtured the county and ward bosses, paying particular attention to the precinct captains, of whom he had at one time over five thousand under his thumb. Such small-town satraps were the key men to hand-pick the county delegates, who in turn elected the delegates to the state convention, who in their own turn chose the delegates to the national convention. Platt also saw to it that helpful rural editors received their share of contracts for official printing, that friendly mayors and legislators in doubtful districts were furnished campaign sustenance, that the "right" candidates were groomed for the assembly. "I don't want any person who wears a high hat and has his shoes blacked," one of his lieutenants explained. "I want a candidate who is down and out, on his uppers, and has fringed clothes, then I can hoist him into office and *he will be mine*." Four years after his disastrous tryst in the Delavan House, Platt had progressed so far in his rehabilitation that he was able to secure the election of his own candidate as speaker of the State Assembly. As his power expanded, businessmen troubled by "unfair" competition, corporation directors with tax problems, underwriters, moneylenders, investment bankers and other victims of political circumstance turned increasingly to him for assistance. To those who sought his help he delivered: a law to be passed, a law to be suppressed, a diplomatic appointment, or a minor state office. Two questions only concerned him: What does a man want? What will he settle for? "A political organization," he wrote, "should be conducted upon the simplest principles. Merit and devotion should be rewarded. Demerit and treachery should be condemned and examples made of those guilty of them." In his rolltop desk there was a row of cubbyholes in which demerit and treachery were duly recorded.

New York politics continued to be Platt's one interest, his hobby, his business, his obsession; and he made himself the master of that limited field. Having taken the measure of all his underlings, he understood their rivalries, knew the size of the vote they could deliver, the relative purchasing power of dollars in rural and urban areas, the strength and weakness of the opposition. Theodore Roosevelt doubted that Platt had "any tastes at all except for politics, and on rare occasions for a very dry theology wholly divorced from moral implications." This also seemed to be the opinion of Platt's New York pastor, the reform-minded Rev. Dr. Charles Parkhurst who one Sunday denounced his congregant from the pulpit as "worse than five Crokers." Indignantly, Platt took his worship elsewhere.

The reverend doctor was more correct in his observation than in his mathematics, for Platt and Croker were much alike. Loyal to their organization, true to their word, they regarded their state or their city as their fief. Moralists condemned them, yet within the context of their times they were ineluctable. Men like Platt, grass-rooted in patronage, established themselves as "honest brokers" between politics and property. Businessmen in an America increasingly dominated by business needed a guide through the labyrinth of politics, while politicians as always needed sustenance and support. Corporations and chiefs of industry found it both easier and more reliable to deal directly with the honest broker than to attempt to buy up legislatures on their own. Platt noted with ironic pride that both friends and foes were beginning to call him "boss." Roosevelt observed the pattern with a mixture of admiration and distaste:

> Big business [he wrote of Platt in his autobiography] contributed to him large sums of money, which enabled him to keep his grip on the machine and secured for them the help of the machine if they were threatened with adverse legislation. . . . When the money was contributed there was rarely talk of specific favors in return. It was simply put into Mr. Platt's hands and treated by him as in the campaign chest.

Increasingly acknowledged as the middleman for special legislation, Platt in the eighties came to be known as the Easy Boss, cold in eye but gentle in voice and manner, guiding his lieutenants with a light if steel-reinforced rein. As New York's Republican party, riven by Stalwarts, Half-Breeds and Independents, drifted rudderless, political managers looked more and more to Platt to take command of the listing ship.

By the time of the 1888 Republican national convention, Platt's comeback had progressed so far that he was named one of his state's four delegates-at-large. Leading contender for the nomination was the colorless elderly senator from Ohio, John Sherman. Blaine's name still rang with the old magic, although at the time of the convention he was in Scotland. Among the lesser candidates were the genial Chauncey Depew and the coldly aloof Benjamin Harrison of Indiana, Civil War general, archprotectionist and grandson of America's ninth president. Sherman failed to gain a majority in the first few ballots, but his nomination still seemed possible until a cable arrived from Blaine declaring that he wanted Harrison. That word was enough for Platt, who swung his New York delegation from Depew to Harrison at a critical moment, with the understanding that in return he would be named secretary of the treasury and given control of federal patronage in New York.

Harrison's slim election victory, in which he received fewer popular votes than Cleveland, was followed by no appreciative gestures toward the Easy Boss. Harrison was willing to make patronage concessions but he drew the line at including Platt in his "businessmen's cabinet." Platt wanted to become secretary of the treasury, not for the juicy pickings, according to his explanation, but for the honor. Turned down by the president after he felt he had been given "a positive pledge," he resolved never again "to trust men from Ohio."

Finding Owego too limited, too public for his increasingly secretive nature, Platt had moved to New York City, settling down at 49 Broadway in the fabled Fifth Avenue Hotel with its central heating, inside toilets and "a perpendicular railway intersecting each story" (later more familiar as an elevator). Built just before the Civil War, the hotel had long been a Republican outpost in a Democratic city. Conkling at the height of his power had strutted there. The Republican State Committee members continued to make it their headquarters. Platt himself later said of it:

> Nobody can take away from the Fifth Avenue Hotel the fame that it for years enjoyed as the place where from every city and county in this State there came, met and conferred the strongest minds in the Republican party and the place from which, after their combined judgment had been finally realized, there went a sentiment in accordance with which popular judgment was moulded and put into effect.*

What he failed to say was that those who came to the hotel did so to confer with him, and that their combined judgment was his judgment. Each weekend he held his "Sunday school class" in a niche near the desk known as Amen Corner. Here upstate leaders joined their city "brethren" to discuss policies and platforms, nominations, patronage, and recruiting, while seated on two plush-covered benches that marked off the Corner from the rest of the corridor. Platt listened, nodding now and then, while the discussion ebbed and flowed, often with some acrimony. Then in his deceptively soft voice he would announce his decision, to which the leaders would bow their heads and intone "Amen!"

Depew was an occasional vistior at 49 Broadway in spite of his Half-Breed deviations. But Chauncey was always dextrous enough to work both sides of the street at the same time. At Amen Corner, he noted admiringly, "were made governors, state senators, and assemblymen, supreme court judges, judges of the Court of Appeals, and members of Congress. Governors . . . took their inspiration and suggestions for their policies from Amen Corner. State conventions would meet at Rochester, Syracuse, or Saratoga, but the eight hundred members would wait before acting to know what had been decided upon in the Amen Corner." Elihu Root, later to become McKinley's Secretary of War, at the New York Constitutional Convention of 1915 recalled those flanking sofas with a reformer's thwarted bitterness:

> Mr. Platt ruled the state; for nigh upon twenty years he ruled it. It was not the governor; it was at 49 Broadway; with Mr. Platt and his lieutenants.†

Platt had not yet become the Autocrat of Amen Corner when in 1886 he maneuvered Theodore Roosevelt into accepting the nomination for mayor of New York City. As a rule the nomination of a Republican mayoral candidate was a token gesture in

* *Autobiography*, pp. 492–93.
† *Our Times: The Turn of the Century*, p. 77.

New York, prelude to a deal with Tammany. But 1886 was a singular year. Not only were the Democrats split into Cleveland and anti-Cleveland factions, but a formidable third-party threat had emerged in the shape of a United Labor candidate, Henry George, advocate of the Single Tax on land, social-minded — not to say socialistic — author of *Progress and Poverty*. So great was George's drawing power that in a straight contest with Tammany he might have won. To avoid the specter of reform, Boss Croker sought out his friendly enemy, Platt. New York's machine Republicans had long been accustomed to working comfortably with Tammany; in fact the Republican enrollment in the city was over a third bogus, with many names introduced straight from the Tammany roster. Croker chose as his candidate the obviously upright and extremely wealthy Abram Hewitt. Platt, equally eager to siphon off George's respectable Republican vote, sent emissaries to Roosevelt, not his usual sub-boss run of Barneys and Sols and Jakes, but respectable, persuasive frock-coated Republicans of the Depew stamp. Roosevelt listened with a receptive ear and eagerly accepted the nomination from a rigged convention at the Grand Opera House "with the most genuine reluctance," pledging himself to fight the good fight "against the spoilsmen who are eating up the substance of the city."

The twenty-six-year-old Roosevelt had come a long way in the six years since he had quit Columbia Law School with the announced intention of being "one of the governing class." Convinced that public affairs needed the active participation of the Best Element, in 1880 he had joined the twenty-first district Republican Club in that wealthy Republican section of Manhattan known as the Terrapin or Brown Stone District. He joined at a propitious moment, for the Republican district leader Jake Hess, a man bound by invisible threads to Amen Corner, was being challenged by his subordinate, a young ex-Tammany worker turned Republican, Joe Murray. The insurgent Joe took the fledgling Roosevelt under his wing, and so dauntless was their combined zeal that Hess found himself forced to accept what must have seemed to him a most unlikely candidate for the assembly from the twenty-first district. Once Roosevelt was nominated, his election followed almost automatically.

When on a snow-blown January morning in 1882 the newly

elected assemblyman from the Terrapin District arrived in Albany, he seemed to his associates a comic figure, a Fifth Avenue butterfly, the dude incarnate. The youngest elected legislator, he sported red dundrearyish sideburns, wore a pince-nez attached to a cord — in their eyes the next thing to a monocle — and spoke with a precise high-pitched "Harvard" accent in which the broad *A*'s sounded like *aw*'s to his colleagues' ward-hardened ears. "Rawther," he seemed to them to be saying. "Mr. Speak-ah! Mr. Speak-ah!" they mimicked him in falsetto behind his back; but the speaker came to respect his ferocious energy in debate, and his fellow legislators soon grew more aware of his flashing teeth and the snap of his jaw than of his broad *A*'s. His views on social and economic questions were still rudimentary, but guided by Democratic leaders who had been prompted by a Democratic Roosevelt uncle to keep an eye on his impetuous Republican nephew, he managed to make his presence felt. In spite of his silk-stocking exterior, there was a dynamism about the neophyte assemblyman that drew men to him, a dynamism Platt innately distrusted.

Roosevelt doubled his majority in the election the following year, and in his second session burst across the front page when he demanded an investigation of Supreme Court Justice Theodore Westbrook for aiding Jay Gould in manipulating securities to gain control of the Manhattan Elevated Railroad. Though Roosevelt's investigation was in the end thwarted, he had made his mark. No longer was he a dude and a silk-stocking society man, but the minority leader in the assembly. Following the tragic death in childbirth of his young wife in 1884, and in his disgust with Blaine's nomination that same year, Roosevelt spent the next two years as a rancher in the Dakota Bad Lands, returning invigorated two weeks before the mayoral election with a wide-brimmed hat and a western manner, both of which he would keep for the rest of his life. "Dee-lighted" with his nomination, confident of victory, he feared only that the "timid good" would drift to Hewitt. Croker and Platt knew better. Hewitt won with 90,000 votes to 67,000 for George, while Roosevelt trailed with a mere 60,000. Since the normal Republican vote in New York ran between 75,000 and 80,000, some 15,000 to 20,000 votes were missing — enough to have swung the election. Where they had disappeared, to whom they had been dealt, no one knew, except possibly Platt and Croker.* In hindsight Roosevelt saw himself as picked to play Curtius and leap into the gulf that was yawning before the Republican party.† He then decided that he was really "a literary feller," married his childhood playmate, Edith Carow, who had attended his first wedding five years before, and retired to Sagamore Hill, the house he had built overlooking Long Island Sound. There he lived the life of a country squire, riding to hounds, hunting, hiking, and with his excess energy in two years writing somewhat superficial lives of Gouverneur Morris and Thomas Hart Benton and a history of New York while completing *Hunting Trips of a Ranchman* and beginning his history, *The Winning of the West.*

The presidential election of 1892 was marked by the emergence of the Populists as a third party; a disparate mixture of the Farmers' Alliance, Greenbackers, Prohibitionists, suffragists, followers of the utopian Bellamy and of George's Single Tax. Although Roosevelt privately considered President Harrison a "cold blooded, narrow-minded, prejudiced, obstinate, timid old psalm-singing Indianapolis politician," he felt obliged to support the president's renomination. Platt, still nursing his grudge against the "White House Iceberg," considered Harrison "unavailable" for a second term because of his "refusal to comply with what were deemed reasonable requests." Again he endorsed Blaine, even though the latter as Harrison's secretary of state had declined to let his name be placed in nomination. Platt's rancor blinded him to the fact that as long as Harrison controlled the party machinery and the party patronage, his renomination could not be blocked. The Easy Boss was to discover that he could not even hold his own state delegates in line, for half of them forsook Blaine.

Three days before the convention Blaine resigned his secretaryship, leaving only surmises as to whether his reason was ill-health, pique at Harrison, or a relapse of his old presidential fever. It made no difference. Though Platt united with Boss Quay of Pennsylvania to raise the helmet of the Plumed Knight,

* Many observers believed that if the votes had been counted fairly George would have won.

† Marcus Curtius, a legendary young hero of Rome, in 362 B.C. threw himself into a chasm that had rent the Forum, after soothsayers had announced it could be closed only by sacrificing Rome's greatest treasure.

though Mark Hanna was on hand to beat a very small drum for Governor McKinley, Harrison was easily renominated on the first ballot. Neither Platt nor Roosevelt took any active part in the election campaign, which despite the Populists was a lackadaisical affair, with Harrison kept at home by his dying wife and the thrice-nominated Cleveland out of courtesy refusing to campaign. Cleveland's election was inevitable, a fact that the Easy Boss may have appreciated at the convention even as he opposed Harrison.

The economic depression that darkened Cleveland's second term brightened Republican prospects for 1896. Hanna's long-range efforts to promote McKinley now roused Platt to belated counteraction. The Easy Boss had resented McKinley ever since the Ohio congressman had profanely rebuffed his emissaries in 1888, and he had come to distrust McKinley's high-tariff obduracy and his ambivalent attitude toward the gold standard. Added to all this was Hanna's upstart refusal to be "reasonable." Platt planned to split the convention vote through a proliferation of "favorite sons." Then in the ensuing deadlock, after McKinley had been sufficiently abraded, Platt would trot out his own compromise candidate, the septuagenarian Levi Morton, a former vice-president and, by Platt's definition, "the safest governor New York ever had." But Hanna had done his spadework all too well, as Platt soon realized, and McKinley's nomination followed on the first ballot.

McKinley's "rising sun of prosperity" seemed unbeatable until it was partially eclipsed by William Jennings Bryan's thunderous Cross of Gold speech. During the summer the Democrats for a time thought they had found in the silver-tongued Bryan a candidate who could beat McKinley and the gold standard. But by November, Hanna's astutely managed advertising scare-campaign carried Republicans to their greatest triumph since Grant's. Though the election brought forth no hallelujahs from Amen Corner, it did increase the Republican majority in the New York Assembly and strengthen Platt's grip on the Organization that he liked to spell with a capital *O*.

The first task of the new assembly meeting in Albany in January, 1897, was to fill the state's vacant seat in the United States Senate. Platt demurely disclaimed any intention of himself being a candidate, maintaining that he never had "any affectation about office-seeking and office holding." Yet somehow word went out from 49 Broadway to the various committeemen, and from them to the front rooms and back rooms of Albany that Platt was the man. Soon every ward and precinct resounced with "spontaneous" demands for the Easy Boss. In 1885 Platt had laid tentative plans to worm his way back into the Senate, only to have them upset by the election of a Democratic state administration. Two years later a senate seat again fell vacant, but his politician's sixth sense warned him that the time was not yet. Now he sensed that the moment had at last arrived. Coyly modest, he let it be known that if all the "practical" Republicans were for him there was little he could do except bow to the inevitable. The banquet that the "Boys" were preparing for the new senator, he assured his followers, would not be a "Platt" banquet but merely one for the winner of the senatorial contest. When the Republican assemblymen caucused in Albany to choose their new senator, the Easy Boss was ensconced in his usual inconspicuous place in Amen Corner. Of the 149 caucus votes, Platt "had to be content with 142," since there were seven recalcitrants who held out for the overly respected lawyer, Joseph Choate. (The names of those seven, properly annotated, found their way into one of the more active cubbyholes of Platt's desk.)

In contrast to Platt's mole-like progress toward his fixed goal, Roosevelt was advancing with strident confidence toward a goal which he himself had not yet determined. Two years of the Sagamore Hill idyll had made him restless for larger horizons than the sea from his window. Above all else, as he admitted to his friend, Massachusetts Senator Henry Cabot Lodge, he wanted to get back into politics. Harrison's election had seemed to offer a way in, and the well-connected Lodge was ready to act as guide. To pay off his nomination obligation, Harrison had made Blaine his secretary of state. It was a department that fascinated Roosevelt, so much so that he would even have been willing to stomach his distaste for the man from Maine to work there as an assistant secretary. But Blaine wanted no part of Roosevelt. To Lodge's wife, who sounded him out on an appointment, Blaine replied that "I do somehow fear that my sleep at Augusta or Bar Harbor would not be quite so easy and refreshing if so brilliant and aggressive a man had hold of the helm." Harrison, importuned by Lodge, did not at first want to appoint Roosevelt to *anything*, but finally agreed to make him one of the four civil service commissioners. It was a job paying $3,500 a year that controlled no patronage and that up until then had gone begging. Roosevelt, to the president's surprise and later regret, accepted it. Until Roosevelt arrived, the civil service commission was a quiet backwater in the aptly named Concordia Building. It would not remain so for long.

Harrison's attitude to civil service was one of lip service, and even then his lips did not move much. His postmaster general, the Philadelphia merchant and Sunday school teacher, John Wanamaker, felt it his civic duty to replace 30,000 fourth-class Democratic postmasters, while other cabinet members prepared to purge their departments with Jacksonian thoroughness. To these expected political manifestations, Roosevelt was the unexpected counterweight. No sooner did he become commissioner than he made the cause of civil service his own, and no Roosevelt cause was ever kept under a bushel. As for the three other commissioners, it was almost as if they did not exist.

Until Roosevelt made his obstreperous appearance the merit system had had little popular appeal. With all his fiery energy the new commissioner for the first time made it newsworthy. Six years he was to spend on the commission. After his first six weeks he announced proudly that he had "made this commission a living force," and he promised that the law would be enforced "up to the handle everywhere, fearlessly and honestly." In Cleveland's administration the Pendleton Law had placed many government employees on classified lists, and the sympathetic Cleveland added several thousand others by executive order. Under Harrison's coldly indifferent eyes, most of his administrators were preoccupied with dismantling this civil service structure. For them the new commissioner stood like a lion in the path, and complaints soon filtered through to the White House. Roosevelt's goal, as he explained in the commission's 1892 report, was to have each man enter "the public service on his merits, after fair trial, in comparison with others of his fellow citizens and be retained as long as he serves the public." The spoils system was "a fruitful source of corruption in national life"— that kept "decent men" out of politics.

Vociferously Roosevelt proceeded to enforce civil service procedure, to lay down to recalcitrant officials that the law was obligatory and not optional. He reformed the examinations and opened many of them to women, he spoke all over the country to marshal public opinion behind the civil service program, he lobbied for additional funds for *his* commission, he greatly improved the distribution of federal offices, and wherever he could be extended the classified system. "No political influence will help you in the least," he told one importunate job seeker, "not both your senators and all your representatives in Congress together could avail to have you certified for our registers." Before long the Mugwumps were rallying to the man they had denounced.

Cleveland's vindicating reelection in 1892 left Roosevelt in an ambivalent position, for as a Republican he had often denounced the Democratic leader. He now wanted to continue as a civil service commissioner, yet hesitated to ask a favor of a man whom he had reviled. Schurz, acting as intermediary, went to see Cleveland, informing him that by reappointing Roosevelt he could deal a blow to the spoils system from which it would never recover. The president agreed to allow Roosevelt to continue the good work.

Roosevelt enjoyed Washington. His public life provided a satisfying outlet for his combative nature. His private life brought him in contact with most of the influential men and women of the day. But, after six years, he found himself growing restive, eager for some newer challenge now that he had established the future of the civil service movement.

As an assemblyman Roosevelt had for a time presided over an investigation into police corruption in New York City. What he learned then convinced him that the city's whole police system needed overhauling. When in 1912 reform Mayor Willian Strong offered to appoint him one of the city's four police commissioners he jumped at the chance. Putting Washington behind him, he arrived at the dingy police headquarters on New York's Mulberry Street one May morning of that year almost at a dogtrot, accompanied by the Danish-born social reformer Jacob Riis and the police reporter Lincoln Steffens. "Where are our offices?" were his first words. "Where is the board room? What do we do first?" What he did first was to have himself elected president of the police board. In the two years that he remained at police headquarters, the other three commissioners faded into the background, protesting at times, sometimes conniving, but little more than shadows. Roosevelt's presence was and would remain front-page news. To his new job he brought his energy, his exuberance, his delight in playing soldier and his unquenchable zeal to make his city and his country a better place. At first he was enormously popular in his explosive efforts to shake up the department. To that corrupt old building he brought a new sense of honesty and honor as well as of efficiency. He saw to it that recruits were appointed by examination rather than pull. Promotions came to be by merit, and the new commissioner made a beginning of civil service. Headlines flashed, as they had always flashed for Roosevelt; Roosevelt On Deck; New Police Brooms Busy; Delinquent Policemen Get Short Shrift From Roosevelt. Not content with sitting in his office, he made sudden visits to station houses and prowled the streets looking for delinquent policemen. Wearing a pink shirt and a tasseled cummerbund, his teeth and eyeglasses flashing, he paced his office giving the orders that made the fusty building hum. Policemen were discharged in droves, much to the anger of Boss Platt who saw his "boys" removed by the Republican hand that should have fed them. "Sing, heavenly muse," Arthur Brisbane wrote in mock heroics in the New York *World*, "the sad dejection of our poor policemen. We have a real Police Commissioner. . . . His teeth are big and white, his eyes are small and piercing, his voice is rasping. . . ."

After a Fifth Avenue dinner party Roosevelt used to like to wander through New York late at night wrapped in a black cloak, his wide-brimmed hat hiding his face, ready to pounce on any dozing or otherwise derelict policeman. Then as the first light flickered in the east he would slip in to Mike Lyons's restaurant on the Bowery for a plate of ham and eggs before heading back to headquarters to sleep a few hours on his office couch in preparation for another strenuous day. Haroun-al-Roosevelt, the newspapers took to calling him. To the public he seemed a Richard Harding Davis character come to life.

But Commissioner Roosevelt's popularity suffered a spectacular drop later in the year when he attempted to enforce the state's Sunday closing law against saloons. Originally sponsored by Tammany, the law had served up until then chiefly as a means by which the police could blackmail those saloon-keepers staying open on Sunday. The large saloons owned by Tammany chiefs were of course unmolested. Other saloon front doors might remain officially closed, but there were always the rear doors, and thirsty householders could "rush the growler" at the side. Though doubtful at first of the law's feasibility, Roosevelt took the legalistic view that it must be obeyed, and dispatched his high-helmeted policemen to enforce it. Even the sacrosanct saloon of "King" Calahan was shut down, to the outraged astonishment of that Tammany master. "I do not deal with public sentiment," announced Roosevelt, "I deal with the law."

In this case public sentiment proved far more a force than the commissioner had reckoned with. Workingmen of New York craved their Sunday beer, and anyone who ordained a dry Sunday could count on their hostility. German-Americans, that large and law-abiding group, were outraged to find their beer gardens closed, and the German societies staged a protest parade. Ferries to beer-blown New Jersey grew crowded each weekend. Dry-mouthed beer lovers muttered about the wealthy sports who could legally wet their whistle at meals, and their resentment was not dimmed by the spectacular raid that Roosevelt launched one Sunday to close down Sherry's. Enemies of reform and enemies of Roosevelt united to make things difficult for the overconscientious commissioner. Hostile legal minds resurrected old blue laws that would have closed down florists, soda fountains, delicatessens and bootblacks on Sunday; and Roosevelt, meeting the challenge dead on, had the police padlock Sunday ice cream parlors. "The law," he announced, "will be enforced in every particular." Even Mayor Strong begged him to go easy, implying that if he did not he was through. Roosevelt found himself baffled at every turn. Finally a judge ruled that since the statute in question permitted a man to take liquor with his meal, "seventeen beers and a pretzel made a meal!"

The press that had welcomed the new commissioner so enthusiastically now turned against him. Platt, meanwhile, was conniving with Commissioner Andrew Parker, a clever, devious lawyer opposed to Roosevelt both personally and politically. Increasingly angered at the removal of "my men" from the police force, Platt hoped to deadlock the board of commissioners and bring Roosevelt to a standstill. In this he was at least partially successful. Parker conspired so actively against Roosevelt that finally Mayor Strong was forced to bring charges against him. When

Parker's duplicity was thoroughly exposed at a public hearing, the mayor ordered his dismissal; but the governor, nudged by Platt, refused to approve the order. Roosevelt in turn refused to make concessions. To his doubting friend Lodge he wrote almost plaintively that "the decent churchgoing Republicans are strongly for me . . . the Platt machine people . . . are on the verge of open war with me."

On becoming commissioner Roosevelt had thought that in a couple of years he could put the police department in good working order. But as his second year spun itself out he found himself at an impasse, frustrated and discouraged. The legislature had passed an amendment to the closing law providing that hotels could serve liquor on Sundays, while defining a hotel as "a structure with ten bedrooms." Two thousand such bar-hotels sprang up in New York within the year, most of them using the spare rooms for prostitution to pay the overhead. But Roosevelt had lost heart for another drag-out fight. As 1896 drew on he concerned himself much more with the coming presidential election than with the obduracies of the New York Police Department. During the summer and autumn he campaigned furiously for McKinley and the gold standard. The Republican victory in November gave him new hopes and new ambitions.

An expansionist to his very bones, he had found events in Cuba increasingly unsettling, and like a war horse he sniffed battle from afar, yearning above all else for a place in the Navy Department. His accommodating friend Senator Lodge approached another Roosevelt friend, William Howard Taft, who had easy access to McKinley through the secretary to the president John Addison Porter. On the day after the inauguration Taft, accompanied by Porter, visited McKinley to urge him to appoint Roosevelt First Assistant Secretary of the Navy. But McKinley was as reluctant at first as Harrison had been to have such a restless and restive man in his administration even in a lesser capacity. When Taft persisted, the president waveringly expressed the hope that Roosevelt "had no preconceived notion which he would wish to drive through the moment he got in." As a man of peace, McKinley had vowed to do his best to avoid the calamity of a war with Spain. He could not help being apprehensive of a firebrand in the Navy Department who clamored for such a war, who yearned to chase the Spaniards out of Cuba, annex Hawaii and even Canada, cut a canal across Nicaragua and heaven only knew what else. But Lodge reassured him that he "need not give himself the slightest uneasiness," since Roosevelt (though he privately considered that McKinley had the backbone of a "chocolate eclair") had promised in writing that his sole aim would be to make the administration a success.

So eager was Roosevelt for his naval appointment that he even turned to Platt about whose "absolute disregard of decency" he had complained earlier in the year. In December he attended a harmony dinner for the man he had labeled "as bad as Croker" and pledged himself not to support Choate's candidacy for senator. The pacific McKinley had no intention of antagonizing the reintegrated Senator Platt, and as a conciliatory gesture had not only accepted a Platt handyman in the Treasury Department but had again placed that old bone of contention, the collectorship of the Port of New York, in the jaws of the Easy Boss. Without the approval of the New York senator, McKinley hesitated to give Roosevelt an appointment. Platt's antipathy to Roosevelt made him slow to appreciate that the translation of that "disturbing element" to Washington was a good way of getting rid of him. "Anybody but that fellow," was his first reaction. But after Roosevelt had harmoniously refused to support Choate, Platt let it be known that he considered the independent police commissioner would probably "do less harm to the Organization as assistant secretary of the navy than in any other office that could be named." Given Platt's *nihil obstat,* Roosevelt's appointment was confirmed.

The speedily resigned police commissioner arrived in the Navy Department at a time when Pulitzer and Hearst were outbidding each other in their yellow-journalistic efforts to whip up a war with Spain over Cuba. A generation had passed since the Civil War, the realities of that sad conflict had become romanticized, and the mood of the country was as pugnaciously expansive as that of the still-young man now expectantly occupying the desk of the First Secretary of the Navy. For Roosevelt, war — any war — seemed, and always would seem, the ultimate test of manhood, the Great Adventure. He soon discovered that his responsibilities and opportunities in the Navy Department were larger than he had anticipated. The elderly Secretary of the Navy John Long was notable chiefly for his lack of energy and his absences from Washington. So the assistant secretary soon found himself acting as the real secretary as he set himself the task of improving the Navy's efficiency and morale, creating propaganda for a larger fleet, and cheerfully preparing for the war with Spain that he considered inevitable. "My chief usefulness," he confided to Lodge at the year's end, "has been that I did not hesitate to take responsibilities . . . and that I have continually meddled with what was not my business."

Even the explosion of the battleship *Maine* in Havana Harbor, though it shook the country and enthralled Hearst, brought no reaction from Secretary Long. Ten days later Roosevelt, taking advantage of his chief's customary absence, sent a telegram to Commodore Dewey, whose Asiatic Squadron was then in Hong Kong, ordering him to coal his ships, make sure that the Spanish squadron did not leave the Asiatic coast, and prepare for offensive operations in the Philippines — an order that outraged Long when he learned of it and that made the subsequent victory at Manila Bay possible.

With the sinking of the *Maine*, in hindsight most probably an accident, McKinley found himself swept into the war he had dreaded by the mindless urgency of popular feeling abetted by the Hearstian slogan that soon became the nation's battle cry: "Remember the *Maine*!" Eleven days after the American war declaration Roosevelt resigned from the Navy Department to organize the First Volunteer Cavalry Regiment. And for the first time he felt his life's real purpose. "I would have turned from my wife's deathbed to have answered that call," he told his military aide a few years later. The war was "my chance to cut my little notch on the stick that stands as a measuring rod in every family."

The country's history might indeed have evolved differently if the First Volunteer Cavalry Regiment had kept its original name of Teddy's Terrors. But the Rough Rider label, quickly and conveniently attached to the unit by newspapermen, gave it the aura of a legend before it got started. Congress had authorized three such regiments to be recruited in the southwest and mountain states, and Secretary of War Russell Alger offered Roosevelt command of the first. Roosevelt refused, on the grounds that it would take a month before he had mastered the science of war. By then the real war might be over, and he preferred to see action first as a lieutenant colonel of the Rough Riders under the command of his friend of the regular army, Colonel Leonard Wood.

Roosevelt ordered his uniform from Brooks Brothers and hurried to Texas to watch his recruits pour in. For all that he was second-in-command, he and everybody else seemed to regard Teddy's Terrors as his private regiment. "Teddy's" abiding fear was that the war would end before he got there and that he and his Rough Riders would miss the fun.

That comic-opera war did manage to last three months, long enough for the Rough Riders to get to Cuba with the martial Roosevelt now in command of the regiment as they advanced to San Juan Hill. The charge up that hill would become the heroic event of a war (in which only 379 were killed) so embroidered by legend that even the participants would grow vague afterward as to just what had happened. Colonel Roosevelt did lead the charge on horseback, most of the Rough Riders following on foot; he was the most conspicuous figure in the field, men died near him, bullets buzzed close to him, and one nicked his elbow. He may or may not have been the first to reach the crest, but certainly he was the most visible of the ridge's conquerors. For what he did that day he felt, and would continue to feel, that he deserved the Congressional Medal of Honor.

Roosevelt had made his mark on civil service and on the New York Police Department, marks that were to prove indelible. With the Spanish-American War he made his mark on history, the one military hero of that unmilitary venture. It had been, as he told reporters, a "bully time and a bully fight." By mid-August he had returned to the United States and was a temporarily quarantined with his Rough Riders at Montaug Point, Long Island. Hints had already reached him that the nomination for governor of New York that year could be his.

Not many miles away, at Manhattan Beach and facing the same Atlantic, the frail and now rapidly aging Platt sat on the veranda of the Oriental Hotel. The year before, in the New York mayoralty election held for the first time under a new charter which consolidated Manhattan, Brooklyn, Queens, Richmond and the Bronx, he had at least evened the score with the reformers who had so irritated and hampered him under Mayor Strong. For this election the reformists under the banner of the non-partisan

Citizens' Union had picked as their candidate the former Republican mayor of Brooklyn and president of Columbia College, Seth Low. Platt admitted to the "sincerest and profoundest contempt for non-partisanship," and when the Citizens' Union requested the cooperation of his organization, he demanded specific pledges in return. Three years before, he had cooperated with the anti-Tammany "good government" group to elect Mayor Strong, only to have the mayor bite the hand that fed him votes. When Low refused to pledge himself to Amen Corner, Platt fielded a "regular" candidate, thus splitting the anti-Democratic vote and making a Tammany victory inevitable. Tammany's Croker produced his candidate, Robert Van Wyck, a pliable nonentity from an old Dutch family. Privately the Easy Boss and the Tammany boss had made their own accommodations, and the result was what they had anticipated. Van Wyck was elected by a minority of the voters, though with a plurality of 80,000 votes over his nearest rival. For Tammany it was a night of triumph, with bands blasting out "There'll Be a Hot Time in the Old Town Tonight" and marchers tramping the streets with banners emblazoned: TO HELL WITH REFORM!

The election left a much divided Republican party and an ominous election-year situation at Albany. In 1896 Platt had forced Congressman Frank S. Black on his organization as candidate for governor over the objections of some of his younger lieutenants. Black was also backed by the Republican Independents and won overwhelmingly. But the Independents were soon alienated when Black appointed a Platt lieutenant, the notorious lobbyist Louis Payn, to the boodle-sensitive position of superintendant of insurance. Another Platt subordinate became commissioner of public works. Black himself initiated a "starchless" civil service law to aid in the selection of more "worthy" candidates for state employment. As his term neared its end he found himself shadowed by the Erie Canal improvement scandal. His chances of reelection seemed negligible, and those of almost any Republican slight.

The ominous autumn was much discussed that August on the Oriental Hotel veranda where Platt met almost daily with the forty-one-year-old chairman of the Republican State Committee, Benjamin Odell, Jr., and the even younger president of the New York County Committee, Lemuel Ely Quigg. Republican prospects seemed bleak, yet as Odell pointed out, there was an optimistic countercurrent of Roosevelt sentiment throughout the state, newspapers were beginning to take him up, he was "in the air." Quigg, at odds with Black, and as a reporter and later a congressman long a friend of Roosevelt's, argued that the returned war hero was the only candidate who could win the election.

Platt, rocking slowly in the wicker chair, agreed "that at best we would have a hard time to elect a governor in 1898." Black was indeed out, but that did not mean Roosevelt was the only alternative. Black supporters would be against him, many of the organization "boys" were uneasy about his reformist impulses, the Sunday beer drinkers had not forgiven him, and the soldiers of the New York National Guard were nursing a smoldering grudge against the Rough Rider colonel who had called them cowards.

Having opposed the Spanish-American War, the Easy Boss was unimpressed by military glory. Even if Roosevelt might prove the silver lining to the lowering election clouds, Platt had a "little might of apprehension" about his "impulsive nature." "If he becomes governor of New York," he mused "sooner or later, with his personality, he will have to be a candidate for the president of the United States . . . I am afraid to start that thing going."

Still lost in his quandary, the Easy Boss sent for Chauncey Depew. For Chauncey the answer was obvious:

> Mr. Platt, I always look at a public question from the view of the speaker's platform. Now, if you nominate Governor Black and I am addressing a large audience — and I certainly will — the heckler in the audience will arise and interrupt me, saying: "Chauncey, we agree with what you say about the Grand Old Party and all that, but what about the canal steal?" I have to explain that the amount stolen was only a million, and that would be fatal. But if Colonel Roosevelt is nominated, I can say to the heckler with indignation and enthusiasm: "I am mighty glad you asked that question. We have nominated for governor a man who has demonstrated in public office and on the battle field that he is a fighter for the right, and is always victorious. If he is elected, you know and we all know from his demonstrated characteristics — courage and ability — that every thief will be caught and punished, and every dollar that can be found restored to the public treasury." Then I will follow the colonel leading his Rough Riders up San Juan Hill and ask the band to play the "Star-Spangled Banner."*

* *My Memories of Eighty Years,* pp. 161–162.

After "a heap of thinking" Platt finally decided to let Quigg go to Montaug Point to sound out the Rough Rider on his amenability. First of all, did Roosevelt want the nomination? Would he as governor agree to "consult" with Platt? Would he refrain from making war on the Organization?

Roosevelt was receptive. He *did* want the nomination. He agreed that he would

> not make war on Mr. Platt or anybody else if war could be avoided; that I certainly would confer with organization men, as with everybody else who seemed to me to have knowledge of and interest in public affairs, and that as to Mr. Platt and the organization leaders, I would do so in the sincere hope that there might always result harmony of opinion and purpose; but that while I would try to get on well with the organization, the organization must with equal sincerity strive to do what I regarded as essential for the public good; and that in every case . . . I should have to act finally as my own judgment and conscience dictated and administer the state government as I thought it ought to be administered.*

Quigg was satisfied that this was "all anybody could expect," even though Roosevelt did not bother to hide certain misgivings about the Organization. The two met Platt and Odell in mid-September at a private room in the Fifth Avenue Hotel for a talk. Reporters could learn nothing except that the talk was "satisfactory." Roosevelt as a regular had had to agree to decline the nomination from his friends in the Citizens' Union who wanted to run him as an independent. With this self-denying understanding, Platt threw the support of the Organization to the Rough Rider. *Aut Roosevelt aut nullus*!

Before the convention met, Roosevelt's technical eligibility came into question. According to the state constitution, a candidate had to have a continuous residence of five years in New York. Boss Croker had turned up documents and handed them over to disgruntled Black adherents, showing that in the preceding March Roosevelt had signed an affidavit that he had been "a resident of Washington" since October 1897 and as such not liable to a New York personal property tax. Roosevelt blamed his lawyers and produced a letter he had written just before he sailed for Cuba declaring that he did not want to do anything in regard to

* *Autobiography*, pp. 295–96.

taxes that might cost him his New York vote. The practical-minded Odell suggested to Platt that since the attorney general alone could initiate proceedings, all that was necessary was to elect a straight Republican ticket and the residence matter could be forgotten. The Easy Boss agreed and ordered that Roosevelt's nomination be carried through.

When Platt, the "delegate from Tioga," entered Saratoga's flag-draped convention hall, delegates crowded round to pay homage to "the old man," while the band played "Hail to the Chief." It fell to Chauncey Depew to place Roosevelt's name in nomination, amid storms of cheers from nine hundred "lusty throats." Without more ado they ratified the Easy Boss's choice 753 to 218.

Even with the Rough Rider leading the campaign, the election outcome remained dubious. Croker, in a customary close-election maneuver, had picked an outstanding and honest candidate, Justice August Van Wyck of the Supreme Court of New York, the distinguished brother of the city's undistinguished mayor. The canal scandal had placed the Republicans on the defensive, and Democrats had a more personal issue in their claim that "Tax-dodger" Roosevelt was either legally ineligible or "morally disqualified." "By nominating Colonel Roosevelt," Boss Croker declared righteously, "the Republicans are trying to escape the consequences of the canal frauds and the other glaring acts of maladministration." Then the quick-tempered Croker tripped himself by refusing to renominate the Democratic Supreme Court Justice Joseph Daly who had served two fourteen-year terms on the bench and who had declined to name a Croker henchman as clerk of his court. Gleefully the Republicans raised the issue of boss rule and "the unsullied ermine," even to the point of nominating Daly on the Republican ticket.

Odell as Platt's chief of staff at first did not want Roosevelt to campaign actively, for he mistrusted the effect on the voters of the high-pitched voice and the high-toned accent. But Roosevelt had long grasped the charismatic quality in himself. A little over two weeks before the election he set out on a Rough Rider barnstorming tour around the state in a two-car private train, carrying with him seven of his old troopers and his old bugler in uniform. He himself wore civilian clothes, but with a black wide-brimmed felt hat that was first cousin to his Rough Rider headgear. At each whistle stop the bugler sounded the charge; then Colonel

Roosevelt would appear on the rear platform to speak briefly on courage, destiny and patriotism, and sometimes even on campaign issues. "He really believes he is the American flag," wrote John Jay Chapman, Harvard man and scholar-poet turned politician. Crowds swarmed to see and hear the Rough Rider. Often as the train pulled away men and women would run along the tracks, cheering and waving their handkerchiefs as if they could not bear to let him out of their sight. At Buffalo Roosevelt was met by a hundred men in Rough Rider uniforms who escorted his carriage to the Music Hall where the bugler again sounded "Charge." "You have heard the trumpet that sounded to bring you here," Roosevelt told his audience as the brazen notes ended. "I have heard the trumpet tear down the tropic dawn on the day that we moved to battle at Santiago, and I know what it means!"— a remark he found too good not to repeat at Fort Henry and several other way stations.

The election was close, though not as close as Roosevelt in his pessimistic private mood had anticipated. He had thought he might win by ten to fifteen thousand votes. His actual plurality was 17,786 out of a total vote of 1,305,636. Platt, saddled with Roosevelt, tried to console himself with the fact that the new governor was "the only man who could have carried our standards to victory this year."

A showdown between the Rough Rider and the Easy Boss was not long in coming. Shortly after the election Platt called on Roosevelt to talk over affairs in Albany. At this time he courteously asked the governor-elect if he had any friend in the assembly he wanted on any particular committee. Roosevelt said he was under the impression that the speaker appointed the committees. "Oh," said Platt, "he has not been chosen yet, but of course whoever we chose as speaker will agree beforehand!" A week after this Platt sent for Roosevelt to say that the governor would be glad to know he was going to have a most admirable new man as superintendent of public works to replace the present superintendent, then taking shelter from a criminal investigation. Roosevelt was not glad. "I told the Senator very politely that I was sorry," he wrote in his autobiography, "but I declined to lose my temper, merely repeating that I must decline to accept any man chosen for me, and that I must choose the man myself."

Yet, though such differences of opinion would persist, Roosevelt was resolved to do all he could to remain on good terms with Platt. "I always did my best, in good faith, to get Mr. Platt and the other heads of the machine to accept my views," he wrote in retrospect, "and to convince them by repeated conversations, that I was right. I never wantonly antagonized or humiliated them. If after repeated and persistent efforts I failed to get them to support me, then I made a fair fight in the open." When Platt came back to New York for the weekend from Washington, Roosevelt would often journey down from Albany to have breakfast with him. The breakfast conferences between the Easy Boss and the difficult governor caused much arching of reformist eyebrows, but Roosevelt saw them as a means of maintaining a tenuously harmonious relationship to the Organization without which, after all, the Republican party could not endure in New York as a party. He realized that to unworldly reformers his breakfasts at the Broadway Hotel had sinister significance, that he would be suspected of having sold out. Yet to him this casual contact with its superficial goodwill was vital. As he explained:

> Any series of breakfasts with Platt always meant that I was going to do something he did not like, and that I was trying, courteously and frankly, to reconcile him to it . . . As long as there was no clash between us there was no object in my seeing him; it was only when the clash came or was imminent that I had to see him. A series of breakfasts was always the prelude to some active warfare. In every instance I substantially carried my point, although in some cases not in exactly the way in which I had originally hoped.*

Roosevelt later estimated that in his differences with Platt he had carried his point nine times out of ten, and the record of his two years as governor seems to bear him out. When Payn's term as insurance commissioner expired in 1900 the governor, though solicited by Platt, refused to renew it since he felt that the venal Payn embodied the very type of "political corruptionist." The most he would do was to offer three or four other names for the Easy Boss to choose from. Reluctantly, Platt gave way.

Increasingly the Easy Boss grew uneasy over Roosevelt. The young governor, with his overabundant zeal and his commitment to reform, had become as conspicuous by how he did things as by what he did. "I have always been fond of the West African

* *Autobiography*, pp. 311–12.

proverb: Walk softly and carry a big stick; you will go far," he announced, and to Platt the announcement had an ominous ring. The governor's popularity had increased enormously since his election. Although he disliked the nickname, people were calling him Teddy with belligerent affection. Outside New York he was still the Rough Rider hero of San Juan Hill. Within the state he had shown himself an able executive, a sponsor of civil service as well as of tax reform and factory regulation, determined in his own words to hold his party "as resolutely against improper corporate influence on the one hand as against demagogy and mob rule on the other." However sour such words sounded in Platt's ears, he had to face the fact that Roosevelt in less than two years had not only rehabilitated New York's Republican party but had even given the Easy Boss himself a veneer of respectability that he had never before enjoyed. It was time, Platt thought, to elevate the Rough Rider "to a higher position."

That higher position seemed an available reality in November, 1899, following the death of Vice-President Garret Hobart. Roosevelt was at once talked of as his successor. Seldom has there been any great popular demand for a vice-presidential candidate, but now, particularly in the West, such a demand seemed to grow up spontaneously. Roosevelt, the Harvard clubman, though he had spent only two years on his Dakota ranch, had succeeded in implanting the image of himself as the cowboy, the rough rider from the great open spaces, the embodiment of western virility as opposed to the effete easterner. For Platt, Hobart's death seemed a rare stroke of luck. His aim now was to exploit Roosevelt's appeal in order to "kick him upstairs" and replace him in Albany by a more tractable if less popular figure. "I want to get rid of the bastard," the uneasy Boss told a crony. "I don't want him raising hell in my state any longer. I want to bury him."

Months before Hobart's death, the will-o'-the-wisp of a Roosevelt candidacy had intrigued Lodge who, unlike Platt, was convinced that the vice-presidency would be a "true stepping-stone for you either toward the Presidency or the Governor Generalship of the Philippines." Roosevelt considered the possibility with little enthusiasm. He told his older sister Bamie that he had no notion of becoming the principal character in a "burial party." The vice-presidency was, he admitted, an honorable post but an empty one with too little to do; one that usually wrote "finis" to a man's political career. "What I should really most like," he wrote Lodge, "would be to be reelected governor, and then be offered the secretaryship of war for four years."

When Roosevelt was police commissioner, Riis once asked him if he had ever thought he might end up in the White House. Roosevelt's eyes flashed anger at the question, his jaw snapped, and he forbade his friend even to mention the matter again. Such thoughts, he told Riis, could kill a man politically by coming between him and his work. Then the commissioner's face seemed to screw into a knot. "I must be wanting to be president," he said, almost as if he were talking to himself. "Every young man does. But I won't let myself think of it. I must not!" Yet the thought persisted. In the summer of 1899, when he travelled to Las Vegas to a Rough Rider reunion, he made the pre-Freudian slip of remarking that he was greeted "as if I had been a presidential candidate." Nearsighted he might be, but his inner eye was fixed on the long-range prospects of 1904, the year when McKinley would have completed his second term.

Not long after Hobart's death, Platt met with Roosevelt to urge him "to take the Vice-Presidency both for National and for State reasons." Roosevelt wrote to Lodge:

> I have found out one reason why Senator Platt wants me nominated for the vice-presidency. The big moneyed men with whom he is in close touch and whose campaign contributions have certainly been no inconsiderable factor in his strength, have been pressing him very strongly to get me put in the vice-presidency, so as to get me out of the state. It was the big insurance companies, possessing enormous wealth, that gave Payn his formidable strength, and they to a man want me out. The great corporations affected by the franchise tax, have also been at the Senator. In fact, all the moneyed interests that make campaign contributions of large size and feel that they should have favors in return, are extremely anxious to get me out of the state. I find that they have been at Platt for the last two or three months and he has finally begun to yield to them and to take their view.*

Early in February Platt began manufacturing sentiment by planting a report in the New York *Sun* that "recent events have made Governor Roosevelt the logical candidate of the party for Vice-President." Enlarging on this, Quigg told newspapermen that he thought Governor Roosevelt's friends from outside New York

* *Theodore Roosevelt and His Time*, vol. I, p. 135.

were planning to sweep the convention with such a wave of public feeling as to make it impossible for him to decline. Five days later Roosevelt replied in a formal statement that "under no circumstances" could he, or would he "accept the nomination for the vice-presidency" and that his "duty" was in his own state. "Senator Platt," he concluded, "cordially acquiesces in my views on the matter." He then wrote Platt that he wanted the organization's endorsement for another term as governor. Platt replied cautiously that he needed time for "mature deliberation" since the "Vice-Presidential question is a very important one and a great deal depends on it." Later at one of his political breakfasts the Easy Boss asked the governor outright what he would do if the convention nominated him unanimously. Roosevelt replied that he would not accept, "and it is in your power to see that I am not nominated."

As winter turned to spring, the organization showed a foot-dragging reluctance to endorse Roosevelt's renomination, hoping — as he put it — "that something will occur to prevent it." Platt and Odell remained ambiguous, while beyond Amen Corner the county chairmen were whetting their knives to cut the governor down. So uneasy had Roosevelt's relations with the machine become that Lodge thought the vice-presidency might be an "honorable opening" to avoid the Albany quicksands. Roosevelt thought otherwise. "I should feel like a coward," he replied, "if I went away from this work, because I ran the risk of incurring disaster and took a position where I could not fail, for the simple reason that I could not succeed." At the April state convention called to choose delegates for the national convention in Philadelphia, both the temporary and permanent chairman endorsed Roosevelt's administration and declared he deserved another term; but the delegates failed to adopt any resolution to that effect. Platt, without tipping his hand, saw to it that Roosevelt was named one of the state's four delegates-at-large, calculating that the Rough Rider's dynamic presence could stampede the delegates into nominating him in spite of himself. Lodge warned his friend that if he went to the convention he would be nominated, and that once nominated he would be unable to refuse. Roosevelt insisted he ought to be there in person to say No to the vice-presidency. "I should be looked upon as rather a coward if I did not go," he explained to Lodge.

The week following the state convention, Roosevelt was in Chicago en route to Galena for a Grant Day speech. There at a press conference he told reporters in carefully chosen words: "I would rather be in private life than Vice-President. I believe I can be of more service to my country as Governor of the State of New York than Vice-President." He did not say, however, as in his February statement, that "under no circumstances" would he accept the nomination. "I thought that this was putting it as emphatically as I could put it," he explained to Bamie, "because the latter is an attitude which a man in active politics, who is sincerely devoted to his party, aught [sic] to be very wary about taking."

After he had cleared his desk in Albany for the summer, Roosevelt left for Washington to voice his objections to the vice-presidency in person. Much to his surprise and somewhat to his chagrin he found the national administration indifferent.

> Teddy has been here: have you heard of it? [John Hay wrote with amused malice]. It was more fun than a goat. He came down with a sombre resolution thrown on his strenuous brow to let McKinley and Hanna know once and for all that he would not be Vice President, and found to his stupefaction that nobody in Washington except Platt had ever dreamed of such a thing. He did not even have a chance to launch his nolo episcopari at the major. That statesman said he did not want him on the ticket — that he would be far more valuable in New York — and Root said, with his frank and murderous smile, "Of course not — you're not fit for it." And so he went back quite eased in his mind, but considerably bruised in his amour propre.*

Officially McKinley adopted the statesman-in-bronze stance that he was neutral as to the choice of his running mate, although at heart he would have preferred Iowa's elderly Senator William Allison. Unobtrusively he let it slip out that he did not want Roosevelt, whose criticism of the administration's conduct of the war had nettled him. The Republican National Committee wanted Elihu Root. Hanna made it known that he wished no part of the "damned Cowboy." Platt shrewdly set about forming an alliance with Pennsylvania's sad-faced cynical dictator, Matt Quay. Neither boss had forgotten his discomfiture by Hanna at the convention four years earlier. Quay felt particularly vindictive toward Hanna since the Pennsylvania boss had recently been deprived of

* Thayer, *Theodore Roosevelt*, pp. 148–149.

his senate seat, with Senator Hanna casting the deciding vote. If Platt and Quay could combine the uncritical western enthusiasm for the Rough Rider with discreet delegate-shifting in the East, then they could run away with the convention and nominate Roosevelt in spite of Hanna. Not only would Quay have his revenge and Platt be free of his obstruent governor, but Roosevelt's strength on the national ticket would carry the New York machine along with it.

Roosevelt arrived in Philadelphia several days before the convention vociferously determined not to be nominated, even though his manner seemed to belie his words. Wearing his wide-brimmed black hat among the multitude of straws, he looked the man from the West, the candidate of candidates.* In spite of the multiplying Roosevelt signs and the furor at the Rough Rider's arrival, Hanna still felt he could stem the tide with a dyke of kept southern delegates. Yet when he appealed to the White House for help in crushing the New York governor, he received merely the sibylline pronouncement that "the President has no choice for Vice-President." Furiously Hanna complained to the national committeemen from Wisconsin that "I am not in control. McKinley won't let me use the power of the Administration to defeat Roosevelt. He is blind, or afraid, or something."

From the West the delegates streamed in to Philadelphia with Roosevelt banners and Roosevelt enthusiasm. Tramping up and down before Hanna's suite, they kept up a steady chant of "We want Teddy." Roosevelt, however brief his sojourn there, fell easily into the cowboy pose. "If the West nominates me, I will take it," he told Odell in one of his shifting moods. Bimm the Button Man, more clearsighted than the politicians, had risked most of his capital by stocking up on thousands of McKinley-Roosevelt buttons and badges.

Just before leaving for the convention, Platt had fallen and cracked a rib. He had gone on to Philadelphia nevertheless, and lay in bed in his hotel groggy from opiates. The night before the opening, with his field-marshals present, he had a showdown meeting with Roosevelt. The Rough Rider, waving his black hat, had insisted that he was not and never would be a candidate, and that if nominated he would stand up in the convention and

* Some saw the hat as a symbol, but it may have been no more than Roosevelt's dislike of formal headgear.

decline. "I can serve better as governor than as vice-president," he reiterated to Platt.

"But you cannot be nominated for governor," Platt wheezed at him; "and you are going to be nominated for vice-president." "I cannot be renominated?" Roosevelt challenged him. "No," said Platt wearily, pointing to Odell. "Your successor is in this room."

With his familiar snap of jaw, Roosevelt told the ailing boss that he refused to yield to any threat; if there was to be war between them he was ready. Then, stalking downstairs, to the room where the New York delegation had gathered, Roosevelt bluntly informed them that a vote for him for vice-president would be a vote for Platt, and that if he should be nominated he would stand up in the convention and denounce the Easy Boss's plot to get rid of him. "There was great confusion," Roosevelt wrote, "and one of Senator Platt's lieutenants came to me and begged me not to say anything for a minute or two until he could communicate with the Senator."

Faced with Roosevelt's adamancy, Platt in seeming acquiescence sent for him again and agreed to have the New York delegation declare for Timothy Woodruff and to give Roosevelt his second term as governor. The Easy Boss's only condition was that if Roosevelt was nevertheless nominated by the convention, he would have to accept. Reluctantly Roosevelt agreed.

As political conventions go, the Republican National Convention of 1900 was a pallid cut-and-dried affair, with Roosevelt providing the one spot of color. Even before Roosevelt arrived, it had been whispered all over the floor that Platt was about to put forward Odell for vice-president and that Roosevelt was out as governor. Beyond rumor was the solid fact that Mark Hanna was still determined to keep Roosevelt out of Washington. On the convention's second day, Quay, in the unaccustomed role of a reformer, rose to propose a rules amendment that would base the number of delegates from each state on the total of Republican votes cast there. This would have almost eliminated the rotten boroughs of the South, the foundation of Hanna's strength. Privately Quay let Hanna know that he would withdraw his motion if the southern delegates would swing to Roosevelt. Outmaneuvered by Quay and Platt, with the western delegates obviously slipping from his control, and with no backing from McKinley, Hanna saw himself forced to acquiesce. On the night before the balloting he issued a statement that "since President McKinley is to be nominated without a dissenting voice, it is my judgment that Governor Roosevelt should be nominated with the same unanimity." Roosevelt, too, had to be persuaded. He was told that without his name beside McKinley's, the West might go to Bryan, that he owed a duty to his admirers, that in fact the vice-presidency was not as dead-end as it had been painted.

After the long-winded preliminary rituals were finally concluded, the convention on its third day was at last ready to vote, and all eyes were on Roosevelt. His presence as he seconded McKinley's nomination seemed to reach to the rafters, a Rough Rider among the politicians, an amateur of youth and vigor among the puffy elderly professionals. With tongue in cheek, but true to his word, Platt had sent the New York delegation to their seats with instructions to vote for Woodruff. It was, as he well knew, an empty gesture. When Roosevelt's name was placed in nomination for vice-president, the hall exploded. Roosevelt pictures and banners appeared from nowhere. Delegates stood on their seats and shouted themselves hoarse, tossed their hats in the air, waved their state standards, while the band struck up the old war-song: "There'll Be a Hot Time in the Old Town Tonight." Only the obedient New York delegation refrained from voting for the Rough Rider on that first overwhelming ballot.

"I am glad we had our way," Platt told reporters as the hall was clearing, then hurriedly corrected himself—"the people, I mean, had their way." Hanna was haunted by a darker thought. "Don't any of you realize" he shouted "that there's only one life between that madman and the White House?"

*Bernard Partridge's hilarious* Punch *cartoon of President Roosevelt making over Taft in his image.*

CHAPTER THREE

# The Image Maker: Theodore Roosevelt

ONE EVENING EARLY in Theodore Roosevelt's elected term he sat in the White House library after dinner with his bulky, amiable secretary of war, William Howard Taft and Taft's *svelte,* somewhat popeyed wife Nellie. The president found himself in one of his playful moods. Leaning back in his leather armchair and closing his eyes, he chanted: "I am the seventh son of a seventh daughter. I have clairvoyant powers. I see a man before me weighing three hundred and fifty pounds. There is something hanging over his head. I cannot make out what it is; it is hanging by a slender thread. At one time it looks like the presidency — then again it looks like the chief justiceship."

"Make it the presidency!" said the ambitious Nellie.

"Make it the chief justiceship," Taft said with ponderous earnestness.

At the beginning of the Republic George Washington had set the august precedent of the two-term presidency. But whether a vice-president succeeding to the presidency should count those remaining months or years as a first term was a question that had never been resolved. Roosevelt, succeeding to the presidency after McKinley's assassination, intended to settle it for himself and for the future when he announced:

> On the 4th of March next I shall have served three and a half years and this . . . constitutes my first term. The wise custom which limits the President to two terms regards the substance and not the form; and under no circumstances will I be a candidate or accept another nomination.*

* *Our Times: America Finding Herself,* p. 461.

Four days after Roosevelt's 1904 election triumph, he sent word that Taft was going to be his successor in 1908. Taft could not imagine himself as president. Later, whenever Roosevelt brought up the subject, Taft would reply: "It's good of you, Theodore, but I'd rather be a judge."

For Taft, in spite of his ambitious wife, to be a judge was all he had really ever wanted. "I love judges, and I love courts," he once said. "They are my ideals, that typify on earth what we shall meet hereafter in heaven under a just God."

William Howard Taft was born to an assured economic and social position in Cincinnati's newly minted society. He entered Yale in 1874 and managed to finish second in his class. Then he studied at the Cincinnati Law School while at the same time working at his father's law office. Neither endeavor was too time-consuming for the genial young man. For some months he examined the workings of the courts from the inside as a law reporter for the Cincinnati *Commercial,* then for his half-brother Charles's newly-acquired *Times-Star.* Charles, bearded and diminutive, and destined to great wealth, was and would remain for his fourteen-year-younger brother a fixed father figure.

In the presidential election year of 1880, Will took his first political step by stump-speaking for Garfield. At twenty-three, he already wore success debonairly like a flower his his lapel. A rising lawyer, one of the most popular of the new-generation Republicans in Cincinnati's Hamilton County, he was at the same time a young man-about-town who could scarcely bear to turn down an invitation to anything. In 1880, after a local scandal that resulted in the surprise election of a reform district attorney, he was appointed assistant prosecutor of Hamilton County, a post which he filled adequately and conscientiously if not spectacularly. The same could be said for his many subsequent appointments. For most of Taft's long life would be spent in appointive office. Only twice would he be elected to anything, once to the bench of the Ohio Superior Court, once to the presidency of the United States. In later life he explained his extraordinary succession of appointed offices to William Allen White. "Like every well-trained Ohio man," he admitted, "I always had my plate the right side up when offices were falling."

Taft was there with his plate in January, 1882, when President

Arthur served him the office of collector of internal revenue for the First District, an appointment that Arthur made primarily to spite Senator Sherman. Pressured to appoint old soldiers and other political hacks and to remove able employees because of their supposed hostility to Arthur, Taft resigned after a little over a year to form a law partnership with an old associate of his father's.

In 1884 he assisted in the spectacular disbarment proceedings against a notably shady Cincinnati lawyer, and the following January was appointed assistant county solicitor, an office undemanding enough to allow him to continue his private practice and remunerative enough for him to marry a charming and sharply intelligent Cincinnati girl, Nellie Herron. Not long after returning from his European honeymoon he was appointed by Governor Foraker to the unexpired Superior Court term of Judge Judson Harmon. Privately Taft and Foraker disliked each other, the young lawyer considering the "double-faced" governor a man of disposable ethics. But Harmon, although a Democrat, had recommended the twenty-nine-year-old Taft, and the governor accepted the recommendation. For Foraker, political considerations outweighed personal feelings. The appointment was a respectable one that would mute the criticisms of his recent teaming up with Cincinnati's notorious Boss Cox. Then, too, the governor with his presidential ambitions was aware of the rising influence of the Taft family and sensed the prudence of keeping on good terms with the politically promising William.

Taft found the appointment deeply gratifying "to a man of my age and circumstance" and later concluded that this was the honor "from which all that I have had since has easily flowed." Judge Taft on the bench was to show himself a thorough rather than a brilliant judge. After serving out the fourteen months of Harmon's term, he was elected to a five-year term of his own. "Power without worry," was how he once defined the satisfactions of judgeship. His satisfaction as a superior court judge was greater than that of his wife, who even before their marriage had visions of Washington. But for him, to be a superior court judge of Ohio was "the welcome beginning of just the career he wanted." Nevertheless, after two years, he began casting sidelong glances eastward at a temptingly vacant seat on the United States Supreme Court. Foraker, the prospect of his third-term election as governor threatened by the so-called Saloon-keepers' Rebellion, was more anxious than ever to keep on the right side of the Tafts. They in turn were not averse to keeping the tricky governor on the left. Though privately queasy, Foraker publicly urged President Harrison to appoint Taft since "his appointment would be satisfactory to an unusually high degree to the Republicans of this State, and no Democrat could justly criticize it." It was a long shot. Taft's own common sense gave him little hope. "My chances of going to the moon and of donning a silk gown at the hands of President Harrison are about equal," he wrote his father. "I am quite sure if I were he I would not appoint a man of my age and position to the bench."

Harrison did not feel he had to go to the length of appointing the legally callow Taft to the High Court merely to please Ohio Republicans, but he was willing to listen to Ohio Congressman Ben Butterworth, who urged him to make Taft his solicitor general. Taft was dubious about leaving Ohio and the unworried atmosphere of the Ohio court, but he viewed the solicitor generalship as a stepping-stone to higher judicial appointment. Nellie Taft had no doubts at all. For in her determined mind she had married a career as well as a man, and the solicitor generalship was her opportunity to get her husband out of the "judicial groove."

The Tafts moved to Washington in 1890. "I am gradually getting acquainted with prominent people here," Will wrote his father, after settling down in Washington, "and I have no doubt that after one year I shall have a pretty general knowledge of the persons who run things." Not long after arriving he met Theodore Roosevelt. But Roosevelt's varied social life was not for him. To Nellie's chagrin, Taft's outlook was legal, his most honored acquaintances the attorney general and the supreme court justices. In arguing the government's cases before the Supreme Court — his principal duty — the two-hundred-and-fifty-pound Taft for all his bulk found difficulty in holding the justices's attention. Nevertheless his period of a little over two years in arguing cases for the government would prove invaluable through the grounding it gave him in constitutional law and procedure, and although his performance was plodding he did manage to win sixteen of the eighteen cases he argued.

When Congress in 1891 created nine new appeals courts in an

effort to break the logjam of litigation in federal courts, Taft pulled every wire he could to obtain one of the new appointments. As a result, or at least subsequently, Solicitor General Taft was translated in March, 1892, to United States Circuit Court Judge Taft of the Sixth Judicial Circuit. With his appointment still hanging in the balance, he had written his father: "I like judicial life and there is only one higher judicial position in the country than that. It would be in line of promotion to the Supreme Court, and I am sure would be a fine position to hold. It would keep me poor all my life if I were to get it, but I don't see that people with very modest incomes don't live as happily as those who have fortunes. The salary is $6,000 a year." Only Nellie remained dubious. "If you get your heart's desire, my darling," she wrote him, "it will put an end to all the opportunities you now have of being thrown with the bigwigs."

Taft's next eight years as circuit judge were, he came to feel later, among the happiest of his life. During those years he also became dean and professor at his old Cincinnati Law School, an undemanding position that gave him much satisfaction, particularly since he was able to introduce the case system to the school. Traveling about pleased him, as did the social contacts, particularly the legal receptions given him at the various cities. As a federal judge he grew in stature and reputation. This world of abstractions, of presiding through musty afternoons, of hearing motions and writing opinions, was for him the best of all possible worlds, one that he never again expected or wanted to leave. He became recognized among lawyers as a precedent-breaker, yet one who stood for the strict interpretation of the Law which he viewed with a capital L as an absolute akin to the platonic idea. His ruling on secondary boycotts in the aftermath of the Pullman strike made him, to his distress, seem hostile to labor, an impression he was never wholly able to eradicate in spite of many later favorable labor decisions.

His move into a wider world came when he received a telegram from President McKinley summoning him to Washington. It was McKinley's intention to make Taft the head of a commission to investigate the Philippines, and subsequently to appoint him governor general of the islands. The president then drew up plans for a second commission to be headed by a civilian who would eventually become the first governor general. When Taft had recovered from his astonishment at receiving a telegram from the White House, he still had no idea what the president really wanted. The brief tumult of the Spanish-American War had scarcely troubled the judiciary calm of Ohio. Taft's own feeling about the war had been one of disapproval. Manifest destiny was no dream of his. On reaching Washington he relapsed into astonishment when McKinley explained that he now wanted him to head the Philippines commission. Taft's first reaction was of dismay at the thought of resigning his judgeship, and he asked the president if it would mean the end of his judicial career. McKinley assured him it would not. "If you give up this judicial office at my request," he told the dubious judge, "you shall not suffer. If I last and the opportunity comes, I shall appoint you." The Supreme Court, unspoken, remained understood. What the Philippines required was a legal mind to reframe the government, a labor of perhaps six months, nine at most. "If I am here, you will be here," the president concluded. Taft agreed to go.

Resigning from the bench to go to the Philippines was for Taft, in his wife's opinion, "the hardest thing he ever did." For Nellie, haunted by the mirage of the White House, it was a way out of the Ohio backwater, an opportunity without limits. For Taft it was a dubious future. He did not know Spanish, he was unused to command, and he felt uncertain of his untried executive ability.

Taft's arrival in Manila as head of the commission was a less than festive occasion, for the military governor, the martial General Arthur MacArthur, failed even to be on hand to pay his respects to his eventual civilian successor. MacArthur, after two years on the islands putting down insurrections, believed in rule by the bayonet. Taft, though cast in the role of a benevolent dictator, believed in granting the Filipinos the greatest possible freedom to manage their own affairs. And in any clash with MacArthur, he knew he had the backing of his friend, Secretary of War Elihu Root. Unlike the army clique, who despised the little brown men, Taft made every effort to cultivate the Filipinos and include them in his receptions and social as well as official life. "We hold the Philippines for the benefit of the Filipinos," he explained in a speech some years later," and we are not entitled to pass a single act or to oppose a single measure that has not that as its chief purpose."

Taft did not officially replace the military governor until the spring of 1901, but following his arrival in Manila he saw to it that MacArthur's power was "cut down to almost nothing." Within a year he had subordinated the arrogant role of the American military and extended civil government, curbed the corrupt Philippine judiciary, improved health conditions, set up schools, and made his portly figure in the tentlike white suit familiar and trusted throughout the islands. "You have made all decent people . . . your debtor," Vice-President Roosevelt wrote him, adding that Taft should be the choice of the Republicans for president in 1904. The governor general replied that his ambition "lies in a different direction" and insisted that Roosevelt himself should be the 1904 candidate.

In 1901, Vice-President Roosevelt had told Taft that "if I had the naming of either President or Chief Justice, I should feel in honor bound to name you." A year later Roosevelt, now president, cabled his Philippines governor general that on January first there would be a vacancy on the Supreme Court "to which I earnestly desire to appoint you." Such an appointment seemed to Taft the fulfillment of his destiny. Yet even as he rejoiced he knew he must decline. As his wife explained in her *Recollections of Full Years*:

> This was not a question which gave Mr. Taft even a shade of hesitation because he knew immediately what he must do. All his life his first ambition had been to attain the Supreme Bench. To him it meant the crown of the highest career that a man can seek, and he wanted it as strongly as a man can ever want anything. But now that the opportunity had come, acceptance was not to be thought of. I had always been opposed to a judicial career for him, but at this point, I have to admit, I weakened just a little. . . . I yearned to be safe in Washington even though it did mean our settlement in the "fixed groove" that I had talked against for so long. Mr. Taft's plain and unmistakable duty held him in the Philippine Islands.

Roosevelt was never a man who took "No" easily. After mulling over Taft's refusal for a month, he wrote that "I am sorry, old man, but . . . I find that I shall have to bring you home and put you on the Supreme Court." Faced with what seemed the inevitable, Taft cabled his acceptance which he tempered by a note presuming "on our personal friendship even in the face of your letter to make one more appeal, in which I lay aside wholly my strong personal disinclination to leave work of intense interest half done."

The prospect of Taft's removal stirred the Filipinos. Manila was soon placarded with signs of "We Want Taft." The pro-consul himself was amazed at his own popularity. One Filipino speaker became so carried away that he was ready to equip the governor general with a halo. "As Christ had converted the cross into a symbol of glory and triumph," he announced, "so had Governor Taft turned a dying people to the light and life of modern liberties." The humor of the situation was not lost on Roosevelt. "All right," he finally agreed, "stay where you are I shall appoint some one else to the court." Six months later, however, when Secretary of War Root was about to retire, Roosevelt ordered his reluctant governor general home to take his place. This time Taft could not say no. He had at least the consoling knowledge that as secretary of war he would have the general supervision of the islands he had come to love. Roosevelt admitted to Taft "if only there were three of you. Then I would have put one of you on the Supreme Court . . . one of you in Root's place as Secretary of War . . . one of you permanently as Governor of the Philippines." Nellie Taft shared none of her husband's hesitancies. To see her husband as a cabinet member was, as she admitted, "in line with the kind of work I wanted my husband to do, the kind of career I wanted for him and expected him to have."

When in February 1904 Taft moved to his ornate desk in the War Department office with its red plush hangings and the solemn gold-framed portraits of his predecessors, it was under the shadow of the autumn's presidential election. On succeeding McKinley, Roosevelt had expressed the conventional pieties about continuing the dead president's policy "absolutely unbroken," and initially he had proceeded with what would be for him caution. He caused his first uproar, a predominantly Southern one, when he invited the Negro leader Booker T. Washington to dinner at the White House — something the politic McKinley never would have done. Then out of what seemed a clear corporation sky he had launched the thunderbolt of the moribund Sherman Antitrust Act to prosecute the railroad aggregate of Hill, Harriman and J. P. Morgan, known as the Northern Securities Corporation. To gain support in his attack on the trusts, he ranged the country on a speaking tour. He had intervened spectacularly in the coal strike of 1902, forcing the obdurate operators to sit down at the bargaining table with union leaders. Through the passage of the Elkins Act forbidding rebates, he had begun his regulation of the railroads. He had bested Great Britain in the Alaskan boundary dispute. And he had warned off Britain, Germany and Italy from dispatching warships to Venezuela to collect their bad debts, even though he considered that country's ruler "a villainous little monkey." He let the "Dagos" know, however, that the United States as custodian of the Monroe Doctrine had the right to exercise "an international police power" in the case of any South American government's "chronic wrongdoing." In line with this reasoning he created the Republic of Panama. Thwarted by the Colombian Senate in his efforts to secure a strip of land for constructing a canal across the Panama Isthmus, he had dispatched a cruiser to the province of Panama to aid the revolution he had fomented there. Within hours he recognized the newly proclaimed republic which as almost its first official act granted to the United States in perpetuity a zone ten miles wide across the Isthmus. "I took the Canal," he later boasted, "and let Congress debate."

After two-and-a-half years as America's youngest president, Roosevelt with his abounding energy was the most popular public figure in the country. Everything he and his exuberant family did was news, and they were always doing something. He himself got up at six and exercised violently before breakfast; he rode a hundred miles on horseback, to set the chair-born generals an example; he read two books a day; he "discovered" writers like Edward Arlington Robinson and W. H. Hudson and Conrad; his Big Stick was the cartoonists' standby. "Teddy"— a name he hated — became a household word — would even become the name of a toy animal after he had refused to shoot a bear cub on a hunting trip.

Roosevelt seemed to embody a boisterous confidence and a fierce joy of life. Yet inwardly he suffered from periods of pessimism and melancholy. To most observers the election of 1904 seemed in prospect a Roosevelt walk-away no matter whom the Democrats might nominate. But as the year drew on, Roosevelt grew more and more apprehensive. Lacking friends and a faction of his own, and with professionals like Hanna and Platt combined against him, he feared he would be eliminated by the Republican convention just as President Arthur had been twenty years before.

"I'd rather be elected to that office than have anything tangible of which I know," he confessed. "But I shall never be elected to it. They don't want me."

One of Roosevelt's more trenchant reasons for bringing Taft back from the Philippines was to employ his skills in the coming campaign. "I have no particular aptitude for managing an army," the secretary of war-designate admitted disarmingly, "nor do I know anything about it." He did not need to know. Roosevelt intended to run his own army. What he wanted in Taft was an astute and trustworthy assistant, an administrator of enhanced reputation deft in the law where the president was clumsy, a source of strength in a critical election year. The War Department was incidental, a place for Taft to hang his hat, not for him to labor in.

Roosevelt was nominated on the convention's first ballot by acclamation. His election was almost as certain, the result never in question except in those dark doubting regions of his mind. After the election he could not longer be derisively labelled His Accidency. "Tomorrow I shall come into my office in my own right," he announced the night before his inauguration. "Then watch out for me." With such a public mandate behind him, he stormed into the White House as he had once stormed into the Mulberry Street office of the New York police commissioner. One observer saw him as "a cross between St. Paul and St. Vitus," proclaiming his Square Deal, intent on remolding conservatism in his own image. Taft in the War Department would be his right-hand man, the old reliable. So confident was Roosevelt of his secretary of war that shortly after his inauguration he left for a hunting trip in the Rockies, assured that all would go well in Washington where he had "left Taft sitting on the lid."

The next four years were all that Roosevelt had promised himself. He believed that a president had the right to do anything not specifically forbidden by the constitution, and he now put that belief into practice. His first term had convinced him that the rich and powerful were often too short-sighted for their own and their country's good, and he saw himself more and more as a progressive conservative, elected both by the people and by destiny to protect conservatism from the old-line conservatives. So great was his popularity at the beginning of his second term that there was even talk in the South of nominating him in 1908 on the

Democratic ticket. It was a popularity that would survive a business depression and the panic of 1907.

With Roosevelt the thought (though at times ill-considered) was the deed, the struggle as important as the goal. "Even if in the end everything should come to nothing," he told the visiting author-journalist H. G. Wells in his high-pitched voice, "*that doesn't matter now.* The effort's real. It's worth going on with. It's worth it. It's worth it even then." Conservation and land reclamation were worth it, simplified spelling was worth it, a pure food law and regulation of the trusts and railroads were worth it, as were all the things he advocated so vociferously in turn. Somehow, everything that Roosevelt touched became a dramatic issue. He was the first president to advocate an inheritance tax, the first to make the White House accessible to labor leaders, the first to entertain a Negro there, the first to endorse the eight-hour day and workmen's compensation measures, the first to involve himself directly in capital-labor disputes, the first to concern himself actively with the conservation of the nation's natural resources and public lands, the first to send the American fleet around the world, a multitude of firsts. Though he considered Bryan "well meaning but cheap and shallow," he would find himself, in opposing his party's reactionaries, adapting much of the Bryan program. His way, he felt with all the emphatic emphasis of his personality, was the broad middle way between radicalism and reaction.

The restless, many-faceted Roosevelt came to place more and more trust in and more and more burdens on his plodding secretary of war. Taft became Faithful John, agreeing to every Roosevelt action large or small, subordinating his own personality until he himself lost sight of it. When the president was absent, his secretary of war became pro-tem president. He supervised his beloved Philippines and he took charge of the Panama Canal construction. For a time he was acting secretary of state until Elihu Root — Roosevelt's close friend since his police commissioner days — took over the office in July 1905.

In Root, the brilliant, sardonic older friend who believed in order and doubted the possibility of improving the world, Roosevelt had acquired a restraining force that he somehow sensed he needed. For Root possessed one of the sharpest intelligences of his age, though his mind was incisive and analytical rather than creative. With his trusted friends, Taft in the War Department and Root in the State Department, Roosevelt felt he could sleep easier at the White House. They called themselves the Three Musketeers, and on memos to the President, Root and Taft signed themselves Athos and Porthos. Roosevelt was of course D'Artagnan.

"I am overwhelmed with work," Taft wrote his schoolmaster brother Horace early in 1906. "Philippine matters, Panama Canal matters, army matters, the disaster at San Francisco . . . together with the session of Congress, where I have to appear before many committees, have all thrown a heavy burden on me." He was being acknowledged by Republican leaders as the able second-in-command. Already there were murmurs of "Taft in 1908!" Nellie found her days stirring, for the Tafts came to know everyone who mattered in Washington. In good time, she was convinced, she would entertain as the First Lady of the Land.

Talk there might be of Taft as the Republican candidate in 1908, but his eye never wavered from the Supreme Court. It was still his ambition to be a justice, he admitted to a friend in December 1905. "I presume, however, there are very few men who would refuse to accept the nomination of the Republican party for the Presidency, and I am not an exception. . . . If I am to be nominated (an hypothesis to me most improbable), it will be done without any organization with which I have any connection." On New Year's Day of 1906, the president offered to appoint him to the Supreme Court to fill a vacancy caused by the resignation of Associate Justice Henry Brown. Of course he would accept. Nellie objected, urging him that in another two years the presidential nomination would be his on the familiar platter. Taft hesitated and continued to hesitate for several months. Root urged him not to take the court appointment, since he was a "presidential quantity." In his own mind Roosevelt would have preferred his secretary of state as his successor, but Root's background as a corporation lawyer would have made him unacceptable to western progressives and Root himself had no yearning to occupy the White House. Taft was second choice. Yet Roosevelt continued to leave his offer open, pointing out to Taft at their next meeting that "you have two alternatives before you, each with uncertain possibilities, and you cannot feel sure that whichever you take, you will not afterwards feel that it would have been better if you had taken the other."

Taft may have had trouble in making up his mind; Nellie had had no trouble at all. She distrusted Roosevelt, who — she felt — was using her husband as a stalking horse to promote a third term for himself by acclamation. Particularly was she annoyed at the frequency with which rumors of Taft's appointment to the Supreme Bench kept cropping up. When a family friend asked nine-year-old Charlie Taft if his father was going to become a supreme court justice, Charlie replied, "Nope."

"Why not?" the friend asked.

"Ma wants him to wait and be president," was Charlie's answer.

By January 1908, Roosevelt was faced with a dilemma. If he did not soon make his choice of a successor known and throw the weight of his administration behind that choice, the public would conclude — as had Nellie Taft — that in spite of his pledge of four years before, he had decided on his own renomination. Finally he told his secretary, William Loeb, Jr., "We had better turn to Taft. See Taft . . . and tell him . . . so that he will know my mind." Loeb at once went over to the War Department to inform Taft that "the president has decided to declare for you."

"I must go over and thank Theodore," said Taft, much moved.

Roosevelt greeted him with a slap on the shoulder. "Yes, Will," he said. "It's the thing to do."

The thing was done! The delegates who swarmed through the mock-medieval entrance of Chicago's barnlike Coliseum for the June Republican National Convention wore Taft badges in their lapels, but underneath their Taft exteriors their hearts still beat for the lost leader. Roosevelt in his biography of Thomas Hart Benton had bitterly criticized Andrew Jackson for his handpicking of Martin Van Buren as his successor. Now, seventy-two years after Jackson, he found himself doing the same thing with his "beloved Will." For the past six months Roosevelt the machine politician had been engaged in the extraordinary effort of crushing Roosevelt the leader. Nellie Taft's fear of a Roosevelt stampede was the secret hope of many a delegate. And, indeed, there was always the possibility that a fortuitously struck spark might set the convention on fire. Roosevelt's pert eldest daughter, Princess Alice, sitting in the gallery with her Aunt Corinne, found herself wishing "in the black depths of my heart 'that something would happen' and that Father would be renominated."

That undercurrent of hopeful uncertainty gave an air of tension to the flaccid convention, even a certain animation to the girdered barn with its placards and crepe paper and tricolor bunting. When on the opening day the Ohio delegation marched in carrying a large silk banner with Taft's portrait on it, there were cheers that sounded almost spontaneous, but at any mention of Roosevelt the cheers were notably louder.

Not until the second day were the indispensable trivialities over. Aloof from the 12,000 delegates and alternates and spectators, the permanent chairman, Senator Lodge, as restrained as his crisp grey beard and tight curly hair, watched with icy blue eyes. His task, his duty, was to keep the delegates in check, to prevent what he himself most wanted — Roosevelt's renomination. This he would do, but on his own terms and with no concessions to Taft family feelings. In his formal speech he knew exactly what informal effects he could conjure up. His mere mention of "the president" brought surging prolonged applause — as he knew it would. He punctuated his speech with such references. Then, on peroration, his metallic Brahmin voice grew edgy as he told the assemblage that "the president is the best-abused and the most popular man in the United States today." The roar that followed stirred the dust in the rafters. In the galleries someone began to bellow "Four, four, four years more!" and the chant spread through the vast sweaty building, from the balconies to the floor. Lodge stood there like a ringmaster, his thin mouth pursed in a smile, making no attempt to halt the demonstration. For forty-nine minutes it went on. "Four years more!" Desperately Taft lieutenants ordered the band to play "The Star-Spangled Banner," but continuing shouts drowned out the lack-luster melody.

Indicating Charlie Taft and the Ohio delegation clustered under their silk Taft banner, Lodge observed under his breath to a friend on the platform: "They say there was no Roosevelt feeling in this convention, but I will show them that there is." It looked indeed as if the convention were about to take the bit in its teeth. Charlie Taft tried to brush off the ominous chant, now accompanied by the tramp of feet. "It's nothing," he told a reporter. "They are working off a little steam." All the Tafts present though, particularly the women, looked worried, shook their heads as Taft's florid campaign manager sidled over to whisper to them.

Then, as if wearying of the charade, Lodge cracked the whip and brought the convention to order. Roosevelt's decision not to be a candidate, he told the delegates, was "final and irrevocable" and "anyone who attempts to use his name as a candidate for the presidency impugns both him and his good faith." "Anyone who would do that," he concluded, "was no friend to Theodore Roosevelt." That closing of the White House door, Lodge admitted later, was "the hardest thing I ever did in public life."

Four primitive amplifiers, hanging directly in front of the platform and ten feet above the heads of the delegates carried the convention proceedings to Roosevelt sitting at the White House telephone, the receiver glued to his ear for the whole tempestuous forty-nine minutes. Archie Butt, his military aide, noted that afterward he was "in as gay a humor as I have ever seen him."

After the Roosevelt renunciation, the nominating speeches of the following day were no more than thin exercises in elocution. The speaker nominating Charles Evans Hughs somehow even forgot to mention his candidate's name. Taft's name brought on a contrived demonstration that, for all the efforts of the Taft managers to prolong it, petered out after twenty-five minutes. Taft with his wife and their immediate friends waited for the returns in the War Department office while young Charlie Taft darted in and out with bulletins hot off the wire. Nellie sat in her husband's swivel chair, almost malignant in her tenseness. When word of the Taft demonstration came, she clutched the edge of the desk. "I only want it to last more than forty-nine minutes," she hissed. "I want to get even for the scare that Roosevelt cheer of forty-nine minutes gave me yesterday."

As the balloting was about to begin, Charlie rushed to her with a bulletin. Nellie "went deathly white" as she read aloud: "a large portrait of Roosevelt has been displayed on the platform and the convention has exploded." She sat there in pallid silence. Taft, flopped down to her right, whistled softly and tapped his fingers on the arm of his chair. Into the silence Charlie dashed with another bulletin which his mother read impassively: "A huge American flag with a Roosevelt portrait on it is being carried about the hall, and the uproar continues with increased fury."

They could not know that the impervious autocrat, Senator Lodge, had already started calling out the roll for balloting. So great was the din in the Coliseum that, polling the states alphabetically, he reached Massachusetts before the reporters were able to gather the results. But Massachusetts with her twenty-five votes for Taft was the bellwether. When Charlie came in with that bulletin, Nellie relaxed in the swivel chair; color came back to her cheeks. The Roosevelt chimera had been held in check after all. Taft received 702 votes to Knox's 68 and Hughes's 67. Then the delegates made the nomination unanimous.

Roosevelt was playing tennis on the White House court when he heard the news, and said he was "deelighted!" The day after the convention he wrote to his friend Sir George Trevelyan that he thought it very rare to find two public men like himself and Taft "so much at one in all the essentials of their beliefs and practices." Taft had gone to Hot Springs, Virginia, with Nellie, to write his acceptance speech. A stream of suggestions and advice from Oyster Bay followed him there. Roosevelt warned him what to say and what not to say, and invited him to Oyster Bay so that they could go over the speech together. To the restrained fury of Nellie and of his brother Charlie, Taft accepted, announcing publicly that he wanted to "get the President's judgment and his criticism." The president did tell him that "you are now the leader, and there must be nothing that looks like self-depreciation or under-subordination of yourself." But with the best will in the world, Roosevelt *knew* that he was the leader still. So did Taft. So did the increasingly disgruntled members of the Taft family.

Taft made his acceptance speech on a broiling midsummer day in front of his brother Charlie's Pike Street mansion, the oldest and finest in Cincinnati. "The chief functions of my administration," he told the loyal but heat-struck crowd, "shall be to complete and perfect the machinery by which the president's policy may be retained." So he saw himself in that summer moment, an epigone.

The Democrats again nominated their aging Boy Orator, William Jennings Bryan, but Roosevelt with his Square Deal had preempted most of the issues — income and inheritance taxes, regulation of corporations — and Bryan's demand for government control of the railroads did him more harm than good. Even without the Rough Rider, a Republican victory seemed foreordained.

Roosevelt entered a political campaign with almost as much zest as if it were a cavalry charge. For Taft it was purgatory. The next four months would be among the most disagreeable of his life. From Sagamore Hill came a steady stream of avuncular instruction and advice for all seasons to the "dear old trump."

For Roosevelt it was almost impossible *not* to act, particularly when he saw "that big generous fellow" doing the wrong thing. Nellie Taft saw condescension in the retiring president where Taft himself still saw only friendship. Roosevelt was the better man, something that the Tafts knew but could not bear to admit, and they reacted with self-justifying resentment. Nellie, with her jealous intuition, had first sensed the invisible rift when her husband was secretary of war. Charlie and the rest of the family were aware of it when it was still too narrow a fissure for Taft to take notice of. Yet reporters observed "a certain kind of indiscreet talk that began about that time, to be heard occasionally in the corridors of the hotel where the Taft family were stopping. It was talk gratuitously critical of Mr. Roosevelt, and it seemed to proceed from, if not originate with, those very close to Mr. Taft." Finally Taft's old college friend, John Hays Hammond, undertook the "delicate mission" of telling Roosevelt that in trying to help Taft "he was keeping himself too much in the limelight" and giving the unfortunate impression that Taft was "forced to rely on the President for everything he did." Roosevelt listened and his jaw snapped, the familiar snap. "I guess you're right," he said finally. "In the future I'll put on the soft pedal."

The soft pedal was not one that Roosevelt was accustomed to, and for all good intentions he could not watch Taft's ineptitudes without offering help and advice. "Hit them hard, old man!" he kept urging the bumbling, stumbling Taft. But all Taft's efforts could not conjure up the Rough Rider vim and zest. Although he could not bend over to place a golf ball on a tee, Taft was to put his foot into his mouth with increasing frequency. With tongue-tripping candor he often succeeded in alienating whole voting blocks. Labor men had labelled him "God-knows-Taft," when after the 1907 panic on being asked what would be the outcome of the unemployment situation, he had replied "God knows!" During the 1908 campaign when he was speaking at the tomb of General Grant, in all innocence and to the rage of the GAR veterans present he somehow brought up the subject of Grant's drinking. "Oh, Lord, I do get angry now and then over the campaign," Roosevelt wrote to Lyman Abbott, the publisher of *The Outlook*. "Of course, I suppose everyone always feels that he could manage things a little differently if he had the doing of them; but certainly I would like to put more snap in the business."

For Taft the 18,000 miles of campaigning, the hundreds of speeches, the nightmare months came to an end on election night in his brother Charlie's Federalist mansion. Most of the Taft clan were there, as was Alice Roosevelt with her husband of two years, Cincinnati's Congressman Nicholas Longworth. An older family than the Tafts with whom they were long-time friends, the Longworths considered themselves the upper-class epitome of their town. In marrying Nick, Princess Alice would find herself caught in the ambivalence of her loyalty to her father and her husband's family's loyalty to the Tafts. She was to experience it first that evening.

As the returns trickled in, it soon became clear that Taft had won a great victory, not as overwhelming as Roosevelt's of four years ago but still impressive enough, with a million and a quarter majority and with 312 electoral seats to Bryan's 162. When the news spread through Cincinnati, marchers convened on Pike Street. A band in front of the house serenaded the president-elect with "Hail to the Chief" and the hurdy-gurdy strains of "Beautiful Ohio." Members of the Citizen's Taft Club cheered and hurrahed on the sidewalk until Taft came out to speak to them. Triple-chinned, beaming, he promised that his administration would be a "worthy successor to that of Theodore Roosevelt."

A telegram from D'Artagnan in the White House congratulated the president-elect "and the country even more." Porthos replied: "It is your administration that the victory approves." Yet Princess Alice, surrounded by felicitating Tafts and Longworths, sensed with rising irritation "an unmistakable attitude, on the part of the members of the Taft family of 'here he is where he ought to be' and 'we don't owe so very much to Roosevelt anyway; he could have got along quite as well without him.' And as the returns came in there was much comparing them with the returns of 1904. Wherever Taft ran ahead of Father's figures, they fairly gloated; so, as far as I was concerned, the stage was set for the first steps that led to the 'breakup of a beautiful friendship.' "

In the interval between the election and the inauguration, the scarcely visible rift between president and president-elect was becoming more apparent to percipient insiders. Outwardly Roosevelt still played D'Artagnan to Taft's Porthos. They were as friendly and agreeable as they had ever been. Yet somehow the vital essence had gone out of their relationship, and both men knew it. Just after the election, Taft let Roosevelt know that he planned no cabinet change. "Tell the boys I have been working with," he said, "that I want to continue with all of them." Several, including Secretary of State Root, did not plan to stay. But Secretary of Commerce and Labor Oscar Straus, Postmaster General George von L. Meyer, Secretary of War Luke Wright — who had replaced Taft for the few months after the election, with the understanding that Taft would keep him on — and Roosevelt's devoted conservation friend, the Secretary of the Interior James Garfield, son of the twentieth president, intended to remain in office. On that assumption Garfield had even renewed a three-year lease on his Washington house.

When the Tafts passed through Washington in December, Roosevelt's military aide, Captain Archie Butt, dropped in on them to discuss his future duties. He found the president-elect laughing his belly-shaking chuckle, his wife looking grim. "I was cabinet-making early this morning," Taft told him, "and I thought I had settled one place at least, and just as you were announced I had told my wife. She simply wiped him off the face of the earth and I have got to begin again. The personal side of politics has always been funny to me, but nothing has been quite as funny as to have a man's career wrecked by a jealous wife." Nellie replied indignantly that she was not jealous at all. "But I could not believe you to be serious when you mentioned that man's name. He is perfectly awful and his family are even worse. I won't even talk about it."

An indolent streak in Taft's nature, never wholly under control, expanded whenever he was under stress. The office that Roosevelt so relished, he approached with foreboding. Just before Christmas of 1908 he wrote a friend that "it is a very different office from that of governor general of the Philippines and I don't know that I shall arise to the occasion or not." "I pinch myself every little while to make myself realize that it is all true," he wrote wistfully to a friend in December. "If I were now presiding in the Supreme Court of the United States as chief justice I should feel entirely at home but with the troubles of selecting a cabinet and the difficulties in respect to the revision of the tariff, I feel just a bit like a fish out of water. However, as my wife is the politician, she will be able to meet all these issues." During the ensuing winter months Taft played golf in Augusta, Georgia, and put aside all thoughts of his cabinet. Finally, to break the silence, Lodge, after consulting with Roosevelt, went to Augusta to try to plot the course of the new administration. He found himself kept at arm's length by Nellie and Charlie. When he did manage to reach the president-elect, Taft told him that his problems would be different from those of the Roosevelt years and he would need other men to solve them. He informed Lodge that he planned to keep only two of Roosevelt's cabinet: Postmaster General Meyer, whom he intended to make secretary of the navy; and Secretary of Agriculture James Wilson. Lodge reported back to Roosevelt that "it was evidently the intention to get rid of every person who might keep President Taft in touch with the Roosevelt influence."

Though hurt and troubled, Roosevelt accepted his successor's cabinet decisions with surface equanimity, merely asking Taft to let those he did not intend to reappoint know as soon as possible so that they could make their alternate plans. Publicly he announced that "Taft is going about this thing just as I would do," but privately he told the rejected Garfield: "Jim, something has come over Will, he is changed, he is not the same man."

Roosevelt in the obscurity of retirement seemed a contradiction in terms. As an ex-president, he would still be a young man. As early as the previous August he had decided on a hunting trip to the remoter parts of Africa, to be followed by a tour of Europe, travels that would keep him outside the United States until at least the spring of 1910. "Down at the bottom," he explained to William Allen White, "my main reason for wishing to go to

Africa for a year is so that I can get where no one can accuse me of running, nor do Taft the injustice of accusing him of permitting me to run the job." But it was a trip, he admitted, he fairly dreamed about, "too good to be true." On the last day of 1908 he wrote teasingly to Taft: "Ha! Ha! *You* are making up your Cabinet. *I* in a lighthearted way have spent the morning testing the rifles for my African trip. Life has its compensations."

Roosevelt's final day in office was as hectic as his other days had been. Members of his "Tennis Cabinet," chiefs of bureaus, congressmen, friends and subordinates, all kept thronging in to wish him well. He signed bills, letters and photographs while keeping up a stream of witticisms. He managed the "Irish switch" of shaking hands with two visitors at a time while calling across the room to a third. Yet he also managed to find time to send his 421st and last message to Congress, with a stinging rebuke about congressional "invasion of executive prerogative." In between callers he dashed off a hortatory memorandum to his successor warning him against dividing the battleship fleet between the Atlantic and the Pacific prior to the finishing of the Panama Canal. Then he scribbled off a note to his son Ted. "I've been full President right up to the end," he wrote, "which hardly any other President has been." When his admiring friend Mark Sullivan left after paying his respects, he accompanied him to the door. Then, as he said good-bye he expressed his simmering doubts about Taft. "He's all right," the almost ex-president told Sullivan. "He means well and he'll do his best. But he's weak. They'll get around him." And in illustration, Roosevelt pushed his solid shoulder against Sullivan's. "They'll — they'll lean against him!"

Doubtful of Taft, aware of the potential rift, Roosevelt in an effort to banish both doubt and awareness had invited the Tafts to a farewell dinner and to spend their pre-inaugural night at the White House. Taft accepted in the same conciliatory spirit, writing Roosevelt that "people have attempted to represent that you and I were somehow at odds during this last two or three months, whereas you and I know that there has not been the slightest difference between us and I welcome the opportunity to stay the last night of your administration under the White House roof. . . . With love and affection, my dear Theodore."

Taft had played golf that afternoon. "The beauty of golf to

me" he once explained, "is that you cannot play if you permit yourself to think of anything else." When he and Nellie arrived at the White House portico at eight o'clock in their White Steamer a light snow was falling. The dinner in the State Dining Room was one that Taft afterward compared to a funeral. Besides the Tafts and the Roosevelts there were only three other couples: the Roots, the bachelor Archie Butt with the Taft friend Mabel Boardman, and Admiral and Mrs. William Cowles. As they sat round the state table like mourners at a feast, Root shed tears into his soup. Only Roosevelt managed to keep things going with his high-pitched monologue which by nature and long practice he could turn on like a hose. Afterward, when the men had retired upstairs to the library for their coffee, they managed to talk more easily. But though Roosevelt still called Taft "Will," Taft in reply called him "Mr. President."

Taft left the White House early in the evening to attend a Yale smoker in his honor at the New Willard Hotel. In spite of the reunion atmosphere with its college songs and cheers, he was unable to shake off the funereal mood. Roosevelt's conservation friend, Chief Forester of the United States Gifford Pinchot, another Yale man who happened to be present, found Taft's smoker speech "curiously full of hesitation and foreboding. I cannot remember a single confident note in the whole of it." The president-elect returned to the White House at about eleven, bade good night briefly to the Roosevelts and went to bed.

By morning, the light snow of evening had turned to a blizzard, with a seventy-mile-an-hour gale howling along L'Enfant's great avenues. The city lay buried, roads blocked, wires down, streetcars and even trains stalled. By breakfasttime the storm still showed no signs of abating. Roosevelt greeted Taft cheerfully in the dining room. "I knew," he told him, glancing toward the window, "there'd be a blizzard when I went out." Taft gave his belly chuckle. "You're wrong, it is my storm," he replied, "I always said it would be a cold day when I got to be President of the United States."

Before leaving for the Capitol the two posed for a photograph on the south portico of the White House; frock-coated, bareheaded, solid men, Taft ponderous, Roosevelt as jaunty as the white rose in his buttonhole. To the chief usher of the White

House, Ike Hoover, Taft seemed "cross and uncomfortable."

Six thousand snow shovelers had been at work since daybreak clearing Pennsylvania Avenue and spreading nine tons of sand between the White House and the Capitol. Taft and Roosevelt left in a carriage drawn by six glistening bays, the top up because of the weather. In spite of the snow, both sides of Pennsylvania Avenue were packed with spectators. Some enthusiasts ran alongside the slow-moving carriage, trying to catch a glimpse of the outgoing and incoming presidents. Applause echoed all along the way, punctuated with shouts of "Oh, you, Teddy!" Roosevelt, alert to any applause, leaned forward, flashing his teeth, waving his hand, bobbling his silk hat. Taft sat back staring straight ahead, his fat face set, in complete disregard of the crowd. As they approached the Capitol, it was announced through megaphones that because of the weather the inauguration would take place in the Senate Chamber.

In his inaugural address Taft promised to carry out the Roosevelt policies, to fight the domination of the trusts, to lower the tariff, to build a "proper" army and navy, to conserve the nation's natural resources, to protect the workman and to complete the Panama Canal. "A bully speech, old man," said Roosevelt, bustling over as soon as Taft had concluded. They clasped hands, with obvious emotion. "Good-bye and good luck," Roosevelt said abruptly. "I'm off," and he hurried toward the exit. Applause, expressly forbidden, broke out all over the chamber as he was leaving.

President Roosevelt, on leaving the Capitol, was once more Colonel Roosevelt, yet even as colonel he could not help but steal the show. A huge and cheering throng followed his double surrey to the Union Station, trudging three blocks through the slush while a brass band played his favorite "Garry Owen" and the old Rough Rider tune, "There'll Be a Hot Time in the Old Town Tonight," and finally "Auld Lang Syne." During a two-hour wait in the station, the colonel held an informal reception in the Union's presidential suite. Then, when the train finally pulled in, he walked through a mass of applauding supporters to the parlor car *Clytie*. He was glad to be a private citizen again, he told them from the car steps, but he had had a "bully time." "Good-bye all," he called out, now waving his wide-brimmed hat as the train began to move. "Good luck to you." And, with the *Clytie* receding, men told each other loudly, "He'll be back! He'll be back!"

While Roosevelt was holding informal court at the Union Station, Taft and Nellie rode back from the Capitol to a large formal luncheon at the White House that was now their house. Nellie as she came through the door noticed the great brass eagle seal embedded in the floor of the entrance hall surrounded by the words "The Seal of the President of the United States." "And now," she thought, "that means my husband!"

After the luncheon, the snow — if not the cold — having abated, Taft in a fur-collared coat, with Nellie wrapped in furs beside him, reviewed his inaugural parade. Once back at the White House, free of visitors at last, the new president eased his bulk into an armchair, stretched out his legs and asserted: "I am president now, and tired of being kicked around." Yet Taft's assertion somehow failed to convince himself. A few days later when an acquaintance asked him how he liked being president, he said he hardly knew yet. "When I hear someone say 'Mr. President,' I look around expecting to see Roosevelt." Often at dinner he would refer to Roosevelt as "the President," much to Nellie's anger who pointed out tartly that what he meant was "the ex-President." "I suppose I do, dear," Taft replied, "but he will always be the President to me, and I can never think of him as anything else."

When on March 23, Roosevelt sailed from New York on the *Hamburg,* Archie Butt was there with a gift from Taft — a gold extension ruler inscribed "Good-bye good luck and a safe return" — and a letter in which the new president had unburdened himself of his doubts:

> When I am addressed as "Mr. President" [he wrote] I turn to see whether you are not at my elbow. When I read in the newspaper of a conference between the Speaker and the President, or between Senator Aldrich and the President, I wonder what the subject of the conference was, and can hardly identify the report with the fact that I had a talk with the two genlemen . . .
>
> I want you to know that I do nothing in the Executive Office without considering what you would do under the same circumstances, without having in a sense a mental talk with you over

> the pros and cons of the situation. . . . I can never forget that the power that I now exercise was a voluntary transfer from you to me, and that I am under obligation to you to see to it that your judgment in selecting me as your successor and bringing about the succession shall be vindicated according to the standards which you and I in conversation have always formulated. . . .
>
> With love and best wishes, in which Mrs. Taft joins me, believe me as ever, Affectionately yours. . . .*

During the election campaign *Punch*'s Bernard Partridge had drawn a cartoon of Taft in a Rough Rider uniform and carrying a Big Stick, a grinning Teddy-mask tied over his face. Impresario Roosevelt, similarly uniformed, stands by applauding hilariously and exclaiming: "There, there, sonny, I've fixed you up so they won't know the difference between us." And indeed it was the Roosevelt mask that Taft had assumed, that Roosevelt had expected him to assume until it became grafted to him. What Roosevelt in his egocentric exuberance did not realize, what Taft in his dependency only vaguely appreciated, was that the assumed mask concealed a man of an entirely different nature and outlook than the Rough Rider.

His successor was only slowly collecting his thoughts. Taft could not feel at ease in the White House. As always when he was under strain, he slept and ate more. He even dozed off at a funeral, and once while having his portrait painted he fell asleep standing up. Newspapermen found him standoffish, in contrast to the vociferous Roosevelt camaraderie. He grew awkwardly self-conscious. When he went horseback riding he imagined people were laughing at him.

For Nellie Taft the fulfillment of her decades-long ambition to see her husband in the White House and herself as First Lady of the land had the quality of a fairy tale, and like a fairy tale the presumption of the wish was soon to be followed by a retributive fate. As First Lady she was tied down by a host of inconsequent problems. The small details of housekeeping bothered her. State dinners, she discovered, were not paid for by the state. Instead of the serenity of her position, she found herself overwhelmed by receptions, dinner parties, musicals, unavoidable functions that

* *TR and Will*, pp. 80–81.

sapped her strength, while always in the back of her mind there loomed the frustrating image of her husband's mask. Two months after she had moved into the White House, while sailing on the presidential yacht somewhat oddly named the *Sylph*, she suffered a stroke. For months she remained in seclusion on the second floor of the White House, seeing no one but her husband and her sister, her nurse, the housekeeper and the doctor. Only gradually did she learn to walk and talk again. It was over a year before she would take part in public receptions, and even then she avoided dinners and social events where she would have to take part in small talk.

While Roosevelt shot lions in East Africa, Taft met his first legislative crisis. He had a delicate balance to keep between the western progressive minority intent on making the Republican party into an instrument of social change, and the eastern majority, for whom Mark Hanna's stand-pattism was still Holy Writ. Thirty western congressional insurgents had joined with the Democrats in an attempt to overthrow the arbitrary rule of Speaker of the House Joseph Cannon, a man whom Taft disliked intensely.

Uncle Joe Cannon, born in 1836, had been in Congress almost as long as anyone could remember. He had been present at the birth of the Republican party, and had helped nominate Lincoln. A wiry little man with narrow calculating eyes, a rapacious nose and a foul mouth, he controlled all committee appointments and alone decided who might have the floor and who might not. Rightly he was called Czar of the House. Even Roosevelt had moved warily in encounters with him. His equivalent in the Senate was the arrogant and imposing Nelson Aldrich, a self-made industrialist and financier from Rhode Island, allied to the Rockefellers by his daughter's marriage.

The Republican party platform of 1908 had promised a tariff reduction, and to Taft's bumbling honest nature a promise was a promise, even though his innate conservativism found the idea of tariff reduction much less acceptable than had the innately progressive Roosevelt. Aldrich and Cannon believed in a high tariff, but they believed in themselves and their authority more, and they came to Taft shortly after his inauguration with the proposal that if the president would use his power and influence to check the Insurgent-Democratic drive against Cannon, they in turn would support the party's platform.

Taft felt he had no choice but to accept. The resulting House tariff bill, the Payne Bill, had enough reductions in it for Taft to overlook its lapses. It did not at all suit the insurgent Senator Robert La Follette of Wisconsin, who complained to the president that the bill was against the public interest and contrary to party pledges. Taft, now uncertain of just where he stood, assured La Follette with clenched-fist emphasis that unless the bill complied with the party platform he would veto it.

Cannon and Aldrich privately regarded the Payne Bill passed by the House as merely a ploy, a preliminary to the bill they really intended to forge in the Senate. For the legislature-elected Senate was still the Millionaire's Club of Hanna's day. Such a body would have no truck with any extensive tariff reductions. The aroused senators made 847 amendments to the House bill, of which approximately 600 raised rather than lowered the tariff. When Taft objected, Aldrich tried to conciliate him by making a few token concessions, placing curling stones, false teeth, canary seed, hog bristle, and silkworm eggs on the free list; but on the essential commodities he was adamant.

Taft, trying to walk a floundering line between the insurgent westerners and the orthodox easterners, found himself swaying first one way then the other depending on who last had his ear. Unlike Roosevelt, he seemed unable either to buy his way through patronage or to apply pressure on his opponents by manipulating public opinion. After months of angry debate the tariff bill was finally passed. Ten progressive senators had voted against the bill with its soaring rates, and its passage brought protests from all over the country. Taft attempted to calm the turmoil by announcing that a conference committee of congressmen and senators would be formed to initiate a compromise bill that would revise most rates downward. So distressed was he over the tariff uproar that he even found difficulty in sleeping, and during the humid summer nights took to wandering through the White House in his size fifty-four pajamas, trying out one bed after the other.

Meanwhile Uncle Joe Cannon and Aldrich carefully loaded the conference committee with members unalterably opposed to any lowering of the tariff. Taft found himself caught in a trap. "I don't think Cannon played square," he wrote plaintively to his brother Horace. He finally signed the pseudo-compromise of the Payne-Aldrich Tariff Bill in August, observing that it was "a sincere effort" if "not a perfect bill." The outraged progressives denounced it as "just plain dishonest."

With the tactless good intentions that were so integral to him, Taft decided to go on a speaking tour of the West and Midwest to defend himself and the party position on the tariff. On a September night in the Opera House at Winona, Minnesota, he read a carefully prepared speech in which he informed his incredulous audience that "on the whole, I am bound to say that the Payne bill is the best bill that the Republican party ever passed." The tariff was the wedge; that speech the final hammer blow. After six months in the White House, Taft had split his party.

There was worse to follow for the president whose most enduring wish was to please everyone. Taft had replaced Garfield by Richard Ballinger, who had worked with the Guggenheim-Morgan Alaska Syndicate to substantiate the so-called Cunningham claims, certain rather dubious claims in the coal lands of Alaska. Although not wholly opposed to conservation, his attitude was much closer to that of midwestern businessmen than to dedicated conservationists like Garfield and Gifford Pinchot. Pinchot, still clinging to his post of chief forester, kept a calculating eye on Ballinger. An intimate of Roosevelt's and a collaborator with Garfield in conserving the country's forests and parks and natural resources, Pinchot had early made conservation his one great purpose. His dream was to have the federal government control *all* natural resources. Roosevelt at the end of his term had written him that "no two men have been so closely identified with so many of the policies for which this administration has stood."

Taft found no such identification. To the new president, Garfield, with Pinchot's assistance, had far exceeded his authority in his zeal to withdraw land from public use. Ballinger, the strict constructionist, could be counted on to right the balance.

From the beginning of the Taft administration Ballinger and Pinchot found themselves in conflict. "The soft pedal is on and on to stay," the new secretary of the interior announced. While Ballinger was commissioner, a young man in the Land Office

Field Service, Louis Russell Glavis, investigating the Cunningham claims, had come to the conclusion that they were illegal. Ballinger insisted they were valid, and when Glavis remained adamant the commissioner removed him from the case. Glavis then went to Pinchot who helped him prepare a report that he then took to Taft. For the president, this smacked of insubordination, and he refused to see Glavis although he did read the report. After reading it he ordered Ballinger to make a rebuttal "as full as possible."

After reading Ballinger's apologia, Taft exonerated him and authorized him to discharge his subordinate. Once outside the Interior Department, Glavis wrote an article for *Collier's* charging that "while in office Commissioner Ballinger urged Congress to pass a law which would validate fraudulent Alaskan claims." Ballinger called the article "a tissue of falsehoods and insinuations," and both sides demanded a congressional investigation.

Angered at the flow of information from the Forestry Service to individuals and publications hostile to Ballinger, Taft ordered all department officials to maintain silence on the controversy. When, despite this order, Pinchot wrote an open letter attacking Ballinger which he sent to the chairman of the Committee on Agriculture and Forestry, the president angrily told his cabinet that this was "a piece of insubordination almost unparalleled in the history of government." Realizing the implication of getting rid of such a close friend of Roosevelt's, Taft nevertheless felt he had no other course but to ask for Pinchot's resignation. Such open martyrdom was what Pinchot had been counting on. The news was cabled across the Atlantic to Roosevelt and reached him by native bearer while he was on a rhinoceros hunt in the Congo. "I cannot believe it," he wrote at once to Pinchot. "I do not know any man in public life who has rendered quite the same service you have rendered." Roosevelt never felt the same toward Taft after Pinchot's dismissal.

It was a foregone conclusion that the Cannon-dominated congressional committee appointed to investigate the Cunningham claims and Glavis's dismissal would find for Ballinger, just as the Democrat-Insurgent minority would find against him. The hearings dragged on for weeks. Ballinger, the strict constructionist, was indeed shown to have been far from strict in his dealings with private interests. But the most sensational aspect of the hearings was the long-concealed and reluctantly admitted fact that a letter Taft had written in exoneration of his secretary of the interior had really been composed by Ballinger and his assistant. What made matters even worse, it was brought out that the president had signed a spuriously dated document to give the impression that his decision to exonerate Ballinger was based on a report by his attorney general.

Roosevelt, as president, had a magnetic, a pied-piper quality, that drew men to him. Most people loved him, a minority hated him, no one could remain indifferent. Taft's unmagnetic presence could inspire affection, but the affection could as readily turn to indifference or dislike. Even before the end of his first year in office, his popularity was wearing thin. He could not grasp that the insurgents were the more vital force in his party. Roosevelt, who grasped it both by temperament and political instinct, wrote from London: "Our own party leaders did not realize that I was able to hold the Republican party in power only because I insisted on a steady advance, and dragged them along with me. Now the advance has been stopped. . . ." After visiting Taft early in his administration the progressive Kansan, William Allen White wrote:

> When I left the White House I knew that I and my kind, the whole progressive lot, were anathema — outlawed from his counsel. He would have none of us. Outwardly it seemed that he did not want to be disturbed. . . . It was not that. He was convinced that we were mad. He was a consistent, honest, courageous, most intelligent conservative. He believed in the existing order. He was nice about it, most felicitous, and could at times smile at it with indulgent condescension. But it was his world. He deeply resented the hands that would touch the Ark of his Covenant.*

When time had dimmed the glitter of the Rough Rider's personality and cast a veil over Taft's ineptitudes, Taft's conservative administration could be seen in historical perspective as not unworthy to be set beside that of the progressive Roosevelt. During his presidency more antitrust suits were brought against corporations than during Roosevelt's more colorful period of trust-busting; his Commission on Efficiency and Economy became the

* *Autobiography*, p. 426.

precursor of the Bureau of the Budget; he placed some eight thousand assistant postmasters under civil service by executive order; his Publicity Act made public the lists of contributors to congressional election campaigns; he proposed a constitutional amendment to legalize a general income tax, and during his administration the Seventeenth Amendment, providing for the direct election of United States senators, was finally ratified. Even in the matter of conservation, Taft's record compared favorably with Roosevelt's, for after Congress had restored him the right to withdraw lands from entry — a right it had angrily taken from Roosevelt three years before — he had withdrawn almost as much acreage as had his predecessor. But to a public responsive to Roosevelt's spectacular posturings, Taft could offer only lethargy.

Roosevelt in Africa remained almost as newsworthy as he had been in the White House. Bwana Makuba — Great Master — the natives called him, at least according to the press. His slaughter of wild animals was encompassing, nor did the papers ever print that behind the near-sighted Rough Rider several sharp-shooters always stood at the ready in case Bwana Makuba missed his target. He and Kermit between them killed 512 animals including seventeen lions, eleven elephants, twenty rhinoceroses, nine giraffes, forty-seven gazelles, eight hippopotamuses, twenty-nine zebras, nine hyenas, and a scattering of such oddly named creatures as the bongo, the dikdik, the kudu, the aardwolf, the klipspringer, and others too numerous to mention, although Roosevelt tried. Returning by way of Europe, the ex-president carried the front page with him as he visited the kings of Italy, Norway and Belgium, the crown princes of Sweden and Denmark, and Queen Wilhelmina of the Netherlands. Franz Joseph, Austria-Hungary's aged emperor, tendered him a banquet. Kaiser William broke all precedent by inviting him to join in reviewing the troops of Imperial Germany.

When the Hamburg American liner *Kaiserin Augusta Victoria*, carrying the Rough Rider, docked in New York he was greeted like a returning hero. Whistles shrilled, foghorns echoed, and an enormous naval parade headed by six battleships sailed down the harbor to meet him. The mayor of New York was at the dock, as was a regiment of Rough Riders. *Life*, the old humorous magazine, burst into verse for the occasion:

Teddy, come home and blow your horn,
The sheep's in the meadow, the cow's in the corn.
The boy you left to 'tend the sheep
Is under the haystack fast asleep.

Taft at once wrote to Roosevelt inviting him to the White House but Roosevelt declined, saying that Washington and the White House were no place for an ex-president. However, ten days after his return, Roosevelt used the occasion of his 30th Harvard class reunion to call on Taft, then at the summer White House in Beverly. In spite of a superficial cordiality, the two men were obviously ill-at-ease and did not see each other alone.

Roosevelt as the squire of Sagamore Hill, surrounded by the stuffed trophies of his marksmanship, announced that he wanted "to close up like an native oyster." Once more, this time as contributing editor to the *Outlook*, he would be merely a "literary feller." Yet the progressives, spearheaded by Pinchot, were soon to be seen on Sagamore Hill's long wooden porch. Senator La Follette, on leaving Oyster Bay, informed newspapermen that Roosevelt was not only the greatest living American but that he was in fighting trim. The disillusioned and still-ailing Nellie Taft, on hearing of the Sagamore Hill pilgrimages, told her husband: "I suppose you will have to fight Mr. Roosevelt for the nomination, and if you get it he will defeat you. But it can't be helped. If possible you must not allow him to defeat you for the renomination. It does not make much difference about the reelection."

Roosevelt left the East, in a private car provided by the *Outlook*, ostensibly to attend the Frontier Day Celebration at Cheyenne, Wyoming, but actually to make a western speaking tour of some five thousand miles through sixteen states. Every time he spoke he was page-one news, relegating the president to pages two and three. The tour was in the nature of a triumph; the return of the lost leader for whom the plain people of the plain states had waited, the Rough Rider who spoke their language if with other accents, the father-figure that Bryan could never be.

It was soon apparent that Taft's swing to conservatism was being counterbalanced by Roosevelt's leanings to insurgency. Where Roosevelt the President had hesitated, Roosevelt the Rough Rider was now unhesitatingly proclaiming the New

Nationalism; a strong centralized government that would regulate big business, unions and agriculture for the common weal, a forerunner of Franklin Roosevelt's New Deal. At the Osawatomie celebration of the John Brown centennial, Roosevelt made the most radical speech of his career, one that had been written for him by Pinchot and which he delivered with only "one or two additions and two or three changes." In it he appealed more directly to the common man than had any president since Andrew Jackson. "The essence of any struggle for liberty," he told a crowd that hung on every word, "has always been, and must always be to take from some one man or class of men the right to enjoy power, or wealth, or position, or immunity, which has not been earned by service to his or their fellows" — a doctrine which, if applied exactly, would have undermined the fortunes of both branches of the Roosevelt family. In his speech he foreshadowed the whole Progressive movement as he proclaimed a "New Nationalism" that "puts national need before sectional or personal advantage." He used his enduring phrase, "the Square Deal" to describe what he defined as not only fair play under the present rules but "having those rules changed so as to work for a more substantial equality of control." He called for graduated income and inheritance taxes, comprehensive workmen's compensation laws, an expert commission to draw up the tariff, control of political activities and expenditures of corporations, stringent conservation measures and federal regulation of the labor of women and children.

Taft was so outraged by the speech that even his golf suffered. Butt noted next day on the course that after one bad stroke "he swore a terrific oath and threw his club twenty-five yards from him in anger. This was so unlike him that even the caddies looked astonished." Taft continued to curse inwardly both at the publicity Roosevelt was receiving and his disregard of president and party in a crucial congressional election year. Writing to Charlie he complained that "Roosevelt allows himself to fall into a style that makes one think he considers himself still the President of the United States. In most of these speeches he has utterly ignored me. . . . He is at the head of the Insurgents, and for the time being the Insurgents are at the top of the wave."

That autumn Roosevelt did go through the motions of campaigning for his party, but he knew it was an empty gesture, that the Republicans with Taft as their wavering leader were slated for defeat. As he sensed in his political bones, the country was in an insurgent mood, ready not so much to vote *for* Democrats as *against* the Republicans. He saw his sourest expectations realized. In the old House of Representatives the Republicans had held 219 seats to the Democrats' 172. In the House elected in 1910, the Democrats outnumbered the Republicans 228 to 161. New York and Ohio, along with twenty-four other states elected Democratic governors. Nineteen-twelve was already casting an ominous shadow

For a year after the elections Roosevelt remained in strenuous semi-retirement at Sagamore Hill. There was no formal break with Taft, but there was no renewal of friendship. Three times the two met in an atmosphere of increasingly strained cordiality. When early in 1911, war with Mexico threatened, the old Rough Rider asked for and received the president's permission to raise and command a cavalry division in case of hostilities. Roosevelt's public break with Taft, which came finally in October, 1911, had its origins in the Panic of 1907. During that year the tottering New York brokerage firm of Moore & Schley had held a large block of shares of the Tennessee Coal & Iron Company, the value of which had fallen to less than the amount of the bank loans for which the stock was collateral. Moore & Schley's collapse would have resulted in widespread bank failures. To save the banks and stem the panic — or so they said — J. P. Morgan and his associates of the United States Steel Corporation, Judge Elbert Gary and Henry Frick, had agreed to buy up the shares of Tennessee Coal & Iron at about double their market value. Even at that price they were getting a bargain, as they well knew. Posing as public benefactors, Frick and the dapper Judge Gary had dropped in on President Roosevelt one morning at breakfast to explain that "out of a sense of duty" they were willing to buy the shares if they could be assured they would not later be prosecuted for monopolistic practices under the Sherman Antitrust Act. Their purchase, they had informed the president with something less than candor, though it would be of little benefit to United States Steel, "would be of great benefit to financial conditions, and would probably save further failure of important business concerns." After consulting with Root and with his attorney general, Roosevelt had told them that the government had no objection to the purchase.

It was a decision that would haunt Roosevelt. As the price of the shares soared, his enemies maintained that either he had been a dupe or that he had sold out to Morgan and the steel interests for past or future favors. He himself later realized that Gary and Frick were not quite the idealists they had made themselves out to be. Then, four years later, Taft's attorney general brought suit against the United States Steel Corporation, charging that it was a monopoly, in part because of its purchase of the Tennessee Coal & Iron Company. The attorney general was merely enforcing the Sherman Act, and there was no malice intended toward Roosevelt. Taft himself had not been even aware of his attorney general's action. But Roosevelt saw it as an impugning of his honor and his intelligence, and he denounced the attorney general for instituting such indiscriminate antitrust suits. "Nothing . . . is gained," he wrote, "by breaking up a huge industrial organization which has *not offended otherwise than by its size*," and he accused the president of "unintelligent toryism." From this point on the two old friends were enemies.

Roosevelt's blast at Taft was like a bugle call summoning the army of the faithful to Sagamore Hill. They came with the fervor of pilgrims to the Oyster Bay shrine, the famous and the obscure, governors and delegations, reborn Populists, farmers, labor leaders, old Rough Riders, Western insurgents, Eastern reformers, conservationists, forward-looking business leaders, backward-looking politicians, professors, authors, idealists, and a fringe assortment of cranks and the chronically discontented. Carloads of mail accompanied them.

Early in 1911, the founding of the National Progressive Republican League had given progressivism a capital P, an identity of its own apart from the Grand Old Party. At an Ohio Progressive Congress held in Columbus in 1912, Brown, Pinchot and Garfield took the lead in demanding the nomination for president of "Robert M. La Follette or Theodore Roosevelt, or any other Progressive Republican." A month later seven Republican governors by prearrangement appealed to Roosevelt to forget his 1904 pledge and come out for the presidency. On February 21 he arrived in Columbus to deliver an address to the Ohio Constitutional Convention. In this, his most radical speech yet, he demanded the recall of judges and of state and municipal officials, and the right of the public both to initiate and through referendum to pass judgment on state laws. Three days later, when questioned by a reporter as to whether he was again a presidential candidate, he struck off a phrase destined to endure as an American political cliché. "My hat," he said, "is in the ring!"

"I told you so four years ago, and you would not believe me," Nellie Taft informed her husband with her old asperity when the news arrived at the White House.

"I know you did, my dear," Taft replied with plaintive humor, "and I think you are perfectly happy now. You would have preferred the colonel to come out against me than to have been wrong yourself." But he told Archie Butt that he had a strong presentiment Roosevelt would beat him at the convention.

Under the strain of his ebbing and Roosevelt's rising popularity, the president put on even more weight. Butt wrote that "his flesh looks like wax, his lips are thin, he is getting unhealthy bags under his eyes." Taft's intention was to avoid any personal attack on his rival, but with his customary unfortunate choice of phrase he referred to Roosevelt and his followers as "extremists not Progressives . . . political emotionalists or neurotics." "Neurotic" — in those pre-Freudian days the polite equivalent of "crazy" — was for Roosevelt the unforgivable word. Equally unfortunate was Taft's belated admission that "I was a man of straw but I have been a man of straw long enough," and his comment that "I don't want to fight. But when I fight I want to hit hard. Even a rat in a corner will fight."

In April, speaking at a rally in Boston's Arena, with the sweat rolling down his face, Taft attacked Roosevelt in language that had cast off restraint. Ten thousand die-hard Republicans led by Governor John Bates cheered him on, encouraging him by singing "We'll hang Teddy's hat to a sour apple tree!" Roosevelt, in Taft's words, had brought "unjust, unfounded charges" against him, trying to discredit him by "adroit appeals to discontent and class hatred. . . . One who so lightly regards constitutional principles" Taft concluded, "could not safely be entrusted with successive presidential terms. I say this sorrowfully, but I say it with full conviction of the truth." After the rally a reporter found Taft at the railroad station slumped in the lounge of the private car that was to take him back to Washington, his head in his hands. Looking up, he said in a despairing voice, "Roosevelt was my closest friend," and then he could no longer control his tears.

Roosevelt replied next day in Worcester, a mere forty miles away, to a crowd of hysterical partisans. The Rough Rider was bull-like in his anger, his face contorted as he denounced the president as "not only disloyal to our past friendship but . . . to every canon of decency and fair play. . . . The assaults made upon me by his campaign managers have been foul to the verge of indecency." Taft, he shouted as he thumped the rostrum, had served under him for seven years without finding fault. "He only discovered I was dangerous when I discovered he was useless to the American people. . . . I do not believe he has given the people a square deal. . . . Every boss in the country is with Mr. Taft." Then finally: "Mr. Taft is president only because I kept my promise in spite of infinite pressure to break it. It is a bad trait to bite the hand that feeds you!"

Archie Butt, as early as November, 1911, sensed that Taft could not be reelected and probably not even renominated. Taft himself thought he would be defeated but hoped, like Cleveland, on a vindicating return to the White House four years later. Meanwhile he would do his best to snatch the bone of the nomination from Roosevelt.

Most politicians had come to take it for granted that an incumbent president could pick himself or his successor in any nominating convention. White House pressure deftly exerted on the bosses, the weight of patronage, and the control of the party machinery and the kept delegates of the South made any other outcome all but impossible. The people's choice by no means needed to be the party's choice. Roosevelt saw in the direct primaries his one hope of circumventing boss-controlled delegates. Agitation for such direct primary legislation grew vociferously. In almost all those states where direct primaries already existed or were then adopted, Roosevelt won overwhelmingly. But in the other states, with their nominating conventions responsive to the bosses, his delegates were few and far between. Roosevelt had used the pressure and patronage of his office to insure his will in

1904 and 1908; now he would find the same forces working against him.

Storming West, the Rough Rider captured the Taft bastion of Ohio. Pennsylvania, supposed stronghold of the bosses, also fell to him. The outcome in the weeks before the convention remained uncertain, even as cries of "cheat" and "fraud!" filled the air. By the time the convention was ready to open in Chicago, the race seemed neck and neck. Of the 1,078 delegates, 241 still remained in dispute, more than enough to swing the nomination.

The credentials of the disputed delegates had been referred to the Taft-controlled Republican National Committee that had already chosen Root as temporary chairman. Though Root had been Athos to Roosevelt's D'Artagnan, he was and would be a regular of regulars. His legalistic mind was appalled at the prospect of a party split, and he could be counted on to apply the rules with an exactness that would cut the ground from under the insurgents. Ten days before the convention, the committee met to rule on the disputed delegates. The sessions, held behind closed doors, verged on a riot, as delegation after delegation was accredited to Taft. Roosevelt supporters shouted "Liar!" and "Robber!", their voices hoarse with impotent rage. "A saturnalia of fraud and corruption," Roosevelt headquarters called it. Of the contested delegates, 233 were awarded to Taft, 8 to Roosevelt.

Taft remained in Washington. Roosevelt at first could not decide whether to go to Chicago, but the trickery of the national committee made up his mind for him. He arrived the weekend before the convention, the Rough Rider colonel, in a new black hat and a wide belt that lacked only its revolver holster. Before his arrival Taft supporters had showered the city with leaflets announcing that "at three o'clock Thursday afternoon Theodore Roosevelt will walk on the waters of Lake Michigan." "Fit as a bull moose," the colonel described himself to waiting reporters, tossing off the incandescent phrase that would give a name and a slogan to a new party.

During that long weekend Roosevelt supporters with Teddy badges swarmed along Michigan Avenue, and gathered in front of the Congress Hotel where Roosevelt had established his headquarters to shout "We want Teddy!" Former Roosevelt troopers wearing their old Rough Rider uniforms roamed the streets looking for the unfortunate wearers of Taft buttons. A rumor spread through the city that when the convention opened, Roosevelt delegates were going to rush the Coliseum and bar it to the Taft delegates. Illinois Congressman William B. McKinley, Taft's campaign manager and a cousin of the late president, had to house and guard the bought Negro delegates to make sure that they stayed bought.

The convention opened dramatically with a contest over the temporary chairman. Root was the choice of the Taft men, and Roosevelt's was Governor Francis McGovern of Wisconsin. Before the balloting could take place, Roosevelt challenged seventy-four of the Taft delegates already approved by the national committee, demanding that at the very least they be barred from voting until the convention had been organized. With these seventy-four delegates the Taft forces would have had enough votes to elect Root; without them Roosevelt would have had a slight majority. The national committee ruled that the seventy-four delegates could vote for the chairman even though their own status was in dispute. Consequently Root was elected by a majority of fifty-seven. Through that initial vote it was clear to Roosevelt that he had lost the nomination, that Root would rule with literal exactness according to the rules laid down by the national committee and always in favor of Taft. So it happened. The Taft majority elected a committee on credentials, and the committee proceeded to seat the seventy-four disputed delegates as permanent members. Root, though weak in health and suffering from dysentery, kept a steady hand on the throttle of the Taft steamroller as it flattened the opposition. The galleries, packed with Roosevelt partisans, grew derisive. "Railroading" was what they called the proceedings. At each Root ruling in favor of Taft there were jeers of "Toot!" "Toot!" "All aboard!" "Choo, Choo!" Some of the galleryites had brought pieces of sandpaper to rub together in imitation of the sound of a steam engine. Roosevelt ordered his delegates to refrain from voting. His lieutenant, Henry Allen, then bade an angry and ironic farewell to the Taft majority, telling them that

> . . . no radical in the ranks of radicalism ever did so radical a thing as to come to a National Convention of the great Republican Party and secure through fraud the nomination of a man

> whom they knew could not be elected. . . . We fight no more. We plead no longer. We shall sit in protest and the people who sent us here shall judge us.*

Taft had picked the junior senator from his own state, the flatulently handsome Warren Harding, to present his name to the convention. Harding, the silver-voiced and shallow-tongued, had long had a reputation as the Ohio harmonizer, the reconciler of irreconcilables. But never before had the Buckeye orator faced such a sullenly hostile audience. He was booed before he opened his mouth. Dapper in a new cutaway and with a geranium in his buttonhole, he attempted — as he had so often successfully done — to summon apt alliteration's artful aid:

> Progress is not proclamation nor palaver. It is not pretence nor play on prejudice. It is not the perturbation of a people passion-wrought, nor a promise proposed. . . .†

Fistfights broke out while he spoke. Wooden seats clattered as scornful Roosevelt delegates stamped out of the hall. Finally amid the shouts and jeers of the balconies and the hiss of scraping sandpaper Harding managed "for one hundred millions of advancing Americans" to name for renomination "our great president, William Howard Taft."

In the perfunctory balloting that followed, Taft was renominated by 561 votes, Roosevelt received 107 and La Follette and the minor candidates 60. Three hundred and forty-four delegates refused to vote. While the balconies hooted the artifact victory, Allen led the remaining Roosevelt delegates from the hall. That same night the Roosevelt delegates and supporters "like a mighty army" marched to Orchestra Hall a mile away where under a huge portrait of Theodore Roosevelt they held their own rump convention. Roosevelt in full fighting trim, eyes narrowed and jaw snapping, gave his heart to them, promising that he would run for president as a Progressive if they would nominate him in a regular convention.

The Progressive Convention that met a month later in the same Coliseum had the atmosphere of a camp meeting. Roosevelt, the Progressive leader, the Bull Moose, seemed to have embodied

* *TR and Will,* p. 261.
† *The Shadow of Blooming Grove,* p. 230.

in his person the reform impulses of a century, from Transcendentalism and Abolitionism to Populism and Women's Suffrage. The Bull Moosers were for the most part from the earnest and neglected middle class, professional plain-livers and high-thinkers, professors, social workers, dissenting small businessmen, farmers, women like Jane Addams (who would second Roosevelt's nomination), clergymen, and of course what Roosevelt himself had labeled "the lunatic fringe." An air of earnest Protestantism hung over the proceedings, which opened with a recitation of the Lord's Prayer. To great applause and much laughter, the stubborn square-faced Hiram Johnson — who would be Roosevelt's running mate — led the California delegation into the hall carrying a banner:

I want to be a Bull Moose
And with the Bull Moose stand,
With Antlers on my Forehead
And a Big Stick in my hand.

Unaware of any incongruity, Oscar Straus, the Jewish philanthropist, marshaled his New York delegation down the aisle bellowing that most belligerent of Protestant hymns, "Onward, Christian Soldiers," a tune that would become the Bull Moose national anthem.

Meanwhile the Democrats, meeting in the sweaty atmosphere of the Baltimore Armory, after forty-six ballots finally nominated New Jersey's long-jawed, progressive-minded Governor Woodrow Wilson as their candidate, a nomination that was practically the equivalent of election. Taft realized as much. "Whether I win or lose is not the important thing" he told the newspaperman, Charles Thompson, his blue eyes blazing. "I am in this fight to perform a great public duty — the duty of keeping Theodore Roosevelt out of the White House!"

Roosevelt, the old campaigner, touring the country in two private railroad cars, the *Mayflower* and the *Sunbeam,* drew such immense multitudes in the West that Thompson thought many of them looked on him as a sort of John the Baptist. He visited thirty-four states and travelled 10,000 miles. Taft characteristically refused to campaign. The Rough Rider preferred to ignore Taft, realistically attacking his stronger opponent. Wilson, he declared, was a good man without any special fitness for the presidency and lacking the slightest understanding "of our industrial and agricultural life." Three weeks before the election, as Roosevelt arrived to make a speech in Milwaukee, an anti-third-term fanatic fired a revolver at him at almost pointblank range. The bullet's impact knocked Roosevelt backward, but its course was deflected by his metal eyeglass case and by the fifty folded pages of the speech he was about to deliver. Though his shirt was wet with blood, his lungs and his heart were uninjured, and he insisted on going on with his speech even though "it may be the last one I shall ever deliver." "I do not care a rap about being shot, not a rap," he told his appalled and anxious audience. "I have had a good many experiences in my time and this is only one of them. What I do care for is my country."

Fortunately for Roosevelt the bullet had stopped short in the fourth rib. Within two weeks, during which all campaigning stopped, he was well enough to resume speaking. Sympathy for him was overwhelming, but not overwhelming enough for him to win the election, whatever his secret hopes. More important for him than the election, though, was his triumph over Taft. Wilson received 6,293,019 votes to 4,119,507 for Roosevelt and 3,484,956 for Taft. The president managed to carry only two states, Vermont (by a mere 235 votes) and Utah.

Alone against Wilson, Roosevelt would have won; alone against Taft, Wilson would have won; together, Taft and Wilson were more than a match for Roosevelt. Yet Taft, though he had kept Roosevelt out of the White House, was sad and bitter at having suffered the worst presidential defeat in the country's history. He tried to console himself with the thought that many Republicans had voted for Wilson to escape the danger of Roosevelt. Roosevelt on the contrary was "all buoyant and good humored." Taft had bitten the hand that fed him, and that hand in turn had knocked him out.

The interim days brought a calm to Taft such as he had not felt in years. "The nearer I get to the inauguration of my successor," he wrote, "the greater relief I feel." In the middle of November he was offered a professorship of law at his beloved Yale. He accepted, and in accepting felt almost as happy as if he had been named to the Supreme Court.

Inauguration Day, 1913, was a warm day, cloudy at first but later with full sunshine, a genial contrast to that bitter inauguration four years earlier. Taft and Wilson, after having their pictures taken together on the White House porch, rode in an open carriage down Pennsylvania Avenue. For once Taft seemed to be thoroughly enjoying himself in public, beaming at the spectators who were applauding more for Wilson than for him. The ponderous man with his ruddy face, triple chin and merry eye seemed far happier than the ascetic schoolmaster on his left. As Taft glanced sidelong at his successor, he thanked his Unitarian God that the man next to him was not Roosevelt.

DRAWN BY F. G. COOPER

# That's All!

*Wilson, as governor of New Jersey, has let Harvey — his self-styled discoverer — and Watterson know he no longer wishes their support for his 1912 presidential candidacy.*

CHAPTER FOUR

# The Colonel from New Jersey: George Harvey

WHEN GEORGE HARVEY was in his cups, a not too uncommon condition, he liked to boast that he had made two presidents and unmade one, a statement that he delivered with a portentous solemnity that alcohol seemed only to intensify. That statement happened to be two-thirds inaccurate. Undoubtedly, without his calculating foresight, Woodrow Wilson would never have become president, but Harvey did not later unmake Wilson, even though he tried. Nor, for all his ponderous assertiveness, did he have any real influence on Harding's nomination at the "Dark Convention" of 1920, although Harvey's was the later-so-notorious "smoke-filled" hotel room where Harding made a brief early-morning appearance on the day of his nomination.

Harvey's solemnity was acquired. Early in life he had developed a weighty manner of speaking and a preternatural seriousness. During the nineties, when he was still relatively young, he drew more precise attention to himself by being the first man in America to wear tortoise-shell glasses. Behind his carefully constructed façade lurked a quick understanding and not-quite-first-rate mind.

He was born on February 16, 1864, in Peacham, Vermont. His father, Duncan, a Yankee of weathered Scots-Irish ancestry, kept the general store and maintained the heretical distinction of being the village's sole Democrat. To bear witness to his aberrant faith, he named his son George Brinton McClellan after the Civil War's battle-shy Democratic general.

Duncan Harvey sold all the county weeklies in his store and

these his son used to pore over with fascination when he had scarcely learned to read. "So far as I can remember," Harvey wrote in after years, "my chief aim in life was to get my fingers into a pot of ink." When he was ten he saved up his pennies to buy a little printing press and started his own paper, *Ariel,* of which he produced seventeen unsmudged copies, none of which sold. During the summer vacation of 1879, when he was fifteen, he became the associate editor of the weekly St. Johnsbury *Republican* at a salary of three dollars a week. The founder-publisher-editor being more interested in courting a girl in neighboring Bradford than in his newspaper, George spent a happy summer on his own as pro tem publisher, editor, reporter, typesetter, printer and deliveryman. At the end of the summer the actual proprietor announced that he had sold out. "It was," Harvey recalled, "a kindly expression of untruth. He did not sell his paper. He did not even give it away. He paid somebody to take it."

On returning to school, George continued as a reporter for the new proprietor of the *Republican* as well as for the *North Star.* When two adventurous young men bought the *North Star,* the sixteen-year-old George was allowed to add editorial writing to his reporting. But the boy felt that "the *North Star* had its limitations, and I had none; so I stepped over into the *Argus and Patriot.*" The editor being a Democrat, George had more scope and more space there to denounce the iniquities of Republican protectionism and the misdeeds of the Hayes administration.

At eighteen, George graduated with half a dozen others from Peacham Academy. Already he had had several small pieces printed by the Springfield *Republican* and on the strength of them he wrote the editor, Samuel Bowles, asking for a job. At that time the *Republican* under Bowles was the spokesman for western Massachusetts and the most noted journal of the three-state rural area that included southern New Hampshire and Vermont. Bowles replied by asking the boy to drop in to see him. Borrowing ten dollars from his elder sister, young Harvey in the summer of 1883 took himself the 186 miles down the Connecticut River to Springfield. Never one to underestimate himself, he determined to ask for fifteen dollars a week. Bowles's coldly polite manner gave him uneasy second thoughts. Diffidently Harvey suggested that he would be happy to take the job at ten dollars weekly. The other, as if he had scarcely heard, observed that the pay would be six dollars. "Finally," said Harvey, "we compromised; on six dollars!"

For a year Harvey bustled about Springfield writing local bits and pieces and learning the workings of a larger paper. At the year's end he again approached his editor, suggesting that he now deserved eight dollars. Bowles did not agree. Harvey quit the *Republican*, though continuing on good terms with Bowles, and with his recommendation in his pocket moved twenty-three miles further down the Connecticut to Hartford and a multifarious job on the *Journal* as reporter, copy editor, part-time editorial writer, and emergency pressroom assistant. Although now earning eight dollars a week he was unhappy with his odd-job routine, and when the editor objected to the political opinions he kept expressing in his writings, he again quit. Heading west for Chicago he found a place as railroad editor of the *Daily News*, a far more important paper than the *Republican* or the *Journal*. A number of transiently eminent writers, the most noted being Eugene Field, worked for the *News*. Its city room atmosphere was stimulating, but Harvey missed the more staid and settled East. When a year later on a trip home he called on Joseph Pulitzer, the proprietor and editor of the New York *World*, New York's and the country's leading Democratic paper, and was offered a job, he jumped at the chance. Quickly he demonstrated that he had a "nose for news" and became one of the *World*'s star reporters. He had not been many months in his new job when he was sent to the Adirondacks where a number of the country's best reporters had gathered to report on General Grant, slowly dying of cancer in a cottage there. Although only just twenty-one, Harvey found himself accepted as an equal by his older colleagues. After Grant's death in June, Harvey was sent to Jersey City to take charge of that state's news. His activities soon led to a special New Jersey edition of the *World*. His name became known, his stature recognized. Even more important than this early recognition was his identification with New Jersey, the state he would make his home.

The New Jersey that Harvey adopted in the autumn of 1883 was a Democratic state, even as the *World* was a Democratic paper. The outsider from Vermont now found himself an insider. But where Vermont in its backwardness had been a relatively clean state, New Jersey under the shadow of New York was indelibly corrupt. Harvey wrote article after article exposing the state's ingrown corruption. Politicians began to wince at the sight of the brash young newcomer. The more upright or at least more knowing political leaders of both parties became his friends, took him into their most important councils, and often turned to him for advice. In 1888 Governor Robert Green appointed him as an aide-de-camp on his staff with the rank of colonel, and from then on for the rest of his days Harvey used that military title. A succeeding governor appointed him to the newly created office of Commissioner of Banking and Insurance. Yet all his political activities were secondary to his work on the *World*. Pulitzer now put him in charge of the paper's uptown Manhattan branch, but he continued to live in New Jersey where he now brought his bride, Alma Arabella Parker, a girl from Peacham. Pulitzer next sent him to Bridgeport to start a Connecticut edition of the *World*, and Harvey made the same quick and brilliant success with it that he had with the New Jersey edition. From New York Pulitzer kept a calculating eye on his young protégé, recalling him to take over the main office as soon as the Connecticut edition was running smoothly. So at the age of twenty-seven Harvey became the managing editor of one of America's foremost papers, responsible to no one except Pulitzer himself. It was the age and the city of great journalists: Whitelaw Reid of the *Tribune*, Charles A. Dana of the *Sun*, James Gordon Bennett of the *Herald*, E. L. Godkin of the *Evening Post*, Charles R. Miller of the *Times*, while George William Curtis still continued to edit *Harper's*.

Harvey's first year as managing editor was a presidential election year. Four years before, in 1888, Benjamin Harrison had defeated President Grover Cleveland's bid for a second term, and Cleveland on leaving the White House was determined to vindicate himself at the next election. But in 1892 in his own state of New York he was opposed for the nomination by United States Senator David Hill, a Tammany-backed machine candidate who as governor four years earlier had secretly supported Harrison. Hill and his cronies prepared to call a "snap" New York nominating convention several months before the usual time to sew up the delegates votes for Hill at the national convention. Cleveland, they reasoned, would cut a poor figure going to the national convention without the delegates of his own state. Harvey — a fervent Cleveland supporter — denounced the "snap" convention in a "scoop" editorial that, though it could not prevent Hill's capture of the New York delegation, did arouse much hostility to him outside New York. Aided by Harvey, managed astutely by the suave New York financier William Whitney, Cleveland was nominated on the convention's first ballot. In this election he overwhelmingly defeated Harrison. Cleveland was grateful to Harvey for his unwavering support, and showed his gratitude by welcoming him into the inner circle of national party leaders, making him an unofficial advisor to the secretary of state. However, Pulitzer, who liked to boast of his intuitive wisdom in first spotting Harvey, was growing increasingly restive at his managing editor's political activity. "My advice to you," he warned, "is to stick to your journalism and never more think of office." Further differences of opinion with Pulitzer plus difficulties with the older members of the staff who continued to resent the promotion of a younger man over their heads, led to Harvey's resignation late in 1893 from the *World*.

During the presidential campaign of 1892 Harvey had developed an increasingly intimate relationship with Whitney. Now he joined him as a confidential business agent. A financier closely linked to political bosses, a deft organizer of monopolies in whiskey and tobacco, Whitney was married to a Standard Oil heiress. His chief interest at the time Harvey knew him was in getting control of the street railway lines as they developed and expanded from city to city. With a group of Philadelphia promoters who controlled the streetcar lines of that city, he and the New York financial manipulator Thomas Fortune Ryan formed a holding company, the Metropolitan Traction Company, that eventually took over street railways in a hundred cities from Maine to Pennsylvania and built up assets — mostly monopoly franchises — worth close to a billion dollars. Harvey worked intimately with Whitney and Ryan, and his association with such transport tycoons gave him a number of sure-fire opportunities for highly profitable speculations. Within five few years of his association with Whitney and Ryan, he had made a fortune. He was not rich by their standards — they were reputed to be worth some 200 million dollars each — nor by that of the elder Morgan, whom he had come to know. But he had made enough to live in opulent independence for the rest of his days. He bought a large estate near the sea at Deal, New Jersey, which he named Jorjalma, a combination of his and his wife's first names, and there he began to entertain in the lavish manner that he became noted for later. "Finance, work in Wall Street, and business promotion," he wrote, "never appealed to me as real rivals of my profession. I was associated with Mr. Whitney, and I knew Mr. Ryan, Mr. Morgan, and other successful financiers, pretty well. I made some money, too, and the creative work I did in building traction lines rested me from the strain of newspaper work. But when I had a chance to buy the *North American Review* I bought it; and then I was happy again."

The *North American Review*, which Harvey took over in 1899, was America's oldest literary and critical periodical. Earlier it had been one of the three or four most distinguished journals in the world, and it was still eminent. Its eighteen earlier editors had included Jared Sparks, Edward Everett, James Russell Lowell, Charles Eliot Norton and Henry Adams. No fewer than ten presidents of the United States had contributed to its pages; generations of Harvard scholars had appeared there. When Harvey took it over it was considered the spokesman of conservative America.

Harvey's predecessor had moved the magazine from Boston to New York and had given it less of a literary and more of a political and economic bias while including some of the world's foremost names in its pages. The newly created department, "By the Editor," Harvey used as his individualistic medium of expression, commenting on current political topics and stamping his personality on the whole journal. Through the *North American Review* he attained national prestige.

Only a few months after he took over the *Review*, Harper & Brothers, America's oldest and most famous publishing house, found itself on the edge of bankruptcy, with J. P. Morgan's State Trust Company its principal creditor. The firm's properties included *Harper's Magazine*, *Harper's Weekly* and *Harper's Bazaar*. The Harper family, who had controlled the firm since 1832, now turned to Harvey as the person most capable of extricating them from their difficulties. With the approval of Morgan, the Harpers elected Harvey their president, while keeping six of the Harper clan as members of the corporation. Harvey's years with Ryan and Whitney now stood him in good stead. He understood finance as the Harpers did not, and by reorganizing the firm, effecting economies, bringing in trusted colleagues from the *World*, and eliminating inbred inefficiencies, he was soon able to put Harper's on a sound business basis. He himself directed the publication of new books, controlled the editing of the monthly *Magazine*, and in a short time assumed the editorship of the *Weekly*. This he completely made over, using it to express his own political opinions more frequently and at greater length than in the *North American Review*. Alert for authors old and new, and notably successful in finding them, he enticed that American dean of letters, William Dean Howells, back to the magazine of which he had once been editor, placing him in charge of the genially intimate "Editor's Easy Chair" and persuading him to contribute short stories as well as articles for the *North American*.

By his midthirties the Vermont boy had become a congenial and convivial man-about-town, a somewhat owlish equivalent of Richard Harding Davis's Van Bibber. He loved to entertain expansively, and some of his semi-public dinners to authors such as Mark Twain and William Dean Howells became international literary events. At one Howells dinner, no less than the President of the United States, William Howard Taft, was present. Mark Twain hailed Harvey as "the Magnificent." Only Henry James demurred from the honor of a dinner, replying to an invitation that "such an occasion would have for me such unmitigated terror and torment, that I shouldn't be able to guard myself, with whatever heroic effort, into being present at it. I should flee to Arizona or Alaska, I should run till I dropped."

Though Harvey now passed most of his time in New York, he still kept his New Jersey residence, still spent his weekends and vacations at Jorjalma and still concerned himself with New Jersey politics and affairs, although his earlier reformist flame now burned more thinly. It was through his vestigial interest in his adopted state that his path first crossed that of Woodrow Wilson's in October 1902, the month Wilson was to be formally installed as president of Princeton.

Some years earlier Harper's had published Wilson's conservative-aristocratic interpretation of George Washington, and the firm was now preparing to print the five-volume edition of his *History of the American People*, so it was natural for an official invitation to his inaugural to be extended to the senior member of the Harper's corporation and Harper family, J. Henry Harper. Having come to regard Harvey as a close personal friend, Harper invited him to the Princeton inaugural. Harvey had once written a letter to Wilson at the urging of Professor Albert Bushnell Hart suggesting that he write a volume in Harper's *American Nation* series. But beyond that, Wilson's name meant little to him and he accepted Harper's invitation, not from any great wish to see the thirteenth head of Princeton but to attend a dinner the evening before at which Grover Cleveland, Mark Twain, William Dean Howells, Speaker of the House of Representatives Thomas Reed, Lincoln's son Robert and J. P. Morgan would be present.

Wilson was seven years older than Harvey, and when he at the age of forty-six stood in cap and gown in Alexander Hall as president of Princeton where he had been professor for so long, he was only at the beginning of his career. Like Harvey a conservative Democrat, he was unlike him in most other things. For this lean, long-jawed professor with the autocratic-ascetic face and eyes veiled by a pince-nez, looked indeed what he was by inheritance, the descendant of generations of dominies and Calvinist preachers.

Wilson's grandfather had been a Scots-Irish immigrant, his father a Presbyterian minister in Ohio who had moved to Virginia, where Wilson was born, and had then taken a church in Georgia. "My earliest recollection," Wilson wrote, "is of standing in my father's gateway in Augusta, Georgia, when I was four years old, and hearing some one pass and say that Mr. Lincoln was elected and there was to be war." The Civil War and Reconstruction shadowed his childhood, disaster impressing on him even more deeply the feeling of being a southerner. It was a feeling he would never lose. His birth land remained in his blood. "The only place in the country," he wrote in his maturity, "the only place in the world, where nothing has to be explained to me is the South."

The Wilson home atmosphere was bookish in a somewhat old-fashioned way, the father often reading aloud to his family from Scott and Dickens. The son attended small private schools of no great merit, then, when he was sixteen, left home for the first time for Davidson, a small Presbyterian college in North Carolina. Even for that primitive level his preparation was inadequate and his health suffered with his grades. At the term's end he left and spent a year at home recuperating in mind and body. Not until the following year did he take up his studies again, this time going north to what was then known as the College of New Jersey, in Princeton. At Princeton he found friends — mostly southerners — and an atmosphere of learning unknown to Davidson. Too frail for actual participation in sports, he became and remained an ardent spectator. His second year — among the most important of his life, in his opinion — brought about his intellectual awakening. He read *The Federalist,* Macaulay's *History of England,* the speeches of Burke and the essays of Walter Bagehot. He practiced oratory, took part in debating and found he had a gift for words. Politics fascinated him and he longed to take part in them. He daydreamed himself as a governor, or "Thomas Woodrow Wilson, Senator from Virginia." On graduating from Princeton he turned to the study of law, entering the University of Virginia Law School in September 1879. "The profession I chose was politics," he wrote later, "the profession I entered was the law. I entered the one because I thought it would lead to the other." However, he soon felt "most terribly bored by the noble study of Law." History, literature and above all political science he found far more to his taste. He became president of the debating club. Politically he saw himself as a Democrat, a nationalist, a free trader, but he found his own party lamentably allied "with every damnable heresy — with Greenbackers as well as protectionists." A social young man, he made friends easily. But again, as at Davidson, lack of success in his formal studies led to a neurasthenic collapse, and after two years he returned to Wilmington, North Carolina, where his family now lived. There in a desultory way he continued his law studies for a year and a half, and after much indecision finally left to practice law in Atlanta in a dingy little office on Marietta Street. His sole client during his first year was a Negro assigned to him to defend by the court. The following spring on a visit to Rome, Georgia, he met his future wife, Ellen Louise Axson, the daughter of a Presbyterian minister, a gentle and charming young woman who shared his interests in art, music and literature, and who helped the indeterminate young man determine the course of his life.

That course was not law. So much was clear to him. "Its practice . . . for the purposes of gain" the young failed lawyer considered "antagonistic to the best interests of the intellectual life." That September he left Georgia for Baltimore's Johns Hopkins University, determined to adopt the teaching profession as one that would give him a moderate income and time for study and leisure. What could be better, he wrote, than to be a professor, "a lecturer upon subjects whose study most delights me?" Yet he could not wholly conquer his older longings. After a year and a half in Baltimore, when he had all but completed his doctor's thesis, he admitted that "I do feel a very real regret that I have been shut out from my heart's *first* — primary — ambition and purpose, which was, to take an active, if possible a leading, part in public life, and strike out for myself, if I had the ability, a *statesman's* career."

As a graduate student at Johns Hopkins he moved among distinguished scholars, but his attitude toward them was prickly, challenging. Ellen enlarged his somewhat arid intellectual horizons by persuading him to read Ruskin, Swinburne, Arnold and Wordsworth. He now became formally engaged to her. His doctoral thesis, *Congressional Government*, was published as a book. Strongly influenced by Bagehot's *English Constitution*, he contrasted the division of powers, the surreptitious committee government and the lack of leadership of the American system with the "perfected party government" of the British cabinet system. His bias was then against popular democracy and in favor of an aristocratic governing elite. Ironically, in the reforms he envisaged, he considered the president a negligible factor.

Wilson's thesis was published even before it had been approved for his doctorate. While neither profound nor original, it was a sustained attempt at a critical analysis of the American political system, and as such caused a sensation. His success in his second career appeared assured. In June of 1885 he married, and that September took his first formal academic post at Bryn Mawr. He stayed there three years, but his initial enthusiasm waned in that blue-stocking bloomer-girl atmosphere. "I am hungry for a class of *men*," he wrote a friend.

When he was offered a professorship at male Wesleyan University at higher pay he left with joyous haste. At Wesleyan, besides his regular courses, he organized the Wesleyan House of Commons debating society and helped coach a winning football team, while still managing to find time to finish a textbook on the development of political institutions, *The State*, possibly his greatest scholarly achievement.

His reputation expanded. He was asked to give a series of lectures at Johns Hopkins. Then in 1890, through the efforts of his college friends, he was called back to Princeton as professor of jurisprudence and political economy. For him it was a happy homecoming. The turbulence of the decade of unrest and depression could not penetrate to the house on placid elm-shaded Library Place, the muted study with its books and its crayon drawings (done by Ellen) of Wesbter, Gladstone, Bagehot and Burke. Princeton was indeed an ivory tower, but from that tower the sharp-eyed Wilson looked down with interested detachment at the agitations of Populism and the Farmer's Alliance, bimetalism, war and Manifest Destiny. Bryan and his "Cross of Gold" speech he found thoroughly ridiculous. On the Spanish-American War he kept his silence. He could afford to be detached. During the depression that followed the Great Panic of 1893 his salary rose; his world felt more secure than ever. Politics intrigued him. Economics did not. He believed in free trade, Adam Smith and the tradition (if not always the practice) of democracy. There was little sign yet of the political liberal-radical in this unworldly conservative professor. Twelve shining uxorious years he passed as a Princeton professor, lecturing on American constitutional law, international law and English common law. Aloof but concerned with his students, witty, voluble, he became one of the college's most popular professors. He led the fight for the honor system in examinations. Football and baseball games found him in the stands, a determined rooter. At one time he helped coach the football team. In his forties, his influence widened. He expanded his own knowledge of America by traveling on lecture tours across the country. He wrote nine books, and articles poured from his typewriter which because of arthritis in his right hand he welcomed instead of a pen. In 1896 the College of New Jersey became Princeton University and he delivered the keynote address, a plea for sound conservative government and an education that would draw much of its life from the best and oldest literature. Always religious, he became an elder of the local Presbyterian church, although he was outraged at the antirevolutionary stance of the Presbyterian Reverend Dr. Francis Patton, Princeton's president. Seven great universities attempted to entice him from Princeton by the offer of their presidencies. The University of Virginia made three such attempts. Twice he worked himself to the verge of a breakdown, and each time he recovered by a leisurely visit to England. He seemed almost too big a fish for the Princeton pond, and devoted alumni raised a supplement to his salary to insure his staying there. There would come a day when the retrograde Dr. Patton would retire or be forced to retire. Professor Wilson did not speculate on this, but others did. Yet, for all Wilson's academic success, he felt that something was lacking, that he was only a "literary politician," once-removed from the real world. In the back of his mind the old dream still flickered of Thomas Woodrow Wilson, United States Senator. But, as he remarked ruefully to his brother-in-law, "in this country men do not go from the academic world into politics."

During the commencement week of 1902, after twenty-seven years as a professor, Wilson was elected president of Princeton. For him it was "like a thunderbolt out of a clear sky," the more flattering because he was the first layman chosen and had been unanimously elected by the twenty-six trustees on the first ballot.

The academic procession on that brisk October day of Wilson's inaugural was the most brilliant Princeton had ever experienced. Ex-President Grover Cleveland led the parade, followed by the varicolored gowns and hoods of more than a hundred college and university representatives. But for an accident President Theodore Roosevelt himself would have been there. Among the throng that sat in Alexander Hall listening to the resonant, slightly anglicized yet vaguely southern voice of the new Princeton president, none was more alert, more impressed than George Harvey. Wilson had entitled his address *Princeton For the Nation's Service*. "It is plain what this nation needs," he said with his crisp enunciation, "as its affairs grow more and more complex and its interests begin to touch the ends of the earth. It needs efficient and enlightened men. The universities of the country must take part in supplying them."

Harvey listened with the rapt attentiveness of a convert at a revival meeting, and, like any convert, his moment of enlightenment was the culmination of a long series of psychological effects. Through the years he had grown convinced that the Democratic party had become "an odds and ends patchwork of theories and expediencies, tainted with Populism, haunted by Bryanesque wildness, unfit to govern since the Civil War." Cleveland had been elected in spite of the party. What the Democrats needed was a candidate to be elected *with* the party. Only a southerner, one acceptable to the North, could lead such a renewal party, restore it to its old preeminence, return it to its great heritage of before the war.

Robert Todd Lincoln, who had been sitting with Harper next to Harvey, remarked at the end of the address that it was the best of the kind that he had ever heard. "Yes," said Harvey. "That man could win the people. I want to know more about him." Harper pointed out that the firm was publishing Wilson's *History of the American People* shortly and that Harvey must already have received advance copies. The two men motored back to Jorjalma, and immediately after dinner Harvey told his guest that he was going up to his library, the Tower. When Harper asked him what he intended to do, he replied that he intended to study Woodrow Wilson.

Harvey stayed in his Tower until midnight, fluttering the pages of Wilson's history. Early next morning he sent a message to his secretary: "Get me everything that Woodrow Wilson has written, or has been written about him." Before that October day at Princeton, Harvey had never read a line that Wilson wrote. Now he devoured him. Here at last was the embodiment of the politician-statesman that he had long dreamed about, who would lead the Democratic party out of the wilderness. When, the following weekend, a guest at Jorjalma asked him what he thought of Princeton's new president, he answered: "I think that he will make a good president of the United States!"

It was a seed of opinion that Harvey would keep private for some years, but indirectly he began to prepare the ground. In his editorials in *Harper's Weekly* and the *North American Review,* without ever so much as mentioning Wilson's name, he outlined a hypothetical Democratic presidential candidate that fitted the president of Princeton in every particular.

Late in 1904, a few weeks after Roosevelt's overwhelming defeat of New York's Judge Alton Parker, the anti-Bryan gold-standard candidate, Harvey became more explicit. Speaking at the 175th anniversary of the St. Andrew's Society in Charleston, South Carolina, he told the members that the Democratic party for the last forty years had drawn its candidates from the West and the East, and all of them, with Cleveland's unique exception, had failed.

Now the party must go back to its southern stronghold, where it had its birth, where until 1861 it produced nine of the country's fifteen administrations. While the party of Jefferson, Madison and Monroe was "in the saddle" there was no question of unfitness to govern. The Democrats must find a leader in the South to reclaim their heritage.

That talk by a Vermont Yankee to an audience of whom many had fought against the Union was a political milestone, indicating as it did the reintroduction of the South to political equality with the rest of the country. From then on southerners began to view the nomination and election of one of their own to the presidency as both possible and practicable. Harvey mentioned no names in his address. Yet from beginning to end he had shaped it to prepare the way for the coming of Woodrow Wilson.

As president of Princeton Wilson saw the opportunity of revitalizing leadership in a university whose old leadership had withered. With dynamic enthusiasm he reorganized the whole administrative structure and replaced the undergraduate curriculum with a coordinated study plan that would be imitated by Harvard and Yale and other colleges across the country. Princeton's first needs, as he saw them, were new buildings, an enlarged staff, a school of science and — his pet project — a preceptorial system. Later he envisaged a graduate school, a school of law, a school of electrical engineering and a museum of natural history. Vast sums of money were needed. He saw to it that those sums were raised.

With his preceptorial plan he aimed to replace rote recitations by counseling and guidance from a group of tutors, as was done at Oxford and Cambridge. "If we could get a body of such tutors at Princeton," Wilson wrote in anticipation, "we could transform the place from a place where there are youngsters doing tasks to a place where there are men doing thinking."

In those early months Wilson carried the undergraduates, the faculty and the alumni along with him. Princeton, so sedately middle-aged, with its arching elms and ivy-covered American Gothic buildings, seemed to have been suddenly reborn. A confident enthusiasm swept the campus, a feeling of new life, a new spirit. "Wilson is Princeton's most valuable asset," alumni told each other almost in wonder. In his Calvinistic self-confidence he thought so himself. What Eliot with his "free elections" had been to Harvard a generation before, he with his "guided education" would be to Princeton.

In 1906, after four years as Princeton's president, Wilson was at the height of his popularity, and the clouds had not yet begun to gather that would shadow his later career there. A leading figure in the academic world, perhaps *the* leading figure, he was still relatively unknown beyond its limits. Harvey now saw it as his self-appointed task to bring Wilson to the attention of a wider public as the next step in his great plan. He found the occasion in a meeting of New York's Lotos Club on February 3, 1906.

The Lotos, if not the city's oldest or richest or most fashionable club, was easily the most distinguished, noted for the dinners it gave in honor of eminent men both American and foreign. Harvey arranged for such a dinner to be given for Princeton's president, then had himself put down as one of the speakers — the chief speaker as it turned out, for after he had finished, the others were scarcely heeded. Owlishly peering through his tortoise-shell glasses, he declaimed in the resonant ponderous manner that was then considered the hall-mark of the gifted speaker:

> For nearly a century before Woodrow Wilson was born, [he began, looking down at the latter's set clerical features] the atmosphere of the Old Dominion was surcharged with true statesmanship. That he is preeminent as a lucid interpreter of history, we all know. But he is more than that. No one who reads, understandingly, the record of his country that flowed with such apparent ease from his pen can fail to be impressed by the belief that he is by instinct a statesman.
>
> If one could be found who should unite in his personality the finest instinct of true statesmanship and the no less valuable capacity for practical application, the ideal would have been attained. Such a man, I believe, is Woodrow Wilson, of Virginia and New Jersey.
>
> As one of a considerable number of Democrats who have grown tired of voting Republican tickets, it is with a feeling almost of rapture that I occasionally contemplate even a remote possibility of casting a ballot for the president of Princeton University to become President of the United States.

> In any case, since opportunities in the National Convention are rare and usually preempted, to the enlightened and enlightening Lotos Club I make the nomination.*

To the American press, Harvey's speech was a nine-day's wonder. Reverberating across the country, it marked the opening of a campaign that would carry Wilson to the White House. For the president of Princeton, the speech awakened and intensified old pre-Princeton ambitions. Now his imagination stretched as far as to picture himself President Woodrow Wilson, in the Old Dominion tradition of Washington, Jefferson, Madison and Monroe, of those first families of which he admitted privately he would have liked to have been born a member. That night, from the University Club where he was staying, he wrote Harvey:

> Before I go to bed to-night I must express to you, simply, but most warmly, my thanks for the remarks you made at the Lotos dinner. It was most delightful to have such thoughts uttered about me, whether they were deserved or not, and I thank you with all my heart.†

On meeting Wilson next morning, his brother-in-law Stockton Axson said: "I see you have been nominated for President of the United States!" Ellen Wilson, standing just behind and still bewildered by the thought, asked:

"Was Mr. Harvey joking?"

"He didn't seem to be joking," said Wilson primly.

Among politicians it was commonly supposed that Harvey was grooming Wilson for 1908. No such political folly entered Harvey's calculating mind. If Roosevelt should overcome his earlier renunciation of a third term, Harvey knew well that no Democrat available could stop the Rough Rider's reelection. And if Roosevelt should stick to his regretted statement and handpick his successor — Root, Taft or whoever it might be — that successor was almost equally certain of being elected. Nineteen-hundred twelve was another matter. Much might happen before then, and much of it Harvey anticipated.

In *Harper's Weekly* of March 10, Harvey published a full page photograph of Woodrow Wilson accompanied by a lead editorial giving thirteen points why Wilson should become president of the

* *George Harvey*, p. 111.
† *Collier's*, Oct. 7, 1916.

United States. Following in Hanna's footsteps, but more subtly, Harvey continued to advertise Woodrow Wilson, to make those liquescent trochees as familiar as Quaker Oats. He used the pages of *North American Review* for a wider and more intellectual discussion of Wilson's capabilities. With his newspaper connections he was able to carry his propaganda afield for a time, so insistently that Wilson protested, fearful that his standing and his Princeton goals might be jeopardized. Wilson at one point even sent Axson to New York to ask Harvey to tone down his campaign. Axson reported back that Harvey had not been frank with him. "He was fascinating and suave," according to Axson, "and I merely got the impression that he intended to go ahead."

As Harvey saw it, before Wilson could swim in the turbid sea of politics he must get used to the water. With this in mind Harvey early in 1906 maneuvered to have the Princeton president appointed a member of the New Jersey Commission on Uniform State Laws — his first public office. He also planted rumors that Wilson might become the Democratic candidate for the New Jersey senate election scheduled to take place when the legislature met in January, 1907. During that summer, while Wilson was in England recuperating from a breakdown, Harvey got together with his long-time friend, the boss of the Newark-Essex County machine, former United States Senator James Smith, Jr., to launch Wilson's candidacy. When Wilson arrived back in mid-October he told reporters that his name had been used without his authority and much to his surprise. "Although I am an old-line Democrat," he told them "and would do any service to restore the party to power, I cannot see that it would be any help for me to accept such an office." When, however, in the November elections the Republicans gained control of the legislature and it was clear that the next New Jersey senator would be a Republican, the Democratic candidacy assumed a symbolic value. Harvey reasoned that Wilson as the unsuccessful Democratic candidate would receive nationwide publicity. The defeat did not matter. The important thing was to make Wilson's name known.

New Jersey Democrats were then facing much the same dilemma as were the Republicans; their parties split between the old-line bosses controlling the party machinery and the insurgents, young Democrats who called themselves progressives, and New Idea progressive Republicans. A conservative Democrat, Wilson still hoped for the support of the progressives once he himself had agreed to his token candidacy. When he found that this was not forthcoming, that the progressives were preparing to label him the tool of the bosses, he lost his political nerve. In his first encounter with practical politics, the academic theorist discovered himself impaled. Despairingly he wrote to Harvey that he doubted his fitness to be a leader of his party in its divided state and he doubted even more that he was a suitable person to be president. All he wanted now was a way out of his dilemma. Unfazed by such a minor contretemps, Harvey drafted a letter to be sent to a key member of the legislature explaining that Wilson had never been a candidate and that he wished his name withdrawn from the Democratic caucus. Wilson's first political gesture had come to nothing.

For Harvey it was a minor skirmish. The real battles lay ahead. Though conservative by nature, and bound by his interests to the world of high finance, he carefully took no sides in the quarrels of the bosses and the progressives. His fixed and unrelenting purpose was to see Wilson in the White House and the Democratic Party restored to its old dominance. To Wilson's persisting doubts, Harvey replied with a list of those who saw the Princeton president as the Democrats' great hope; the archcapitalist August Belmont; his associate Thomas Fortune Ryan, who had supported Princeton and would now support Wilson with his dubious millions; Adolph Ochs, the publisher of the New York *Times*; the courtly, influential Colonel Henry Watterson, editor of the Louisville *Courier-Journal* and known throughout Kentucky as "Marse Henry"; William Laffan, publisher of the reactionary New York *Sun*; Cleveland's gold-standard secretary of the treasury, and his comptroller of the currency; and a selection of Wall Street bankers, utility magnates and conservative businessmen.

They found the Princeton president's views highly to their taste, for he was against Roosevelt's "trust busting" theatrics, against the "socialistic" supervision and regulation of business by the federal government, against the labor movement and its abrogation of the right of freedom of contract, for state's rights as opposed to federal power. Yet in one respect Wilson had changed greatly from the young graduate student who believed that the presidency should be merely a ceremonial office and the president a figurehead, a temporary constitutional nobody. He now saw the chief executive as the political leader of the nation, who could appeal directly to the people over the sectional and limited interests of Congress. "The nation as a whole has chosen him [the president] and is conscious that it has no other political spokesman," he wrote in 1907, as if he could already foresee himself in the White House. "His is the only national voice in affairs. Let him once win the admiration and confidence of the country, and no other single force can withstand him, no combination of forces will easily overpower him. . . . If he rightly interpret the national thought and boldly insist upon it, he is irresistible."

One morning early in 1907 Harvey sent for his most trusted lieutenant on *Harper's Weekly*, William Inglis. There, in the privacy of his editorial office on Franklin Square, he unveiled his strategy.

Inglis was to give most of his waking moments to Wilson's candidacy for president. Wilson must be made known. By 1910 the country would be disgusted with the Republicans. That would be the year to run Wilson for governor of New Jersey. Until then Inglis was to advertise and exploit Wilson in every conceivable way.

Harvey was well aware that after the Democratic fiasco with the "safe and sane" Judge Parker in 1904, the party would in 1908 turn left for the third time to the ever available Great Commoner, William Jennings Bryan. In that year of assured Republican triumph, Harvey would not have wanted the nomination for his protégé if it had been offered. Nevertheless it was his strategy to keep Wilson in the public eye as a *possible* candidate. With this in mind he approached his early mentor, Pulitzer, to suggest that the *World* endorse Wilson for the 1908 Democratic nomination. Equally interested in and amused by Harvey's "professional candidate," Pulitzer agreed to run an editorial endorsing him if Harvey would write it. Harvey returned to his office and finished it in a few hours, then took it to Pulitzer who remarked that it sounded like a speech. "Well," Harvey told him, "I did my best to write it in the *World*'s own style!" Pulitzer laughed heartily. The editorial appeared in the *World* on January 18, 1908:

FOR PRESIDENT

If the Democratic Party is to be saved from falling into the hands of William J. Bryan as a permanent receiver, a Man must

> be found — and soon. There must arise a real leader around whom all Democrats uninfected by Populism, and thousands of dissatisfied Republicans, may rally.
>
> Certain personal attributes are essential to successful candidacy. Known fidelity to high ideals. Unquestioned integrity. Veracity. Courage. Caution. Intellectuality. Wisdom. Experience. Achievement. Breadth of mind. Strength of body. Clarity of vision. Simplicity in manner of living. Eloquence. Human sympathy. Alertness. Optimism. Enthusiasm. Finally and practically: Availability!
>
> One Democrat who unquestionably meets these qualifications is Woodrow Wilson, President of Princeton University.

Only a handful of people knew that Harvey was the author, but the editorial drew national attention to Wilson, transforming him from an academic figure to one of the leaders of the conservative Democrats. Such editorials could not make Wilson the candidate that year over Bryan, but Harvey's subtle mind ranged beyond the party disaster he foresaw in November 1908, to 1910 and the governorship of New Jersey. Wilson meanwhile dissociated himself completely from Bryan, whom he considered "the most charming and lovable of men personally, but foolish and dangerous in his theoretical beliefs." When talk arose about nominating the president of Princeton for vice-president, he refused bluntly to consider any such possibility. After a reporter in Pittsburgh asked him if he was a candidate for the presidential nomination, he grinned his arch, toothy grin and replied that while he appreciated "most heartily Colonel Harvey's kindness in bestowing on me such an honor, I must say I think there are other wires taller than mine which will attract the lightning."

Shortly before the convention Wilson sailed again for England, a country he found a perpetual source of refreshment and renewal. At this time he was in dire need of both, for neurasthenia had again overwhelmed him after his last two stormy and embittered Princeton years. In Wilson's day less than half of one per cent of the country's young men went on from high school to college. For a land lacking an established aristocracy, attendance at college had become a substitute of sorts, a hallmark of an elite. This became particularly true of the old established eastern universities, dominated by the big three: Harvard, Yale and Princeton. The goal of college life was a social one. "It is not what you learn," it was said of the four-year college interlude, "but the friends you make" — or, more pertinently, the clubs. They were the Eastern measure of all things mundane: at Harvard, Porcellian; at Yale, Skull and Bones; at Princeton, Ivy. The studies pursued, the examinations taken, were in the nature of an obstacle course, to be accepted good-naturedly as the fee paid for admission to the social and athletic world. A gentleman's grade was a passing C. "Greasy grinds," high school boys who burned the midnight oil in regions beyond the clubs, were felt to be contemptible outsiders, "untouchables" in Brahmin Harvard's terminology, "birds" at Princeton where three out of every four undergraduates came from the more exclusive preparatory schools. It was the Princeton of the golden-boy athlete, Hobey Baker, a place the young Scott Fitzgerald would find just this side of paradise. Wilson in a mood of exasperation described his college as "just what they say it is, a fine country club where many of the alumni make snobs of their boys."

That narrow and excluding social gradations should exist within Princeton was a denial of Wilson's ideal of a university. Unable within his academic limits to face the fact that end-of-the-century America set small stock on concerns of the mind, that the colleges served their primary function as finishing schools for the sons of the wealthy, he held to the medieval idea of a university as a democracy of scholars with its only legitimate object intellectual attainment. For him the sixteen clubs ranged sedately in their elegant buildings along Prospect Avenue were the very symbol of all that was wrong with Princeton. Ivy, Cap and Gown, Colonial, Tiger Inn and the rest had grown from modest eating clubs to lush and exclusive establishments for which the college itself was merely an academic background. "We must *reintegrate*," Wilson told the trustees in his 1906 annual report —"and create a college comradeship based on *letters*." He now proposed to take over the clubs outright, purge them of their privilege and exclusiveness and convert them into quads much like Oxford and Cambridge colleges but without their scholastic autonomy.

In four years Wilson had transformed Princeton. He had reorganized the curriculum and raised the academic standards. His preceptorial plan had been a brilliant success So far had he been able to go. But in his plan to transform the clubs into what he considered socially useful adjuncts of the college, he was challenging the mores of plutocratic America and he was doomed to defeat. The trustees first voted approval of his plan, then, under pressure from wealthy indignant eastern alumni, reversed themselves. The undergraduate clubmen resisted him on the campus, backed up by their elders. Another than Wilson might have compromised, but his nature found that impossible. Calvinistic in his self-righteousness, he could see no middle way. He was *right*, and he did not compromise with wrong. Yet, by the time he sailed for England in the early summer of 1908, broken in spirit, he had been compelled to face the rejection of his quad plan. It was his first defeat. The forces of social privilege had been too strong for him.

The battle over the clubs marked the beginning of Wilson's transition from an academic convervative to a militant political progressive. Returning refreshed from England in September, 1908, he found himself almost at once engaged in a controversy with Princeton's graduate school dean, Andrew West, that would prove as bitter and long-drawn-out as the quad struggle but with much wider ramifications. What was essentially a difference of opinion between two stubborn men over the control and location of a new graduate school, Wilson transformed, both in his own mind and that of the general public, into a ringing crusade for social democracy.

Next to Wilson, West was the most outstanding member of the Princeton faculty, a classical scholar of international reputation who during President Patton's lax regime was one of the professors who dominated Princeton affairs. Since 1896 his most cherished, most zealously pursued goal was to found a separate graduate school of intellectual luster that would transform Princeton into a university. In 1900 the trustees finally agreed to such a school, at the same time making West dean, with control over all graduate courses, fellowships and appointments. The school was at first enthusiastically endorsed by Wilson.

West developed plans for housing his graduate college along the lines of Wilson's quad plans, a great quadrangle on the English model with a resident master, where graduate students would live and eat and have their conference rooms. But his idea, as opposed to Wilson's, was to build the new college off-campus, apart from the undergraduates. Wilson's preceptorial plan, of which West completely approved, had taken precedence over other developments. But when that was in working order, West expected that Princeton's next project would be his graduate college. Much to his chagrin he found his cherished project pushed into the background, possibly indefinitely postponed, by Wilson's quad plan. The rivalry of the two men now came out into the open. West disliked his arbitrary president. Wilson sharply disapproved of his graduate school dean's independence, and endeavored to restrict West's autonomy. The conflict was made inevitable by their two natures. Neither man could brook a challenge to his authority. "The trouble is," West told Wilson to his face, "that I have not hit it off with you."

The issue between the two headstrong men was obvious, and in retrospect trivial, but behind its Gothic façade two rivals struggled for power. After the rejection of the quad plan, with Dean West as one of its leading opponents, the question of the graduate school and its location shifted from the indefinite to the immediate. Wilson, who had done little or nothing to further the new school, now wanted it on the campus. West wanted his quadrangle on Bayard Lane a short walk from the campus. That short walk was destined to become a national issue.

In 1909 Wilson persuaded the trustees to divest West of most of his authority and place control of the graduate school's curriculum and appointments in the hands of a Wilson-dominated faculty committee. West countered by presenting Wilson with a letter from his lifetime friend William Cooper Procter, the enormously rich head of the Procter & Gamble soap firm, offering half a million dollars for a graduate school on condition that it be built off the campus, distinct and apart from the undergraduate college. In those days a half million dollars was an enormous sum of money. Faculty and trustees were divided as to its acceptance. The majority of the alumni were in favor. When the trustees finally agreed to take Procter's offer, Wilson informed them that he could not accede to accepting gifts on terms that took Princeton's educational policy out of the hands of the trustees and faculty and permitted it to be determined by those who gave money. He offered the trustees the choice of refusing Procter's offer or accepting his resignation. They in turn referred the whole question to a special committee of five to be appointed by Wilson.

Though Dean West's English-patterned graduate college was essentially a variation of Wilson's quads, Wilson now twisted the issue between them to that of social privilege versus academic democracy, maintaining that West's college was intended to extend the exclusivism and privilege of the clubs to the graduate quadrangle. West of course had no such intention, but Wilson in his rage and frustration over the defeat of his quad plan had come to view the academic scene through the distorting glass of his own dogmatic intransigence. Where he might justly have appealed to a wider public over the club issue, he now falsely appealed over the graduate college. When one of the editors of the New York *Times,* Henry Brougham, offered to write an editorial about the controversy, Wilson sent him a letter of great length that formed the substance of the editorial, "Princeton," that appeared in the *Times* of February 3, 1910. "At Princeton," Brougham had written with savagely indignant inaccuracy, "the scene of a battle fought a century and a third ago for the establishment of the American democracy, is in progress to-day a struggle not less significant for the future of American youth and of Government in the United States. It is the more significant, though pitched in academic halls, because it will decide the issue whether the American colleges shall henceforth fall short of their democratic mission." The exclusive and benumbing touch of special privilege was upon the colleges, and the outcome of the Princeton controversy would determine whether they would continue to foster "mutually exclusive social cliques, stolid groups of wealth and fashion, devoted to nonessentials and the smatterings of culture."

With the editorial Wilson was made to seem to Americans all over the country the champion of democracy. A week later, and before the committee of five could meet, the chagrined Procter withdrew his offer. Wilson was delighted. "At last," he wrote, "we are free to govern the University as our judgments and consciences dictate." With the vindictiveness that was part of his Calvinistic nature, he now began a movement to oust West.

All that spring Wilson visited alumni groups and associations to speak about the graduate school controversy. He found the alumni for the most part hostile. In New York they listened in frigid silence and without applause to the man who, they felt, had capriciously thrown away a half million dollars. While Wilson proceeded from city to city, the board of trustees voted not to allow him to poll the faculty, the majority of whom would probably have sided with him. All Wilson's resentment and suppressed rage finally boiled over in an impromptu speech he made to the Pittsburgh alumni on April 16. Suddenly the Burkite conservative, the professor who disapproved of labor unions and "trust busting" as restraints on trade, who even three years before had considered the 1907 Panic as caused by "the blundering and unintelligent activities of the government in its attempts to regulate business," found himself the radical tribune of the people, carried away by the eloquence of his passion as if he were speaking in tongues.

"How does the nation judge Princeton?" he asked in rhetorical fury. The university was not an instrument for the pleasure of Princeton men but intended for the service of the country. And it would be judged by the country's standards. America "expects of Princeton what it expects of every other college, the accommodation of its life to the life of the country." Like the Protestant churches, "with more regard to their pew-rents than to the souls of men," the privately endowed colleges were serving the "classes" rather than the "masses," pandering to the desires of wealthy students and alumni. As a result the future would not be for the private institutions but for the state universities who were seeking to serve the people, who were "constantly sensitive to the movements of general opinion, to the opinion of the unknown man who can vote." Wilson in his new vision saw the strength of the nation as coming "from the great mass of the unknown, of the unrecognized men, whose powers are being developed by struggle." Lincoln himself would not have been as serviceable to his country if he had been a college man because the process "to which the college man is subjected does not render him serviceable to the country as a whole."

Never before had Wilson said such things or perhaps even thought them. "What we cry out against," he told the stunned Pittsburgh audience, "is that a handful of conspicuous men have thrust cruel hands among the heartstrings of the masses of men upon whose blood and energy they are subsisting." Universities made men forget their common origins and universal sympathies, but "the great voice of America does not come from the seats of learning. It comes in a murmur from the hills and woods and the farms and factories and the mills, rolling on and gaining volume until it comes to us from the homes of common men. Do these murmurs echo in the corridors of universities? I have not heard them."

Swept along by his own rhetoric, Wilson announced his determination with "every power that there is in me to bring the college that I have anything to do with to an absolutely democratic regeneration of spirit." Nor would he cease his crusade until college men were saturated with "the same thought, the same sympathy that pulses through the whole great body politic." Dean West's graduate college was a challenge to democracy. "Will America tolerate the idea of having graduate students set apart?" Wilson asked finally. Not at all. "Seclude a man, separate him from the rough and tumble of college life, from all the contacts of every sort and condition of men, and you have done a thing which America will brand with contemptuous disapproval."

The men of the farms and factories and mills could not have been less concerned with the location of Princeton's graduate college inside or outside the campus, or whether undergraduates and graduate students might mingle socially. But Wilson had taken a matter of academic policy, turned it inside out and with ringing words transformed it into a national issue. What matter that logic made nonsense of his claims? To the country he stood forth in Pittsburgh as the leader of the forces of democracy against the powers of exclusivism, snobbery and reaction.

In the end it was West who had the last word. A month after Wilson's Pittsburgh outburst, West's elderly friend Isaac Wyman of Salem, Massachusetts, died leaving his entire estate of between two and four million dollars to Princeton for the building and endowment of a graduate college along the lines proposed by West, who was named as one of the estate's executors. Up until then Wilson had stubbornly rejected all efforts to compose his differences with the dean. But to reject such a sum as this, he knew was out of the question. "We have beaten the living," he remarked, "but we cannot fight the dead. The game is up."

As Wilson realized, the majority of the trustees, the alumni and the students were ranged against him. Either he had to accept the Wyman bequest and West's control of the graduate college or resign. For the moment he chose not to resign, but the bright and hopeful days were long since over, and it was clear by commencement that he and Princeton had reached a parting of the ways even as he was being impelled forward as candidate for governor of New Jersey.

As early as May, 1909, Harvey had written confidently in *Harper's Weekly* that "we now expect to see Woodrow Wilson elected Governor of the State of New Jersey in 1910 and nominated for President in 1912." In January 1910 Harvey again sent for Inglis and told him:

> There has been nothing to do in a political way for Wilson these past two years; but the effect of the publicity has been on the whole satisfactory. The time has come now to proceed on a political line. On Saturday I lunched by appointment with Senator Smith at Delmonico's and we put in the entire afternoon discussing the situation. Although one of the shrewdest political observers I have ever known, I doubt if the senator quite appreciates the smash which is going to overwhelm the Republican party next November. But he does think there is a possibility of carrying New Jersey if a strong candidate shall be named. He agreed with me that if the Democrats could be held in line, Wilson would make a most effective appeal to Republican and Independent voters. There are several candidates, however, who have always been his friends and supporters and to whom he feels under distinct obligations. But he is very uncertain respecting the party workers and rank and file as to Wilson. He is going to think it over, however, and talk with a few of his lieutenants, and we are to meet again next Saturday.*

Harvey's nebulous presentiment of half a dozen years earlier now began to take form in the divisive year 1910: the fragmentation of the Republican Party under the inept Taft; the return of Rough Rider Roosevelt to rally his progressives; the emergence of the Democrats from the shadow of Bryan. Boss Smith owed his seat in the United States Senate to Harvey, who had brought to Smith's earlier candidacy the potent backing and financial support of William Whitney. A week after their Delmonico luncheon, Smith and Harvey met again. Smith at this time "came up to scratch in fine shape," promising that his organization would spring into line whenever Harvey gave him the word that Wilson was ready to accept the nomination.

Wilson, then in the midst of his graduate school controversy, did not wish to be diverted or seem to be running away from a fight.

* *Collier's,* Oct. 7, 1916.

Harvey spent a night at Prospect, the square-towered president's house on the Princeton campus, trying to persuade the reluctant Wilson to commit himself. Finally Harvey asked him: "If I can handle the matter so that the nomination for governor shall be tendered to you on a silver platter . . . what do you think would be your attitude?"

Wilson walked up and down the floor for some minutes in deep thought. Finally he said slowly: "If the nomination for governor should come to me in that way, I should regard it as my duty to give the matter very serious consideration."

Equivocal though the answer was, Harvey accepted it, as did Smith, who agreed to leave the matter of the nomination dormant until Harvey returned from his annual trip to England. Though the most powerful Democratic leader in New Jersey, the Newark-Essex boss was far from absolute, and he found his subordinates restively eyeing the Democratic gubernatorial nomination that with each passing month seemed more and more the prelude to election. Smith himself had large hopes for Wilson. "We have the opportunity," he told a friend, "of electing the next president of the United States by nominating and electing Woodrow Wilson as governor of New Jersey." Smith could see practical considerations as well. Wilson, the conservative intellectual, would be a respectable front for the less-than-intellectual, less-than-respectable Democratic machine politicians now being challenged by the progressive insurgents. Then too, as the other bosses had pointed out, Wilson was bound to run far ahead of his party, gathering in the votes of disenchanted New Idea Republicans and making possible a Democratic legislature that might once more elect Smith to his old senate seat. One assurance Smith did demand for his endorsement, and that was that Wilson if once elected governor would not "set about fighting and breaking down the existing Democratic organization." Wilson replied that he would not, so long as he was left "absolutely free in the matter of measures and men."

As the dragging weeks brought no word from the absent Harvey, and no declaration by Wilson, Smith found himself faced with incipient revolt from his own party workers. When Harvey belatedly returned at the end of June, Smith called him at once to tell him that the New Jersey situation was "hot" and that he could not keep his men in line another week unless Wilson came out and agreed to accept the nomination. Thoroughly alarmed, Harvey tried to arrange a dinner meeting with Wilson on Sunday night at Jorjalma. Smith was to be present as was "Marse Henry" Watterson. But Wilson, spending the summer at Lyme, Connecticut, replied nonchalantly by telegram to Harvey's urgent invitation that there was no Sunday train from Lyme and consequently he could not come. The frantic Harvey dispatched Inglis to bring Wilson back by any means possible. Inglis took the train to New London, rented a car, and raced across bumpy back roads to catch Wilson just as he was going to church. Wilson agreed to return with him, and the two reached New London only ten minutes before the New York express.

For all the hurried impromptu arrival of the chief guest, the dinner at Jorjalma went off most amiably. Harvey and Smith impressed on Wilson that the New Jersey party leaders were willing to nominate him for governor "by acclamation" if only he would come out and declare his candidacy. To Wilson the distant prospect of the White House grew ever more intriguing. "The question of my nomination for the governorship of New Jersey," he later wrote a friend ". . . is the mere preliminary of a plan to nominate me in 1912 for the presidency." His immediate reaction was to go along with Smith and Harvey. Yet there were the trustees who had stood behind him in his controversy with West, and he felt he must consult with them before turning his back on Princeton. Those four men all agreed, however, that he had no obligation to the university or his supporters that should keep him out of politics. A week after the Harvey dinner, he announced that he would accept the nomination. As he confessed to a friend, after what he had taught his students about the duty of educated men to undertake public service, he did not see how he himself could avoid it.

If the rank and file Democratic party workers of New Jersey had been able to express their unimpeded choice at this time, they would have picked not Wilson but the former mayor of Trenton, Frank Katzenbach, who had been the Democratic candidate for governor in 1907 and whom they felt more entitled to this year's nomination than any academic outsider. Harvey realized that Smith's support alone was not enough, that Wilson also needed the support of Robert Davis, a former plumber and East Side Tammany ward leader, who had made himself absolute boss of Jersey City. Smith and Davis had been enemies in the past. Harvey managed to persuade them to lay aside their differences in the common cause of nominating Wilson. Since Wilson had met only Smith, Harvey felt it was high time for him to get to know the state's other Democratic leaders, and he arranged a luncheon for Wilson with the other bosses and with interested corporation officials at New York's Lawyers Club.

The politicians all agreed that Wilson was far stronger than his party and would easily win in the November election. The business leaders agreed to support the politicians. Wilson agreed to accept their support.

On July 15, just two months before the New Jersey Democratic Convention, Wilson sent an open letter to the Trenton *True American* and the Newark *Evening News* formally announcing that if "as many well informed persons" had assured him "a decided majority of the thoughtful Democrats of the State" wished him to accept the nomination he would consider it a duty "as well as an honor and privilege to do so." A decided majority of the Democratic progressives, however, wanted nothing to do with an academic amateur, whom they saw as merely a respectable front for the State House ring of the Smith-Davis machine. As one progressive assemblyman wrote, "the fact that George B. McClellan Harvey is Wilson's chief sponsor should be enough to finish Wilson."

In the face of such opposition Wilson remained silent, but his earlier condemnation of Bryan and of state regulation of business and his antilabor opinions were spread across the state by the progressives. Finally he did break his silence to say, in obvious contradiction to his earlier statements, that he had always been a warm friend of organized labor. He remained quietly in Lyme for the summer, while continuing to receive situation reports from Harvey on the campaign's progress. Earlier he had expected that with the announcement of his candidacy all the other Democratic candidates would withdraw, and he was much put out when he found that he would not receive the nomination on the promised silver platter. Particularly was he disturbed by the tenacity of Katzenbach's candidacy. Harvey tried to hearten him with the encouraging thought that full party agreement was not desirable, since it would then appear that the Democrats were completely controlled by the bosses.

Smith and Davis did their primaries work well, producing the solid blocs of delegates they had promised. Yet on the eve of the convention, held in Trenton on September 15, a week before Princeton's fall term, Wilson, in the face of unrelenting progressive-insurgent opposition, was by no means certain of being nominated. Smith, on arriving at the convention, had taken command, occupying Room 100 of the Trenton House, the traditional headquarters of the bosses of both parties. Never had he spent a busier night than that one before the convention opened, persuading the persuadable, rounding up the "hungry patriots" with such tried hands as his son-in-law Boss Nugent and the racetrack fixer known as the "Duke of Gloucester." Harvey had come on from New York with Inglis and taken a suite in the same hotel. That evening, all through the waning hours, politicians moved like nocturnal animals through corridors and lobbies rancid with cigar smoke. Wilson himself had gone from Lyme to his home in Princeton to await the results.

Smith, making his rapid calculations, saw the odds as even. But by the first grey of morning Harvey's hopes and courage had begun to ooze. Inglis, who had managed somehow to get to sleep, was wakened by a hand on his shoulder and saw Harvey looking down at him, ashen-faced. "We're up against it," he told Inglis:

> This man Silzer from New Brunswick has got the big northern counties away from us, and the senator can't get them back. We have got to put Wilson over on the first ballot or we never can. The cold fact is that at this moment we haven't the votes and we've got to get them. I have just left the senator. He is lying down in his clothes, but can't sleep. I must if I can, for a little. Have a cup of coffee and wake me at a quarter before eight. And, Bill, for God's sake, don't let a whisper get out about Wilson being in Princeton. If we should be beaten and it should get out that he had come over to Princeton, he would be the laughingstock of his enemies if not of the country, and I would be responsible. Can't you see it would be a personal tragedy? It simply must not be. Now, don't fail me.*

Wilson in Princeton was playing golf when the convention opened in the Trenton Opera House. By lunchtime, but before the balloting had begun, Harvey's hopes and spirits had revived. He told Inglis:

> It's all right, if Smith can hold Essex solid, and I guess he can.

* *Collier's*, Oct. 14, 1916.

> Get your automobile and bring Wilson to my room in the hotel. Don't let anybody see him if you can help it. If he's nominated, a committee will call for him. If by chance he should fail of nomination, you get him back to Princeton without letting a soul know that he has been here. If he makes a speech, he'll win them all. But we've got to have him here, so that he can make his speech right away. No power on earth can hold that tired crowd for one hour after it finishes its work.*

Inglis raced to Princeton, got out of the car in the gravel driveway in front of Prospect, but before he could reach the steps Wilson opened the door, smiled, and said: "I am ready." He appeared calm and unruffled, well-rested. Instead of the politician's still-conventional frock coat, he wore a grey sack suit. His imperturbability, his easy poise continued for the rest of the afternoon which he spent in Harvey's room, refusing all refreshment, even tea and toast. In the Opera House, that "gigantic sweat-box," the balloting had begun. At the mention of Wilson's name there was sustained applause, and strategically-placed Princeton students gave their college cheer: "Siss-boom-ah-h-h! Wilson! Wilson!! Wilson!!!" It soon became clear to seasoned politicians that Wilson would have a small majority, possibly 50 in a total of 1,333 delegates. Before the first ballot had concluded, a number of anti-Wilson delegates, anxious to get on the bandwagon, began to switch their votes. The final Wilson tally was 749 to 584. Then a motion was hurried through to make it unanimous. Wilson, still resting in Harvey's suite, was notified at once. "I am ready," he told the news bringer with the same calm, and was at once driven to the Opera House to make his acceptance speech.

He faced a sweated-out unenthusiastic audience. Most of the delegates had never set eyes on him before. The large sullen progressive minority had been whipped into line for the sake of party unity. Unconciliated by the progressive platform, they viewed the bosses' candidate with seething ill-will. Suddenly they heard this renegade professor saying:

> I did not seek this nomination. It has come to me absolutely unsolicited. With the consequence that I shall enter upon the duties of the office of governor, if elected, with absolutely no pledge of any kind to prevent me from serving the people of the state with singleness of purpose.†

* Ibid.

† *Wilson: The Road to the White House*, p. 167.

Sullen lethargy gave way to enthusiasm as the mellifluous voice, with what Harvey called its "fascinating articulation," flowed on. Wilson was declaring his independence of the bosses, and the thought electrified the progressives, brought them to their feet. "Thank God, at last, a leader has come!" Joe Tumulty, the young insurgent from Jersey City, exclaimed. Harvey and Smith exchanged imperturbable glances.

Great tasks lay before the Democratic party, Wilson told the delegates. Americans had to reconstruct their economic order, and in so doing would reconstruct their political order. As he concluded, with a conventionally fervent peroration on the flag, the delegates cheered themselves hoarse. Some even tried to carry him out of the hall on their shoulders. A squad of policemen had to form a hollow square to get him to the car where Harvey and Inglis were waiting. Smith and Davis and the lesser bosses were as warm as the progressives in their enthusiasm, reasoning coldly that rectitude, even the stiff rectitude of a schoolmaster, was in the end bound to be tempered by gratitude.

As the car with the three men in the back seat pulled away from the Opera House and crossed State Street, Wilson turned to Harvey and asked: "What was my exact majority?" Harvey looked at him through weary, bloodshot eyes. "Enough," he said.

The new Wilson was enthusiastically received by the progressives of his own party and by many of the New Idea Republicans. In the practical aspects of the campaign, however, the neophyte professor felt obliged to fall back on the professional skills of the boss triumverate of Smith, Nugent and Davis. His first campaigning efforts were ambiguous, as if he were attempting to gloss over what were, for the progressives of both parties, the real issues. Soon he found himself accused of evasiveness, of insincerity, of hypocrisy. Stunned by such taunts, he confronted his critics in a speech at Newark on September 30th in which he turned his back on his conservative past. Gone were the measured words, the vagueness, the caution, as he denounced the singular hospitality of New Jersey to corporations, called for their state control, and then, moving on to what he had previously opposed all his adult life, he came out for direct primaries and the direct election of United States senators. The people of New Jersey, he told his audience, were in the midst of a great political revolution and he, Woodrow Wilson, represented the cause of regeneration.

With his growing political awareness, Wilson knew he could not be elected without the support of independents and New Idea Republicans. Conviction and political expediency in equal measure impelled him down the progressive road. By mid-October, with the forgetful zeal of a convert, he had become so oblivious of his past that he could say: "I am and always have been an insurgent." Even Theodore Roosevelt, later his arch-enemy, felt that Wilson as the state leader of the progressive movement deserved to be elected. His campaign speeches carried far beyond New Jersey, and it became clear to a larger America that in that small eastern state a new personality was emerging in Democratic politics, the first of any stature since William Jennings Bryan. For all Wilson's adopted Progressivism, the Democratic machine continued to back him loyally and skillfully. And in spite of his condemnation of bossism in general, he remained on friendly terms with the New Jersey bosses.

The Republican bosses, seeing their power base erode in the Taft-Roosevelt feud, had put forward as their nominee for governor former State Commissioner of Banking and Insurance Vivian Lewis, a man of progressive leanings, though not identified with the New Idea faction. Nevertheless, it was clear that most of the New Idea Republican insurgent votes were going to Wilson. Harvey took no active part in the campaigning, remaining at Deal, paying weekly strategy visits to Smith and replying at length to Wilson's frequent requests for advice and aid. The grateful Wilson wrote to Harvey that he did not deserve such true and disinterested friendship. Harvey continued to back Wilson in *Harper's Weekly*, writing that the people would render a verdict "as between this most exceptional man responding to a call of civic duty, and the group of men whose impelling advantage is mere lust of power which they have wielded so long to personal advantage and to the shame of the State."

Wilson won by 49,056 votes, carrying a Democratic legislature in his wake. Among other things, this legislative victory opened up the prospect of the election of a Democratic United States senator. Smith had been elected to a single term in 1892, and after the Republican interlude-years was eager to return to the Senate. Since political enemies had started the rumor that Governor Wilson would merely be Senator Smith's advance agent, Smith had promised before the Trenton convention not to be a candidate for the Senate if this would hurt Wilson's chances. Harvey advised Wilson not to make this offer public since it might damage him with the party regulars. Not hearing from Wilson, Smith concluded after Trenton that Wilson had no real objection to his candidacy.

In 1907 the New Jersey legislature had enacted a law allowing senatorial candidates to submit their names to a popular referendum. The referendum was in the nature of a public opinion poll, for it was not legally binding on the legislators and was looked on by party leaders as a joke. In 1910 no prominent Democrat was willing to enter this informal primary, since there seemed little prospect of a Democratic legislature's being elected in November. Two candidates did at last appear, a Newark lawyer of dubious repute, and a wealthy talkative eccentric known as "Farmer Jim" Martine. Scarcely ten percent of the eligible voters bothered to go to the polls, and Martine received 48,449 votes to his rival's 15,573. Politicians laughed off the results. Martine did not begin to take himself seriously until the unexpected election of the Democratic legislature. Smith was equally surprised at the election results and, considering Martine no more than a buffoon and assuming no opposition from the governor-elect, he decided to make a bid for his old senate seat. Wilson did object, pointing out that Smith's election to the Senate would be considered payment for service rendered in the gubernatorial contest. Admitting that the primary was a farce and Martine a fool, Wilson suggested naming a compromise candidate. Smith refused to consider anyone but himself, and the two men parted with overt hostility.

Although Wilson thought as little of the primary result as did Smith, he soon found himself under great pressure from his progressive supporters of both parties who insisted that Martine, however personally negligible, was the primary winner, and to deny him his place was to deny the progressive principle of direct election of senators. Much distressed, Wilson turned to Harvey:

> I have learned to have a very high opinion of Senator Smith. . . . But his election would be intolerable to the very people who elected me and gave us a majority in the legislature. . . . It was no Democratic victory. It was a victory of the "Progressives" of both parties, who are determined to live no longer under either of the political organizations that have controlled the two parties of the State. . . .

> It is a national as well as a State question. If the independent Republicans who in this State voted for me are not to be attracted to us they will assuredly turn again, in desperation, to Mr. Roosevelt, and the chance of a generation will be lost to the Democracy; the chance to draw all the liberal elements of the country to it, through new leaders, the chance that Mr. Roosevelt missed in his folly, and to constitute the ruling party of the country for the next generation.*

Wilson undoubtedly expected Harvey would show the letter to Smith in an effort to persuade him to drop his candidacy. Shortly after his meeting with Wilson, Smith did discuss the matter with Harvey. Both men agreed that in a knock-down fight Wilson would probably win, but this in no way altered Smith's determination to claim what he felt was his right. "Well, by God," he told Harvey finally, "I guess I'll let him beat me."

In the question of the senatorship, the bosses who had originally sponsored Wilson now devoted their best efforts to defeating him. But Wilson in turn went over their heads to appeal directly to the legislators and the people. Even before his inauguration the governor was developing an astonishing deftness in political in-fighting, a deftness that brought him eager allies. Most of the New Jersey newspapers supported him. To the progressives he seemed more and more the longed-for leader. The issue as he shaped it went far beyond the senate race. It became his challenge to the authority of the bosses. Given his nature, this challenge was in one way or another unavoidable. He now fell back on his progressive supporters; Smith on the party machinery.

In the emotional stress of this struggle, Wilson saw himself, as he had in Pittsburgh in the spring, as the tribune of the people. Less than two months after he had expressed his "very high opinion" of Smith, he was stumping the state in impassioned efforts to smash the Smith-Nugent machine. His Calvinistic nature saw this local issue elevated to a matter of high principle, of God and freedom.

> Does not your blood jump quicker in your veins when you think that this is part of the age-long struggle for human liberty? What do men feel curtails and destroys their liberty? Matters in which they have no voice. . . . You can see the dust of the plain

* *Wilson: The Road to the White House*, pp. 212–13.

> gather, and then as they take heart and realize that the fort is hard to take or not, life is not worth living unless it is taken. . . .*

A week after the inaugural, the New Jersey legislature convened to choose the new senator. Wilson had massed the great majority of the voters behind him. The lesser politicians, with their instinct for victory, deserted the old leader. In the final vote only three assemblymen remained loyal to Smith. Martine the clown was overwhelmingly elected and Smith left Trenton a tearful, broken old man.

Smith's defeat established Wilson's national reputation. Throughout the country he was now seen as 1912's most probable Democratic presidential candidate. As the friend of both men, Harvey had remained apart from the struggle, though after Smith's downfall *Harper's Weekly* hailed Wilson as the "Knight Errant of the New Democracy who as such will be nominated for President in opposition to William H. Taft." In March the *North American Review* published an article on "The Political Predestination of Woodrow Wilson." Yet Wilson's turnabout, his unfurling of the progressive banner that would eventually metamorphose into his New Freedom, sent Harvey's own plans a-glimmering. For Harvey's goal had been to nominate Wilson with the support of wealthy conservatives by gaining the allegiance of just such political machines as Wilson was in the process of destroying. By the time Wilson became governor, Harvey had succeeded in gathering under one canvas the Democrats opposed to Bryan, the supporters of Cleveland, the conservative financial Democrats such as Ryan, Belmont and Morgan, and the big bosses in New York, Illinois and Indiana. It was a coalition that fell apart at the sound of Wilson's progressive trumpet. For Wilson, in spite of all he had said in the past, was drawing closer and closer to the Bryan wing of his party.

The three-month legislative session following Wilson's inaugural was the swiftest, the most eager in its reforming zeal, that the state had yet seen. Personally taking command, the governor forced passage of his bills through all incipient opposition. His four chief measures were a direct primary law "to make the government in every part a people's government"; a law regulating

* Ibid.

public utilities; a corrupt practices act; and a workmen's compensation law. The direct primary act, known as the Geran Bill, required party primary nominations of all elected officials and delegates to conventions. As such it was a body blow at the bosses, a triumph for the progressives. At the end of the session late in April there was already an organized movement underway to make Wilson his party's presidential nominee in 1912.

Wilson's original astonished delight at finding himself mentioned as a presidential candidate had given way to calculated anticipation. From Trenton he found his gaze straying south more and more to Washington. After the session's end he made his first open bid as a candidate by going on a speaking tour of the West. Everywhere he drew large crowds. During the summer, while a Wilson machine was taking shape in New Jersey, Harvey was spending his usual months in England. In his absence the first rift in his relationship with Wilson became apparent. It began rather as a feeling on Wilson's part than from any particular incident. The governor, wearing his new progressive cloak, did not fancy being under obligation to a man with a Wall Street label. As he told a reporter who visited him at his summer home at Sea Girt: "I wish that I could rid myself of the support of *Harper's Weekly* and Colonel Harvey. I do not know why Harvey insists on supporting me. It does me great injury." Newer faces were replacing the old in the Wilson circle, men like the hawk-faced Georgian, William Gibbs McAdoo; and Wilson's former student, the crippled New York lawyer William McCombs; and the shadowy Texan, Colonel Edward House.

Harvey came back to America late in August suffering from bronchitis. Hoping to relieve it, he went to Maine where in a spell of foggy weather he developed pleurisy. Not until October could he return to Deal. Yet, though a semi-invalid, he managed to write one of his strongest articles, later to appear in the *Independent,* calling for Wilson's nomination for president. On returning to New Jersey in October he found Wilson campaigning to elect a Democratic legislature the following month. Aware that Boss Smith was devoting whatever strength he had left to thwarting Wilson by electing a Republican legislature, Harvey felt he should warn the governor and sent Inglis from Deal to arrange a meeting between them.

Inglis thought Wilson much changed from when he had last

seen him at the convention. His bonhomie had given way to a formal though affable reserve, and he was surrounded by a respectful entourage from whom he kept his distance. Inglis told him he had a message from Harvey, and Wilson, smiling without warmth, took him alone into the library. When the governor heard Inglis's message, the smile vanished. "What does he want to see me for?" he asked abruptly. Inglis said he did not know. "It cannot be very important," Wilson broke in, "or he would have told you what it is. I can't see him." When Inglis, shocked by the refusal, persisted that Harvey would not have sent him on such a journey if it were not important, Wilson reiterated impatiently that he could not see him. "I have had a hard campaign; I am tired, and I must have some rest," he concluded. Nor would he give a definite date as to when he could see Harvey.

Harvey accepted the rebuff with good grace, explaining to Inglis that the governor was harassed on all sides and might have temporarily lost his perspective in the preelection tumult. As Harvey had predicted, the Democrats did lose the legislature, the clandestine aid furnished the Republicans by Smith and Nugent giving the opposition party a majority. Chagrined as Wilson was, he could take comfort in the election analysis in *Harper's Weekly*, for Harvey explained away the defeat as a concealed victory. The masthead of his editorial page he inscribed with the slogan: "FOR PRESIDENT, WOODROW WILSON." In his lead editorial he declared that Wilson had transformed New Jersey into a solid Democratic state. Only the treachery of the Smith-Nugent machine in Essex County had prevented an even greater triumph in 1911 than in 1910, for everywhere, except in that renegade county, the Democrats had increased their earlier lead. Harvey now excoriated his old friend Smith, while proclaiming that Wilson was stronger than ever.

Harvey and Wilson finally met with Watterson on December 7 in New York's Manhattan Club. Harvey asked if there was anything left of "that cheap talk during the gubernatorial campaign" about his advocating Wilson on behalf of the "interests."

"Yes," said Wilson, with great positiveness, "there is. I lunched today with two of the young men in my literary bureau, and they both declared it was having a serious effect in the West."

"Have you thought of any way to counteract this harmful effect?" Harvey asked him.

"I have not," Wilson replied. "In fact I am greatly perplexed how to do it. . . . I have not yet been able to devise a way to meet the situation."

"Is there anything I can do," Harvey asked again, "except of course to stop advocating your nomination?"

"I think not," said Wilson. "At least, I can't think of anything."

"Then," Harvey told him, "I will simply sing low."

After a few more words the two men parted with frosty politeness. They would not meet again until Wilson was in the White House. In the next issue of *Harper's Weekly* Harvey removed the Wilson slogan from his editorial page. Rumors at once spread of a rupture between them. Joe Tumulty, who had become Wilson's private secretary, warned the governor that Harvey had been deeply hurt and that the incident might cause a break in their relations. Somewhat contritely Wilson, on December 21, wrote Harvey a note marked "personal":

> Every day I am confirmed in the judgment that my mind is a one-track road and can run only one train of thought on time! A long time after that interview with you and Marse Henry at the Manhattan Club it came over me that when (at the close of the interview) you asked me that question about the "Weekly" I answered it simply as a matter of fact, and of business, and never said a word of my sincere gratitude to you for all your generous support, or of my hope that it might be continued. Forgive me, and forget my manners!

Harvey replied:

> I think it should go without saying that no purely personal issue could arise between you and me. Whatever anybody else may surmise, you surely must know that, in trying to arouse and further your political aspirations during the past few years, I have been actuated solely by the belief that I was rendering a distinct public service. . . .
>
> Whatever little hurt I may have felt as a consequence of the unexpected peremptoriness of your attitude toward me is, of course, wholly eliminated by your gracious words.*

Wilson answered a week later, describing Harvey's letter as "generous and cordial" and saying that he was more than ashamed of hurting a true friend, "however unintentional that hurt may have been." He thanked Harvey for his generous praise and continued support that heaped coals of fire on his head, and con-

* *Wilson: The Road to the White House,* pp. 363–64.

cluded that "you have proved yourself very big and I wish I might have an early opportunity to tell you face to face how I really feel about it all."

Harvey replied in kind:

> Thank you sincerely for your most handsome letter. I can only repeat what I said before — that there is no particle of personal rancor or resentment left in me. And I beg of you to believe that I have not said one word to anybody of criticism of you.
>
> I *have* to print a word of explanation to the *Weekly*'s readers, but it will be the briefest possible.*

Both men were ironic, both in their degrees hypocritical, for Wilson's private wish was to get rid of the Harvey label, while Harvey had not forgiven the cold rebuff at the Manhattan Club. On January 8 the Democratic leaders gathered in Washington at the Raleigh Hotel for their ritual Jackson Day dinner. Harvey was present; sharp political eyes noted that he failed to greet Wilson. A few days later Wilson and Harvey attending a banquet in Philadelphia, though not twenty feet apart, ignored each other. Ostensibly forgiving, Harvey was merely waiting for a suitable moment to make the Manhattan Club incident public. His opportunity came through Colonel Watterson. Shortly afterward, on a lecture tour of the South, Marse Henry confided to the publisher of the *Atlantic Constitution* that at the right moment he and Harvey were going to expose Wilson as a base ingrate. At the same time he wrote to Harvey warning him not to say anything yet. "*On no account* make the first move," he told him. "You hold a full and winning hand . . . I have a perfectly definite plan and have thought it out in every detail. . . . I am an old hand at the bellows at this sort of business, and *know I am right*."

Even as he was writing this letter, Watterson received a message from Harvey urging him to make the Manhattan Club incident public at once. Watterson told him to wait. "In my judgment it would spoil all to give it out prematurely or in the loose form of an interview. My plan is to treat it much more seriously. I propose immediately on reaching home to write to Governor Wilson a letter fully and frankly explaining why I can go no further in the support of his candidacy. In this I shall give as my pivotal point his treatment of you, making common cause with you. This

* Ibid., p. 364.

cannot fail to result in a correspondence in which we have everything to gain and he everything to lose."

On December 29 Watterson, on a visit to Charlotte, North Carolina, had told his story to James Hemphill, the editor of the Charleston *News & Courier*. Harvey kept urging him to break the news. Finally Watterson gave Hemphill a report to print. "All sorts of rumors are flying about," Watterson declared. "One has it that Col. Henry Watterson was a party to the breach between the two eminent Easterners. . . . The other has it that Wilson found Harvey's support a handicap with the Democratic radicals and rudely demanded of Harvey that he stop it."

Wilson was much distressed by the implication of this report, and through his wife attempted to reach some sort of reconciliation with Watterson, her cousin by marriage. Meanwhile Harvey in the January 20 issue of *Harper's Weekly* published a statement "To Our Readers":

> We make the following reply to many inquiries from the readers of *Harper's Weekly*:
>
> The name of Woodrow Wilson was taken down from the head of these columns in response to a statement made directly to us by Governor Wilson, to the effect that our support was affecting his candidacy injuriously.
>
> The only course left open to us, in simple fairness to Mr. Wilson, no less in consideration of our own self-respect, was to cease to advocate his nomination.
>
> We make this explanation with great reluctance and the deepest regret. But we cannot escape the conclusion that the very considerable number of our readers who have cooperated earnestly and loyally in advancing a movement which was inaugurated solely in the hope of rendering a high public service are clearly entitled to this information.

The statement was released to the press four days before it appeared in the *Weekly*. To those outside the gossip circles of Eastern politics it came like a bolt from the blue. Wilson's enemies rejoiced. He seemed then and there to stand convicted of the basest ingratitude. The New York *Sun* welcomed the occasion to denounce the New Jersey governor. Hearst's papers printed a highly fictional version of the Manhattan Club conversation. According to the formerly sympathetic Richmond *News-Leader,* Wilson had "dropped the pilot." President Taft felt that "the Harvey-Wilson episode is going to stir up the Democratic politics for some time. It shows Wilson in a perfectly bloodless chase for the White House and willing to sacrifice friendship."

That Wilson's action was not the direct affront Harvey had made it seem was made clear by Colonel Watterson's forthright account "regretfully" given in his *Courier-Journal* of January 17 and then distributed by the Associated Press throughout the country. Hurt and aggrieved, intensely loyal to Harvey, Marse Henry could not nevertheless endure the misrepresentations that Hearst and his ilk were fostering. There had been nothing, he wrote, of a discourteous, or even an unfriendly, nature at the Manhattan Club. Wilson's statement that Harvey's support was injuring his candidacy was in reply to a direct question. Watterson's chief grievance was over Wilson's "autocratic" and "tyrannous" manner which had made him feel that Wilson was not the man to make "common cause with his political associates." This milder response resulted from Ellen Wilson's letter. "Col. Harvey was *by far* his [Wilson's] ablest advocate," she wrote, prompted by her husband, "and we felt that whatever harm such championship might do in certain quarters (owing to the inflamed state of the public mind toward Wall Street) was more than counterbalanced in other quarters. . . . Woodrow was really doing violence both to his feelings of friendship and gratitude to Col. Harvey and, in a sense, to his own judgment, in saying what little he did. Doubtless, that was why he said it so badly. . . . Woodrow wrote to Col. Harvey and received a very friendly letter, yet one that showed he had been deeply wounded. . . . He was Woodrow's first political friend, the one who started it all. His speeches and editorials have all been *wonderful* and one among *my* very dearest treasures. In short, this matter involves something far more important than politics, viz., friendship."

Marse Henry's account indeed blunted the edge of the attacks on Wilson and gave his friends the occasion to defend and, they hoped, vindicate him. As the New York *World* remarked editorially: "Gov. Wilson may or may not be the wisest choice for the Presidential nomination. But his gratitude or ingratitude to Col. Harvey will not be the paramount issue in the Baltimore Convention."

That Harvey in his resentment determined to drive Wilson from public life, as Wilson's most inclusive biographer, Arthur Link, maintains, depends on a somewhat one-sided reading of the Harvey-Watterson-Wilson correspondence. But if Harvey actually felt that way after his Manhattan Club rebuff, it was a transitory feeling. Though he and the New Jersey governor had reached a parting of the ways, Harvey still kept an interest in his particular creation. He took no part in the preconvention presidential campaign in which McComb became Wilson's manager, but he refused the requested endorsement of the three other leading candidates: Governor Judson Harmon of Ohio; Speaker of the House of Representatives Champ Clark; and the southern congressman, Oscar Underwood. Clearly, Wilson and Clark were the foremost contenders, but behind them lurked the enigmatic figure of the aging Bryan. Was he hoping for a convention deadlock with the weary delegates finally turning to him once the other candidates had exhausted themselves battering against the convention's two-thirds rule? Many politicians thought so, and at times he thought so himself.

At the opening of the convention Bryan had forced through an astonishing resolution declaring that the Democrats "were opposed to the nomination of any candidate for President who is representative of or under obligation to J. Pierpont Morgan, Thomas F. Ryan, August Belmont, or any other member of the privilege-hunting and favor-seeking class." Although Nebraska had declared for Clark, and Bryan cast his vote with the rest of the delegation, he remained personally neutral between Clark and Wilson.

Sweaty days succeeded each other with desperate slowness as the Democrats balloted in Baltimore. It was a marathon session. Harmon had faded early; Clark, though holding a majority of the delegates, lacked the two-thirds necessary for nomination. Wilson, if he yielded at all, was prepared to yield to Underwood. Not until the forty-sixth ballot would the delegates finally choose a candidate. From the outset Clark's managers had been negotiating privately with Boss Murphy, and finally, on the tenth ballot, the New York delegation switched from Harmon and it seemed that with New York support Clark might be nominated in a rush. On the fourteenth ballot Bryan rose to explain to the convention that he was now shifting his and his delegation's vote from Clark to Wilson since he would not support any candidate backed by Boss Murphy and indirectly by the Morgan-Ryan-Belmont combination. Senator Carter Glass of Virginia felt at the time and afterward that Bryan by his shift had not the slightest idea of contributing to Wilson's nomination but merely hoped to defeat Clark and prolong the contest until he received the nomination by default.

Harvey, accompanied by Inglis, attended the convention more as a noncommittal observer than as a participant. Yet politicians kept seeking him out, asking his advice. Detached as he was, there were two moments in those heat-struck days in which he held Wilson's fate in his hand. The first was after the adjournment that followed the fourteenth ballot when a troubled and sweaty Bryan collared Inglis and asked to be taken to Harvey immediately.

"Harvey," said Bryan, wiping the sweat from his face. "Do you think New York will go for Wilson?"

Harvey looked at him thoughtfully and said he did not think so. "Well," Bryan replied with unmistakable disappointment, "I didn't know but they might." To Harvey the point of Bryan's question was clear. If Boss Murphy's delegation declared for Wilson, Bryan would then repudiate him. And with Bryan's veto, Wilson could never gain a two-thirds majority. Tammany's support would be the kiss of death.

The following noon, as Harvey and Inglis were having lunch in their hotel dining room, Harvey spotted Boss Murphy, Roger Sullivan the boss of the Illinois Democratic machine, and Democratic National Chairman Norman Mack at a nearby table. When Harvey was leaving, Sullivan caught sight of him and shouted to him to come over. Inglis recalled:

> We hardly sat down when Mr. Sullivan said abruptly: "Well, colonel, what do you think of your candidate now?"
>
> The Colonel made no response for a full minute while all three eyed him keenly, particularly Mr. Murphy. Then he said slowly: "I suppose, Roger, that you are thinking of going to Wilson."
>
> "What makes you think that?" asked Mr. Sullivan sharply.
>
> "Never mind. I think so. If there is any question about it, I will leave it to Mr. Murphy."
>
> Mr. Murphy said nothing, and the colonel continued: "Now, gentlemen, it doesn't matter what my attitude toward Mr. Wilson is, but I can tell you what his is toward you. You can throw your delegations to him if you like, and if you do so you probably will nominate him, but I can tell you this, you will have your labor for your pains. He will never recognize you in any way and will

never have a thing to do with either of you. Now remember what I tell you."

"Well," continued Mr. Murphy, "that settles it so far as I am concerned. I believe Harvey knows what he is talking about and has got it right."*

When Harvey and Inglis returned to their rooms, Inglis confessed that he was still in the dark. "Doesn't it occur to you," Harvey asked him, "that Bryan thought that I might suggest to Murphy, just as Sullivan clearly has been urging him, to throw New York to Wilson, and that Bryan then would have an excuse to repudiate Wilson upon the same grounds that he has repudiated Clark? Well, you can bet your last dollar it isn't going to happen now. Murphy is a one-idea man. He believes what I said — which was the exact truth — and he will never go to Wilson. Brother Bryan will have to bark up another tree."

After the thirtieth ballot, the first in which Wilson finally forged ahead of Clark, Bryan sent his brother Charles after Harvey who returned with him and spent half an hour in Bryan's suite.

Bryan certainly is a wonder [Harvey told Inglis on his return]. His rooms were full of people, so he took me into his bathroom and we have been there ever since, each with a foot on the side of the tub. Do you know what he wants to do? He wants to adjourn the convention for thirty days. He has heard, and he is right, that Sullivan is going over to Wilson on the next ballot. That means Wilson's nomination, if it happens. The only way to head it off is by adjourning for a month or so as soon as the convention meets. Bryan said he could not make the proposition himself without queering himself with the whole country, but he told me that if the suggestion should come from either the Clark or the Underwood people he would support it. He expects me to convey that information to whichever side I consider most available.

But, [Inglis queried] will they do it?

They would, undoubtedly. Postponement is the only possible chance for either of them. Now, understand, I said they would. I also say they won't, for the simple reason that not a living soul except yourself is going to know that Bryan would support the proposition. He is convinced in the back of his head that I have a grudge against Wilson and want him defeated. Consequently he has no doubt that I will give the tip. I did not say that I would or that I wouldn't; but, of course, I shall do nothing of

* *Collier's*, Oct. 21, 1916.

> the kind. We are going to sit here until there is just time to get to the press seats in the convention and we are not going to answer any calls or see any living human being. Then, William Inglis, we are going to slip over to the hall by the back way and you are going to see Woodrow Wilson nominated for President of the United States.*

From the press section Harvey and Inglis could look down on the convention floor at Bryan, surrounded by a throng of shirt-sleeved delegates, mopping his domed forehead and occasionally stealing a glance toward Harvey who with averted eyes kept doodling on a scratch pad. The minutes slipped by and the moment that Bryan was waiting for passed, the last moment in which Wilson might still have been defeated.

Wilson was finally named on the forty-sixth ballot, after the collapse of the opposition brought about his unanimous nomination. Several weeks later, Inglis was talking with Louis Seibold, the political correspondent of the *World*. "Do you know," Seibold remarked, "that the man most surprised at Wilson's nomination was William Jennings Bryan? I was talking with him just as he was entering the hall that morning, and he told me confidentially but positively that the convention was going to adjourn right off the bat for thirty days!"

The week after Wilson's nomination his name once more appeared on the editorial pages of *Harper's Weekly* after a seven-month absence. Harvey wrote:

> Intelligent choice . . . was restricted to Speaker Clark, the sturdy representative of the Old Order, and Governor Wilson, the virile champion of the New. . . . The foundation of Mr. Wilson's two thirds was the feeling that he was a winner, enhanced by admiration of his exceptional intellectual capacity, consideration of his freedom from entanglements, and respect for his moral courage. . . . If the Democrats cannot elect Woodrow Wilson, they could not elect anyone.
>
> No Democratic national canvass since Jackson's has been inaugurated more auspiciously.

In the election campaign McCombs, though his health had been much impaired by the strain of the nomination struggle, became campaign manager and chairman of the Democratic National Committee. McAdoo was named vice-chairman of the all-important New York headquarters. The two men remained

* Ibid.

extremely jealous of one another. Louis Brandeis, the liberal Boston lawyer, filled the gaps in Wilson's economic knowledge by supplying a program for dealing with trusts and monopolies. Wilson himself supplied the ringing phrase "The New Freedom," a slogan precedent that every liberal president would afterward follow. Harvey made no offers of aid in Wilson's campaign, nor did he attempt to resume any personal relations with his former friend. But he did remain on friendly terms with Tumulty, and through Tumulty Wilson often turned to him for advice and campaign ammunition.

The frail McCombs collapsed in August and McAdoo took charge until October. Finding McAdoo sitting at his desk on his return, McCombs ordered him out of the office. So great was the dissension between the two men that McCombs, with Wilson's knowledge, asked Harvey if he would draw a curtain before that part of his mind that related to any acrimony or bitterness toward Wilson and come in to help make the first Democratic president in twenty years. Harvey agreed, moving to a suite of rooms at the Waldorf and spending the last three weeks of the campaign with Inglis at the New York headquarters directing publicity and smoothing over the differences between McAdoo and the ailing McCombs. In the *Weekly* issued three days before the election, he reprinted six predictions that he had made in the past six years about Wilson's political advancement, all of which had come true. He now made a seventh, that Wilson in the election would gain a more than three-hundred-vote majority in the Electoral College. Wilson's actual majority turned out to be 339. So confident was Harvey of Wilson's victory that he wrote him a letter of congratulation the day *before* the election:

> I shall be busy getting out a paper tomorrow night, so I am going to write a line now.
>
> First, I want to compliment you upon your canvass. I can recall none to equal it in effectiveness. Never before to my knowledge has *every* utterance of a candidate added strength. That surely is an achievement.
>
> My congratulations go to our country. To my mind, it is probably unnecessary to say, your election is the greatest thing that has happened since Lincoln's. Nor am I sure that it *was not as essential* as his was.

Wilson was, however, a minority winner with only 44 per cent of the popular vote. Roosevelt alone would easily have beaten him.

> A mighty task confronts you, of course. As to that, I have no fears. I have more than hope. I have implicit faith in *you*. It is most comforting, I assure you, to feel that way — and I am more eager, I truly believe, for your great and enduring success as President of the United States than you yourself can possibly be.
>
> So with full confidence I tender my best will and wishes to you, and my felicitations to the first Southern-born lady to occupy the White House since Eliza McCardle.*

Wilson replied with a formal though cordial note of thanks, but there was no hint of renewing old ties. Between the November election and the March inaugural Harvey had no political function. He was not consulted, nor did he expect to be, about the affairs of the new administration. He was not asked to join the presidential party at the inauguration ceremonies. The goal that he had set for himself on that bright October day ten years before had been attained. That in itself was enough for him. In recognition of this he brought out a voluminous special edition of *Harper's Weekly*, setting forth the whole story of that decade from the Lotos Club speech through the New Jersey gubernatorial campaign of 1910 to the election victory of 1912. "The Triumph of an Idea" Harvey called his chronicle, which was at the same time a farewell to his editorship, for a few weeks later the *Weekly* was sold and passed to other hands.

Wilson as president would have liked some sort of reconciliation with Harvey, but he was too proud and unbending to approach his old friend directly. Through a third person he let it be known that Harvey would be welcome to call at the White House. Harvey, however, would accept nothing less than a direct invitation. With the same circuitousness Wilson offered him the post of ambassador to France after McCombs had declined it, but Harvey rejected both the manner and the substance, preferring to stay in America and edit his *North American Review*. For six months after the inaugural he had nothing but praise for Wilson's New Freedom. Of the president, he wrote in the autumn of 1913:

> All that had been predicted of the effectiveness of Woodrow Wilson has been realized. No President of the United States has demonstrated greater capacity for true leadership. None, barring Lincoln, was confronted at the outset by a larger number of

* *George Harvey*, pp. 218–19.

perplexing problems. None has met his difficulties with more sagacity or overcome them more skillfully.*

Harvey's first difference with Wilson came in the administration-supported law to exempt labor unions from offenses against the antitrust act. Harvey claimed that this would make it lawful for one class to do that which was forbidden to the other. He was also disturbed over Wilson's refusal to recognize General Victoriano de la Huerta as president of Mexico. Huerta had overthrown and murdered his predecessor Francisco Madero. Nevertheless, Harvey felt that since Huerta was firmly established as head of state, recognition had become a practical rather than a moral matter. "What legal or moral right," he asked "has a President of the United States to say who or who shall not be President of Mexico?"

The outbreak of the First World War brought Harvey and Wilson closer again and finally brought about their meeting. August 1914, was for Wilson a private as well as a public tragedy for in the week of that "incredible European catastrophe" Ellen Wilson died after a lingering illness. Bryan, on becoming Wilson's secretary of state, had been pushing his treaties for the Advancement of General Peace, and thirty such had been prepared, with additional nations signifying that they were receptive to the idea. Now, with the war, that embryonic League of Nations plan to bring about "the parliament of man, the federation of the world," lay in ruins.

In spite of his personal grief, Wilson the public leader carried on, asking Americans to be neutral in thought as well as in deed. Harvey in his September *Review* called on the country to "Uphold the President," and pleaded for another Democratic majority in the November congressional election since the president's hands "should be strengthened by a vote of confidence, not weakened by seeming division. Now, more than ever before, or perhaps ever again, it behooves our country to stand behind its leader united before the world."

Following the editorial, Harvey on a visit to Washington received a telephone call from Presidential Secretary Tumulty to say that "President Wilson would be greatly pleased and obliged if the Colonel could make it convenient to call at the White

* Ibid.

House that afternoon." Harvey excused himself with a fictitious previous engagement. Then on the following Sunday, October 4 — celebrated all over the land as "Peace Sunday" — Harvey, while again in Washington, received another call from Tumulty who this time came in person to escort him to the White House. That evening Wilson's secretaries informed newsmen officially that:

> Colonel Harvey on the invitation of the President, spent an hour with him at the White House this afternoon, discussing the general situation.*

Afterward Harvey told his friends that there had been nothing personal in their talk, that they had chiefly discussed Europe. But as Harvey left he laid his hand on Wilson's shoulder and said with his ingrained solemnity: "Mr. President, Washington will always be known as the Father of his Country. But this war, which involves directly or indirectly all the world, will afford you, sir, opportunity to achieve a still higher position, a greater fame. For you, sir, may become the Father of the Peace of the World!" Following this meeting Harvey worked actively in the campaign to elect a Democratic majority, Tumulty writing to thank him for his efforts. On Wilson's birthday on December 28, Harvey wrote him a note of congratulation and good wishes. Tumulty replied: "The President warmly appreciates your message of birthday greeting, and he asks me to thank you cordially for your generous words."

Harvey continued to write articles in the *Review* on all the aspects of the war, urging support of Wilson, yet at the same time demanding preparedness for what he considered the inevitable entry of the United States. As the war progressed, Harvey moved ever closer to the Eastern pro-Allied war group whose spokesman was Theodore Roosevelt, while Wilson still followed the populist-isolationist-pacifist tradition of the West. After the *Lusitania* had been sunk in May 1915, Harvey still expressed his confidence that "a more dependable President than Mr. Wilson could not be desired," but when Wilson limited his protests to writing notes, Harvey's misgivings grew. "We hope to continue to support the President," he wrote in August, 1915, "but what we wish to make certain of is that he recognizes the need of a change of method. Words having borne no fruit in the case of the Germans, recourse

* Ibid.

must be had to acts." At the same time Harvey grew increasingly impatient with what he considered Wilson's indecisiveness in dealing with the revolutionary situation in Mexico. "It is the bitter truth," he concluded "that our Administration has come to be regarded as anaemic rather than American."

Although by 1916 Wilson had made some concessions to the preparedness advocates, such concessions seemed to Harvey inadequate, and he was outraged when the president replaced his energetic secretary of war, Lindley Garrison, with the pacifist Progressive Newton Baker. In that presidential election year it was obvious that Wilson would be renominated, probable that he would be reelected. But by September Harvey still had not made up his mind whether to support Wilson, whose campaign slogan was "He kept us out of war!" or the more warlike stance of the Republican candidate Charles Evans Hughes. Finally, while still proclaiming himself a Democrat, he came out for Hughes, repudiating the Wilson administration for its "criminal blundering with respect to Mexico, and its fatuous timidity in dealing with belligerent powers."

After Wilson's reelection, however, Harvey again pledged his fullest support to the president. The euphoria of the election was brief, for by mid-February Harvey was calling for immediate war against the "infamous autocracy" that was Germany and its "dastardly rulers." When the German government announced the resumption of unrestricted submarine warfare, the psychological climate of America made war inevitable. Wilson recognized this, first with reluctance, then with the enthusiasm of his inborn self-righteousness. His War Message of April 2 with its resounding phrases, Harvey found a "great message of Patriotism . . . for the Nation . . . glorious, for patriots inspiring, for the President noble."

In the autumn of 1917 Harvey started a weekly journal of opinion, the *War Weekly,* which he saw as a means of urging on and encouraging the President. His faith, though wavering, still persisted, and he maintained that Wilson would be all right "if only he can be made to feel that the Nation is behind him in pushing things vigorously to a 'fight to the finish.' " But as the war expanded, as Baker's ineptitudes in the War Department grew increasingly apparent, Harvey turned from his role of sympathetic critic urging the country to "Stand by the President" to the gadfly of the Administration for whom Secretary Baker had become "Newtie Cootie . . . a chattering ex-Pacifist . . . seated on top of a pyramid of confusion which he has jumbled together and called a war machine." So caustically did Harvey now treat Baker and Attorney General A. Mitchell Palmer, that Palmer at one point was prepared to have him arrested under the newly enacted anti-sedition legislation.

Harvey's growing estrangement with the Wilson Administration brought him into close and friendly contact with Theodore Roosevelt, now the mouthpiece of the anti-Wilson forces and Wilson's most embittered critic. The final parting of the ways came after the Armistice when Wilson left for Europe to head the American delegation to the Peace Conference. For this and for Wilson's determination to bring the United States into his cherished League of Nations, Harvey never forgave him. And what had been political grew personal. The two former friends came to hate each other.

Following the Armistice, Harvey changed the name of his *War Weekly* to *Harvey's Weekly*. In it, week after week, he led the attack against the League. In articles and cartoons, in prose, verse and pictures, in petitions, in venomous paragraphs, with mordant wit and sometimes with less than wit, *Harvey's Weekly* denounced Wilson's internationalism. To the advocates of the League, *Harvey's Weekly* proposed an *International Hymn*:

Our foreign countries
The lands of Chimpanzees
Thy name we love, etc.

Most Americans, without understanding too much about it, had by the end of the war taken the League of Nations and their country's participation in it for granted. Even conservative Republicans like Taft, Elihu Root and Hughes were for it, as were such notable Americans as President Lawrence Lowell and ex-President Charles W. Eliot of Harvard. Those who, like Harvey and Senators Henry Cabot Lodge and William Borah, opposed the League's "entangling alliances" and stood out for "nationality" against "internationalism" were at first in a determined minority. Yet a groundswell of reaction against what Harvey termed "Wilsonism" was in evidence even before the Armistice. In the November 1918 midterm election the Republicans, in spite of Wilson's personal appeal, won majorities in both houses of Congress. Nevertheless, when Harvey met with a congressional group opposing the League at the home of Connecticut's Senator Frank Brandegee in May, 1919, with Wilson still in Europe, the outlook of the oppositionists seemed "lamentably gloomy." Senator Philander Knox, one of those present, suggested that "as a last resort" an appeal for funds should be made to Henry Frick of the United States Steel Corporation and Andrew Mellon, reputedly next to John D. Rockefeller the world's richest man. Harvey was sent to "pull the leg" of both financiers. He reported back that "the desired reservoir has been found and that it was rich and deep." Later he admitted that each man had contributed five million dollars.

In June, 1919, Wilson returned to the United States from Paris with the Versailles Treaty and the Covenant of the League of Nations to present them to the Senate for ratification. But it was soon clear that without amendments or reservations to guard American rights and sovereignty, as understood by the more recalcitrant senators, the covenant — inextricably intertwined with the peace treaty — would never receive the necessary two-thirds vote in the Senate. Wilson stubbornly refused to change so much as a comma in the covenant, and when he found he could not persuade the senators individually to his point of view, he determined to "appeal to the country." On September 3 he started out on his doomed transcontinental railroad tour in his blue car *Mayflower* to defend the League in twenty-six major cities and daily at a dozen or so whistle stops. Following him with houndlike doggedness were three anti-league senators — Borah, Hiram Johnson, and the English-hating James Reed. In the sweltering somnolent weather Wilson drove himself beyond his limits until he was overwhelmed by insomnia, blinding headaches that sometimes made him see double, moments of hysterical tears. Halfway through his tour his exhausted body gave out and he woke to find his left side paralyzed by a stroke. He would never again function actively as a president. For another year and a half he would remain in the White House, a remote invalid, inaccessible even to his associates, while his dream-child, the League of Nations, was rejected by the Senate, and his countrymen in the postwar reaction turned with growing bitterness against him. In his remoteness he continued to hope and expect that the presidential election of 1920 might vindicate him and the League of Nations in the person of the Democratic candidate, James Cox.

As the election neared, *Harvey's Weekly* came out for the Republican candidate, Senator Warren Harding, the affable mediocrity from Ohio, while continuing its biting attacks on the man Harvey had made president. When the slow-witted Harding showed signs of wobbling on the League issue, Harvey was dispatched to his home in Ohio to keep him on the straight and isolate path. Harvey also wrote a number of Harding's campaign speeches and even — after Harding's inevitable election — composed the substance of the president-elect's inaugural address, leaving Harding to provide his own characteristic fustian and alliterative trimmings.*

Wilson and Harvey were now enemies, searing in their hatred for each other. For Harvey it was like the old fairy tale of the fisherman and his wife. His wish had come true, that wish of so long ago, and in its coming true it had destroyed itself. While the pitiable wreck of a president huddled in his wheelchair in the White House, a mute spectator of the campaign that would torpedo the last of his hopes, *Harvey's Weekly* with each issue gloated over the diminished days of the fallen leader: "Only 237 Days More"; "Only 230 Days More!" and so on, with "damnable iteration." Finally on February 26, 1921, the *Weekly* exulted for the last time: "Only SIX Days More! And we can put it even more cheeringly than that: Only 144 hours more!"

* As a reward for his support President Harding appointed Harvey ambassador to England, a post that eight years earlier he had hoped to receive from Wilson.

**"N-nothin' to it, I tell you!"**

*The scandals that occurred while Daugherty was Attorney General were as nothing compared to the scandals that gathered around his name afterward.*

CHAPTER FIVE

# The Back-Room Boss: Harry Micajah Daugherty

A MAN'S DESTINY is determined by many a petty event, even the looseness of his bowels. For if it had not been for such eliminatory urgency, Warren Gamaliel Harding would not have become President of the United States. But for his impromptu encounter with Harry Daugherty outside a privy in October 1899, Harding might have passed his remaining quarter century as a convivial small-town booster, editor of a local paper and ephemeral state politician.

Both men were attending a Union County Republican rally at the crossroads village of Richmond, Ohio. Harding, recently nominated as the Republican candidate for state senator from the 13th District, was unknown to Daugherty. Harding knew Daugherty well enough, for Daugherty, the former chairman of the Republican State Committee, was a power in Ohio, a back-room boss, the man who had nominated McKinley for governor six years before. Richmond's night before had been a boisterous one, with the bar of the Globe, the town's single hotel, packed elbow-close and every room in the ramshackle wooden building occupied for the first time since that day in 1896 when presidential candidate McKinley had passed through and made a campaign speech. Like most small-town Ohio hotels of its day, the Globe lacked both plumbing and running water. Its sanitary accommodation was a two-hole privy on the far side of the back yard beyond the kitchen.

Early the following morning Harding had hurried across the fly-blown yard to the wooden sanctuary with the half-moon cut in the door. It was while he was occupied inside that Daugherty stepped outside with a morning-after thirst and headed for the rusty pump in the middle of the yard. After a few swings, he managed to fill the tin dipper chained there. As he was killing his thirst, Harding emerged.

Harding was then thirty-four years old, just under six feet tall, with massive, if slightly stooped, shoulders and a bronzed complexion that radiated, or seemed to radiate, health and vitality. A swatch of white hair swept across the forehead, and the rest of his head seemed dusted with powder. Virile, with a square regular face and firm jaw, he could have donned a toga and starred in an amateur production of *Julius Caesar*. "Why," a rustic supporter would exclaim later on seeing him at a banquet, "the son of a bitch *looks* like a senator." That first glance before the half-moon door impressed Daugherty as well. The other introduced himself with warm-voiced affability as Warren Harding, the editor of the Marion *Star*, and ceremoniously offered Daugherty a plug of tobacco. Daugherty, observing the etiquette of rural Ohio, bit off a chaw and handed the plug back. Harding then took a bite himself. They chatted a few minutes by the pump in the morning sunlight. Then Harding ambled back to the dining room at a more relieved pace. Daugherty continued to meditate on the graceful, receding figure. "Gee," he mused — for Daugherty mused in the vernacular — "what a great-looking president that man would make!"

The bright morning gave way to an afternoon of rain. Restricted by the weather to the lobby or the bar, the politicians reminisced about past campaigns and traded smoking-room stories while waiting for the evening's rally. Daugherty made a point of talking with Harding, warmed to the younger man's genial presence, and finally to the surprise of the other politicians suggested that Harding make the first speech of the evening.

Until Harding appeared on the stage of Richmond's over-optimistically named Opera House, he had been an unimpressive speaker, awkward and stagestruck at best, a filler-in at Fourth-of-July orations. But faced with his first important audience, he found within himself the gift of political glossolaly. Those at the Richmond rally, impressed by the easy, handsome editor, found themselves carried away by the bland polysyllabics of his silver voice. And Harding, as he spoke, for the first time felt his own power. As Daugherty watched and listened, his conviction of the morning grew. A man like that could go a long way. It was a thought that he would store in the political filing cabinet of his mind, to remain dormant but never wholly forgotten for the next two decades. Before Daugherty could project himself into the career of someone else, he had first to burn out his own ambitions. Harry Micajah Daugherty was born and brought himself up in Washington Court House, thirty-five miles southwest of Columbus, a typical small Ohio county seat with its domed central courthouse and the row of loafers in front of it. Alert for every opportunity, legitimate or otherwise, he managed to put himself through high school and then work his way through the University of Michigan. Stronger than an ethical sense was his will to succeed, as he demonstrated while still a student when he and his brother Mally tapped the telegraph wires under a culvert a few miles from Washington Court House to pick up advance results of horse races in order to make sure-thing bets. After a few enterprising weeks they were caught, but before then they managed to make a handsome profit.

Unabashed by this contretemps, he came back to Washington Court House with his Michigan degree, and read law in a local lawyer's office. After passing his bar examination he had to wait until his twenty-first birthday before he could be admitted to the bar. At first most of his cases were criminal, and within four years he had built up the largest practice in Fayette County.

With success, his interest turned from criminals to corporations. Together with another young lawyer-lobbyist he set up the firm of Daugherty & Todd. "Handsome Harry," the courthouse hangers-on began to call him, more out of tribute to his dapper aggressiveness than to his physical self. He was stocky; his ears lay close to his square head; his bulldog neck supported a pugnacious jaw and a thin mouth that turned down ominously at the corners. He wore his hair parted in the middle; before he was thirty it was thinning. Most singular were his eyes, one of which was brown, the other blue. A cast in the brown eye, compounded by a tic, made him seem to look round rather than at anyone.

Always a cloud of rumor and suspicion would blur the Daugherty outline. Shortly after Harry's admission to the bar, he was brought before its grievance committee and charged with unethical conduct. He was rescued by Fayette County's Judge John Mayberry who stopped the proceedings, explaining that he wanted to protect the reputation of a young lawyer. In later years, when Daugherty was one of the back-room engineers controlling the Ohio legislative machine, Judge Mayberry's son, as clerk of the House of Representatives, would function to their mutual profit as the gravedigger for the bills Daugherty opposed.

In 1889 Daugherty was nominated and elected to the state legislature with the backing and financial support of Governor Foraker, the oratorical Fire Alarm Joe, who considered the new assemblyman his Fayette County outpost. Daugherty served two terms, the last time he would be elected to public office. In his second term he was enough of a presence, or at least pulled enough strings, to be made speaker of the House of Representatives.

Fire Alarm Joe caused a national sensation in 1892 by opposing the venerable John Sherman's reelection to the United States Senate. With senators still elected by vote of their state legislatures, Foraker took Daugherty's backing for granted. However, when the Fayette County Republican Convention endorsed Sherman, Daugherty stood up and pledged his support. Then, that same evening, he met Foraker's manager in Columbus and assured him of his unqualified allegiance. Shortly before the legislative vote, Sherman's manager drew a number of five-hundred-dollar bills from Columbus's Deshler Bank. A suspicious young teller secretly inked a small W on each bill before passing them over the counter. Foraker, for all the usual exactness of his political calculations, to his surprise found himself defeated. Even more surprisingly, he found his Fayette County outpost had voted against him. Following Sherman's reelection the marked bills began to surface in the state capital, proof to Fire Alarm Joe that the staid senior senator had bought off his opposition. The Columbus *Press-Post* accused Daugherty in its front page of switching his vote to Sherman for "seven crisp $500 bills." Daugherty, forced to defend himself on the floor of the house of representatives, told the assembly:

> I do not claim to be so honest that I cannot sleep at night—
> But I didn't get any of those crisp $500 bills.*

The assembly appointed a committee to probe the charges. After

* *The Shadow of Blooming Grove,* p. 112.

a week's investigation the members reported themselves "unable to find one iota of evidence that would lead us to believe that H. M. Daugherty either received, asked or was offered any consideration for his vote for John Sherman." Friendly legislators crowded round to congratulate Handsome Harry and for once he was so overcome that the tears ran down his cheeks. But outside the capital the inked bills were not so readily passed over.

After Daugherty had given up his seat in the assembly, he opened a second office in Columbus, becoming a much-sought-after corporation guide through the morass where business and politics meet. Although his right hand was always aware of what his left hand was doing, the two hands were able to act independently. Through his legislative connections he became a deft instigator of "milker bills," whose surface intent was to regulate or restrict the activities of various large corporations. Alarmed company executives would then engage Daugherty to kill the bills he had secretly spawned. The journalist Mark Sullivan, who knew Daugherty during most of his adult life, thought of him as a man of high talent and low tastes, a competent lawyer who might have been an outstanding one. Such a goal was not within Daugherty's temperament. Too restless by nature to pore over legal briefs or unearth precedents from musty tomes, he preferred the marketplace excitement of manipulation and intrigue to the leather-bound respectability of a law office. He knew law, but he knew men better, their foibles, their weaknesses, their strengths. And he knew when to flatter, when to bluster, when to offer friendship, when to compromise and when to retreat. Never did he meet a man, as he said himself, whom he considered unfathomable.

In 1893 he was made chairman of the Republican state convention that nominated McKinley for his second term as governor. Yet for all his lobbying success and his growing fortune, Daugherty retained an itch for political office. By instinct a man of the back rooms, he lacked the dignity of a McKinley, the good-fellow air of a Harding, Foraker's fiery boom-ta-ra, or Hanna's relentless resources. When he came out onto the open platform it was to face defeat. In 1895 he managed to get himself nominated for attorney general but lost the election. Four years later his attempt to challenge Hanna's personal candidate for governor, Judge George Nash, was flattened by the teamwork of

Hanna and Boss Cox. William Howard Taft, who liked Daugherty, thought he had a facility for creating enemies. Twice as a candidate for Congress he ended up an also-ran. Whereupon a Columbus wit remarked that the only election Harry could win would be to the Order of the Tin Can. Defeat embittered rather than discouraged him. An acquaintance, who knew him in his lobbyist heyday, wrote that he was "what we used to call a fringe politician. He was the fly on the rim of the wheel. You'd always find him outside, looking in. When a good office was to be filled, Harry would always be among those mentioned — he'd see to that — and that let him out. He kept himself surrounded by we-men but they couldn't deliver the vote."

On Harding's election to the state senate several weeks after his casual encounter in front of the privy, Daugherty wrote to congratulate him, saying that he would consider it a compliment if the new senator would call on him during the session. Harding paid the compliment and Daugherty returned it. The new senator with his permanent smile and his back-slapping camaraderie soon became one of the most popular legislators in Columbus. Yet though Daugherty sometimes attended the convivial poker evenings that Harding liked to hold in his hotel room, there was no particular intimacy between them. Daugherty, lobbying with molelike persistency, had little time for such amenities. Life for him was real and earnest, and the grave of bills inimical to his clients was indeed his goal. Even Harding's election as lieutenant governor in 1905 did not bring them closer. The seed planted that morning in Richmond still remained dormant.

In 1904 Hanna died, and in accordance with his dying wish — still potent beyond the grave — the legislators, encouraged by Boss Cox, elected his old lieutenant, Congressman Charles Dick, to succeed him. In 1907 Congressman Burton, long opposed to the Cox machine and disgusted by a new series of Cox scandals, set out to organize a Republican reform group that would oust Cox's lieutenants from the September convention and remove Dick from his chairmanship of the State Executive Committee. Burton found practical if incongruous support in Harry Daugherty, who now stepped forward in the role of the foe of the bosses and the people's friend. Harding, the regular of regulars, led the Marion delegation to the convention and was elected to the committee on resolutions. He took a poor view of Burton's efforts to rock the Republican boat, and an equally poor view of Daugherty as a reformer. "The amiable and talented Mr. Daugherty shuddering about bossism is a spectacle to amuse all of Ohio," he editorialized in the *Star*. "We like Daugherty, but he held a high seat in the bossing procession, when there was Hanna absolutism in this state, and never said a word." The convention endorsed Dick "without reservation" and left Daugherty out on his usual limb. The following year he was back in the fold in time for the presidential nomination, joining with Cox in support of Taft against the opposition of the diminished and fading Senator Foraker.

The year 1910, when the differences between Taft and Roosevelt were beginning to fragment the Republican party, found Daugherty with quixotic persistence hoping and plotting (the two were simultaneous with him) to take Dick's place in the United States Senate. In 1910 a Republican assembly itself seemed doubtful. Nevertheless, when the state convention met in Columbus, Daugherty was there, moving paunchily in the shadows, buttonholing delegates to support him for the senate seat that the assembly would be filling in January. But the chief business of the convention was to pick a candidate for governor, and Harding was coyly available. With Foraker and the regulars backing him and Boss Cox belatedly throwing him his support, he was nominated on the third ballot.

The Republican nomination that year was a Greek gift. Faced with the popular Democratic governor Judson Harmon and with the growing fissures in his own party, Harding did not have a chance, although in the euphoria induced by his nomination, the glory of being Marion's first citizen, he failed to grasp the inevitable. The landslide for Harmon was so devastating that Harding momentarily lost faith in the democratic process itself, writing to the *Star's* sub-editor that he was through politically, since such things were bound to happen as long as every Tom, Dick and Harry had the right to vote.

It was the rancorous year 1912 that finally brought Harding and Daugherty together in mutual allegiance to Taft. As the president's fortunes declined, Harding had grown more intimate with him. Harding's *Star* increased its devotion. "Ohio for Taft?" he asked rhetorically after Roosevelt had announced his hat was in the ring. "Nothing surer in political life." It did not seem so sure when Roosevelt captured thirty-four of the forty-two Ohio delegates to the Republican National Convention. The six Ohio delegates-at-large, however, having been selected by a carefully rigged state convention, remained Taft-true. Among these six were Daugherty and Harding. Taft at length asked Harding to present his name in nomination at the national convention. "I think I was more honored by that request than by my own nomination," Harding wrote a decade later when he himself was president. In that controlled convention, Harding faithfully performed his burning-deck role even though his feet became well-blistered in the process.

At the Ohio Republican state convention held the following month, the machine-picked Taft majority tried in vain to persuade the Progressives to compromise. Harding in his mellow voice pleaded for Taft and harmony, only to find himself howled down again by Roosevelt supporters. They even hooted him when, assuming an aggrieved manner, he told them that he "wouldn't want to belong to any party that wouldn't endorse its standard-bearer." Some of the Taft-true considered again giving Harding the nomination for governor, but the experience of two years ago had cleared his senses. He could see and smell defeat in November.

Already the "traitorous" Walter Brown had resigned as chairman of the inner-circle Republican State Central Committee, taking ten of the twenty-one committeemen over with him to the Progressives. The chairman of the State Executive Committee and its more important members followed. No politician could be found to stick his head in the noose of the executive committee, for that was what the chairmanship had come to seem. The Republican Party of Ohio resembled a collapsed building, the pieces visible, the structure gone. But what was disaster to the party was for Daugherty his great opportunity. "For the benefit of the party" he was willing to assume the "most uninviting and herculean task" of directing the executive committee — whose members still included Harding and Charlie Taft. At the same time he became chairman of the skeletal central committee. Seventy of the eighty-eight county organizations had gone over to the Progressives and others were preparing to follow. Daugherty proceeded to raise a campaign fund, to drive out "the traitors," to determine "who were for the flag and who had it under their feet." Some of the Progressive "deserters" were planning to run on both the Progressive and Republican tickets. Daugherty obtained a ruling from the sympathetic state supreme court that no candidate could appear under two party designations. During those months of battle he was relentless in ousting the Bull Moosers from the county committees. He and Harding were much together, though with an odd diffidence Daugherty did not yet call him by his first name.

Daugherty saw as his goal, not the election of Taft — which he knew was impossible — but the defeat of Roosevelt. In this he was more successful within Ohio than Taft was nationally. Wilson of course carried the state. Nor was it surprising that Ohio elected a Democratic governor and eighteen of the state's twenty-one congressmen. But Daugherty had whipped the state organization into line so relentlessly, had employed the manna of Washington patronage with such astuteness, that Taft managed to defeat Roosevelt by 277,000 votes to 229,000 in Ohio. "Well, the mad Roosevelt has a new achievement to his credit," Harding wrote in a post-election edition of the *Star*. "He succeeded in defeating the party that furnished him a job for nearly all of his manhood days after leaving the ranch, and showed his gratitude of the presidency, at the party's hands. The eminent fakir can now turn to raising hell, his specialty, along other lines."

A few weeks after the November debacle Daugherty wrote Harding, for the first time calling him by his first name:

> One great thing resulting from this war we have had and that is that we are better friends than ever and understand each other thoroughly and will hang together through thick and thin.*

To Harding, back in Marion, his political career seemed at end, and he resigned himself without too much resignation to spend the rest of his days as a small-town editor-publisher.

The 1912 election was the culmination of the Progressive movement. Those who had politics in their blood, like Daugherty, were the first to sense the turn of the tide. For by 1913, to the dismay, and bewilderment of the reformists, the mood of the electorate had begun to change. In the municipal elections of that year, the regulars rallied to defeat Brand Whitlock's Toledo independents, the voters of Columbus repudiated their reform administration, while, most spectacularly of all, Boss Cox's machine returned to power in Cleveland. Progressives still thought of themselves as the wave of the future, but the more pragmatic, like Mark Hanna's son Dan, began sounding out the

* *The Shadow of Blooming Grove*, p. 241.

Daugherty-backed regulars for a merger that would again present a united front against the Democrats.

Any such reconciliation brought up the problem of the aloofly conservative Senator Burton, whose term would expire in 1914. Nineteen-fourteen was the first year in which the seventeenth amendment took effect, providing for the direct election of United States senators. It was not a prospect that pleased Burton, who had become increasingly at odds with his own party both in Washington and in Ohio. The thought of a strenuous nomination campaign followed by an even more strenuous election was too much for him. He suffered from black periods of depression. In one of these he decided to withdraw from public life altogether.

Foraker saw Burton's withdrawal as clearing the way for his own belated vindication. Dan Hanna, now back in Republican good graces, saw Foraker as a "peril to his party," a Standard Oil-spattered conservative to replace an honest one, a Roosevelt-hater whom the returning Progressives would never accept and who could never be elected. Hanna begged Burton to change his mind. Once more visions of political sugar plums began to dance in Daugherty's head. He would be the compromise candidate, the healer! He was, he let it be known, receiving so many letters and telegrams urging him to run for the Senate that he might find himself forced to accede. It took a rapier thrust from Dan Hanna to puncture Daugherty's self-inflated balloon and bring him back to earth.

To play both ends against the middle was Harding's nature, and it had become his second nature. By his genial manner and unanchored oratory he managed to be friendly with those who were among themselves mortal enemies. To many in 1914 he seemed the ideal compromise candidate to knit up the raveled sleeve of Ohio politics. Harding, however, had been badly burned four years earlier as candidate for governor, had had the humiliation of a victory parade in Marion the night before the election and an overwhelming defeat next day. This time he would agree to run only if he had the support of Dan Hanna and most of the erstwhile Progressives. "I am not seeking any nomination," he wrote with his customary coyness. "I have, however, never declined to honor any draft made upon me by my party and would not do so now." Hanna pledged his support. In after years Daugherty liked to imagine that he had been responsible for urging the reluctant Harding into the senate race and a career that through its set of curious chances would carry him to the White House six years later. "I found him like a turtle sunning himself on a log," he told Mark Sullivan, "and I pushed him into the water." Most of the actual pushing was done by Dan Hanna.

A third candidate for the nomination now appeared, a non-entity congressman by the name of Ralph Cole. But the only real contest was between Harding and Foraker. Harding refused to attack his old friend and mentor, and Fire Alarm Joe, with the blind optimism common to politicians, felt so sure of regaining his old seat that he scarcely bothered to campaign. He had behind him the renovated Cox machine, the votes of the Grand Army of the Republic, the prestige of two former terms in the Senate. Ominously, though, he had to face the hostility of the Anti-Saloon League and the hardshell Baptists because of his opposition to a national prohibition amendment.

"The Senatorial campaign has been quiet, but that is natural and proper," Harding wrote with relief. "The Senatorship is not to be decided by sensationalism." As he had all his life, he suffered from profound periods of self-doubt. Could he possibly be nominated, he kept asking himself? Was he worth nominating? When such moods overwhelmed him, the brash Daugherty could always be counted on to shake him free of them. Meeting a bedraggled and discouraged Harding one rainy afternoon in Columbus, Daugherty listened while the other explained almost tearfully why he could not win over the great Foraker. Daugherty gave him a hearty slap on the back, bet him two suits of clothes that he could beat Fire Alarm Joe hands-down, and told him to name the tailor.

Daugherty proved to be right. Harding won out by 12,000 over Foraker, with Cole trailing unmentionably in the rear. Whichever party might win in November, the election promised to be a close one. The Republican nominee for governor was Congressman Frank Willis, known as the "highball" candidate for his deft straddling of the liquor question — part booze, part water. Harding's Democratic opponent, State Attorney General Timothy Hogan, had in two terms in office made a unique and brilliant record in prosecuting grafting Ohio politicians. Even in the Bible-belt regions, his inherited Catholicism had seemed a dead issue. Unfortunately for his prospects, it would become a very live one in the coming campaign.

Harding regarded Hogan as a friend, an old picnic companion, and never during the campaign did he attack him or his religion. On the other hand, to those who did assail Hogan's Catholicism, he gave his silent apostolic blessing. All was fair, after all, in love and politics — and he had long proved both those points. Scurrilous propaganda sheets like *The Menace, The Defender* and *The Accuser* appeared like mushrooms all over Ohio, supported from unknown sources and warning that the Pope was about to take over the Buckeye State through his Knights of Columbus and his faithful attorney general. Signs on fences, walls and billboards, even freight cars, proclaimed:

> Read *The Menace* and get the dope.
> Go to the polls and beat the Pope.

Harding's friend, the Marion lawyer Hoke Donithen, managed his campaign. After the nomination Daugherty participated only casually. During most of *The Menace* agitation he stayed in his Columbus office, occasionally talking with other members of the executive committee and sending an encouraging note to Marion, but doing little else. He made no speeches, and just before the election went on a week's vacation.

To those outside Ohio, Harding's smashing victory in November was an astonishing demonstration of innate political strength. Hog-caller Willis managed to defeat Democratic Governor Cox by only 29,270 votes in a total of 1,129,233, while Harding had a margin of more than a hundred thousand over Hogan. Examined more closely, the figures showed that some 70,000 Democrats who voted for Cox refused to mark a cross after the papist attorney general's name. Outside Ohio, where the figures were not examined closely, the legend remained of Harding the powerful vote-getter, in the state that was the "Mother of Presidents."

If Harding had retired after his first senate term, or even had he managed to get himself elected to a second term, he would scarcely have been remembered a decade later beyond the limits of Marion. In the seven sessions that he served in the Senate he championed no measures of even temporary significance; his name was never connected with any important or semi-important legislation. In all he introduced 134 bills, most of them about local Ohio matters such as changing the name of a lake steamer or securing a Civil War veteran's back pension. His few public bills concerned themselves with such significances as amending the McKinley Memorial Birthplace Association Act, providing for an investigation of influenza and other diseases, and celebrating the three hundredth anniversary of the landing of the Pilgrims. (The persistently annoying issues of women's suffrage and prohibition he managed to straddle.) Almost half the time his seat was empty, and he usually avoided being present wherever any vote was taken that might antagonize a minority group. Mentally anchored in the Ohio landscape, he found the European war at first too remote to concern either him or his country. After the sinking of the *Lusitania,* however, he demanded immunity from submarine attack for all American vessels, even ammunition ships. Yet he was careful not to take too positive a stand about anything concerned with the war for fear of alienating the potent Ohio German-American minority.

Harding was appointed to the Committee on the Philippines, and his first speech in the Senate — not delivered until January, 1916 — was a hundred-per-cent-American "white man's burden" oration demanding retention of the Philippines by the United States. He was a Chautauqua speaker and became well-known for "preaching Americanism" — whatever that might mean. In the days before amplifiers he had a mellow, carrying voice, an engaging presence, an ability to mouth sonorous banalities that signified little and passed for patriotic fervor. Chambers of commerce and such organizations liked to listen to him, and he liked to tell them what they liked to hear.

He soon came to enjoy the clublike atmosphere of the Senate and the convivial life of Washington. And he was popular — a good sport, a good fellow, friendly, kind to animals, with not enough convictions to disturb anyone else's. He entertained well on pleasant poker evenings at his new house on Wyoming Avenue. His cellar was well-stocked. Though he was not rich, the twenty thousand effortless dollars that his *Star* brought him in each year plus his $5,000 salary enabled him to live well. Young Assistant Secretary of the Navy Franklin Delano Roosevelt enjoyed his golfing company; Nicholas Longworth came to Wyoming Avenue on poker evenings, sometimes with his wife Alice Roosevelt Longworth, who was not averse to taking an occasional hand, though she remained resolutely averse to extending the hand of friendship to the Hardings in her own home.

Harding the Chautauqua Speaker, the flag-waver, the preacher of Americanism, was at least making himself known. A month before the Republican national convention of 1916, the New

York *Times* named four favorite sons of Ohio as potential candidates — Burton, Herrick, Willis and Harding — in case that chill leading figure from New York, Governor Charles Evans Hughes, should fail in his bid. From Oyster Bay, Roosevelt had announced that he would not be a compromise candidate, and the Old Guard Republicans determined to see to it that he could not change his mind.

It was a senatorial election year in Ohio as well as a presidential year in the rest of the country. Among other hopefuls edging forward to confront the Democratic incumbent, Senator Atlee Pomerene, Daugherty, the aging political bridesmaid, emerged from the backs to claim the candidacy as a reward for his burning-deck stance in 1912. Newton Fairbanks, chairman of the state central committee, agreed that after such "herculean" efforts, Daugherty should be nominated unopposed for his "more than thirty years of hard, unselfish, loyal, and unrewarded service in the ranks of the party." Between Daugherty and the other aspirants, Harding himself preferred to remain neutral. "I think Daugherty is somewhat annoyed because I have not come out in an interview or an editorial in favor of his candidacy," he wrote his friend Malcolm Jennings that summer. "He has had my sympathy all along, but I have not felt at any time that I could take an open and conspicuous part in his behalf."

To defeat Wilson in that war year would first of all require a return of the prodigal Progressives to the regular Republican fold. As an apparent gesture of cooperation the Progressives were holding their convention in Chicago at the same time as the Republicans, and for all their self-assertiveness, it was hoped they would accept the Republican nominee as their own. In the search for a soothing-syrup temporary chairman, the Republican choice fell on Harding, the easy speaker, the harmonizer, the orator who with his mellow voice and glittering generalities would offend no one. He was duly elected, and on the strength of his ambivalent oratory made keynote speaker as well.

As chairman, the debonair and genial senator from Ohio managed adroitly. But as keynote speaker he found himself suddenly out of his depth in an apathetic sea of delegates most of whom would in their heart of hearts have preferred Teddy Roosevelt to any man living. Harding spoke for almost two hours to his unresponsive audience. His words were leaden. Alliteration's art failed to aid him. "A convention of oysters probably would compare to advantage with the animated churchyard that listened to Harding's key-note speech," wrote the correspondent of the New York *Times*. The minutes dragged by. Harding's collar wilted, as did the McKinley geranium he wore in his buttonhole. "There had been talk," the *Times* correspondent continued, "of Harding setting the convention aflame with his oratory, so that lightning would strike him when the moment came, if it should ever, to name a dark horse. But nobody could stampede this convention and Harding could not stampede any convention."

There was no dark horse. Hughes was nominated on the third ballot. The Progressives went on to nominate Roosevelt by acclamation, the colonel telegraphed his refusal, and the frustrated and furious delegates knew that the Progressive party was dead. Most of them, whatever their private thoughts, would end up by supporting Hughes.

Harding's humiliation outlasted the convention. On being chosen chairman he had seen himself moving into statesman's row, into the ranks of those national leaders he had so long admired — Foraker in his prime; Hanna; McKinley. But after his keynote speech, received so coldly and so derided in the press, he had been reduced to the ranker's level of a small-town senator. "Since the rousting [sic] I received at Chicago," he wrote Jennings, "I no longer harbor any too great self confidence in the matter of speech making." To his mistress he had written earlier that he was finally awakened to his utter incapacity and incompetence.

Yet the Chicago fiasco had a less durable effect on outsiders than on himself. In the aftermath of Wilson's victory in November, the Ohio Republicans were swept out of office. Harding alone remained, with four more years to serve in the Senate. Still playing his role of harmonizer, he had written to Roosevelt before the election expressing his "very great satisfaction" at the colonel's declining the third-party nomination and at his pledge to support Hughes. It was the beginning of a curious rapport between Harding and the man whom he had referred to four years earlier in the *Star* as "Theodore Rex . . . the buncombe man."

Harding, for all his impressive figure, continued to remain conspicuously silent in the Senate. "I do relatively little talking in Congress," he admitted. In all the wartime sessions, nothing he ever did or said had the effect on legislation of a comma or a semi-colon. (After the war declaration of April, 1917, he did introduce an amendment to the draft bill that would have allowed Colonel Roosevelt to resume his Rough Rider role and raise three volunteer divisions. But Wilson had the amendment stricken out.)

In the outburst of chauvinistic frenzy following Wilson's war declaration, Harding's voice remained surprisingly muted. He was all for America, all for the Allies, but he was too prudent to forget his German-American constituents back in Ohio. At one time he announced that he favored a dictator to coordinate the war effort, but changed his mind at the sobering thought that such a dictator would be a Democrat. As the war neared its climax in 1918, his overimaginative friend Frank Scobey, the former Ohioan turned Texas land speculator, wrote urging him to make a bid for the presidency in 1920.

"It is very comforting and satisfying," Harding replied, "to have a good many people think well of one for the big office but none of this has any strong appeal for me. I am inclined to think I should like to stay in the Senate but I am not letting the matter worry me to a sufficient degree to keep me awake nights."

The growing war-weariness of the country showed itself in the 1918 midterm elections. If only by a small margin, the Republicans managed to take control of both houses of Congress, but the shadow of 1920 already was creeping over the Capitol. In Ohio Republicans again gained control of the state, except for the governorship, where Hog-caller Willis, the professed prohibitionist, was knifed by the wet Boss Cox machine. Ohio politicians began to count on their fingers. Every Republican president elected since the Civil War had been born in Ohio or had at least come from Ohio.* If Hughes had managed to carry Ohio in 1916, he would have been elected. Ohio was a key state with a strong Democratic counterbalance. An Ohio candidate would be a logical choice to swing the balance, and Harding was the one Ohio Republican still intact in high office.

Such small-talk logic scarcely carried beyond the state's boundaries. Outside Ohio the one Republican choice, the only choice, was Theodore Roosevelt. Twelve years older than when he left the White House, in 1920 the Rough Rider would still be only sixty-two. "I don't like him. I once despised him," the gross and formidable boss of Pennsylvania, Senator Boies Penrose, told a

* If one assumes that Roosevelt inherited his first term, and was reelected to the second.

group of Republican leaders assembled in Washington. "But that doesn't alter the fact that Theodore Roosevelt is now the one and only possible Republican candidate in 1920. He will surely receive the nomination." Roosevelt realized this as fully as did Penrose. Grateful to Harding for sponsoring the "Roosevelt" amendments to the draft act, touched by Harding's letter of condolence after his aviator son Quentin was shot down overseas, he even considered taking Harding on as his running mate. It would have been an innocuous gesture of conciliation to the regulars over a sinecure office that Roosevelt himself scorned and that seemed made for Harding.

Indeed Harding would have been supremely happy as a vice-president fainéant presiding over the Senate. Daugherty would have been equally happy at the promotion, for it would have left vacant a senate seat in the year that might at last be *his* year. Eight years ago he had singed his feet on that deck whence all but he had fled, and he had failed as yet to get his political reward. His relations with Harding were at this point somewhat strained, for he was engaged in a vituperative struggle with the erstwhile Progressive, Walter Brown, who, having returned to the Grand Old Party, was now with the help of Boss Cox's successor Rud Hynicka and the wets attempting to seize control of the party from the politically dry Daugherty and his regulars. For Harding, who had been attempting without much success to reconcile and unite the two hostile groups through his amorphous Ohio Republican Central Advisory Committee, Daugherty's feud against Hynicka was distressingly like a replay of 1912. "We cannot have a successful Republican party in Ohio," he wrote to Daugherty, "if we map our course with a view to taking reprisals and everlastingly baring to public view the grievancies [sic] of campaigns which have passed. . . . You know my attitude as well as anybody in Ohio. I am always seeking to harmonize and think a great deal more of party victory than I do of the promotion of any personal ambitions."

Stung by this reproach, Daugherty defended the purity of his actions, replying to Harding's "unfortunate" letter that "I thought you knew me well enough to know that I never play any cards under the table in politics or anywhere else." Harding's answer to this was so cool that he reverted to their earlier last name basis:

> The trouble with you, my dear Daugherty, in your political relations with me, is that you appraise my political sense so far below par that you have no confidence in me or my judgment. Pray do not think because I can and do listen in politeness to much that is said to me that I am always being "strung."*

And to a mutual political friend, he wrote:

> I will make no arrangement of any kind in the future with Daugherty. I felt myself under very great obligation to him and have highly valued his political friendship. He is a brilliant and resourceful man, but his political hatreds have come to a point where they bias his judgment and I do not always think him a trustworthy adviser.†

If Theodore Roosevelt had lived, he would have been nominated and elected in 1920, and the history of the United States would have been very different. But on the night of January 6, 1919, he died in his sleep. Harding was among those members of Congress appointed to attend the funeral. Daugherty, with his ferret nose for politics, had already wired him insisting he attend. All personal differences seemed to dissolve before this vast alteration in the climate of the American political scene. The president-to-be had gone and there was no direct Republican succession.

The closest to a successor was Major General Leonard Wood, Roosevelt's old friend and Rough Rider comrade-in-arms. Several months before his death, Roosevelt had told his 1912 floor manager, Henry Allen, that if he was unable to run for president in 1920, he hoped the convention would choose Wood. After the Rough Rider's death, his sister Corinne asked the general to take over the leadership of the Roosevelt forces.

Wood had had an astonishing military career. On graduating from Harvard Medical School he had gone to the Arizona Territory as a civilian contract doctor in the Army Medical Corps. Twenty-four years later he had become the army's chief of staff. As first military governor of Cuba, he had ruled that island with a compassionate efficiency that had won over the initially distrustful natives. Later he was equally successful as governor of the Philippines' Moro Province, a position he held until he was appointed commanding general of the Philippines Division. After the outbreak of the war in 1914, he had visited colleges across the

* *The Shadow of Blooming Grove,* pp. 309–10.
† Ibid.

country preaching preparedness to undergraduates, and in 1915 over Wilson's objections had organized the first Business Men's Training Camp at Plattsburg. He and Colonel Roosevelt became the country's foremost advocates of preparedness, and Wilson regarded them both with disapproval and personal dislike. Although Wood was the army's senior general, Wilson after making his war declaration refused to allow him to take any command in Europe, and reduced him to training a division of recruits at Camp Funston. Even then, the President would not permit Wood to go overseas with his division, the 69th, when its training was completed. To most of the country Wood seemed an upright soldier, a victim of personal spite.

More avuncular than stern, Wood had a commanding presence, an easier air of authority than a martinet like Black Jack Pershing. Although no politician, and with a distaste for those who were, he had not been above playing politics in the past. A Republican, his party ties were of the loosest, and neither the party bosses nor the dogmatic liberals fancied him. To Republicans at large he was enormously popular, and they would have rejoiced in his nomination. One of the earliest Wood supporters was the Ohio Republican party treasurer, Colonel William Cooper Procter, who stood ready to float the general with his Ivory Soap millions. Procter would eventually take over the management of Wood's campaign.

Harding's ambition was a limited one. He hoped to serve another term in the Senate. Then, in 1926, at the age of sixty, he planned to return to Ohio as the leading citizen of Marion, the little town that had once looked askance at him and at his heredity. He would reconstitute certain ancestral acres in nearby Blooming Grove, he would "bloviate" — that old Ohio term for not doing very much and enjoying it — spend half a not-too-strenuous day at his *Star*, spend convivial evenings at poker and elsewhere. With luck he would no longer be impeded by his ailing and domineering wife. The responsibility that a president must bear was for him an abhorrent thought. He sensed himself unequal in intellect, in education, in force of will, to occupy the White House.

Shortly after Roosevelt's death, he revived his dormant state advisory committee. Roosevelt's death had robbed the erstwhile Ohio Progressives of their leader, and Harding was able to absorb Walter Brown into his committee as well as to come to terms with Bob Wolfe and Dan Hanna, who had flaunted the Progressive banner in their respective newspapers. Daugherty was also on the committee. He and Harding had settled their differences months ago. "Daugherty has been a typical scrapper for what he thinks the right course," Harding wrote in November, 1919. "I have always felt I could depend on Daugherty, though he did give me a little annoyance during the trying period we passed through last winter." The presidency brought no gleam to Harding's eye. But in the back of Daugherty's mind the seed was sprouting that had been implanted so long ago at that casual Richmond encounter. Giving up the lurking will-o'-the-wisp notion of being elected to anything, he now saw his role, the at-least-possible role, of becoming the power behind the White House, the man who if he could not occupy the seats of the mighty might at least fill them.

In the spring of 1919, AEF veterans and former rookies of the Plattsburg Camps joined with other zealous young amateurs to form the Leonard Wood Non-Partisan League. Within a month the league had 60,000 members and branches in every state. In October Colonel Procter became the league's chairman and put his massive fortune behind the general's candidacy. Dan Hanna and Walter Brown pledged their political and financial support as did the Standard Oil executive H. H. Rogers and James Duke, the tobacco king. Procter set up elaborate headquarters in New York, Washington, and Chicago and proceeded to sell Wood to the public. John King, Irish by birth, Republican by choice, the suavely tough boss of Bridgeport, Connecticut, became Wood's campaign manager. Left to his own back-alley devices King, with Procter's money and his own gall, might have cornered a majority of the delegates. His strategy was to deal directly with the state bosses. But his way was not Procter's, who naively felt that the process of securing the nomination should be like the soap he advertised, ninety-nine and forty-four hundredths percent pure; millions for advertising but not one cent for graft. For Walter Brown and Dan Hanna, the Wood boom seemed the opportunity they had been waiting for to capture Ohio's Republican party. Hynicka stood by, ready to assist with his renovated Cox machine. Harding found himself in a dilemma. If he declared for another senate term, Brown and Hanna would proceed to garner Wood delegates that might have gone to him. Wood's nomination might even kill Harding's chances of keeping his senate seat, since with the general in the White House, Republican patronage would go to Brown, and Harding would have no jobs to promise or provide. Yet if he announced himself a Buckeye favorite-son candidate, he might fail and lose his senate seat as well.

Meeting in secret session, the advisory committee, pressed by Hanna and Hynicka, named a subcommittee to smoke out Harding as to his intentions. The returned Progressives wanted no part of Harding as a presidential candidate "because he has not shown himself to be the type of man needed for the place." They would, however, support him for another term as senator. Harding, with the wary Daugherty beside him, refused to be smoked out. He would, he told the subcommittee, make his decision in his own good time. But the strain of such plotting and counterplotting, invigorating though it might be to Daugherty, told on Harding's less buoyant nature. "I could be happy without even returning to the Senate," he wrote Jennings. "I grow so weary of the conspiracies, insincerities, and petty practices of politics that I have moments when I am inclined to make a sweeping gesture and tell all of them to 'go to hell'. . . . I think you know as well as anybody that I do not take myself excessively seriously and do not think my participation in public affairs utterly essential to the continued existence of sane government. I really do not care a rap about higher political honors and do not mean to aspire to them."

Daugherty had other ideas, as he wrote to Colonel George Christian, Harding's Marion neighbor and home-town booster:

> Now I think we should without Harding knowing about it canvas & keep in touch with the big field. We need say no more that he would not be a candidate for the Presidency. He will of course not say that he is. He don't now have to do much talking or know much. Presidents don't run in this country like assessors you know. He had at home the same troubles that McKinley & Hanna & Taft had. In a way at the right time I will make this clear.*

In the intricacies of Daugherty's mind the pattern was emerging. Scarcely daring to believe it himself, he began to construct the mosaic of his grand design. No other candidate would be able to touch Wood's total of delegates, and yet — with the opposition of the eastern bosses — he would (unless Daugherty guessed wrong) still not get a majority. Procter would overdo it with his soft soap and hard money campaign, and there would be a reaction. Closest contender to Wood was Governor Frank Lowden of Illinois, but

* *The Available Man,* p. 348.

Lowden had his own drawbacks. He would not reach Wood's total, and in a bitter convention fight the two would cancel each other out. The convention would deadlock. Half a year before it occurred to anyone else, Daugherty saw this blunt fact staring him in the face. Other lesser candidates like Hiram Johnson would have too many enemies. Somewhere, somehow, a dark horse would have to be brought out of the Republican paddock, a compromise candidate, a harmonizer. Daugherty saw that emerging dark horse as Warren Harding. His strategy was deceptively simple. In the intervening months he made his contacts with political bosses in all possible states, praising Wood, praising Lowden, praising Johnson, praising favorite sons while collecting second — and third — and fourth — choice pledges for Harding. The odds were long, but Daugherty had the steely nature of a born gambler. As he explained in his retirement:

> Harding's campaign from the beginning was a one-man-managed campaign, carefully planned, if I know what it is to plan a campaign. Without his knowing it I traveled all over the country to get the situation at first hand. I did this at my own expense. . . . Harding did not know much about what I was doing; I never bothered to tell him, just went ahead, and when I learned what the situation was I told him about it. . . . The real work was done months before the convention when the pins were set up all over the country for second, third, and fourth choices for Harding among the delegates and influential men of the various communities. . . . The simplicity of his campaign was so pronounced that nobody knew about it until we began to collect the second, third, and fourth choice votes when we got the convention tied up. This was part of the game and we nominated Harding by the use of these second, third, and fourth choices in the tie-up.*

Daugherty's immediate task was to persuade the reluctant Harding to make the race. The version of events that he gave in his apologia is simplified but basically accurate. He had met Harding in Columbus on an evening in November after the close of the Congressional session, and the two men went to Daugherty's upstairs library where they talked for the next six hours. Harding was still most reluctant to give up his Senate seat for a long chance at a high office he neither wanted nor felt himself fitted for. "What would you do in my place?" he finally asked, wilting under the other's persistence. "I'd go into the big circus," Daugherty told him:

* Letter to Ray Baker Harris. Harding papers.

"And do you think I have a fighting chance?"
"I think you have the best chance."
"How do you figure it?" he asked.
"On this line," I answered. "Neither one of the leading candidates can win. General Wood is backed by a powerful group of rich men who wish a military man in the White House. . . . But there's not enough money in the world to buy the nomination for a man who wears epaulets in 1920."
"Lowden's a power to be reckoned with," Harding suggested.
"Sure. The best man on the list, too, I like him. He'd make a fine President. But he'll never have the prize of a nomination."
"Why?"
"He's too rich."
"Nonsense."
"Besides, he married Pullman's daughter. No party will name a railroad magnate for the office of President". . . .
"Come down to brass tacks," Harding ordered. "Am I a big enough man for the race?"
"Don't make me laugh! The day of giants in the Presidential chair is passed [sic]. Our so-called Great Presidents were all made by the conditions of war under which they administered the office. Greatness in the presidential chair is largely an illusion of the people."*

Daugherty finally persuaded Harding to take the plunge, and the two of them walked back through the early-morning darkness to the house where Harding was staying. "We had it out," Daugherty told Harding's business associate, the former Republican State Executive Committee chairman, Charles Hard, a few days later. "I can't say when he will announce. I had all I could do to overcome his will. We had one hell of a time. But listen. While Harding did not absolutely promise, I say to you and you can rely on it — *he will be a candidate.*"

To make assurance doubly sure, Daugherty arranged for his 1916 successor as chairman of the state central committee, Newton Fairbanks, to make a public declaration for Harding. On December 1 at a banquet of the Roosevelt Club of Toledo, Fairbanks proposed Harding as a candidate. Harding, who was present, had no idea of what Fairbanks was intending to say. He did not make his own official announcement until December 16, declaring rather coyly then that he had been reluctant to have his name used but that his first obligation was to the Republicans of Ohio. Lowden announced his candidacy next day. Wood had already

* *The Inside Story of the Harding Tragedy*, pp. 17–18.

announced his, as had favorite sons Hiram Johnson of California and Miles Poindexter of Washington.

In the capital, Republican National Chairman Will Hays, at a meeting of the National Association of Republican State Chairmen, issued the formal call for the 1920 convention. The chairmen, most of them representing the Old Guard, used the occasion to discuss how they might best stop the Wood boom. Of the various countercandidates, Lowden and Harding were those mentioned most frequently. As far as Harding was concerned, politicians had come to have a superstitious regard for Ohio, a regard that had only increased following Hughes's 1916 defeat. Meanwhile Daugherty had opened a minuscule Harding headquarters in a shabby Washington hotel with himself as director and his hanger-on, Jess Smith, as secretary. From here he launched his countrywide undercover campaign.

Prudently Daugherty left Ohio in charge of Hard, counting on him to secure a solid slate of favorite-son delegates. He himself crisscrossed the West and South in his travels, praising favorite sons while touting Harding as an alternative, picking up promises of second, third and fourth choice, and here and there a first choice delegate — one each from Alabama, Arkansas, Florida and Mississippi; two from Louisiana and Kentucky; the promise of five from Missouri plus eight concealed ones. Several revisionist Harding historians have made out that Daugherty claimed too much in claiming credit for Harding's nomination, that in his frenetic travels he was unaware of the wider ramifications of the campaign. Indeed, Harding's own political correspondence in the months before the convention is enormous. He was not the passive figure that the self-vindicating Daugherty later tried to make him out to be. Nevertheless, without Daugherty's Mephistophelean energy, Harding left to himself would never have received the nomination. Hard, who had managed Harding's business affairs during the senatorial years, wrote in 1959, eighteen years after Daugherty's death: "Again, and again, and again I say, Harding would never have been nominated but for the leadership of Daugherty."

Harding's immediate need was to demonstrate his base strength by securing the solid support of Ohio's convention delegates. Ohio's peculiar ballot law required delegate candidates to indicate their second as well as their first choice. On behalf of Wood, Hynicka approached Harding with the disarming suggestion that the Wood forces might have their delegate candidates file for Harding for second choice if Harding in turn would instruct his candidates to make their second choice Wood. Procter even was willing to have the Wood delegates make Harding their first choice on the first ballot. To Harding it seemed more than reasonable, a harmonious means of bringing an end to the constant feuding between Daugherty and Hynicka. The deviousness of the offer escaped Harding, but it did not escape the devious Daugherty. On the first ballot Harding would indeed receive Ohio's forty-eight electoral votes, but on the second and subsequent ballots all Ohio's votes would go to Wood. Nudged by Daugherty, Harding finally replied that he would "think over" the proposition, but a month later he openly came out against Wood in Ohio, announcing that he wanted only delegates who would stand by him to the end. Let Ohio's choice be decided at the primaries!

Wood's managers entered him in every state with a primary contest for delegates except California. Harding's meager funds would permit no such expansive gesture. The only other state he planned to make a primary contest in was neighboring Indiana. Wood, Johnson and Lowden forces were all campaigning for delegates there, but Daugherty was openly confident that Harding would not only beat his wealthier rivals in Indiana but would carry his own state solidly. In this euphoric mood he made a statement in New York that would subsequently enter American folklore. As he was packing his bag in his room at the Waldorf Astoria, two reporters called. One of them, trying to draw him out, said that since Daugherty could not produce a tabulation of delegates sufficient for Harding to win the nomination, he presumed that Daugherty expected Harding to be nominated by a small group of weary political managers in some back hotel room at two in the morning. "Make it 2:11," Daugherty quipped back.

The casually spoken numbers had an indelible effect. Two A.M. might have been forgotten; not so the electrically specific 2:11. Daugherty was quoted as saying:

> I don't expect Senator Harding to be nominated on the first, second or third ballot, but I think about eleven minutes after two o'clock on Friday morning of the convention, when fifteen or twenty men, bleary-eyed and perspiring profusely from the heat, are sitting around a table some one of them will say: "Who will we nominate?"
>
> At that decisive time the friends of Senator Harding can suggest

him and can afford to abide by the result. I don't know but what I might suggest him myself.*

It was just a quip. Neither Daugherty nor the reporters believed it, but that 2:11 quotation — with cigar smoke gratuitously added — has ever since become a cliché of politics; The Smoke-filled Room at 2:11 A.M., metonymy for sordid political manipulation.

The quip seemed even less credible six weeks before the convention, when the Ohio primaries were held. Harding had written Scobey confidently that "the great rank and file of the state is very cordially behind me." The returns showed he had overestimated. Wood succeeded in capturing a quarter of the forty-eight delegates, and Daugherty himself was defeated as delegate-at-large. The results in Indiana a week later were even more of a disaster. There, in the one state outside Ohio where Harding had campaigned actively, he managed to gather only ten percent of the vote, trailing behind Wood, Lowden and Johnson, and winning not a single delegate.

The undaunted Daugherty had to work hard to revive Harding's drooping spirits. After all, as he pointed out, Harding had still won a majority victory in Ohio. Indiana mattered far less than those quietly collected second and third and fourth choices. Daugherty trotted out all the old arguments: Wood and Lowden would fight each other to a standstill; Johnson was too radical; Root too old; the dealer's odds were still on Harding.

In after years, that Republican national convention held in Chicago the second week of June, 1920, evolved into a legend. According to the legend, the convention was dominated by sinister economic and political forces intent on nominating and electing an innocuous candidate, a presidential puppet, behind whose back they could carry on their predatory activities. Oil, lumber and other interests, eyeing the government's vast natural resources, saw lush opportunities with the right man in the White House. A reactionary senate clique wanted no more Teddy Roosevelts with their Big Sticks, no more scholastic Wilsons, but a president who thoroughly understood the basic principle that Congress proposes and the president disposes. So, the legend continues, after three frustrating days when the convention had at last arrived at its predicted deadlock, a group of Old Guard senators got together in a hotel room to sort out the presidential possibilities and pick *their* candidate, the man who would "go

* *New York Times*, Feb. 21, 1920.

along." There in a haze of cigar smoke they shuffled through the possible names, dealing and discarding as if they were playing poker. At a time conveniently close to 2:11 A.M. they came up with their choice, Senator Warren Harding of Ohio. He was biddable, a man who had sat with them for five years with closed mouth, and yet who had a certain reputation outside the Senate for vapid oratory, a man who had spread himself in attacking Wilson's League of Nations and who had even coined the word "normalcy," a man with no discernible political philosophy except that of party regularity, who once nominated would undoubtedly get elected; a second and diminished McKinley.

Certain facts have seemed to corroborate the legend. There was indeed a 2 A.M. meeting in Harvey's hotel suite, and Harding *was* nominated the following morning. He *was* the least or among the least of American presidents. The corruption in his administration, if no greater than in that of certain more esteemed Presidents, *was* far more apparent, and its repercussions lasted a decade after his death. Yet the legend of Harding and the Dark Convention is essentially a false one. He was not nominated by a cabal of senators; he was nominated, with the luck that is always the concomitant of success, through Daugherty's foresight and astute spadework in the grass roots. The cigar-smoking senators agreed or half-agreed on what was basically a *fait accompli*.

At the opening of the convention Harding was not the unknown that the legend made him out. He might well have been described as a run-of-the-mill politician, yet in the *Literary Digest* poll taken a few weeks before the convention he ranked sixth in the list of possible Republican candidates. Wood was of course first, with Johnson second, and Hoover a surprising third. Lowden followed Hoover and was followed in turn by Hughes and then Harding, with Coolidge and Taft ending the poll in that order.

Yet for all his poll-topping popularity, Wood was in serious trouble before the convention opened. Colonel Procter had parted with the more politically astute King and, while rejecting the latter's backstairs political deals, had blanketed the country with Wood posters, pamphlets, buttons, billboards and books. So much money did he spend that Johnson's friend Senator Borah brought the matter before the Senate Committee on Privileges and Elections. Although the committeemen, meeting a week before the convention, failed to find anything sinister in Procter's lavish efforts, they did bring out that he had spent a recorded $1,773,303 and probably several times that amount off the record. Such figures did Wood the lasting damage of branding him as the rich man's choice. Lowden's chances seemed even more eroded when it was discovered that his manager had paid two uncommitted Western delegates $2,500 each "for nothing in particular but to create sentiment for Governor Lowden." Lowden was unaware of the bribery in his name, but he could not avoid the responsibility.

When the convention opened on Tuesday, June 6, in the sweaty atmosphere of Chicago's Coliseum, Wood had by far the largest block of delegates, though still lacking about 150 to reach the 490 necessary for nomination. Through the tedious preliminary ritual of the first two days, Daugherty instructed his Harding workers to "smile, keep in good humor" and make no enemies. Jauntily wearing Harding badges, they met all incoming trains, carried bags and summoned taxis for bewildered newly arrived delegates while talking up the man from Marion. Daugherty had brought the seventy-five members of the Republican Glee Club with him, and each evening he sent them to serenade the headquarters of the other candidates. Harding, his self-doubt growing as his modest campaign fund diminished, considered dropping out of the race and sought temporary solace in the arms of his young mistress, Nan Britton. No self-doubts troubled Daugherty who with a staff of over five hundred of his best workers set up a complete roll of all delegates, their hotels, their room numbers and their candidate choices from first to fourth. Every rival headquarters had its undercover Harding observer. Daugherty saw to that. Seeking out Lowden's manager, Toby Hert, he offered to lend him a number of Harding votes on the early ballots, to help to beat Wood, and Hert, with his fingers crossed, accepted them. There was a Byzantine air of intrigue to those two preliminary days of the convention, a complication of comings and goings, of rumors and counterrumors, of sleek if sweaty politicians on their private missions from one hotel room to the other. But Daugherty's instinct for the fundamentals was sound.

Not until Friday afternoon at 5 o'clock did the balloting finally get underway. Wood led at the start with 287½ votes, followed by Lowden with 211½ and Johnson with 133½. Harding with 65½ was in sixth place but could have been in fourth if he had claimed the thirty or forty undercover votes on loan to Lowden. On the two subsequent ballots Wood's total was raised from 303 to 314½ — still 177 short — while Lowden reached 289. Somewhere in the shuffle Harding lost four votes.

At this point, over the loudly voiced objection of the delegates, the temporary chairman, the supercilious elderly Senator Henry Cabot Lodge of Massachusetts, adjourned the convention. With that adjournment, Harding had given up any hope of winning. William Allen White ran into him in a hotel elevator, boozy, unshaven, and looking "like the wreck of the *Hesperus.*" Daugherty on the other hand was buoyant as a gambler counting on a run of luck. While the convention nominating speeches droned on, he had been making his behind-the-scenes contacts at the Coliseum, or buttonholing key figures on the streets or in the hotels. He spread his workmen out fan-wise to talk Harding to each delegation, to find out where the delegations would be after the adjournment. During the evening he sent the Columbus Glee Club out again serenading. And everywhere he passed the word along that good old Harding was the man to break the deadlock. "We made it a Harding night," he later wrote, "of good cheer and friendly gestures for every candidate."

Meanwhile a meeting did take place in a smoke-filled room, but contrary to the legend it decided very little. The room was one of the suite on the thirteenth floor of the Blackstone shared by George Harvey and Will Hays, the chairman of the Republican National Committee. The dominant figure present was Senator Lodge. From 8 P.M. until morning Old Guard senators and party leaders wandered in and out of the Harvey suite, pouring themselves drinks and talking at random through coiling smoke. Lodge himself was pledged to Wood, but he had come to feel that it was now "impossible and undesirable" to nominate either Wood or Lowden. Someone suggested Senator Philander Knox, Roosevelt's attorney general and Taft's secretary of state, with Johnson as vice-president. An emissary was sent to the Johnson headquarters and returned with the frustrating answer that Johnson would accept Knox as vice-president if he himself received the presidential nomination. In any case Knox himself was too old, too ailing. As for Governor Calvin Coolidge, hailed as the hero of the Boston Police Strike, Lodge would have none of him. "Nominate a man who lives in a two-family house!" he had said a few weeks earlier. "Never! Massachusetts is not for him!" So it went on, the shuffling, dealing and discarding. Governor Sproul of Pennsylvania was too closely linked with the railroads. Hughes, sorrowing over the recent death of his daughter, had already declined. Hays, when his name came up, declared that as chairman of the national committee he could not bid at his own auction. Daugherty was not present at any time. He did not even know the meeting was taking place. Finally New York's Senator James Wadsworth left the room, fed up with "listening to a lot of footless conversation." Afterward he maintained that the alleged president makers in the Harvey suite were "as futile as chickens with their heads cut off!"

Yet no matter how many times the political cards were dealt, the Harding card always remained. No Republican presidential candidate had ever been elected without Ohio's vote, and this year the Democrats might well pick Governor James Cox of Ohio as their nominee. There was that argument. There was the further argument that Harding was experienced politically, popular in the Senate, presidential in appearance, the "logical candidate," the one who had the least marks against him. At about 1 A.M. those still in the Smoke-Filled Room decided by a "standing vote" that it would be the wise course to nominate Harding just as soon as this could be brought about." The decision was a tentative one, more the recognition of the course of events that seemed to make Harding the most available candidate, rather than the later-depicted plot of a group of Old Guard senators to foist a pliant tool on the convention and the country. Before the morning's balloting they would pass the word to the undercover Lowden delegates and to the favorite-son delegates they controlled to shift to Harding. There was scarcely more to it than that. As Connecticut's Senator Frank Brandegee explained, with more bluntness than elegance: "There ain't any first-raters this year. This ain't 1880 or any 1904; we haven't any John Shermans or Theodore Roosevelts; we got a lot of second-raters and Warren Harding is the best of the second-raters."

At about two in the morning — close enough to Daugherty's 2:11 A.M. to accommodate the legend — Harvey, the only nonsenator present, sent for Harding. The Harding that received the message, and who had been alerted to the discussion going on, bore little resemblance to the shambling unshaven man White had seen earlier in the elevator. Shaved and showered, trailing an odor of bay rum and confidence, he appeared on the threshold to be met by the owl-eyed Harvey, his solemnity reinforced by his usual dose of alcohol. Harvey led him into one of the bedrooms.

> We think [he told Harding in his self-consciously impressive voice] you may be nominated tomorrow; before acting finally, we think you should tell us, on your conscience before God, whether there is anything that might be brought up against you that would embarrass the party, any impediment that might disqualify you or make you inexpedient, either as a candidate or as President.*

Harding asked for a few minutes to think it over and retired to an empty bedroom. What Harvey had in mind behind his solemnity he never revealed. Undoubtedly he had seen the flyers that an elderly fanatic, Professor William Estabrook, Chancellor of Wooster College, Ohio, had been distributing at the various Chicago headquarters announcing that Harding's father was a mulatto and his great-grandmother a Negress. It is less likely that he had heard anything of Harding's love affairs. But Harding could not be certain. In any case, after ten minutes of self-communing, Harding opened the door to tell Harvey there was no impediment.

While Harvey and the senators were shuffling and dealing on the thirteenth floor of Blackstone, Wood, trim and at ease in his high-collared khaki uniform in spite of the heat, was at his headquarters in the Elizabethan Room of the Congress Hotel with two of his military aides, his confidential secretary John Himrod, his manager, Frank Hitchcock, who had been Taft's campaign manager in 1912 and had taken over when King left, his old Cuban quartermaster general Chauncey Baker, General E. F. Glenn, and the Massachusetts industrialist and inventor John Hays Hammond. At least three times that night the general would be taken up on a high mountain and shown the political kingdom. Each time he would turn away. Early in the evening the ailing Penrose called from Philadelphia and asked to speak to Wood. Himrod, who answered the telephone, covered the mouthpiece and asked Wood across the room if he would take the call. Wood said he would not, but that he would receive any message. Penrose's message was blunt. If Wood would give "us" three cabi-

* *Our Times*, vol. VI, pp. 63–64.

net members, he would be nominated on the morning's ballot. "Now, General," said Glenn as Himrod relayed the message, "one word will make you President of the United States!" Wood turned and said softly to his secretary: "Tell Senator Penrose that I have made no promises and am making none." Penrose replied that he was sorry, but "we" intended to have a Republican president this time and to name three members of his cabinet. Two Republican elders arrived a little later with a similar proposal that received a similar rebuff. "Shady business, gentlemen," Wood told them, "and I'll have nothing to do with it."

The most bumptious arrival in the Elizabethan Room that evening was the gilt-edged, gold-toothed millionaire from Oklahoma, Jake Hamon, who explained bombastically that the fifty southwest delegates he controlled would be enough to conclude a bargain for the seventy-five Pennsylvania delegates. He had come to offer his delegates to Wood in exchange for being allowed to name the secretary of the interior and the ambassador to Mexico. At this, Wood for once lost his temper. Striding across the room he shouted at Jake: "I am an American soldier! I'll be damned if I'll betray my country! Get the hell out of here!"

As the languid and sticky night wore on, those in the Elizabethan Room grew more and more aware of the forces combining against Wood. Hitchcock, who had been an old hand at buying up Southern delegates in 1908 and 1912, turned to the general with his last hope: "There is only one thing. We can pull something off by buying some of those delegates. That," he added, regretfully, "you wouldn't allow."

No, Wood told him, he would not.

The cards had been dealt for the last time, and as far as those in Harvey's Blackstone suite were concerned, Harding was to have his chance. But there was still no conspiratorial certainty about it. At 3:30 A.M. a reporter caught the Kansas senator and future vice-president, Charles Curtis, coming out of the Harvey suite and asked him who it was going to be. "We are going to try to put Warren Harding over," Curtis told him. 'We'll try him out for a few ballots tomorrow but if he doesn't show strength we'll switch to Governor Sproul."

Just before the convention opened on Saturday, the odds that the day before had been 10 to 1 against Harding had dropped to 5 to 1. Curtis called his Kansas delegation together to let them know that if Wood could not make it in the next ballot or two — "it had been decided" to give Harding a play.

In the morning's first ballot, the fifth of the convention, a shift in the political weather was apparent. Wood's total dropped to 299, 16 New York favorite-son delegates switching to Lowden to carry him 4 beyond Wood. Daugherty still kept his reserves in line for Lowden, but scattered votes began to drift to Harding, giving him a total of 78, 12½ above his previous high. Daugherty, his face a mask, watched the pattern develop according to his plan. On the sixth ballot Wood's floor leaders, summoning all their reserves, barely managed to tie Lowden with 311½ votes. Johnson, in third place, continued a downward course. Harding gained another 11 votes.

On the seventh ballot the temperature inside the Coliseum was 102. Wood gained ½ vote and topped Lowden by that margin. Harding was now in third place with 105 votes. With the eighth ballot Daugherty began gathering in his concealed delegates. On that ballot Wood lost 22 votes, Lowden was down to 307 and Harding had pushed ahead to 133½. Restless delegates began to wander in the aisles, some munching sandwiches. Daugherty, now ready to gamble all his chips, sent orders out to muster every available Harding vote, every delegate hidden or held back, every midwinter promise.

Before the balloting could begin, Daugherty found his plans challenged, himself faced with disaster. Something was going on backstage, something that was apparent in the manner of the frosty and aloof Chairman Lodge when he recognized Lowden's floor manager, Hert, who promptly made a motion to adjourn. New York and California seconded the motion. Lodge put the motion to the delegates, and to a thundering chorus of Noes pronounced that the Ayes had it. Daugherty, flushed with rage, his good eye flashing, pushed his way to the rostrum, shouting at Lodge: "You cannot defeat this man this way! This motion was not carried! You cannot defeat this man!" Lodge tried to put him off with the devious explanation that they needed the recess to swing Johnson's followers over to Harding by offering Johnson the vice presidency. "A fool's errand!" the tricked but unfooled Daugherty told Lodge.

The convention adjourned at 1:40, not to meet again until four. During those two hours Wood and Lowden met privately.

Both agreed that Harding's nomination would be a disaster to the party, both agreed that the best immediate solution would be to adjourn the convention for the weekend. They approached Johnson who, contemptuous as ever of Harding, agreed to cooperate. Later Procter met Hert at Lowden's headquarters. Hert said that the combined Wood-Lowden forces still had a majority of the delegates, and suggested that they could combine if Wood would agree to accept the vice presidency under Lowden. Procter said that the general more than any other man deserved first place, but he would be glad to have Lowden in second place. Hert refused, but agreed to the adjournment.

While this was going on, Harvey and his friends were back in the Smoke-filled Room still debating possible choices and wondering now whether it might not be possible to swing the delegates to National Committee Chairman Hays. With this in mind Harvey called the chairman of the Connecticut delegation, J. Henry Roraback, to ask if he could get his delegates to switch to Hays. Roraback replied that, while Wood was Connecticut's first choice, Harding was the state's pledged second choice. Harvey warned that Connecticut's switch to Harding would start a real stampede. "Nothing would please me more," Roraback answered curtly. His answer squelched the Hays boom.

Daugherty in the meantime was bustling in and out of the various headquarters, firming up his commitments, encouraging the hesitant, admonishing the dubious, a leader at last among leaders, impervious and assured, masking the doubts that haunt all gamblers. He telephoned Boss Penrose who, at last convinced that Harding was the man, had prepared a statement to the press to that effect. Daugherty, fearful that if the statement appeared in the afternoon papers before the balloting there would be an outcry that Harding had been picked by the bosses, ordered him to hold off. Penrose obeyed.

Four o'clock found the delegates in their seats, the rostrum still empty, the heavy atmosphere electric. Word had passed that it would be Harding! But the minutes dragged by; quarter-past four, half-past four. Procter at the Coliseum waited for Hert to settle the matter of adjournment, but Hert could not be found. Vainly Procter sent a messenger in search of him. The delegates were growing restive. Some of them climbed on their chairs. There were whistles and stamping and shouts of "Play Ball!"

Lodge, from the wings, said he could not hold back the convention any longer. Hays begged for just another ten minutes "in the name of party harmony." At 4:50 there was still no sign of Hert, and Lodge stalked to the rostrum and ordered the secretary to call the roll for the ninth ballot. The roll proceeded with alphabetical regularity, and at first with no change — Alabama, Arizona, Arkansas, California. Then, suddenly, the Connecticut delegation switched its votes from Lowden to Harding. The break Daugherty had so long counted on had come! The Illinois delegation continued to cast its votes for Lowden, but Kansas now switched to Harding after the delegates had been told by Curtis that Wood was through. Unless an adjournment came promptly, the Harding parade could not be stopped. When Kentucky was called, Hert appeared from nowhere to announce dramatically that his state was switching to Harding. He made no mention of adjournment. The balloting continued. As Hert turned to leave, Procter cornered him in the aisle. What about the adjournment, he wanted to know? "It's off!" said Hert. "You damned liar, aren't you going through?" Procter shouted. "No," said Hert, edging away. What neither Lowden nor Procter knew was that Hert would have rather seen Wood defeated than Lowden nominated. And he had just succeeded in defeating him.

By the end of the ninth ballot, Harding with 374½ votes was still 119 short of the majority, but the end was obvious. The balconies were beginning to chant "Harding! Harding!" Harding postcards, carefully supplied by Daugherty, fluttered down from the rafters and balconies like snowflakes. Harding's wife, her puffed arms tightly folded, was sitting in a box in the front balcony, her right arm gripping two enormous hatpins. Seeing her from the floor, Daugherty — who had just sent a message to the Pennsylvania manager asking for the delegation's votes on the next ballot — made his way to the box and sat down beside her, whispering hoarsely that they had the votes, that on the next ballot her husband was going to be nominated. At the word "nominated" she started forward, almost leaping from her chair and driving the hatpins deep into Daugherty's side. He felt the sting and then a dizziness as if he were going to faint, as if he were smothering. Over and above the pain he could feel blood trickling down his leg into his shoe, and wondered if the hatpins had pierced his lung. Moving unsteadily from the box, as if the floor were tilting under him, he heard Lodge's clipped Yankee voice echoing out of nowhere to call the tenth ballot. All the states seemed to be for Harding now — Arkansas, Colorado, Illinois, Indiana, Maine, Massachusetts; 440 votes and only 53 more needed for the nomination. As Daugherty padded uncertainly along the aisle he could hear the swish of blood that filled his shoe. From some remote region in space he heard the clerk call out "Pennsylvania," and then a bass voice reply "Pennsylvania casts sixty-one votes for Warren Harding!" The balconies cut loose, streamers and papers floated down, the gabble of the crowd turned to a roar. Fortune's wheel had stopped, and Harding had won! Daugherty tottered to an anteroom, examined his side and discovered that his lung had not been pierced after all. When he took off his shoe, he found it full of sweat, not blood. He was not even aware of what was happening some minutes later when the delegates bolted and nominated Governor Calvin Coolidge as vice-president.

The Republican nomination that year was the equivalent of election. No Democratic candidate could have stemmed the tide, not even Herbert Hoover, whom the Democrats had earlier wanted to nominate before he turned Republican, certainly not Governor Cox of Ohio and his debonair running mate ("flighty," Senator Lodge called him) Franklin Roosevelt. Americans in one of their periods of anger and frustration were voting against, not for. They were voting against the stubborn invalid Wilson, against his crusade to Keep the World Safe for Democracy that they had so embraced and that had turned out so shabbily, against the wartime regimentation and peacetime High Cost of Living, against shortages and strikes and disorders and foreign entanglements, against the League of Nations, against the not-so-brave new world that was the war's inheritance. Wilson, the broken man, had come to personify to his countrymen all the strife and disillusionment, the high hopes shattered, the bloody sacrifices that had come to nothing. He was the scapegoat, just as in another twelve years Herbert Hoover would prove to be another scapegoat. Even so, the size of Harding's victory was astonishing. He carried thirty-seven of the forty-eight states, with 404 electoral votes to Cox's 127, the most overwhelming electoral victory in a hundred years. In the popular vote his percentage was the highest ever recorded by a successful presidential candidate.

The four months between the election and the inaugural Harding spent at the customary prepresidential task of picking his cabinet. He was proud of his selections: Charles Evans Hughes as his secretary of state: Herbert Hoover, secretary of commerce, over the objections of the Old Guard; as secretary of agriculture, Henry Wallace, Iowa agriculturist and father of a future Democratic secretary of agriculture; Andrew Mellon, "America's leading financier," secretary of the treasury. Even that later-so-discredited figure, Senator Albert Fall, seemed an acceptable choice at the time as secretary of the interior. Only Daugherty, as prospective attorney general, brought out any extended hostile comment. "It won't be long before Harry Daugherty is selling the sunshine off the steps of the Capitol," one cynic observed. But this was the post that Harding had promised him, the seat of power that would vindicate him for all his Ohio humiliations, that would allow him to walk down Broad Street, Columbus, and if he met Dan Hanna make any scurrilous suggestion he wished. Daugherty's appointment drew personal as well as public protests. Senator Wadsworth on a visit to Marion told Harding that it would be a disappointment to the members of the bar, and would be not only a mistake but dangerous. The president-elect replied with deep feeling: "Harry Daugherty has been my best friend from the beginning of this whole thing. I have told him that he can have any place in my cabinet he wants, outside of secretary of state. He tells me that he wants to be attorney general and *by God he will be attorney general!*"

Daugherty and Fall were the two cabinet members who subsequently cast the deepest shadow on the Harding administration. The legends of the Ohio Gang and Teapot Dome were to make the name of the Harding administration a synonym for graft and corruption. Yet both legends reduced a series of grey and complicated facts to a theoretic black-and-white simplicity. Fall may have been merely a man with a blurred ethical sense who acted according to his lesser lights, rather than a betrayer of his trust and his country. The same may be said for Daugherty, although today's Harding descendants see him as the chief culprit in their president-ancestor's denigration and have not hesitated to label him a thief. Yet Mark Sullivan, when he was engaged in writing the final volume of *Our Times*, spent two days with the seventy-five-year-old Daugherty in his retirement. He did not believe then or later that Daugherty had ever deliberately betrayed his chief. "I felt that he lived by a code of his own," Sullivan wrote; "if his code did not happen to be identical with the world's conventions, so much the worse for the world's conventions." But "Daugherty, when in Harding's cabinet, and at all times in respect to Harding, prized Harding more than he prized anything else. To suppose that, in this respect or as respects any action of his, he would consciously have done for his personal benefit a thing that would bring discredit on Harding would be to indict not only his morals but his loyalty and his intelligence."

Daugherty's code as head of the Department of Justice was the ambiguous one of the Ohio political jungle. Shady figures operated in his shadow, and he must have been aware of their activities: the sleazy grafting of his "bumper," Jess Smith, who had an unofficial office in the Justice Department; the gross irregularities of the Bureau of Investigation (later the FBI) under his detective friend William J. Burns; the traffic in liquor and liquor permits; the influence-peddling; the sticky-fingered activities of lower-level Ohio politicians who had moved to Washington in Harding's wake and who owed their appointment to Daugherty as patronage dispenser. Daugherty had spent most of his own savings on Harding's election campaign, yet he lived on a scale in Washington double or triple that of his salary. Twice while he was attorney general he was investigated by Congress. "The Department of Easy Virtue" one investigating committeeman labeled Daugherty's Justice Department. After Daugherty's resignation had been forced by President Coolidge, he twice went on trial for conspiracy, and each time the jury failed to agree. At his second trial, the jury stood 11-1 for conviction, and it was commonly believed that the stubborn holdout had been bribed. Nevertheless most of Daugherty's assistants in the Department of Justice, young lawyers of unquestioned probity, never in the scandal years lost their belief in Attorney General Daugherty's basic honesty.

Daugherty's second trial was due posthumously to Jess Smith, who had committed suicide when his graft world began to tumble about his ears. Shortly before his death he had deposited $50,000 in dubious money with an Ohio bank belonging to Daugherty's brother Mally. Smith had two other accounts in the bank, but this, "Jess Smith Extra No. 3," was described as a "political account," a joint account with Daugherty who had used it during Harding's nomination campaign to deposit contributions and make disbursements. Smith's $50,000 deposit, Daugherty explained, was merely a return of money that he had borrowed earlier. That mysterious deposit was the basis of Daugherty's indictment, since it was alleged that the money had been paid to Smith as a bribe. Conveniently, the records of Extra No. 3 had been destroyed by Daugherty. So strong was the circumstantial evidence against the resigned Attorney General that only a full and detailed explanation would have cleared his name. Yet at his trial when the time came for him to take the stand in his own defence, he remained seated, picked up a pencil and with cool deliberation scribbled a note. This, handed to the judge, read:

> Having been personal attorney for Warren G. Harding before he was Senator from Ohio and while he was Senator, and thereafter until his death,
>
> And for Mrs. Harding for a period of several years, and before her husband was elected President and after his death . . .
>
> And having been attorney for the Midland National Bank of Washington Court House, Ohio, and for my brother, M. S. Daugherty
>
> And having been Attorney General of the United States during the time that President Harding served as President,
>
> And also for a time after President Harding's death under President Coolidge,
>
> And with all of those named as attorney, personal friend and Attorney General, my relations were of the most confidential character as well as professional,
>
> I refuse to testify and answer questions put to me because: The answer I might give or make and the testimony I might give might intend to incriminate.*

This refuge in what would later be referred to as the Fifth Amendment alibi, seemed to strip the remaining shreds of honor from Harding's tattered reputation, as if his friend's silence had been necessary to protect his dead self. Daugherty had made a president, and with his last non-testimony he had demolished his creation.

* *Our Times,* vol. VI, p. 354.

*As in the children's game, Papa Stearns "packs his bags for Boston" leaving the somewhat too sharp-nosed Calvin to his White House inheritance.*

CHAPTER SIX

# Lord Lingerie: Frank Waterman Stearns

TWO THINGS THERE were that Frank Waterman Stearns cared about more than anything else in life, with the selfless affection that some men give to their God or their country or their mothers and a few to their wives. He could in a pinch explain why he cared for Amherst College, but his feeling for Calvin Coolidge was not to be explained. Nor did he ever think about his feelings. Loyalties, in his opinion, needed no explanation. Amherst, that little hill college in the obscurely western part of Massachusetts, was his *alma mater carissima,* the setting of his lost youth that endured so poignantly as an after-image. What he remembered most vividly was the college in late spring, the sudden softness of maple and elm buds on College Hill after the formidable winter, Sugarloaf Mountain and the serrated peaks of the Holyoke range in the blue distance, the square-towered chapel through the haze of greenery, with the seniors sitting on the fence in the half-light of evening singing "The Bulldog on the Bank, and the Bullfrog in the Pond." When he tried to conceive of the Heaven in which he so firmly believed, he felt it must be something like his senior year at Amherst. "One may live a long time," he wrote in after years, "without finding out all that there is to Amherst College."

If Amherst was his *alma mater,* Calvin Coolidge was his *almus filius.* In this man not quite young enough to have been his son, this rufous Yankee with the abrupt laconic manner and the nasality of the Vermont hill country, he had found something that he sensed was missing in himself. To Coolidge he would give an austere and bloodless devotion beyond the flesh-and-blood devotion he gave to his own son and his two daughters. When Coolidge was merely a state senator from Northampton, a mousy and slightly comic politician mincing along the corridors of the gilt-domed State House, Stearns saw him as a figure of destiny, an Amherst man who would one day be president of the United States.

Frank Stearns, the Tremont Street drygoods merchant-prince, was not, in Cleveland Amory's later term, a "Proper Bostonian," but he was the next best thing; he was recognized by Proper Bostonians. Beacon Hill dowagers patronized his emporium, a conveniently brisk walk across the Common. R. H. Stearns became an institution rather than a store, a byword as well as a standby for imperiously white-haired old ladies who knew they could find at Stearns' what had mostly vanished in Boston, from corsets and long underwear to hatpins and 240-thread-count pocket handkerchiefs and the finest grade of satin. Stearns' first-floor glove counter became an informal meeting place for Boston matrons. Stearns saleswomen (not ladies, not girls) remembered offhand the glove and shoe and stocking and corset sizes of dozens of Boston women. One saleswoman is said to have remembered the stocking sizes of over five hundred customers. A Victorian decor and a Victorian residue of merchandise endured at the Tremont Street store a generation after the old queen was in her grave. Amory, writing in 1947, observed that Stearns still bravely displayed "along with sleeker trends, all manner of old-time merchandise, including pearl chokers, Queen Mary hats, cameo brooches, high-necked, long-sleeved nightgowns, etc."

Dick Stearns, the founder of the store and father of Frank Waterman, was a Lincoln farm boy who had first seen Boston as he rode into the city on his father's cart with a load of vegetables. Like Dick Whittington so long before him, he was fascinated by the first sight of a city, and though he would never be Boston's mayor he would end up one of Boston's leading merchants, respected, trusted and distantly recognized. When he had become of age he left his father's scrabbled acres for a clerking job with the Boston merchant C. C. Brewer at $150 a year. Within that year he was promoted to first salesman, and after two years he left to start his own business with his minute savings plus the small credit that an uptight and enterprising young man might command in Boston.

In his first shop he acted as buyer, salesman and porter, rather like his older contemporary the fine grocer Samuel S. Pierce, who had started his one-man enterprise by first delivering his groceries in a wheelbarrow borrowed from the Brattle Street Church. From their small beginnings both Sam Pierce and Dick Stearns aimed at the carriage trade, making a specialty of carrying only goods of the highest quality. The carriage trade in Boston knew quality and a bargain. Both young men prospered. Those who patronized one store were likely to patronize the other. Like William Dean Howells's Silas Lapham, Richard Stearns rose quickly, but unlike Lapham he never overextended himself. Soon he was known to more out-of-town buyers than any other merchant in the business.

Frank, on graduating from Amherst, first went to New York where he worked briefly as a salesman in the wool trade in order to gain an independent experience of the business world in a larger environment. But he soon returned to Boston and the Tremont Street store as his father's trusted adviser and in time (which moves slowly in Boston) his successor. R. H. Stearns Company with its carriage trade continued to thrive. Yet, though Frank Stearns could easily have afforded a Silas Lapham mansion on the water side of Beacon Street, he preferred to live in suburban Newton, just as he had once preferred Amherst to Harvard. Although his house was a brick replica of a Georgian mansion, he sent his son to Newton High School. Proper Bostonians had long deserted their public school system, and a more socially ambitious man than Stearns would have enrolled his son at Milton Academy or one of the newer Episcopalian foundations that were attempting to transplant the English public school into the alien American earth. Stearns nursed no social ambitions, even though his family tree was as well-rooted as any in proper Boston. For was he not a Mayflower Descendant, and would not his son be in his good time, a member of the Society of the Cincinnati? What is more, he had removed from the austere Congregationalism of his father to the more genial Episcopalianism that Phillips Brooks had succeeded in making palatable and indeed more than palatable to Back Bay Boston. His exclusion from the *Social Register* failed to concern him. He was a member of the class of 1878 at Amherst. Calvin Coolidge — J. Calvin Coolidge he then called himself — did not graduate until seventeen years later. If they had both gone to Harvard, the odds would have been against their meeting.

But the close-knit quality of the Amherst alumni community made their eventual meeting almost inevitable. Once they had met, Coolidge came to fill a gap in the older man's life, to supply a purpose beyond the marketing of lingerie and gloves. "As an individual, my feeling towards him is that of a father," Stearns wrote after he had become Coolidge's political sponsor; "as a public official, it is much like that of a son."

J. Calvin Coolidge, the monosyllabic Yankee who arrived as a freshman at Amherst in September 1891, would have seemed an unlikely prospect to fill a gap in anyone's life. He had been born in Plymouth Notch, Vermont, one of those hill towns that had been drained of their strength in the mid-nineteenth century by the migrations to the richer, easier farmlands of the West. The Vermonters who remained and kept to the granite-strewn acres were those too deeply rooted in the past to change horizons even for the better. A wax-works museum, William Allen White called Vermont, the only state whose population had decreased since the Revolution. Plymouth, so shadowed by hills that the sun set in summer at five o'clock, could have been the setting for Edith Wharton's *Ethan Frome*. Yet in the archaic Notch where, it seemed, Lord Amherst's redcoats had passed only yesterday, the Coolidges were old-fashioned. John Calvin as a boy at school spoke with a twang that was the inheritance of generations of psalm-singing nonconformism and that rang strangely even among the rustic pupils of the one-room school he attended. No school, no college, no later high position in state or country would modify that atavistic twang. Coolidge was said to have pronounced "cow" as a three-syllable word.

When he was twelve his mother died. "The greatest grief that can come to a boy came to me," he wrote in his *Autobiography*. "Life was never to seem the same again." A year later, on a bitter winter day with the temperature thirty degrees below zero, his father harnessed the horse and sleigh and drove him the twelve miles to Ludlow, where he enrolled him in Black River Academy. It was a pinchbeck school, one of scores of such grandiloquently named academies that dotted the New England landscape in the wake of the Greek Revival. John Calvin at first boarded in the village, a reticent farm boy, diligent rather than brilliant, at times overwhelmed by the homesickness that he kept to himself or half-revealed to his younger sister Abbie. On Saturday afternoons he worked in a Ludlow carriage shop that made perambulators and toy wagons. Whenever he could, he went back to Plymouth Notch.

Four years he remained at Black River Academy, until with four other boys and four girls he graduated in June, 1890. Three months before that his sister Abbie had died following a sudden attack of appendicitis. Her death was his second great sorrow, not to be expressed in words. Six weeks afterward he wrote his father only that "it is lonely here without Abbie."

Since the little academy's diploma was not acceptable for admission to most colleges, John Calvin spent his summer — when he was not hoeing or haying — in preparing for the Amherst entrance examinations. The boy and his father chose Amherst as being near and inexpensive. But on the short journey there to take his examinations, John Calvin came down with a cold that forced him to return to Plymouth Notch. College receded. For a time his father considered apprenticing him to a pharmacist. But that spring, as J. Calvin Coolidge, he enrolled for a term at St. Johnsbury Academy, Vermont's leading preparatory school, and received a certificate entitling him to be admitted to Amherst College without examination.

The Amherst that Coolidge entered in September, 1891, had 336 students, most of them the sons of well-to-do rural and small-town New England. J. Calvin was a peripheral figure, more rural, less prosperous. During his four years, he remained almost to the end obscure. Even in his senior year he felt his own oddness. "I am from the country and am glad of it," he wrote his father, " 'the men of the mountains always beat the men of the plains' but I do not always want to remain a rustic in my ideas and appearance." The shy monosyllabic boy from Vermont would have liked to be one of the boys, but he lacked both the instinct and the personality. "A drabber, more colorless boy I never knew than Calvin Coolidge when he came to Amherst," a classmate recalled in the years of Coolidge's fame. "He was a perfect enigma to us all." J. Calvin wrote to his father that "I don't seem to get acquainted very fast."

Amherst was a fraternity college, and most of the freshmen were "rushed" almost on arrival. At Black River Academy J. Calvin had written his father that "the societies are a great factor at Amherst and of course I want to join one if I can. It means something to get into a good society." But no eager sophomores of the nine fraternities knocked on his door. He remained among the nonfraternal rejects, in the unkindly Greek-derived phrase an "Ouden," a nothing. Not until his senior year, when a classmate who had belonged to Phi Gamma Delta at another college started to form an Amherst chapter, was he asked if he would care to join. He replied simply, "Yes."

In his four Amherst years he took no part in athletics or social life, nor did he try out for the undergraduate paper, though he did write an Indian-legend story for the literary journal. He continued to suffer from homesickness, and inwardly he still mourned for his dead sister. "We must think of Abbie as we would of a happy day," he wrote his father, "counting it a pleasure to have had it and not a sorrow because it could not last forever." Amherst's most famous professor, the religious moralist in the guise of a philosopher, Charles Garman, imbued the young Coolidge with a rigid ethic that he would carry with him for the rest of his life.

By his senior year J. Calvin had achieved a certain modest reputation as a debater. He became a zealous brother in his new fraternity. An average student, he finally managed to graduate cum laude. In his last months he blossomed out. A modest blossoming it was, but in his dry laconic Yankee way he had managed to impress his fellow students as a wit of sorts, for he was elected Grove Orator, the senior chosen to give the humorous oration on class day. Delivered in his deadpan Yankee voice, it produced applause, cheers and raillery. Read long afterward in cold print it is the humorous equal of most such orations. During those last months Coolidge, in his secretive way, had submitted a manuscript in the contest for a silver medal offered by the National Society of Sons of the American Revolution for the best essay on "The Principles Fought for in the War of the American Revolution." His essay won the prize, and after his graduation it won a gold medal — worth $150 — in a national competition with the silver medal essays of forty other colleges. Six months before graduation he had written his father:

> I have not decided what I shall do next year, shall probably go into the store or go to a law school at Boston or New York. That is about as far as I can get, and think you will have to decide which I shall do.*

* *Your Son, Calvin Coolidge,* p. 68. f.n.

On receiving his diploma he recorded that he intended to study law, although where or how he was still uncertain. Years later when he had become president, one of his classmates, recalling the diffident senior he had known, wrote:

> I was not one of those who expected Coolidge to have any spectacular career. I did not think he would become famous. The last place in the world I should have expected him to succeed was politics. He lacked small talk, and he was never known, I suspect, to slap a man on the back. He rarely laughed. He was anything but a mixer. The few who got in personal contact with him had to go the whole way.*

The summer following his graduation Coolidge spent on his father's farm, determined on a law career but still undecided as to how to go about it. Three more years at one of the urban law schools like Harvard or Columbia seemed far too costly to both father and son. Coolidge decided to fall back on the early-republic tradition of Clay and Webster and Lincoln, of the young man starting out on his own in a fusty law office off the courthouse square reading Blackstone and Coke. In September, 1895, he was again in Amherst, and a classmate took him to the office of Hammond & Field, the best-known law firm in Northampton seven miles away. John Hammond and his junior partner Judge Henry Field were both Amherst graduates, and Hammond, who had gone back to Amherst for his fortieth reunion that June, had listened to Coolidge's Grove oration with much amusement. Coolidge, given a florid introduction to Field by his friend, stood there mutely, saying only two words at the end of the interview: "Good morning!" Field offered him a tentative opening, a desk in the office where he could read as much as he wanted and learn what he could, but the judge added that he himself would have little time to devote to a student. The *Daily Hampshire Gazette* for September 17, 1895, noted that

> J. Calvin Coolidge of Plymouth, Vt. and a graduate of Amherst, class, '95, is to take a position in the law office of Hammond and Field.

So the new clerk, whose sandy hair was already beginning to recede, arrived at his desk or rather table in the outer office. He gave the appearance neither of great energy nor of idleness. Judge Field did not think he worked too hard; but then, he was

* *Calvin Coolidge: The Man from Vermont*, p. 71.

being paid nothing. Sometimes when the judge came out of his private office he would find his clerk turned round in the swivel chair staring out the window. The newcomer said little, but he attended every session of the county court, and he observed. "I guess we've added the Sphinx to our staff," the judge told his partner.

The half-rural, half industrial city in which Coolidge now made his unspectacular appearance had a population of about 15,000, a majority of the inhabitants Yankees, with a solid Democratic bloc of Irish and French-Canadian mill workers. Like all such small industrial cities it had its self-conscious elite of bankers, lawyers, and mill and property owners. Usually its mayor was a Democrat. Northampton's most unusual institution was Smith College for young women, then just completing its second decade. With industry tempered by adaptability, plus a prudent marriage, a clerk from a firm like Hammond & Field might hope to rise into the elite by his midforties.

On first coming to Northampton, Coolidge lived briefly in a lodging house, then rented a furnished room on Round Hill from Rob Weir, steward of the city's Clarke Institute for the Blind. For twenty months he sat in the outer office reading Kent's *Commentaries* and student textbooks in between helping to prepare writs, deeds and wills. At Christmastime Judge Field was surprised to learn from the columns of the *Springfield Republican* that his outer-office sphinx had won the gold medal of the Sons of the Revolution. When he asked his clerk why he had not mentioned it, Coolidge explained: "Didn't know you'd be interested."

No one would be aware that Field & Hammond's industrious apprentice suffered from occasional attacks of homesickness for his Vermont hill country. To those who noticed his inconspicuous figure he seemed a "queer duck," an "odd stick." One of the few who knew him then described him as "splendidly null, apparently deficient in red blood corpuscles, with a peaked, wire-drawn expression. . . . As he walked there was no motion of the body above the waist. The arms hung immobile." Sometimes he would lunch at Rahar's Inn, a three-story brick building on a side street favored by law clerks and young men starting out in the world, but otherwise he eschewed company, avoided entertainments, and showed no interest in sports or hobbies. The thirty dollars his father sent him each month, he managed to live on. "Not much was left," he wrote forty years later, "for any unnecessary pleasantries of life." And pleasantries were unnecessary. Untroubled by restlessness, he seemed for the most part just content to "sit around." In the long isolating evenings he read the speeches of Lord Erskine, of Webster, of Choate, so different from his own monosyllabic manner. He read Macaulay's essays and Carlyle's, and perused the historian of "manifest destiny," John Fiske. In his autobiography he wrote that he "was soon conversant with contracts, torts, evidence, and real property, with some knowledge of Massachusetts pleadings." The claim seems true enough, for in June, 1897, he appeared before a county committee consisting of Hammond and two local judges, and after Judge Field had presented the motion for his admission to the bar and the committee had asked him a few questions, he was admitted to practice in the Massachusetts courts.

For a time he continued to arrive at his outer office table at Hammond & Field's. Then one morning, without explanation, he and his books were gone. He had not gone far. With a few hundred dollars inherited from his grandfather he bought some law books and furniture, and on February 1, 1898, he opened his own law office of two small rooms on the second floor of the new Masonic Building. "I was alone," he recalled. "Of course I had acquaintances that I might call friends, but I had no influential supporters who were pushing me along, sending me business." His first year he made $500, enough to make himself independent of his father. His office cost him $200 yearly. He spent $150 for board, $120 for his room, $50 for clothes, $50 for such frivolous items as cigars, and an occasional beer or dinner at Rahar's. The $95 deficit he was able to make up from his earlier savings. But the next year he earned $1,400, part of it as counsel for a local savings bank. His expenses remained the same. Yet, like many a young lawyer with time on his hands, his mind wandered to politics. The political scene had long been his quiet preoccupation, one of the few topics that could bring him out of his shell. His Republican allegiance to the party of business, of respectability and sound money was as inherent a part of him as his Yankee blood. So it was only natural that he should do his bit in 1896 against William Jennings Bryan and his free-silver heresy.

Not long after Coolidge had taken his place in Hammond & Field's outer office, Judge Field was nominated and elected mayor of Northampton, while his partner was chosen district attorney. Their apprentice handed out cards and ballots and took a minor part in the campaign. In the summer of 1896, the *Northampton Daily Hampshire Gazette* published an article Coolidge had written attacking Bryan and free silver. Shortly after being admitted to the bar, he was one of five men chosen from his ward to serve on Northampton's thirty-five-man Republican City Committee, responsible for selecting candidates for city office. No one was too impressed by the prissy young lawyer who somehow seemed never to have been young. Yet there were two qualities Calvin Coolidge possessed that gave him a headstart in politics. He was consistently lucky, and he had the common touch. Just in picking his lodgings, he was lucky, for Weir's house was in Ward Two, the upper-class ward of the city and the ideal one for a young Republican politician to start off. Living in a Democratic ward, he would not have been able to make that modest start. Beyond his luck, for all his inbred Yankee reserve, he had a knack of getting along with ordinary people, with those classified sociologically as upper-lowers and lower-middles. With the Hammonds and the Fields he would never feel at social ease, but with the local cobbler, the deliveryman, the grocer, the news vender, the druggist, even the tavern keeper, Coolidge sensed a sub-rational tie that he had felt with the rustics of Plymouth Notch. Among such people he could talk easily in his laconic way. They in turn warmed to his cold personality, finding in him none of the politician's backslapping condescension. He was in some basic earth-bound sense one of them, and to him they would give their support and their loyalty. None of this was apparent in the pinch-faced young lawyer who, motionless from the waist up, minced along the street each morning under the plumed elms from Round Hill to the Masonic Building.

In October, 1898, he represented his ward as a delegate to the Republican county convention, and was himself nominated Ward Two's city councilman. Two months later he was elected as one of Ward Two's three council members, a post that paid nothing but that could be a first rung in the ladder of a political career. The Republican party in Massachusetts, however, resembled an escalator more than a ladder. As the astute local commentator Mark Hennessey noted in 1935, the Commonwealth was for years "steadfastly Republican nationally. . . . Occasionally she elected Democratic Governors, usually on issues which divided the ranks of the Republicans." There were Republican bosses, but none in the sense of a Platt or a Penrose. Venality was more decently masked than among the Massachusetts Democrats. Republicans were more the party of perquisites and protection than graft. The legislature was not bribed; rather it was selected and coaxed. If a young Republican politician followed the rules, he could be counted on to ride the escalator as far as his talents and his corporate standing — which often amounted to the same thing — could take him. From a councilman or mayor of a small city, it was only a step to the Beacon Hill chamber of the House of Representatives with its codfish totem; a step more to the Senate. For those more politically qualified there was the lieutenant governorship. It was an unwritten Republican law that after three annual terms a Massachusetts governor should make way for his lieutenant governor. Retired to the fastness of State Street, or to some sinecure in the banking or insurance world, the ex-governor would still be known as "Governor" to the end of his days.

After the death of an Irish-American Democratic fellow councilman, Coolidge introduced a resolution of respect. He was probably quite sincere; he was certainly astute. Northampton's Irish and Democrats took friendly note of the gesture. The young lawyer was on the escalator. A year later he had in his mousy way progressed sufficiently to persuade the twenty-one councilmen and aldermen to elect him city solicitor, a none-too-arduous post that paid $600 a year. He was reelected the following year, but the third year a more ebullient Democrat defeated him. Republicans, however, looked after their own in Massachusetts, and Coolidge was appointed to fill the term of the deceased clerk of courts for Hampshire County. It gave him the respectable sum of $2,300 a year but barred him from private practice. Rather than be limited to a dead-end position, he declined to run for election to the post that autumn. In the presidential election year of 1904, Coolidge was chosen chairman of the Republican City Committee among whose members he had sat seven years earlier.

He was thirty-two years old, modestly successful, with the promise of further success, his feet planted on the lower level of the escalator. And now, rather oddly and for the first time, a young woman entered his life. She, Grace Goodhue, a teacher in the Clarke School, lived in a teacher's residence a few doors below him. One autumn morning in 1904 while she was watering the flowers in the yard she happened to glance up at the Weir house and saw Coolidge, in long underwear and with his hat on, standing in front of a mirror shaving. She laughed, and then turned away, but the figure in the long underwear had heard her laughter. Some days later Rob Weir introduced them, and Coolidge explained that he wore a hat when shaving because he had a lock of hair that kept getting in the way. They seemed unlikely prospects, the gracious young woman and the graceless man. All they apparently had in common was a Vermont heritage, for she was a Burlington girl, a Phi Beta Kappa graduate of the University of Vermont. She was vivacious, witty, kind, with a sparkling presence that made up for the fact that she was no great beauty. People liked her instinctively. In her quiet way she was attractive — far too good for Calvin Coolidge, Northamptoners who knew them both would say. Yet somehow after that unpropitious first encounter they began to appear together, took trolley and buggy rides, on weekends attended picnics and church socials, which he hated but went to for her sake. He even tried unsuccessfully to skate and to dance. Finally he made up his Yankee mind. "I am going to be married to you," he told her one day. They were married on October 4, 1905. It was a rainy day. "I don't mind, if I get the girl," Calvin remarked on observing the weather. Such pithy remarks, usually in words of one syllable, would later be collected and give him a certain fugitive reputation as a wit.

The couple went to Montreal for a two-week honeymoon. But after a week Calvin had had enough. "Grace, gotta be getting back home," he told his bride. "Running for school committee, gotta get back and make a speech." The election took place two months after Coolidge's marriage. There were two other candidates, one a Republican and one a Democrat. With the Republicans splitting their ticket, the Democratic candidate nosed out Coolidge, with 934 votes to the latter's 840. It was Coolidge's last electoral defeat. One neighbor admitted afterward that he had not voted for him, since he felt that a school committeeman should have a child in the public schools. "Might give me time!" was Coolidge's monosyllabic reply.

Following their marriage, the Coolidges lived for several weeks in the Norwood Hotel until it closed down. Its closing gave them a chance to buy most of their linen and tableware at bargain prices. For years the Coolidge knives, forks and spoons would bear the "Norwood Hotel" stamp. While the couple were still staying at the Norwood, Coolidge returned from his office one afternoon with an old russet-colored bag containing fifty-two pairs of socks, all with holes in them. "Is that why you married me," his wife asked him, "to get your socks darned?" "No," he replied solemnly, "but I find it mighty handy."

They spent the winter and spring in the home of an absent Smith professor, then in the summer rented half a duplex house at 21 Massasoit Street for which they paid $27 a month. This would remain their permanent home even through Coolidge's presidential years. The side street was quiet, shaded by fast-growing Norway maples. The house was commonplace, respectable, of the type occupied by anonymous small-middle-class Americans across the country. Downstairs a front hall opened into a bay-windowed parlor which in turn opened into a dining room. Beyond was the kitchen. Upstairs were three bedrooms and a bath. Coolidge himself had tended to the furnishings. The parlor had mission furniture, an Axminster carpet, a framed sepia reproduction of Sir Galahad, a photograph of Plymouth Notch. Conspicuous over the white-painted mantel was the embroidered quotation that might have served as Coolidge's motto:

> A wise old owl sat in an oak,
> The more he saw, the less he spoke;
> The less he spoke, the more he heard,
> Why can't we be like that old bird?*

The Coolidges had not been living there long before their first son was born.

Meanwhile politics had not forgotten the sphinx of Ward Two, nor had he forgotten politics. "An enigmatic little devil," Judge Field observed, and Northampton's inner Republican circle agreed. But the Republican managers had also begun to sense in Coolidge the indefinable quality of a vote-getter, that would make him a plausible candidate in 1907 to beat the local Democratic incumbent for his seat in the Massachusetts House of Representatives. Coolidge was nominated by the Republicans without opposition. The escalator moved up a notch.

In his mousy way Coolidge campaigned hard, visiting every voter in the district, paying particular heed to the Irish Democrats, ringing every doorbell and quacking at each opened door: "I want your vote. I need it. I shall appreciate it." On election

* The original version from which this was adapted appeared in *Punch* in 1875:

> Here was an old owl liv'd in an oak
> The more he heard, the less he spoke;
> The less he spoke, the more he heard
> O, if men were all like that wise bird.

day the votes came to him, enough Democratic votes thrown in to give him a surprising victory over his popular opponent.

As one of the four representatives of Hampshire county, Coolidge received $750 a year plus travel expenses. It was not a position very eagerly sought after, except by those who hoped to make a career of politics. These regarded it as an apprenticeship on the escalator. For Coolidge, Boston with its State House was his first experience of a metropolis. As he left for the first session of the legislature, Judge Field went with him to introduce him to the members of the Republican State Committee. In Coolidge's pocket was a letter of introduction to the Speaker of the House of Representatives, John Cole, which read:

> This will introduce to you the new member-elect from my town, Calvin Coolidge. Like the singed cat, he is better than he looks. . . .*

The new representative made no great impression on the party leaders to whom he was introduced. "What in hell can a fellow like that do down here?" one of them remarked. Another told Judge Field: "I shook hands with your friend and he gave me a cold!" Coolidge stayed at the Adams House where many of the out-of-town legislators stopped, in a small dollar-a-day back bedroom. Friday afternoons he returned on the Boston & Maine to Northampton. Beyond his fellow legislators he knew almost no one. In the evenings in his room under the sickly gas jet he read the *Evening Transcript* and sometimes the *Manual for the General Court* or a history of the United States. But he gave more attention to legislative business than did most of the legislators, studying bills, attending drawn-out committee meetings and hearings. Seldom missing a session, he was always on hand to vote. "He was an obscure member of the House," his authorized biographer wrote; "his name rarely appeared in the Boston newspapers except on a roll call; but he soon acquired a reputation for faithfulness and reliability. . . . He did not care for the theatre or enjoy symphony concerts, and he must have had some lonesome evenings. But after all, it was what had happened at college." "David Harum," his fellow legislators called him behind his back, but they grew to accept him.

State elections were then held annually in Massachusetts, and in 1908 Coolidge barely managed to get reelected. His second term he served in faithful obscurity although he did get appointed

* *Calvin Coolidge: The Man from Vermont,* p. 96.

to several of the more important committees. Yet some of those sharp-eyed leaders who regulated the escalator were beginning to eye Calvin Coolidge. Senator Murray Crane, the paper manufacturer of Dalton, twenty-five miles west of Northampton, had early in Coolidge's legislative career become aware of his Northampton neighbor. "Find out all you can about a man named Coolidge there," he instructed a subordinate on his way to Northampton. "You will save trouble in looking him up now. He is one of the coming men in this country."

By the time Coolidge had taken his legislative seat in the gilt-domed State House, Crane was the Republican boss of Massachusetts, a businessman who had drifted into politics in the manner of a Hanna rather than of a Platt. Rich from his heritage in the century-old Crane paper mills, he represented the western Massachusetts elements of his party and much disliked Senator Henry Cabot Lodge, the supercilious and superficial spokesman of Brahmin Boston. Lodge might preen himself on his intellect and look on Crane and his kind as barbarians, but Crane by his persistence had become the real leader of his party in the commonwealth. A weedy little man, with a sad rat-tailed moustache and muddy complexion, Crane was anything but a commanding presence. "Uncle Murray," did not pretend to be a glad-hander, he could not make a speech, but he knew how to "gumshoe" behind the political curtains, and he was thoroughly acceptable to the party of entrenched property. "He was honest according to his lights and leading," William Allen White wrote, "a little more honest than the times demanded." Three times he was elected governor, emphasizing efficiency and economy more than anything else in his administration. When the 78-year-old United States Senator George Frisbie Hoar died in 1904, the then-governor appointed Crane to finish out the senate term. Two years later the legislature elected him in his own right. He also reached the inner circle of Republican national committeemen.

Crane's Boston lieutenant was William Butler, a textile manufacturer and former state senator who kept a judicious eye on the legislature. Coolidge had met and admired Butler, who in turn had called Crane's attention to the Northampton legislator. In time Coolidge came to be known as Uncle Murray's man. It had a different connotation than in Pennsylvania or New York or Ohio. For no Crane or Butler ever would or could persuade Coolidge to violate his Vermont ethical sense; and this they understood. But his thoughts on propriety and property were theirs, and they would find him sympathetic. Republicans in Massachusetts, with certain exceptions like Charlie Innes, the leader of Back Bay Boston's lone Republican ward, were not open to bribery or the more obvious forms of graft. A Democratic vote in the Massachusetts legislature could be bought for $50. Republican votes could not be bought, but they could be persuaded.

The Republican escalator operated on the tacit understanding that an elected official, except in unusual circumstances, would serve two terms and then advance or retire — with the exception of the governor and lieutenant governor, who were usually granted a third term. After two terms Coolidge paid his silent adieu to the Great and General Court of Massachusetts. For almost two years he remained a private citizen, his law practice, like his family, growing modestly; for he was counsel for a bank and for the Springfield Brewery, and he was also the father of a second boy. Each morning the wise old owl walked from Massasoit Street to the Masonic building to sit most of the day behind his oak desk. Then in 1909 the Democratic mayor of Northampton announced that he was retiring at the end of the year. No Republican hopeful showing any eagerness to bell the Democratic cat, the Republican City Committee unanimously picked Coolidge as its candidate. Fortunately his opponent had tactlessly announced his "dryness" from the platform of the local Congregational church to the anger of those Irish and French Canadian wards that Coolidge had gone to great pains to cultivate. Coolidge was elected by a scanty 187-vote majority. Fifteen years after his arrival, the Yankee from Vermont had become mayor of his city.

Financially the office was scarcely rewarding, the mayor receiving $800 a year, which Coolidge refused to allow increased. But the election had again demonstrated his vote-getting ability. As he wrote his father:

> At least 400 democrats voted for me. Their leaders can't see why they did it. I know why. They knew I had done things for them, bless their honest Irish hearts.*

The Republican escalator, more by Coolidge luck than by design this time, had carried him a notch further. Small though his salary might be, he was a prominent citizen, a voice in his party. When he took his oath of office on January 3, 1910, he began a

* *Your Son, Calvin Coolidge,* p. 111.

period of public office-holding that would end only with his leaving the White House nineteen years later. His record as mayor was a respectable one. He reduced the tax rate by 50¢, raised teachers' salaries slightly, increased efficiency in the police and fire departments, and enforced the licensing laws. He was reelected against the same opponent, this time by a plurality of 256 votes. Coolidge's second term opened larger vistas. There was talk of him as a candidate for state senator from the Berkshire-Hampden-Hampshire district, a seat then occupied by Senate President Allen Treadway who was considering running for Congress. The foolhardy notion of opposing the senate president never crossed Coolidge's mind. "I want to go to the senate sometime," he told Treadway, "but I don't care when. When you are all through, let me know."

Treadway's decision to run for Congress was the signal Coolidge had been waiting for. He now announced that he was a candidate for Treadway's vacant senate seat, and in September, 1911, he received the endorsement of the three Republican county organizations of his district. Progressive restiveness had divided Republican Massachusetts enough for a Democratic governor, Eugene Foss — a wealthy Republican turncoat — to have been elected the year before. All the signs pointed to his reelection in the 1911 winter of Republican discontent. But Coolidge's western outpost was a safe Republican bailiwick and his nomination was the equivalent of election.

According to a fellow Republican legislator's judgment Coolidge "looked upon himself as a cog in the government, to do his part, to follow the leaders." While never in opposition to his party's leadership, he was always willing to put himself out for others in small ways, and he managed to win the goodwill of a number of his Democratic colleagues. Behind his mask of modesty he took great pride in his title of "Senator." Labor leaders found him considerate and cooperative. His most noteworthy act in his first term was to head a special committee that settled the 1912 Lawrence textile strike after months of violence Though at times showing indications of being mildly progressive, he remained faithful to Taft and the regulars in the 1912 Republican split. Massachusetts, while going for Wilson that year, gave more votes to Taft than it did to Roosevelt. Coolidge, faced with a Bull Moose opponent as well as a Democrat for his senate seat, nevertheless managed to win handily.

"I thought a couple of terms in the Massachusetts Senate would be helpful to me," Coolidge wrote in his *Autobiography*. He could scarcely consider himself a success at this middle point of his life. He was forty-one, and old for his age. His law practice, when he could find time for it, consisted mostly of petty cases. No corporation heads knocked on the door of his Masonic Building office in the six months that he hibernated there. Politics had come to seem more attractive to him than the law, but his second term would bring him as far as the escalator could carry him. Or so it seemed. Yet fate, or luck, or whatever one might call it, had higher things in store for the sandy-haired Vermonter on his passive escalator ride. He had by this time become a knowledgeable legislator, a reliable if unspectacular party man, and by this time his "singed cat" aspect had become familiar in the corridors of the State House.

Destiny now touched Calvin Coolidge, oddly and unspectacularly, by bringing him into indirect contact with Frank Waterman Stearns. A bill pending in the Massachusetts House would have extended the Amherst town sewerage system. The treasurer of the college wanted the bill amended so that the college system could be connected to that of the town — with great saving to the college. He wrote to Stearns and asked him as an Amherst trustee to see if Coolidge could help in the matter. Yet so inconspicuous had Coolidge remained outside of his small political pond that Stearns, for all his obsessive attachment to Amherst, had never heard of his fellow alumnus. Stearns sent an Amherst classmate, the Boston lawyer Arthur Wellman, to see Coolidge at his State House office where the senator, wary of visitors, kept the only chair, except for his desk chair, locked in the cupboard. Coolidge was cold, nasal, monosyllabic. To Wellman's question as to whether he would modify the Amherst sewerage bill, he quacked: "No, I won't!"

Stearns, after taking in Coolidge's response, was — as he later wrote —"mad as a wet hen." The bill hung fire until the next session. When the following year Wellman appeared at Coolidge's chairless office with the same request, he received the same reply: "No, I won't." Then, after a painful silence, Coolidge added with a dry cackle: "Your bill was signed by the governor about a week ago." Coolidge had not forgotten his alma mater. In his silent way he had arranged everything. "Twa'n't any use to introduce it last session," he explained to Wellman. "Too near the end!"

The voluble Stearns was awed by such taciturn activity, and later at a dinner at the Algonquin Club took pains to meet Coolidge who merely extended a cold limp hand and muttered "How-di-do." Then at the end of the evening as he was leaving he edged up to Stearns to quack at him: "Ever anything you want up on the Hill, come up and see me."

Normally the end of Coolidge's second term would have marked the end of his political career. Retired to Northampton he would continue to be addressed by the courtesy title of "Senator" and his mail would be addressed to the Hon. Calvin Coolidge. That was all. But in 1913 the president of the state senate, Levi Greenwood, decided that he would run for lieutenant governor. There were no outstanding replacements for the senate presidency, and Coolidge — if he could surmount the third-term barrier — was as outstanding as any. He talked with Uncle Murray and the western Republican leaders, and they agreed to offer no opposition to his third term. The Republican party of Massachusetts was still riven by the Bull Moose split of the year before, and as the summer wore on Greenwood came to the conclusion that it would be more prudent to resume his old seat in the senate than to venture further up the escalator. Coolidge's hopes appeared stillborn.

Greenwood was right about his further chances, for the whole Republican state ticket went down to defeat that year as the Irish Democrat David Ignatius Walsh was elected governor, and with him a complete Democratic administration. Only the legislature remained narrowly Republican. What Greenwood had not counted on, however, was the strength of the opposition within his own senatorial district. An outspoken opponent of votes for women, he found himself defeated by enraged suffragists who campaigned against him with venomous efficiency. Greenwood's defeat was an example of what would later be termed "Coolidge luck." For Uncle Murray and his cohorts readily determined that the regular Coolidge would be the next president of a Massachusetts senate where the entrenched Republicans still outnumbered the Democrats 21 to 17. Coolidge himself pulled every wire he could, and by this time he knew where the wires were hidden. The Boston *Sunday Globe* observed that

> the Presidency of the Senate is settled. . . . . Coolidge came to town last Wednesday and showed his fellow Republicans that while some of them were talking through their hats, he could lay down

16 out of the 22 Republican votes in the upper branch of the legislature, and the other candidates and near candidates tumbled all over themselves to get out of the way of the steam-roller.

Coolidge will make a good presiding officer. He doesn't need to consult a specialist when anything bobs up that requires nerve. He can state a humorous legislative proposition without smiling. As to the political advisability of selecting Coolidge, that's a question on which there is a difference of opinion among Republicans.

With the governor and the lieutenant governor and the attorney general all Democrats, Senate President Coolidge became the highest ranking member of his party within the Commonwealth. At the next election he was reelected to the senate by an almost two to one margin over his opponent, showing himself, as the *Daily Hampshire Gazette* observed, "the best vote-getter in the state, and he will be heard from later." That same year, 1914, Governor Walsh defeated the Republican candidate, Samuel McCall, by a small margin, although the Republicans carried the remainder of the state ticket, even electing the Republican speaker of the house of representatives, Grafton Cushing, lieutenant governor. Cushing, a suave and wealthy Harvard-educated Bostonian, would be next in line for governor, but just behind him on the escalator stood the rufous little man from Vermont. That escalator, once its equilibrium had been reestablished, might be expected to carry Coolidge to the lieutenant governorship and then to the governor's chair, and finally at the end of the line to a gilt-edged berth in a bank or insurance company. What he lacked primarily was a sponsor, and that sponsor, in the person of Stearns, was not long in appearing.

To Stearns it had long been a source of regret that most Republican leaders in Massachusetts were Harvard men who acted as if no other college existed. Equally good if not better men, he was convinced, came from his beloved college in the Berkshires. He was much impressed by Coolidge's inaugural senate address with its pithy almost aphoristic style so at variance with his own effusive volubility. Coolidge had said:

> Do the day's work. If it be to protect the rights of the weak, whoever objects, do it. If it be to help a powerful corporation better to serve the people, do that. Expect to be called a standpatter, but don't be a standpatter. Expect to be called a demagogue, but don't be a demagogue. . . . Don't hesitate to be as reactionary as the multiplication table. Don't expect to build up the weak by pulling down the strong. . . .*

* *Have Faith in Massachusetts,* pp. 7–8.

Not long afterward Stearns stopped in at the senate chamber during a busy session with Coolidge presiding. As soon as Coolidge noticed Stearns, he motioned to him to come and sit beside him on the rostrum. Stearns later wrote an account of the incident:

> It was evidently a day on which they were rushing through bills for final action, and the whole business was droning along. Behind the chair of the President of the Senate was a corridor, separated from the rostrum by portières. While I sat there, three different Senators, one after another, stuck their heads through the opening in the portières, saying, "Mr. President, I think we ought to do so-and-so." In each case he answered, "No," and the Senator simply said, "All right, just as you say." This entire absence of effort to impress me was different from the action of any politician that I had ever met, and it finally interested me so much that I began to look him up.*

For Stearns, his encounter with Coolidge was in the nature of a revelation. Here at last was the Amherst man he had been looking for, the man who would put the college on the political map. He had a hundred reprints made of Coolidge's inaugural address and distributed them to Republicans of importance across the Commonwealth. Then he arranged for a testimonial dinner. As he explained to Coolidge:

> A number of your Amherst College friends have watched with interest the work you are doing for the Commonwealth, and will be pleased if you will accept the invitation to be present at a dinner in your honor, which seems the best way they can make you know their interest and appreciation.
>
> Some of us feel that the duty of good citizens is not wholly met by using care in the selection of proper candidates for the Legislature and by voting for them at election time. We have the feeling that perhaps it would be acceptable to our Senators and Representatives if they could be in real touch with citizens in various walks of life, — teachers, clergymen, doctors, lawyers, business men, — and that if such acquaintance were more common, it would work to the advantage of the state.
>
> Perhaps at this dinner you will say something that will help us, if we are right in this idea, to make it effective. We suggest as a place for the dinner the Algonquin Club, and for time, May 12th at 7 o'clock.†

Sixty-seven were present at the banquet, most of them Amherst

* *Calvin Coolidge: The Man from Vermont*, p. 130.
† Ibid.

graduates. An undercurrent of talk followed the banquet, concerning Coolidge as the next Republican candidate for lieutenant governor. "A good many people have spoken to me about it," Coolidge wrote his stepmother. "I have no plans except to try to do what is given me to do." The view from the upper reaches of the Republican escalator was still hazy after the Progressive debacle. For a time Coolidge even considered a prominent public appointment. When a vacancy occurred on the Public Utilities Commission, he allowed friends to sound out Governor Walsh. For the Democratic governor there would be the party advantage of shunting aside a proven vote-getter; for the Republican senator there would be the personal advantage of a well-paying sinecure with a pension at the end of the road. If Coolidge's friends had not arrived at the executive chamber fifteen minutes *after* Walsh had made the appointment, Coolidge might have ended as obscurely as his long-forgotten predecessor and successor as senate presidents.

Whether or not this rebuff helped Coolidge make up his political mind is not known. But in 1915 the Coolidge luck still held. The year looked propitious for the Republicans. Progressives and the Old Guard were burying their differences, and after a five-year interlude it seemed that Massachusetts might again elect a Republican governor. McCall saw himself as his party's logical choice. Not so Lieutenant Governor Cushing, who felt he had a better claim than last year's defeated candidate. The ensuing McCall-Cushing contest for the Republican nomination left the lieutenant governorship open. Cautious Cal waited. He knew that if he announced his candidacy while the legislature was still in session, he would lose control of the senate as the other senators began to maneuver for his place. But as soon as the legislature had adjourned, he handed Stearns a note to give to the newspapers. It read "I am a candidate for Lieutenant Governor, Calvin Coolidge."

The effect on Stearns was electric. At last, in his sixtieth year, he had discovered his ultimate purpose in life, to further the larger career of the reticent Yankee who, he rapidly convinced himself, was another Lincoln and "greatest American." For a first step, Stearns formed a committee to take charge of the Coolidge campaign. As he explained in a long letter to Coolidge just after the latter's announcement:

I can shout pretty loud and pretty persistently when I am deeply interested. I certainly am this time. All I want to do is the best for you. . . . You will know me better as time goes on. One of my ways of making myself effective where I have a strong admiration and belief in a person, especially a young person, is to put them in the fore-front and back them up in every conceivable way that I know how. . . . Now here is a chance for you to have a laugh if you want to. You will think that for an old codger like me, I am getting sentimental. Never mind, a little sentiment does not hurt once in a while. . . . This is personal and it is also because I believe that it is for the great good of the State, and later of the country, that it should be so. If later it shall so develop that my relations to you are confidential and more than ordinarily friendly, I shall feel that I have received still another degree, which I shall value very greatly.*

Stearns proceeded to shout loud. He drafted the advertising department of R. H. Stearns in the Coolidge cause. He dug deep into his own pocket and coaxed more money from the pockets of other men of wealth. By mid-summer the campaign was rolling, and already he felt in his bones that this was only the beginning, that with his help and by God's grace (as interpreted by Garman), Calvin Coolidge would end up in the White House. In July he wrote to an Amherst professor:

Just now, in addition to what little an old man can do for the dry goods business, I am spending all my spare time working for Calvin Coolidge. You know I never go half way on anything and I have become convinced that the salvation of the Commonwealth and the country demands that Calvin Coolidge should be kept in active public life and as near the top as possible. Just for the minute it does not seem best to push him for anything higher than Lieutenant-Governor of Massachusetts, but later, of course, he must be Governor and still later President. Just think what a time we will have at Commencement when the President of the United States, a graduate of your class, '95, comes back to Commencement.†

Of course Sterans would have got nowhere without the acquiescence of Crane, but Uncle Murray was more than willing to tool up his well-oiled machine for the faithful Coolidge. Coolidge's opponent for the nomination was Guy Ham, a florid orator of the McKinley-baroque school that had begun to go out of fashion. Coolidge was no orator, but as Crane said, "that Yankee twang

* Ibid.
† Ibid.

will be worth a hundred thousand votes." Ham was orotund but Coolidge was folksy. In the primaries McCall defeated Cushing by 6,000 votes, while Coolidge led Ham by 25,000.

McCall and Coolidge formed a curious team, the urbane easy orator, slightly progressive, who fancied himself as "the scholar in politics" and the flinty clipped conservative. It was said that McCall could fill any hall and Coolidge could empty it. Yet in that year of Republican resurgence, McCall managed to defeat Walsh by a mere 6,313 votes while Coolidge topped the ticket with a majority of over 50,000.

Immediately after the election Coolidge wrote Stearns:

> In so far as my own fortunes could be shaped by anyone but myself, you are responsible for my nomination and election, above all my nomination. It was your endorsement that made my candidacy accepted at its face value. If my public services are hereafter of any value, the credit should be shared with you.*

Stearns replied:

> As I look at it, your campaigns have only had an auspicious opening. They are in their early stages as yet. As long as I have health and strength, you can count on me. . . . I am almost staggered by the realization that every step now must be taken with great care, because the opportunity is wonderful and the need almost beyond words.†

"Under the custom of promotion in Massachusetts," Coolidge wrote in his *Autobiography*, "a man who did not expect to advance would scarcely be willing to be lieutenant governor." But Lieutenant Governor Coolidge had two more terms to wait before he would reach the escalator platform. In the public eye he had become a character, a Vermont nephew of Uncle Sam, and somehow he inspired trust. When he spoke he quacked, but he used maxims that the press always found quotable. Continuing the habit of his apprentice days at Hammond & Field, he would sit for long periods at his desk, silent, remote, staring out the window. Gamaliel Bradford, observing the new lieutenant governor, found no sense of quick and eager response in the man. Coolidge's was "a pinched, drawn face, not hard but anxious, the face of a man perpetually faced with problems too big for him. The face had New England written all over it."

* Ibid.
† Ibid.

From this time on Stearns fussed over Coolidge like a mother hen, publicized him, entertained him at his summer home in Swampscott and at the suite he kept in Boston's Hotel Touraine, paid his political bills and would have contributed to his personal ones if the lieutenant governor had been willing — which he was not, even though his official salary was a mere $2,000. He took Coolidge for his first visit to Washington and there introduced him to Senator Lodge, who was condescendingly cordial, though in later years he would remark that he had known Calvin Coolidge only as long as it was necessary to know him.

As the Republican National Convention of 1916 neared, Coolidge was careful to disassociate himself from any candidate. Stearns went to Chicago as an alternate delegate-at-large with nothing to do but to wander through the sweaty June days creating sentiment for Calvin Coolidge. To anyone who listened — and there were not many — he would announce that Coolidge and only Coolidge ought to be the next president of the United States. He became one of the minor comic figures of the convention, fluttering through the hotel lobbies and headquarters like a nervous floorwalker, an unlikely politician with a plump anxious face, guileless eyes behind rimless bifocals, a melancholy drooping white moustache, and an expansive watchchain linked across his little pot belly. To Uncle Murray it was laughable to hear Lord Lingerie — as they called him behind his back — suggesting that Calvin Coolidge should be the next president. To Senator Lodge it was grimly laughable. "Calvin Coolidge!" he remarked when somebody relayed the news to him. "My God!" Unabashed by laughs and rebuffs, Stearns persisted. Mr. Coolidge — he and Stearns would always remain "mister" to each other — would at least become known, would be groomed and ready for 1920 or 1924 or whenever the magic inevitable date might be that would summon him.

Governor McCall, as an older man, let his lieutenant represent him at most of the Commonwealth's public functions, and Coolidge's prim Yankee features grew familiar from the Berkshires to Cape Cod. The wise old owl became almost voluble from the number of speeches he had to make. He wrote them all himself, and they were typically Coolidge — sparse, Anglo-Saxon-derived, with aphorisms that verged on clichés and that were the pattern of his thought. For reasons unfathomable to more sophisticated men like Crane and Field, he remained consistently popular with the electorate, leading his ticket in every election. Nominated without opposition for their second term, McCall and Coolidge were reelected easily, McCall with a plurality of 46,240 votes to Coolidge's 84,930. In the first war-election, in 1917, McCall and Coolidge were again nominated, Coolidge without opposition. McCall's majority was this time 91,413, Coolidge's 101,956, and Cautious Cal had even come within 2,500 votes of carrying Irish-Democratic Boston. He was now two-thirds of the way through his three-year apprenticeship, and the upper escalator platform lay just beyond. With sober realism he estimated his chances. As he wrote his stepmother just before the 1917 election that was itself a foregone conclusion:

> You do not want to feel too certain about next year or about my being Governor. It is very largely a matter of chance. It is rather an accident that I am Lieutenant-Governor. As I told you, many things may happen in a year, so you do not want to consider anything political as assured beforehand.*

With the governorship in sight for his protégé, Stearns now turned over the management of R. H. Stearns to his subordinates in order to devote his whole time to promoting the further career of Calvin Coolidge. Bearing this in mind he gave up his Newton home and moved to a castellated brick mansion in the Back Bay. Until then he had been wary of too close association with Brahmin Boston, that inbred elite who patronized his store while at the same time patronizing him, but now he felt it essential to be nearer the State House and the city in order to assume full command of his obsessive project. Coolidge became more than a son to him, for the Vermont Yankee embodied the hopes and dreams he could not find in his own son. He arranged luncheons and dinners for Coolidge to meet the right people; he reprinted the litutenant governor's aphoristic speeches by the thousands; he distributed hundreds of Coolidge photographs framed and autographed; he wrote Coolidge dozens of long hortatory letters to which he received replies of two or three lines; he fussed about Coolidge's health and his reluctance to take vacations. And all the time he lived in the glow of his dream.

It took all the efforts of Stearns and Crane to get Coolidge

* *Your Son, Calvin Coolidge,* p. 139.

elected governor in 1918. That climactic year, with the war rushing to its conclusion, made an election seem incidental, made it seem even more so after Boston and Massachusetts were swept by the great autumn influenza epidemic. Because of the influenza the Republicans were unable to hold their regular convention. They were further handicapped by the unpopularity of United States Senator John Weeks, running for election that year against the opposition of the suffragists, labor and the wets. His opponent was the popular ex-Governor Walsh. For once Coolidge's grass-roots popularity seemed to wilt. He was elected by a mere sixteen thousand votes. Weeks was defeated.

But for the Boston Police Strike that occurred eight months after he was sworn in as governor, Coolidge would have ended up at the top of the escalator as just one more of a line of Republican governors who performed their task with reasonable conscientiousness and efficiency and who retired to plush obscurity. Who now remembers Samuel McCall, or Coolidge's successor Channing Cox or for that matter Murray Crane? Who remembered them a decade after they left office? Once again it was Coolidge luck, destiny or blind chance that made the Massachusetts governor's name a byword across the nation.

Nineteen-nineteen was a year of strikes: the steel strike; coal strikes; textile strikes; maritime strikes; actors' strikes; the Seattle general strike; even a rent-payer's strike. Not that police strikes were unknown, for there had been one in Montreal, and even in law-abiding Britain, the police of London and Liverpool had walked out.

The Boston police had their grievances, mostly concerned with the High Cost of Living, as inflation was then known. Industrial wages had doubled. Theirs had remained the same except for a belated $200 raise that brought their minimum wage to $1,100 a year, out of which they had to buy their uniforms. Beyond that was the even larger grievance of the two-platoon system that kept them on twelve-hour shifts. They were overwhelmingly Irish-Catholic, they were pugnaciously discontented, and in the mood of the time they were ready to strike for their demands.

Police Commissioner Edwin Curtis, an old-line Bostonian, had once been Boston's youngest mayor and had watched with dismay as the Irish took political control of what he considered *his* city. The Republican legislature, also observing this attritive process, had passed a law requiring the Boston police commissioner to be appointed by the governor, and Curtis returned twenty-four years later to police the city he had once governed. A martinet, enamored of discipline, he saw his policemen as an army and himself as a general entitled to prompt, cheerful and unquestioned obedience. The police owed allegiance to him and possibly to God, otherwise to no one.

Boston's mayor at that time was Andrew J. Peters, a Yankee Democrat in the attenuated tradition of the 1850s such as one occasionally still found in Massachusetts. When the Irish Democratic leaders fell out among themselves, as sometimes happened, he was elected as a reform mayor. Though wealthy enough to be personally honest, he was incapable of reforming anything, nor did he have the understanding or the impulse. Secure in his position in the *Social Register,* he preferred sailing his yacht on summer afternoons to sitting at his desk at City Hall. To the professional pols he was a joke with a Harvard accent. During his solitary term, bagmen wandered through the corridors of City Hall and even made their deals in his office anteroom. He never knew. His avocations were golfing and yachting, and he took a deep if dubious interest in little girls.

Through the heat-struck summer months the policemen of Boston began organizing themselves into a union which they called the Boston Social Club. Curtis at once issued an order stating that policemen could not consistently belong to a union and perform their sworn duty. Nevertheless the Boston Social Club applied to the American Federation of Labor for a charter. Curtis at once promulgated Rule 35 of his department's list of rules and regulations: "No members of the force shall join or belong to any organization, club or body outside the department."

Undeterred, the policemen refused to withdraw their application, and on August 11 their Social Club was transformed into Boston Police Union No. 16807, of the American Federation of Labor. Curtis at once charged the eight officers and leaders of the new union with insubordination and ordered them placed on trial. They in turn warned him that if he did this the police would strike. Curtis found the men guilty but postponed sentence. Then on August 29 he found eleven more leaders guilty, and again suspended-sentence — in order, he later said, to give his men a chance to withdraw from the federation. Then he announced he would pass sentence on September 4, three days after Labor Day.

From his City Hall office on School Street, Mayor Peters observed the oncoming strike with the paralyzed awareness of a rabbit observing an oncoming snake. He could neither give orders to the commissioner nor the police. The most he could do was to appoint a Citizens Committee of Thirty-four to "investigate and advise." The committee, a cold bread-pudding of old Bostonians with a few wealthy Irish and Jewish merchants to give it flavor, was headed by James Storrow of the ultraconservative brokerage house of Lee, Higginson & Company. It proceeded to investigate, meeting daily with the president and leaders of the police union, and finally advising that a compromise could be worked out if the policemen would drop their affiliation with the American Federation of Labor. Commissioner Curtis wanted no advice. He knew how to handle his police. The most he would agree to was to postpone his decision until the following Monday.

A hundred yards up Beacon Hill from City Hall, Governor Coolidge in his high-ceilinged office at the State House viewed the Boston imbroglio with detachment as he leaned back in his official chair smoking his post-prandial cigar and staring out the window. Each afternoon he napped in that chair. Years ago when he had been a student at Black River Academy, several more mischievous boys had pitched an old stove down the stairs one evening after he had gone to bed. Next day one of the masters asked him if he had not heard the noise, and he said that he had. When the master asked him why he had not done anything, he replied: "It wa'n't my stove." The looming police strike "wa'n't" his strike. If there should be one, it would be up to Curtis and to Peters.

Curtis was convinced that when the chips were finally down, the majority of the police would remain loyal to him, and he so advised Peters. The mayor in turn was convinced that whether Curtis was right or wrong there was nothing that he, Peters, could do about it. The governor was convinced that the best thing he could do was nothing. "If you saw ten troubles coming down the road, nine would run into the ditch before they reached you." Of course there was always the dark tenth chance, but the odds were computably safe against it. When the Committee of Thirty-Four, baffled by the intractable commissioner and the irresolute mayor, came to him, he sent them away, telling them merely that he would keep "carefully informed of conditions."

The committee's compromise then called for the appointment of a subcommittee of three to study and report publicly on police wages, hours and conditions. The police would not be permitted to affiliate with the American Federation of Labor, but they might have their own local organization. There would be no recognition of the right to strike. Meanwhile, there would be no disciplinary action taken against any of the union leaders. Curtis refused to listen. The men who disobeyed him must be disciplined, and that was that. Claude Fuess in his definitive biography of Coolidge admits that at that point "a single word from him [Coolidge] would probably have led to a compromise, but that word he would not utter."

That terse and threatening weekend, the governor left Boston to attend "Welcome Home" receptions to returning soldiers at Abington and then Andover. No one seemed to know where he spent Saturday night, but on Sunday morning he set out for Northampton. On Monday he kept an engagement to address the state convention of the American Federation of Labor. In an uninspired address he failed to mention the threatened police strike, but two hours before he spoke Commissioner Curtis had suspended the nineteen recalcitrant patrolmen. Coolidge arrived back in Boston late that afternoon in time for a Union Club dinner with Storrow, Peters and several members of the citizen's committee. Before the dinner Coolidge met the other two privately. They asked him to defend the compromise plan. He declined to interfere. They then begged him to call out the state guard, that combination of the over-age and the unfit that had taken the place of the national guard when the Yankee Division was called into active service in 1917. Again the governor declined. While this and various other hectic conferences were taking place, the policemen in a secret ballot voted 1134 to 2 to walk out at 5:45 P.M. Tuesday. By Tuesday morning the strike seemed all but inevitable. Curtis felt that in the event of a strike he would have enough loyal men left to protect the city and told the mayor so. Peters and Curtis met again in the governor's chamber at five o'clock. Once more the mayor begged the governor to call out the state guard. The police commissioner still maintained this would not be necessary. The governor again refused to act, but ironically pointed out to the ingenuous Peters that the mayor of Boston had the authority to call out the state guard units within the city's boundaries.

At just after five o'clock the police began to quit their stations, often to the accompaniment of cheers from the crowds that gathered round the station steps. Of the 1544-member police force, 1117 walked out that damp and chilly afternoon. A world-city was without police protection. At first, so strong is habit, there was no more than a feeling of uneasiness in Boston. The five o'clock commuters continued on their suburban ways as usual. Then groups began to congregate here and there on street corners. A few unwary passersby had their hats knocked off. Someone unbolted the spare tire from the rear of an auto parked near Tremont Street. There was nothing to stop him. Others followed his example. It was a little like Hallowe'en in the tougher parts of the city, unruly, prankish. Then about midnight the mob turned ugly. Streetcars were stoned and the passengers forced to leave, fruit stands were plundered, then store windows smashed. Soon sixty thousand dollars worth of merchandise was strewn over the streets. Belated or overcurious pedestrians found themselves held up; several women were pushed into doorways and raped. Dice games sprang up on Boston Common within view of the long windows of the Governor's Chamber, although Coolidge was long since in bed with instructions that he was not to be disturbed. After 3 A.M. the unprotected city grew calm. But no one knew what to expect on Wednesday.

Late Wednesday morning Peters made use of his newly discovered powers to call out the state guard within Boston. He also asked the governor for three thousand additional troops. Coolidge at once complied. Before the afternoon's end guardsmen were patrolling the downtown streets. The mayor then told reporters plaintively that in the crisis he had "received no cooperation from the police commissioner and no help or practical suggestions from the governor." He called on citizen volunteers, who were supplied with badge and revolver and the authority of policemen. Harvard's President Lowell freed his students from classes so that they could play at cops and robbers. Finally Peters, with the authority he claimed he had found under an old statute, dismissed Curtis.

That Wednesday an uneasy quiet lay over the city, but from

all over New England professional criminals were converging on Boston. Tuesday night had been a rogues' carnival. Wednesday turned grimmer. As it grew dark the mob gathered in and around Scollay Square — Boston's tenderloin — while striking policemen moved about encouraging the violence that was not long in coming. A crowd of young toughs in South Boston taunted and abused a company of guardsmen, showering them with bricks, stones and bottles until the panicky soldiers opened fire, killing three and wounding ten others. In a round-up of crap shooters on Boston Common, guardsmen killed a sailor. Eight persons died before the strike ended.

By Thursday morning order had generally been restored in the city, although the superintendent of police still advised all shopkeepers to board up their windows. Some 4,800 guardsmen patrolled the streets, augmented by metropolitan and state police and eager volunteers. Meanwhile Crane in Dalton was becoming increasingly alarmed at the governor's inaction and the effect that this might have on his chances in the November election, and he was equally troubled that Peters might reinstate the policemen and claim credit for having settled the strike. He expressed all his doubts and troubles over the telephone to Butler who at once arranged to have lunch with Coolidge at the Union Club. During their long, lunchtime discussion, the governor asked Butler what he thought he ought to do. Butler told him he ought to call out the state guard and take over the Boston police department. Coolidge monosyllabically agreed. After lunch they left for the governor's office where the governor proceeded to issue two executive orders, one calling out the state guard, the other taking over control of the Boston police department and reinstating Commissioner Curtis. Then he turned and asked Butler: "What further damage can I do?" When Butler suggested that it might be tactful to let the mayor know what he had done, Coolidge replied: "Let him find it out in the papers!"

Coolidge had taken charge when it was no longer necessary to take charge, but outside the city it seemed that a resolute governor by his prompt action had saved a city from anarchy. The strike had been front-page news across the country, universally condemned by Democrats and Republicans alike. Senator Lodge thought it the first step toward a Soviet America. President Wilson called it a "crime against civilization" and sent Coolidge a telegram of congratulation. The striking policemen were themselves having second thoughts and now voted overwhelmingly to return to work with conditions as before the strike. American Federation of Labor President Samuel Gompers sent telegrams to Peters and Coolidge requesting that the strikers be taken back pending arbitration. But Commissioner Curtis, reinstated in office, issued an order that none of the patrolmen who had failed to report for duty could report back under any circumstances. Coolidge in turn called the conduct of the police "desertion of duty" and made it clear that they could never resume their old jobs. In replying to Gompers's telegram, he stated he had no authority to interfere in the discipline of Curtis's department. On Saturday Gompers telegraphed back:

> The question at issue is not one of law and order, but the assumption of an autocratic and unwarranted position by the Commissioner of Police. . . . Whatever disorder has occurred is due to his order in which the right of the policemen has been denied, a right which has heretofore never been questioned.*

Coolidge on Sunday sent off a long reply just in time to hit the Monday headlines. His telegram read in part:

> . . . . I have already refused to remove the Police Commissioner of Boston. I did not appoint him. . . . Your assertion that the Commissioner was wrong cannot justify the wrong of leaving the city unguarded. That furnished the opportunity; the criminal element furnished the action. There is no right to strike against the public safety by anybody, anywhere, any time. . . .†

And so on, for another 150 words, but one blunt incandescent phrase swept the country: "There is no right to strike against the public safety by anybody, anywhere, any time. . . ." At the beginning of that week, scarcely anyone outside Massachusetts had ever heard of Calvin Coolidge. By the week's end he had become a national hero, his flinty impassive features reflected back from every Sunday rotogravure section. At last, it seemed, a man had dared to take a stand against the turbulence and disruption of the postwar year, a man who in voice and features might have been a direct descendant of Uncle Sam. Cautious Cal was transformed into Law and Order Coolidge with his atavistic Yankee eccentricities a trademark.

* *A City in Terror,* pp. 190–91.
† Ibid., p. 191.

On the very day that Commissioner Curtis was suspending the eighteen police union leaders, Stearns was conferring with the editors of Houghton Mifflin about publishing *A Collection of Addresses and Messages* by Calvin Coolidge, most of them made while he was lieutenant governor and headed by his inaugural address as senate president. Stearns agreed to pay the cost of printing including advertising — about 75¢ a copy — and to distribute most of them himself as political reminders. It was decided to rename the book *Bay State Orations*. Then a few days later some editorial genius at Houghton Mifflin had the inspiration to adopt a phrase taken from the senate inaugural speech, *Have Faith in Massachusetts*. Immediately after the police strike one of the Houghton Mifflin partners came in hot haste to Stearns imploring him: "You must let me spend some more money, work nights and get that book out now." With the addition of several police-strike utterances, *Have Faith in Massachusetts* was printed and bound and ready for delivery by mid-October.

Stearns set about getting a copy into the hands of congressmen, governors, mayors, judges, of every politician of any note in the country. The first printing of 3,000 was soon followed by a second 5,000. Other printings followed. All in all some 65,000 copies were financed and distributed by Stearns who also agreed to contribute $18,000 for an advertising campaign to bring the book to a large audience. Seventy-five hundred copies were actually sold. The rest were given away. But those who had for years looked on Lord Lingerie as a garrulous old fool, now began to consider him a prophet. Coolidge's Amherst classmate, Dwight Morrow, confessed to Stearns that "for the past two or three years, when you have talked about Calvin, I have thought YOU were crazy. I want to say now that I was the one who was crazy."

Coolidge admitted in his *Autobiography* that his chief mistake in the police strike was having failed to call out the state guard until after the rioting. Yet if he had done so, he would never have been a brief national hero, never have become his party's next vice-presidential candidate. The two nights of violence were necessary as a dramatic prelude to the emergence of Coolidge. His luck held. The eyes of the nation focused on Massachusetts in November when Coolidge came up for reelection. It was a law-and-order election, with Republicans urging the voters to "Remember September the 9th." In the largest vote ever yet cast in Massachusetts the governor was reelected by an overwhelming 125,101 majority. "Such an impressive victory in a doubtful state and upon what is becoming a great national issue," the *Literary Digest* commented, "has naturally thrust Governor Coolidge into the limelight for the Republican nomination for President in 1920."

Within a few days of Coolidge's second inaugural, Stearns had opened a Coolidge presidential campaign headquarters in Washington's Hotel Raleigh and was planning a second one in Chicago. All in all he raised about $65,000 in campaign funds, a minuscule sum compared to the treasuries of Wood and Lowden. Then at the end of January and without telling his sponsor, Coolidge announced that he refused to enter any contest for Massachusetts national convention delegates since he did not wish to have the governor's office "used for manipulative purposes." Undaunted, Stearns evolved a plan to send unpledged delegates who in case of a stalemate would vote for Coolidge. Crane had come out for Coolidge, and even Senator Lodge — possibly with his fingers crossed — announced that Massachusetts ought to support him. But in March Coolidge stated bluntly: "I have not been and am not a candidate for president." Stearns still refused to give up, even though his plan for an unpledged delegation failed to work out. There were indeed the four unpledged delegates-at-large headed by Lodge and Crane, but of the thirty-one ordinary delegates, eight regarded themselves as for Wood. Nevertheless there were hopeful signs. Senator Harding came to Boston in May, and he said in an interview that if he were from Massachusetts he would be for Governor Coolidge for president.

In preparation for the June convention, Stearns had a small pamphlet of sixty pages printed containing excerpts from Coolidge's speeches and bound in imitation black leather with *Law and Order* stamped in gilt letters on the cover. These he planned to distribute to each delegate and alternate and to anyone else who was willing to read or listen.

Stearns arrived at the Chicago convention, the Dark Convention of 1920, with his son Foster and several bails of *Law and Order*. In the *Literary Digest* poll Coolidge had ranked seventh in a list of possible candidates, but no one in Chicago except for Stearns took his candidacy seriously. His name would be placed in vanity nomination along with a number of other favorite sons like Judge Jeter Connelly Pritchard of North Carolina, Senator Miles Poindexter of Washington and Senator Howard Sutherland of West Virginia; but that would be all. Stearns had become so noted for his Coolidge monologue during the hot preliminary days, that delegates began to turn on their heels in the hotel lobbies when they saw him coming. However, they were all supplied with *Law and Order* and in most cases with *Have Faith in Massachusetts.* "Nominate a man who lives in a two-family house?" Lodge exploded when he heard of Stearns' meandering crusade. "Never! Massachusetts is not for him." When Coolidge's name was placed in nomination, the applause lasted just one minute. Wood's name had brought on a forty-six-minute demonstration. On the first ballot, Coolidge had thirty-four votes — twenty-eight from Massachusetts, one from Kentucky, two from New York, two from South Carolina and one from Tennessee. That was the highwater mark of the Coolidge tide. Subsequently, until the tenth ballot which nominated Harding, Coolidge's vote dropped by degrees to twenty-three, then stabilized at twenty-eight.

Harding's Saturday afternoon nomination was a relief from the frustrations and the overpowering heat. For the great majority of the delegates, tired and sweaty and ready for adjournment, he was a second or third choice, but at least the convention would not run over into the following week. Hotels and restaurants had jacked up their prices for the convention, and many delegates were short of money and impatient to get away from Chicago. Even as the applause and tinsel demonstration for Harding began to fade, delegates were beginning to drift out of the Coliseum and down Michigan Avenue. The convention's acting chairman, Governor Frank Willis of Ohio, in spite of his hog-caller's voice, could barely make himself heard above the tramp of feet and the slap of folding seats. Under the platform, in an interlacing of wooden beams, a group of senators who formed the inner circle of the party had gathered hastily to decide on the vice-presidential candidate. Their choice was Senator Irvine Lenroot, whose Wisconsin progressivism was counted on to balance Harding's old-guard conservatism.

The word went out to the diminished hall. A delegate stood up and in inaudible tones moved to nominate Lenroot for the vice-presidency. Willis, pounding his gavel, waited for the seconding motion. In the back of the Coliseum a red-faced man standing on his chair was waving his arms, bellowing in a voice even louder than Willis's. Willis recognized him. He was Judge Wallace McCamant, leader of the Oregon delegation and an admirer of Calvin Coolidge who possessed no less than three copies of *Have Faith in Massachusetts.* Even his mighty bellow could not make itself heard clearly above the din until suddenly the remaining delegates became aware that the bull voice was not seconding Lenroot but nominating Coolidge. "A far more spontaneous and enthusiastic roar of approval ensued," Oswald Garrison Villard reported in the *Nation* "than Harding got at any time." It was as if by this spontaneous and independent gesture all the frustrations, disappointments and strain of the past week had been suddenly released. Wood's men, Lowden's men, could at last shout defiance at those who had beaten them. The delegates were now welded into a unified mob, intractable, not to be stopped. In the politician's ominous cliché, the convention had taken the bit in its teeth and was running away. Calvin Coolidge had become, astonishingly, a symbol of man's independence! He was overwhelmingly nominated.

Coolidge with his wife was following the convention's course in the shabby two-room suite on the fourth floor of the Adams House that he had expanded into when he was first elected governor. Shortly after eight that evening the telephone rang and he put down his cigar to answer it, listened for a minute in silence. Then he hung up and turned without expression to his wife. "Nominated for vice-president," he said in his psalm-singing voice. "You aren't going to take it, are you?" she asked him. "I suppose I shall have to," he said, immobile, unsmiling. "Mr. Coolidge was always sentimental," his wife wrote fifteen years later, recognizing the exultation behind that prim granite face.

Stearns alone was disappointed. He saw the vice-presidency as a dead-end post that could lead nowhere except through the accident of death. Another friend of Coolidge's grasped the situation with more clarity. "If Calvin Coolidge were nominated for the vice presidency, I wouldn't take the presidency for a million dollars," he told a reporter at the convention. "Because I would die in a little while. Coolidge has always been lucky politically. Everything comes to him in a most uncanny and mysterious way. Excuse me from the presidency with him in the vice-regal chair."

And so it happened twenty-nine months after Coolidge took his oath of office as vice-president of the United States. During those months of semi-activity he went to a number of public dinners, partly from reasons of economy, partly to kill time. The poker-playing gaiety of the Harding era was not for him. Beyond presiding over the Senate and sitting silently at Harding's cabinet meetings, he did little. At times he grew morose. His set occasional speeches were little heeded. Their most constant reader was Frank Stearns. He had still not given up, could not in fact give up the dream of the White House for his political son. Week by week he dispatched long rambling hortatory letters to Coolidge, going on page after page with advice, suggestions, admonition, encouragement. "Why not take some comfort out of some of these things," he wrote in typical fashion when Coolidge had complained of his "barren life," "be glad to see folks, let them know that you are glad to see them and try for six months to take it for granted that just plain common folks, the backbone of the country, feel it an honor to meet the Vice President of the United States and are certain in their own minds that they now have the best Vice President the country has ever had and they will be mighty glad to have your friendly acquaintance even if you were not Vice President of the United States. I know how folks feel and I am not making any mistake whatever. It is of enormous importance to the country that you assume your position of leadership, which you certainly have. Nobody can destroy it but yourself. I cannot imagine any way in which even you can destroy it unless you persistently for years make folks feel that you are not interested in them. I know you are. Let them know it."

For Stearns, Harding's sudden death in the summer of 1923 with its consequences was like a dream come true. Even the stage setting was unique. Coolidge, spending his vacation in the family homestead at Plymouth Notch out of range of telegraph and telephone, had gone to bed at his customary early hour on the day of Harding's death. Shortly after midnight he was wakened by his father coming upstairs and calling him by name to tell him that the president was dead. Since his father was a justice of the peace, he was able to give his son the oath of office at once. That stark inaugural in the farmhouse parlor lighted by a single kerosene lamp, with father and son facing each other across the table with the family Bible on it, was a Currier & Ives lithograph come to life, a homespun myth, harking back to the earlier simpler days of the Republic, that would make him in his day and in spite of the contempt of the intellectuals one of the most popular presidents.

In the several weeks that it took the widowed Florence Harding to leave the White House, the Coolidges continued to live at the Gresham, where Stearns joined them shortly after their return to Washington.

> We had a suite of rooms next to the Coolidges [Stearns wrote his son]. The hallways were filled with newspaper men from early morning until late night. They tried to make me talk about Mr. Coolidge. At first I refused to say anything, but finally was persuaded . . . that they certainly would write something and that I had better try to get them to paint a true picture rather than an imaginary one. I also found out that the one thing they wanted to know was who controlled Mr. Coolidge. The only person they could think of was myself. They seemed to have no other person in mind, so I set about convincing them that I did not control him. I think the public has the picture quite correctly and they understand that if I do not control him nobody does, and that therefore he comes to the Presidency freer of entanglements than any man who has come into that office.*

By a happy combination of fate and foresight Stearns had attained his goal. Although he had been whispered into half a dozen high positions within the presidential gift, he wanted nothing that a Hanna or a Harvey or a Daugherty might have claimed. He had no secret ambition to be a cabinet member or a senator or an ambassador, nor did he aspire to the confidential intimacy of a Colonel House. He wished no patronage or appointments. It was quite sufficient for him during the Coolidge years to stay at the White House whenever he wished as an honored an intimate guest. In wandering with pride down those historic corridors, his watchchain stretched expansively across his tight little stomach, he gave the external impression of a floorwalker surveying his domain. His satisfaction with his creation was all-sufficing. He liked to refer to himself as "the President's errand boy." "I don't want anything outside of what I have," he told reporters.

* *Calvin Coolidge: The Man from Vermont,* p. 314.

*The Medieval Gnome and the beaming FDR.*

CHAPTER SEVEN

# The Medieval Gnome: Louis McHenry Howe

ROOM 1702 IN the Congress Square Hotel! [reporter at Chicago's 1932 Democratic National Convention wrote in the marvel of his discovery.] Keep that number in mind. In all human probability a candidate for President is being nominated in that room this day. And it is by no means improbable that Room 1702 may be the anteroom to the White House — one has that strange feeling in passing its threshold — the feeling that destiny is at work within these walls.

Hunched down within the depths of an overstuffed chair is the most singular personality in American politics. I defy anyone to find his counterpart outside the pages of Charles Dickens or Victor Hugo. A diminutive, incredibly thin, gnome-like individual who seems scarcely to belong to this day and age. There is something utterly medieval about him. His head, full domed and thinly-thatched, is overlarge for his body. His forehead is high and furrowed.

His eyes are set back deeply under heavy brows. His face is narrow and points from high cheekbones to subtle chin. The whole face is amazingly creased and wrinkled.

This amazing man is Louis McHenry Howe, the closest man alive to Franklin Roosevelt; his alter ego; the real head and directing mind of the Roosevelt drive for the Presidency.

Every moment of his waking and sleeping hours has been spent in Room 1702 or in an adjoining room. Day or night he has not taken a step out of that place. I doubt if he has even glanced out the window upon the stirring panorama of Michigan Avenue and Grant Park — the surging crowds, the marching bands, the squadron of Army airplanes. . . . These spectacles leave him cold.

His one and only interest is to finish the job and get back to Governor Roosevelt's home in New York's East Sixty-Fifth Street, his home also, and to his books and private papers. To get the job done he applies the inexhaustible energy and concentration

> that is the astonishment of all who watch him work. He sleeps maybe four hours in the twenty-four, and eats when his nervous energy permits, a sandwich and a glass of milk. Anything serves. Food means nothing. The only thing that means anything is votes for Roosevelt — that and the insistent calls of the Albany wire. Personal appearance means even less. His clothes hang on him, baggy, unpressed; his trousers confined perilously by a buckled belt. But there is nothing baggy about his intelligence.
>
> He is a rare bird in political life, this curious little man who serves his master with the unhesitating fidelity of a loyal dog; this remarkable Louis McHenry Howe, who presides in this new throne room where history is in the making.*

Louis Howe had had to make the best of a bad body. "I am," he admitted in his middle years, "one of the four ugliest men, if what is left of me can be dignified by the name of man, in the State of New York. I am wizened in the Dickens manner. My eyes protrude from too much looking. Children take one look at me on the street and run." A glib reporter had labeled him "the medieval gnome," and he relished the offhand slur that would in time become a newspaper cliché. He was perhaps more ancient than medieval, an Alberich with the same obsession for power. Yet he was wise enough to know that if it should come to him, it must come indirectly. "He loved power," Eleanor Roosevelt wrote of him, "but he also recognized realities and he decided that in the end he would exercise more power through someone else." "I am hated by everybody, I always have been hated by everybody, I want to be hated by everybody," he once told a friend.

At forty, when most men's lives have taken their final form, Howe was a failure. A petty political manipulator who knew Albany's legislative ways and byways, he had as his sole source of income a part-time job as a state-house reporter for the New York *Herald* and the *Morning Telegraph* while the legislature was in session. Yet for all his shabby insecurity he had been born to wealth and a relatively established position. His parents were proper New Englanders who had settled in Indianapolis to be readily absorbed into the newly-minted elite of that burgeoning city. At the outbreak of the Civil War his father, Edward Porter Howe, had joined the 101st Indiana Volunteers as a private and by the war's end had risen to captain. After the war Captain Howe married Eliza Ray Sharpe, "Lide," a widow eleven years his senior

* *The Man Behind Roosevelt*, pp. 178–79.

with two almost-grown daughters. Her father had been president of the Bank of Indiana and she had money of her own. Her new husband, after being appointed adjutant general in charge of paying off the discharged Indiana soldiers, became secretary of the Franklin Insurance Company. He prospered and used both his own money and his wife's to speculate in the postwar real estate boom. At first all went well. He bought a large and handsome house in the best neighborhood, with a library and in the rear a stable. In 1871 his son Louis was born, a frail mite with a pinched pathetic face and spindly arms and legs, asthmatic, prone to bronchitis. The child could never romp with the other children of the sedate upper-class street. Daily he was taken to the doctor's. Since he could not run about, his father bought him a little pony-drawn phaeton.

Except for their boy's health the Howes' future looked serene. Then the postwar bubble burst in the Panic of 1873. Within a year Howe had lost everything. Reduced to bankruptcy, with judgments of over $16,000 against him, he fled Indiana with his wife and five-year-old son to Saratoga Springs, New York, where Lide's half-sister's husband ran a small sanatorium-boarding house known grandiloquently as Dr. Strong's Remedial Institute. He and his family spent a year under the charitable Dr. Strong's roof while he attempted vainly to earn a living as a free-lance writer. Finally he managed to find a job as the solitary reporter on the local Republican weekly, the *Saratogian*, writing up the local trivia. The pay was small, but enough at least for Howe to support himself again and to rent a minute house. After six years of such reporting he optimistically bought the little sheet known as the Saratoga *Sun* and tried to turn it into the Democratic rival of the *Saratogian*. In that Republican community, official advertising — the life blood of rural papers — and most local printing went to the *Saratogian*. Captain Howe barely managed to survive. Soon he was forced to move back to the shelter of the Remedial Institute. Not until Louis was seventeen had trade expanded sufficiently for his father at last to be able to buy a house. But gradually, as advertising came into its own with the dawning consumer age, the *Sun* shone more brightly and Captain Howe achieved a modest prosperity as well as recognition as spokesman for the Saratoga County Democrats.

Because of Louis's health much of his childhood had to be spent quietly indoors. Left to himself he read omnivorously, uncritically

— Kipling, Stevenson, W. W. Jacobs, the medieval romances of Anthony Hope. His father passed on to him the books that arrived to be reviewed in the *Sun*. For some years his mother tutored him at home, then sent him across the street to attend the Temple Grove Seminary for Young Ladies. As he grew older he took to writing occasional verse, often of a religious nature, and his little poems appeared from time to time in the *Sun* or the *Saratogian*.

Whatever his physical deficiencies, Louis was a sociable boy and at adolescence he struggled against his asthma and bronchitis. In spite of the truss that he was forced to wear because of his weak spine, and would have to wear all his life, he learned to ride a bicycle, to skate and play golf and tennis. At sixteen he wore the scarlet and black uniform of the Saratoga Toboggan Club, taking part in the junior races down the steep slope behind the town and out over the lake. His bicycling turned out to be his misfortune, for one day while riding he caught his foot in the spokes and was thrown into the gravel. Ever afterward his face bore black-pitted scars.

Weak though he was in body, grotesque in features, he nevertheless developed a gaiety and a charm that overcame his physical handicaps. Demand for him grew as an impromptu speaker, and in spite of his truss he danced gracefully. Often he was found leading the "germans" at the Saturday night dances at the Grand Union and United States Hotels. Loving music, he sang in the choirs of the Second Presbyterian and the Bethesda Episcopal Churches. With his deft mind he easily became a whist expert, and even managed to earn pocket money by giving lessons in that fashionable accomplishment. Despite his diminutive ugliness he was a ladies' man, a "gay blade." And if he could not afford to gamble much, he nevertheless paid periodic visits to Richard Canfield's casino. Horse racing fascinated him. He could never resist a small bet.

Captain Howe, with the aim of sending his son to Yale, transferred him from Temple Grove to a boy's private school, the Saratoga Institute. But by the time Louis graduated his father found such additional expense too burdensome, and the boy went to work as reporter and printing salesman at the *Sun*. He did not feel it as a deprivation. Saratoga sufficed him. In adolescence he had developed a passionate interest in the theater. Saratoga during its season was a theater town, with such stars playing there as Otis Skinner, Edwin Booth, DeWolf Hopper and Ada Rehan. They in turn inspired an active amateur group in which Louis took a leading part as producer, director, scene designer, coach and even at times as actor, although to his regret his roles were limited to comic ones. He himself wrote several comedies and staged them at the Remedial Institute. When the local high school players needed a director for their annual play, they turned to him.

By the time he was twenty-one he had become co-editor and co-proprietor of the *Sun*. With the aging captain's increasing bad health, Louis took over more and more of the duties of the paper. As a reporter he developed an intricate knowledge of local politicians, an instinct for unraveling the seams of politics. He made a habit of probing into old documents, of ferreting out the dubious motives behind the high-flown phrases. Captain Howe had served for some time as local correspondent for the New York *Herald* and the *Evening Telegram*, and this twin assignment he now passed on to his son.

By the early nineties the *Sun* seemed an established success, so much so that in 1891 Louis and his father took a cruise to Europe and the Mediterranean. The following year Grover Cleveland was elected to his second term as president, and the captain's Democratic loyalty was rewarded by his appointment as Saratoga postmaster. He now spent his days at the post office, leaving his son in possession of the newspaper.

In the summer of 1896 Grace Hartley, a Vassar student, came with her mother to the Remedial Institute from Fall River, although there was nothing wrong in the blooming Grace's health. Her mother was born a Borden, a noted Fall River family that had become unhappily notorious several years earlier after the trial of Lizzie Borden for murdering her parents. Louis was at once attracted to this smart and handsome young woman. She admitted afterward that she was not all impressed by him at their first meeting. Yet despite his flawed face and gnomish exterior he soon showed himself an enjoyable companion, witty, gay, eloquent, amusing and somewhat pathetic. She saw much of him that summer, and more the following summer. After she had left, he wrote her regularly and even made periodic trips to Fall River to see her. By slow degrees she fell in love with him. Her mother did not approve. In 1898, when she returned briefly for the third time to Saratoga, they became engaged. By then the war with

Spain had broken out, and Louis was trying unsuccessfully to get himself assigned to the Philippines as a war correspondent. When Grace left on her birthday, he took the train part way with her, and by the time they crossed the Massachusetts line he had persuaded her to elope with him. They journeyed on to Vermont, were married by a justice of the peace, then had a brief candlelit dinner at a country inn. That same night Grace went on to Boston and Louis returned to Saratoga. The parting was symbolic of their marriage, made up of successions of such partings. He managed to visit her in Fall River several times that winter, and eventually her mother discovered their secret. The mother insisted on a second and formal wedding, and this took place in May, 1899, at Fall River's Episcopal Church of the Ascension.

For all her earlier disapproval the mother was determined to make the best of her daughter's marriage. She bought the young couple a large, gracious house not far from Captain Howe's and only a brief walk to the *Sun* office. Set in a green expanse of grass with a garden and a circular summerhouse, furnished with antiques from Fall River, the house had an airy graciousness about it that seemed full of promise for the future. That promise did not last the year. McKinley's election had lost Captain Howe his post office. The printing business had fallen off in the Cleveland depression and the Democratic *Sun* was beginning to set in that stubbornly Republican community. Louis had to mortgage his gift house to keep the paper going. But by the year's end the paper's creditors had taken over. For a few months after losing control he continued as editor, then was demoted to reporter and salesman at $10 a week. Grace was expecting a baby in June. Some months before this she had returned to Fall River. Meanwhile Louis's parents, without other resources, moved in on him, as did his half sister. Grace returned briefly with the baby on several occasions, but each time the combined household was too much for her, and she fled to Fall River. In September, 1901, the new *Sun* publisher discharged his reporter. Grace refused now to return to Saratoga at all. "I married you for better or worse," she wrote Louis. "I couldn't go through another entire winter like last winter." Yet, with the tie of the child between them, neither wanted to dissolve the marriage. When he could scrape together enough money for the fare, he would still take the train to Fall River. He managed to pick up a few dollars here and there playing faro or betting at the races. At one point he even considered becoming a bookie. Only his part-time job as local correspondent for the *Herald* kept him from destitution. He covered the Saratoga race track, the goings and comings and petty gossip of notable visitors and the inevitable local scandals. Sometimes he was lucky enough to write an outside book review and once he sold an article to *Town and Country* for $15. In the winter of 1901–1902 he had a real stroke of luck when the *Herald* sent him on a trip to the West Indies. So well received were his rather lurid feature stories on that voyage that in September 1902 he was asked to join the *Herald's* editorial staff. Grace and the child stayed in Fall River while he moved into a Manhattan boarding house. His waspish temperament and unruly temper made him enemies in the big city. After a few months his health gave out, and when later he returned expectantly to New York no editor was willing to take him on. In 1904 he found a last-resort job in Saratoga at $15 a week as secretary of a newly formed Business Men's Association. To Grace in Fall River he wrote encouragingly that he hoped to board the old people out for the winter. She was not tempted to return.

At last Howe's fortunes took a modest turn for the better when the *Herald* editor gave him a job as assistant to the paper's staff man at Albany. It paid a handsome $40 a week. The only difficulty was that it lasted no longer than the legislative session, sometimes a mere two months. Grace and the child came for a time to Albany to share furnished rooms with him. Her Albany days were empty, for her husband passed most of his waking hours at the capitol or the Press Club or rummaging through old newspaper files. He spent so many hours in the capitol's musty basement going through old records that other reporters took to calling him "the water rat." Gradually he achieved a reputation as a knowledgeable political reporter, earning as much as $75 a week. Yet he was growing old before his time. In his late thirties his face looked like a withered apple, his hair was sparse, his shoulders stooped. Broken in health, he weighed less than a hundred pounds. His clothes, flecked with cigarette ash, were baggy, his three-inch high collar was usually smudged, and his fingernails black. Daily he chain-smoked three to four packs of Sweet Caporals, his breath sour from nicotine, the fingers of his right hand stained yellow-brown. A racking cough seemed always about to shake him to pieces. His nerves were edgy, his temper short. "Mein Gawd!" was his favorite expletive — a relic of a German course he had once taken.

In 1906 Boss Murphy determined to foist William Randolph Hearst on the people of New York as their next governor. Thomas Mott Osborne, the wealthy, independent and erratic mayor of Auburn, led a group of reform Democrats to oppose Hearst and Tammany. In the campaign Osborne hired four newspapermen as political field-workers, among them Howe. Excited by his new job, Howe rushed from town to upstate town conferring with political leaders during the day and writing long confidential reports to Osborne each night. Though Tammany brushed aside the amateurish opposition to win the nomination for Hearst, he was overwhelmingly defeated in the election by the Republican Charles Evans Hughes.

The defeat of his party made Osborne even more determined to wrest control of the upstate Democrats from Tammany. He set up an Albany headquarters in the struggle. Howe with his energy and political insight seemed just the man to take charge, as his *Herald* contacts gave him in addition a listening post inside the capitol. After hesitations that would prove typical of him, Osborne finally hired Howe at $40 a week. Howe had hoped for $50, yet his new prospects delighted him. "I feel the turning point has come in our fortunes, dear," he wrote to Grace who had returned to Fall River. A week later he was writing her: "Isn't it funny Osborne wants me to be practically his private secretary. That is the kind of job you have always been poking me up to getting."

Osborne's enthusiasm for reform waxed and waned, as did his enthusiasm for his importunate little assistant. In 1908 he angrily discharged Howe on a week's notice. Louis was desperate. His doctor had just warned him that he had only a few months to live, and he begged Osborne to take him back, even offering to work for nothing. Out of pity or goodwill Osborne did take him back as a private investigator and lobbyist at his old salary. Off and on he continued to work for Osborne, adding to his store of practical political knowledge, yet with little practical benefit to himself. But for his meeting with the debonair newly-elected senator from Dutchess and Columbia Counties, the twenty-nine-year-old Franklin Delano Roosevelt, he would have ended up as a peripheral Albany character, mean-tempered, a little comic, a little pitiable, his name forgotten the month after his funeral.

Six feet two inches tall, assured in manner as in clothes, Franklin Roosevelt was thought handsome in spite of his high nose and long chin. Tammany's Big Tim Sullivan, on seeing the new senator stride across a hotel lobby with his head thrust back, remarked to another boss: "You know these Roosevelts. This fellow is still young. Take my advice and drown him before he gets old and tough."

In 1910, Roosevelt, the desultory young lawyer, married his toothy distant cousin Eleanor. Dependent on her modest income and on his mother Sara for financial support, he was not much further ahead in a career than on that June day six years earlier when he received his diploma from Harvard's President Eliot. By this time he had three children, but still lived under the shadow of his dominating mother. Then, in this unsuspectedly portentous year, John Mack, the Democratic district attorney of Dutchess County, dropped in to see him on some minor legal matter. Mack mentioned that the Democratic state assemblyman from the Dutchess County district, former Lieutenant Governor Lewis Stuyvesant Chanler, was going to run for senator. Perhaps Franklin would like to try for his place. Franklin would! He had become bored with the city and was only waiting for a good excuse to abandon the law. Faced with the magic name of Roosevelt and the money behind it, the Poughkeepsie ward bosses overcame their plebeian doubts. Then, in that churning year of progressivism, Chanler decided it would be more prudent to stick to his safe seat in the assembly. Roosevelt took him out to dinner several times, trying unsuccessfully to persuade him to change his mind. But at the prospect of Albany, Franklin's political instinct had quickened. The senate nomination was one the loyal Democratic leaders were now willing to offer him, since there seemed few takers for that dubious honor. Only once since the Civil War had the largely agricultural district gone Democratic. Nevertheless, in the last election it had not gone Republican by very much. Franklin was faced with the choice of either accepting the left-handed nomination or giving up his vague political notions and retiring to the status of a country gentleman like his father. A month before the election he appeared casually at the Poughkeepsie Democratic headquarters in riding habit to announce that he had decided to accept. County Chairman Edward Perkins looked at the slim arrogant figure in the shiny boots with dismay. "You can't wear that outfit campaigning!" he almost shouted.

In the term then coming into use, young Roosevelt appeared more a "progressive" than a Democrat. He was, he announced in his acceptance speech, pledged to no man, influenced by no special interests. So he entered politics, contemptuous of grafters and ward-heelers as only a man of independent income could be, convinced that the only way the political scene could improve would be through participation of the better people.

Dutchess, Putnam and Columbia Counties had never seen anything like the effervescent political month that followed. Candidate Roosevelt toured the district in a rented fire-engine-red Maxwell with huge brass headlights, the top removed, the sides and hood plastered with American flags. He bumped down remote back roads to hamlets where no politician had yet penetrated, speaking at crossroads and station platforms, setting up drinks at country inns and local saloons. Although he found public speaking difficult at first, he soon acquired the knack as well as a convenient arsenal of pet phrases. "My friends," he began to call the farmers gathered at the crossroads, who may at first have looked askance at his accent and manner. But his ever-ready laugh, his warmth and undeniable charm usually broke through their rustic reserve. "Call me Franklin," he would urge some plodder along the road. "I am going to call you Tom." Nor did he disdain the regular Democratic leaders in the towns with their intimate knowledge of the electorate.

On election day he carried his traditionally Republican district by 15,708 votes to 14,568 for his opponent. Four things had combined to make his election possible: the magic of a presidential name; a year that was not a Republican year; the money he had spent, a modest few thousand dollars, but far more than had ever before been spent in the district; lastly, his winning manner, his ability to make many strangers think he was indeed their "friend."

The newly-elected senator rented a brownstone town house near the capitol and moved to Albany with his family and staff of servants. By contrast most legislators lived in back-street hotels or rooming houses, the most they could afford on their $1,500 salary, plus the petty graft they could pick up. "The scene in Albany spread before Roosevelt's eyes the paradox of state governments," Finis Farr wrote, "though expensive, inefficient, staffed then as now mostly by drones and petty thieves, they yet seemed to fill a vital need against the government of Washington."

Almost as soon as Roosevelt arrived in Albany he found himself embroiled in a row with Tammany Hall. Nineteen-ten, with the Republicans split between Taft and the Progressives, had been a Democratic year, and in New York the Democrats gained control of both houses of the legislature. Since Tammany made up the majority of the Democrats, Tammany chieftain Charles Murphy expected the upstate Democratic minority to knuckle under. United States senators were still chosen by legislatures. To fill Senator Chauncey Depew's seat, vacant that year, Murphy sent in the name of one of his henchmen, former Lieutenant Governor "Blue-eyed Billy" Sheehan. Outraged by this Tammany ukase, twenty-one reform-minded Democrats refused to accept Sheehan, and put forward their own candidate. Roosevelt was not the leader of these 'young Turk" insurgents, but his house provided a convenient and comfortable meeting place, and as the only senator among them he soon assumed the role of informal spokesman. As reporter Howe recorded in the *Herald*:

> Twenty-one men, so little reckoned with in politics that their very names, until yesterday, were practically unknown outside the limits of their home districts, these men successfully defying the weight of Tammany Hall, blocking the progress of one of the most carefully planned political moves in recent years, standing unterrified by threats and unmoved by the most cunning politicians, such is the amazing feature of the struggle at Albany today.*

The name of Roosevelt dramatized the struggle, echoed it beyond the borders of New York State, and the neophyte senator received more than his due as a potential giant killer. As such rebellions usually did, this one ended with an ostensible concession that was really a Tammany victory. Murphy withdrew Sheehan in favor of another Tammany stalwart, Justice James O'Gorman. Roosevelt remained among the diminished diehards. That ten-week struggle was his political initiation. In it he learned much about the labyrinths of politics while at the same time building up a reputation as a Democratic progressive. Rexford Tugwell saw Roosevelt's anti-Tammany struggle as committing him to the support of a progressive program, "some of which he liked, and some of which he did not, but none of which he could hence-

* *The Man Behind Roosevelt,* p. 27.

forth altogether escape. Conservation he embraced with enthusiasm, woman suffrage he had doubts about and gave in to with some reluctance. In between he supported labor legislation with some reservation and the various items of good government with various degrees of readiness. But all of it was part of the role for which he was cast; he could not, if he wanted to, escape. But on the whole, although he had some qualms . . . he found his new-found philosophy congenial. He also, being then, as ever, shrewd in sizing up the long-run future, saw that progressivism — Democratic progressivism — was good politics. How right he was!"

During those abrasive winter weeks in the assembly, Howe many times observed Roosevelt from the press gallery. One could scarcely help but notice that conspicuous figure, jutting above the anonymity of his fellow legislators, slim, poised, handsome, with wavy hair that was enough, in one reporter's opinion, to "set the matinee girl's heart throbbing with subtle and happy emotion." To Howe, ugly and poor and no longer young, the new senator in the immaculate cutaway must have seemed to have been granted all the gifts of fortune that the rumpled reporter had been denied.

In the middle of the senatorial fight Howe went to Roosevelt's town house to interview him. Roosevelt received him in the library, a paneled room with a large fire blazing in the hearth over which was carved a coat-of-arms. Howe particularly noticed the crest — a hand holding a club — and thought at once of the other Roosevelt's Big Stick. While his visitor scrunched in a leather armchair near the fire, Roosevelt paced up and down, his head thrown back as he announced his determination to stop Sheehan. "You can tell your paper that we are in this fight to a finish and we are in it to win," he told Howe, striking his clenched fist into his hand. "From that moment we became friends," Howe wrote long afterward, "and almost at that very first meeting, I made up my mind that . . . nothing but an accident could keep him from becoming President of the United States." After this meeting Howe determined to hitch his battered wagon to the ascendant Roosevelt star.

The campaign of 1912 brought Roosevelt and Howe together. Before the end of 1911 Roosevelt had gone on a political pilgrimage to Woodrow Wilson and returned convinced that the New Jersey governor, the scholarly anti-boss, was the bright hope of the Democratic party for the 1912 presidential election year.

In the spring of 1912, Osborne organized the New York State Wilson Conference, an organization of Democrats supporting Wilson. Roosevelt became chairman of the conference's executive committee and asked Howe to handle the publicity. Louis gave up his newspaper job to devote all his time and energies to it. Boss Murphy wanted no part of Wilson, and Tammany had more than sufficient strength to insure a complete slate of anti-Wilson delegates to the Democratic National Convention at Baltimore in June. Osborne and Roosevelt did lead a protest demonstration in the convention hall after the New York delegation had switched its support from Harmon to Clark, and Roosevelt could at least claim that he was one of the original Wilson supporters in his state. If the New Jersey governor was elected, he would have an obligation to reward the New York senator's early allegiance. After Wilson's nomination Roosevelt telegraphed his wife in high excitement: "Wilson nominated this afternoon all my plans vague splendid triumph."

Following the convention, Roosevelt and Osborne transformed their conference into the independent anti-Tammany Empire State Democracy, and Howe was assured of his old role as publicity director. By August, however, their resistance effort had foundered, Osborne withdrew his financial support and the Empire State Democracy withered away. Howe was left without a job and without resources. "Now I am in a hole" he wrote appealingly to Roosevelt "because there are five long months before Albany and the price of living has not gone down any. If you can connect me with a job during the campaign, for heaven's sake help me out, for this mess is a bad business to me."

The letter arrived opportunely. Roosevelt at Hyde Park, while making preparations for his reelection campaign, had come down with typhoid fever, and the doctors forbade him even to leave his bed. It would be no easy election, for Tammany was out to see that none of those twenty-one insurgents would ever appear in Albany again. Louis Howe, with his energy, and devious knowledge of upstate politics, seemed the answer. From his sick room Roosevelt telephoned him. "You have so many ideas on how to run a campaign," he told Howe, "I'm going to give you a chance to put them into practice and I'm flat on my back and the doctors say I have to stay here. You run the campaign. You'll have a check book and a free hand. Now, go to it."

Even though Howe's salary was only $50 a week, this seemed

his long-hoped-for and almost despaired-of opportunity, his belated beginning. His sharp-honed political instincts sensed the future promise of this imposing young man with his famous name, his assured position, and his charm, his astuteness and his surface brilliance. Howe complemented the Roosevelt qualities with his capacity for sustained intellectual effort, his application, his ability to devote long drudging hours to the task at hand, his intimate knowledge of politics that the younger man would only gradually acquire. He and Roosevelt were, to his mind, an ideal team. Just after the Democratic convention he had written to Roosevelt, addressing him as "Beloved and Revered Future President," but beneath the playful salutation lay an abiding conviction of the other's destiny.

Nineteen hundred and twelve brought with it the climax of Progressivism. Just as two years before, the absent Roosevelt took his stand as a Democratic progressive, bipartisan in his concern for his constituents, against the bosses. Howe showed himself a whirlwind campaigner on his own, cruising the rural areas in an open car, a canvas cap on his head and with his wife beside him in a duster and hat and thick veil. As soon as he had signed up with Roosevelt he had sent for her, installing her and their baby son in a boarding house near Vassar. In his campaigning he knew enough not to make set speeches, but he talked informally with farmers by the score. From his temporary headquarters he sent out hundreds of personal letters under Roosevelt's forged signature. He ran full-page advertisements in county papers extolling his candidate as the friend of the farmers and of labor, the enemy of the bosses. When Tammany rumors spread that Roosevelt had opposed Sheehan because Blue-Eyed Billy was a Catholic, Louis at once lent Roosevelt's car and chauffeur to a local priest "to take the Archbishop up from Fishkill" with as much publicity as possible. Deftly he sowed seeds of discord among the Republicans. Carefully he arranged for a mass distribution of $5 bills to workers on election day. "Keep that temperature down," he scribbled to his bed-ridden leader, "so you can get on the job. I am having more fun than a goat. They will know they have been to a horse-race before they are done. Your slave and servant, Louis Howe."

Roosevelt failed to get a clear election majority by almost a thousand votes, but he won easily over the divided Bull Moose and Republican candidates, beating even Wilson's margin in his district by a few hundred votes. Howe was now a Roosevelt figure.

"From then on," Elliot Roosevelt wrote, "Father and Louis were two halves of a single political being." But Eleanor objected to the constant presence of the scruffy little man who filled her house with the fumes of his Sweet Caporals, spilled ashes on her carpets and talked over her head in the incomprehensible jargon of politics.

An expectant Roosevelt had gone to Washington for Wilson's inauguration. On that March morning at the Willard Hotel he ran into the new secretary of the navy, Josephus Daniels. Roosevelt congratulated him. He in turn asked the young man, whom he had got to know at the Baltimore convention, how he would like to come to Washington as assistant secretary. "How would I like it?" Roosevelt replied in the idiom of his cousin Theodore. "I'd like it bully well. It would please me better than anything in the world!" At once he wrote to Howe: "Dear Ludwig; . . . Here is the dope. Secretary — $2,000 — Expect you April 1, with a new uniform."

"I am game," Howe wired back, "but it is going to break me." Actually he was transformed by such a stroke of fortune. What he had vainly hoped for in Osborne, he had found at last in Roosevelt. The new position was one such as he could scarcely have imagined in his years of poverty. He, the political strategist, would guide the still inexperienced young man to what he had already mapped out as his ultimate goal. Both he and Roosevelt were acutely conscious of the precedent and pattern of Cousin Theodore, who had also started out as a belligerent reformer in the New York assembly, also served as assistant secretary of the navy. Far earlier than Roosevelt, Howe understood how indispensible they each were to one another. "Always in the background," Josephus Daniels wrote of the grotesque little man whom he considered the strangest he had ever met, "he knew all the tides and eddies in the Navy Department, in the administration and in the political life of the country. . . . Even in 1913 he expected to see 'Franklin' occupy the White House, and to further that ambition he devoted his every effort. His one and only ambition was to steer 'Franklin's' course so that he could take the tide at the full."

In 1912 the navy was held in little popular esteem, so little that Wilson felt free to appoint a known pacifist, a rural southerner as its secretary. So it was not particularly noteworthy that the briefless young lawyer of three years before, whose qualifications were that of an amateur sailor in the Bay of Fundy and a collector of naval prints, should find himself nautically in the second rank of the Washington bureaucracy, particularly since he was a Democratic Roosevelt. For him, as for Howe, it was just another rung on the political ladder.

When Roosevelt and Howe crossed the threshold of the assistant secretary of the navy's spacious office, they had little or no idea of what lay ahead of them. "I can still see us as we entered for the first time," Howe told his confidential secretary, Lela Stiles, years later. "Though a newspaperman I had never learned what the duties of a secretary to the assistant secretary of the navy were. So, standing beside Franklin's desk, I blotted his signature as he signed official papers for several days."

Howe was not so much Roosevelt's secretary as his political manager and watchdog, his buffer, shielding his superior from importunate lesser contacts, taking charge of the tedious intricacies of patronage, drafting letters to New York constituents, wheedling postmasterships from the complaisant assistant postmaster general, doling out shipyard jobs to the politically sanctified, coordinating all efforts into building a New York machine that could challenge Tammany. "From 1913 on," Kenneth Davis wrote "Howe lived through Roosevelt — his life had practically no meaning for him apart from Roosevelt. . . . Howe *was* Roosevelt (Roosevelt was never Howe), and a manifestation of his *necessary* acceptance of the other's domination was the fierce possessive jealousy with which he guarded his special relationship."

The new assistant secretary of the navy did not find the work too demanding. Though Secretary Daniels was himself no deepwater sailor, he had no intention of letting his subordinate take over the department as Theodore Roosevelt had once done. He did not, however, object to Roosevelt's making tours of inspection, and the assistant secretary was assiduous in visiting navy yards and installations and vessels. Crusty admirals in Napoleonic fore-and-aft hats and gold stripes halfway up to their elbows snapped to attention and saluted as he was piped aboard. He thoroughly enjoyed the ranks of marines drawn up in his honor, the bands playing, the guns booming salutes. He even designed an assistant secretary's flag for himself.

Washington in that quiescent time was still a village where everyone above a certain level knew everyone else. Roosevelt, of course, knew everyone. He found the same congenial company and many of the same people he had known at Harvard and in New York.

His job interested him, at times intrigued him, but did not overtax him. The details could safely be left to Howe and to the permanent secretaries and clerks. There was always time for social life, for congenial hours at his clubs or on the fairways of Chevy Chase with such "good spirits" as Senator Warren Harding of Ohio. Eleanor later said that it was Howe who saved her husband from the snobbishness and total dedication to pleasure-seeking represented by the Metropolitan and Army and Navy Clubs.

It was during these years that Franklin fell in love with his wife's part-time social secretary, Lucy Mercer, nine years his junior, of impoverished gentility and much charm. The affair reached a crisis in 1918 when Eleanor found a packet of Lucy's letters to him. She agreed to allow her husband a divorce, but the devoutly Catholic Lucy refused to consider marriage under such circumstances. Sara threatened to cut off her financial support, always essential to her son. Then, too, Franklin may have been nagged by second thoughts as to how a divorce might affect his political future. Whatever the reasons, he went back to Eleanor, though they never lived together again as man and wife.*

Politically, Roosevelt and Howe bided their time, while doing their best to snatch up every possible bit of patronage. Howe had a nose for available jobs. By judicious publicity he encouraged the impression in New York State that the assistant secretary of the navy was the person to write to for independent Democrats who needed help in Washington. With Cousin Theodore's example still in mind, Franklin in the summer of 1914 suddenly declared himself a candidate for the United States Senate in that first year of the popular election of senators. Once more taking his familiar stand against Tammany, he asked the voters of New York to make their choice between "reactionary politics and politicians" and "intelligent progressive and honest administration in government." Howe was away at the time or he might have prevented such folly. "My senses have not yet left me," Roosevelt wrote him, but Howe undoubtedly thought that they had. Though battered by events, Tammany was ready for Roosevelt. Boss Murphy, not to be outdone by the assistant secretary of the navy's respectability, named as his candidate the ambassador to Ger-

* Although he agreed to give up Lucy, they later managed to see each other. Long since married and a widow, she was one of three women with him when he died.

many, James W. Gerard, a wealthy businessman who was also a Tammany stalwart. Although Howe must have realized the hopelessness of the contest from the outset, he went to work with his old zeal, plotting publicity campaigns, forwarding releases to the rural press, playing up his carefully cultivated friendship with labor leaders by mailing out hundreds of personal letters with union endorsement.

Meanwhile Roosevelt had left Washington for a prolonged vacation at Campobello. Much to Howe's distress, he failed even to appear at the formal opening of the campaign at New York's Cooper Union four weeks before the balloting. Howe vainly begged him to send a "ringing message" with some plausible excuse for his absence. In spite of Howe's exhaustive efforts the campaign was poorly planned, poorly financed, poorly run. Even the Howe-Roosevelt patronage beneficiaries wavered. Gerard won the nomination by a two to one margin, although it did him and his party little good, for the Republicans swept the November election. A chastened Roosevelt campaigned for the Democratic regulars, including Gerard. He had learned one lesson that he would not forget: Never meet the Tammany Tiger head-on!

Established in a permanent position at last, Howe was able to have his wife and son and daughter living with him. The advent of the war brought him heavier responsibilities, for the details of Roosevelt's tasks fell to him. His particular field was labor relations and here he created lasting goodwill for his chief. Daniels placed Roosevelt in charge of all labor matters and he in turn handed them to his assistant. When strikes threatened at navy yards or installations, Howe hurried there at once. As troubleshooter he found himself responsible for procurement of labor, for obtaining key items of ship construction, and at one point he was even investigating prostitution and gambling in naval towns. By May, 1917, he had become a special assistant to the assistant secretary at $400 a month and was rated an expert in the Bureau of Supplies and Accounts where he concerned himself with price control and general purchases. His political activity faded as, following the 1914 defeat, the hopefully built-up Howe-Roosevelt machine disintegrated. By 1916 he and Roosevelt had practically given up on New York politics. Yet Howe never wavered in squeezing out the last ounce of publicity for the assistant secretary while remaining himself obscurely in the background.

Following the president's war declaration the eastern seaboard elite had rushed to volunteer almost en masse. Theodore Roosevelt, in his sixties as belligerent as ever, was intent on raising and leading a volunteer division. His sons were almost at once in uniform. Franklin felt no such martial promptings. His duty, he maintained, was at his desk. Yet with Theodore's Cuban example before him, he could not fail to be aware how useful an active war record could be in politics. By August 1918 he was angling for a commission. "The more I think of it, the more I feel that being only thirty-six my place is not at a Washington desk, even a Navy desk," he told Eleanor. Howe counseled prudence. "I wonder," he told Eleanor in turn, "if he knows that it has been practically decided to accept no volunteers whatever under the new draft and that married men with children are not going to be called."

As the 1918 election and the war's end simultaneously neared, the disarrayed New York Independents tried to persuade the conveniently absent Roosevelt to run for governor. Even Tammany was willing to go along. But Howe the realist knew the time was wrong and urged the upstate leaders to support Al Smith, then president of the New York Board of Aldermen and one of Tammany's honest men held in reserve by that organization. Roosevelt on his return readily endorsed Smith who managed to breast the year's anti-Democratic tide to win election by a small majority.

In the war's aftermath, with the country's longing to return to an imagined prewar era that the Republican presidential nominee, Warren Harding, would label "normalcy," there seemed little future either for Roosevelt or the Democrats. Roosevelt thought his party's best hope would be to nominate a distinguished nonpolitical figure like his earlier friend and dinner companion, Herbert Hoover, Wilson's food administrator. By January of 1920 he was writing of Hoover to Hugh Gibson, the first American ambassador to the recreated Poland: "He certainly is a wonder and I wish we could make him President of the United States. There could not be a better one."

As the June Democratic convention neared, several newspapers began booming Roosevelt as a presidential possibility, much to Howe's dismay, who feared a premature draft for a hopeless contest that would lead to political oblivion. The leading candidate, the president's son-in-law, William Gibbs McAdoo, was handicapped by his position as the "crown prince" of the Wilson administration and failed to win or persuade the necessary two-thirds of the delegates. After forty-four ballots the convention finally chose Ohio's governor, the relatively unknown James Cox, a Wilson supporter who was at the same time acceptable to the urban bosses. To balance their candidate Cox's managers wanted an Easterner, a Wilsonian, a progressive. Franklin Roosevelt seemed the ideal choice. Cox's manager sought out Tammany's Boss Murphy. "I don't like Roosevelt," Murphy told him. "He is not well known in the country. But this is the first time a Democratic nominee for the presidency has shown me courtesy. That's why I would vote for the devil himself if Cox wanted me to. Tell him we will nominate Roosevelt on the first ballot as soon as we assemble." And he might have added that Roosevelt was expendable, while Tammany's golden boy, Al Smith, was not. On hearing the news of Roosevelt's nomination, Hoover — by then having proclaimed himself a Republican — wrote him a warm letter saying that although they were not of the same "political tribe," he wished "an old friend" and "great public servant" the best.

Vaulting up from assistant secretary of the navy to vice-presidential candidate like Cousin Theodore before him, full of an enthusiasm undampened by Howe's doubts, Roosevelt prepared a speaking campaign he intended to contrast with Harding's McKinley-inspired determination to stay on his own front porch. In three months of campaigning he visited thirty-two states and made over a thousand speeches, traveling in his own private railroad car with a party of reporters, and Eleanor as the sole woman aboard. Although the Democratic tide was fast ebbing, he himself was well received wherever he went. A reporter found him "the figure of an idealized college football player, almost the poster type in public life, . . . making clean, direct and few gestures; always with a smile ready to share, sincerely, one is sure, in the audience's humor. He speaks with a strong, clear voice, with a tenor note in it which rings — sings, one is tempted to say — in key with . . . that intangible utterly charming and surely vote-winning quality." Populist farmers at whistle stops, confusing him with Cousin Theodore, would bellow out "I voted for your old man, an' I'll vote for you!"

While Roosevelt toured the country, Howe remained in Washington, in his chief's phrase, "keeping the shop." Despite the exactions of his office, the long hours, the shouldering of others' responsibilities, his years at Washington had been good years. He had at last a happy if modest family life with his wife and children. He had become a recognized minor actor on the Washington stage. Much to his sardonic pleasure he was considered a person of mystery within his department. Admirals nudged each other in the corridors when he passed. Although his health grew increasingly wretched, compounded now by heart trouble, he found refuge in a small cottage on isolated Horseneck Beach near Fall River where he spent two to four weeks each year and to which he retreated spasmodically when he felt near collapse. Though the Roosevelt social world was beyond his reach or wish, he had his own relaxations. He sang in the choir of St. Thomas Episcopal Church, he was active in the Drama League Players, mostly as a director but sometimes in comedy parts. He painted with watercolors, and still wrote occasional light, and sometimes more serious, verse. In spite of his salary increases, however, he never managed to get out of debt.

Late that summer he joined Roosevelt, then speeding in his railroad car on a second tour of the West. He helped with speeches and press releases, and went out of his way to curb his temper and keep cordial relations with the newsmen aboard. On this tour he first came into contact with Eleanor Roosevelt. She had never liked the profane grubby little man with his inevitable half-smoked Sweet Caporal, and though she treated him politely she had always remained cold and offhanded. Through this barrier Howe managed to sense her loneliness and lack of self-confidence. He knew her anguish over Lucy Mercer. Because he sensed her intelligence and latent social awareness, he tried to share some of his own insights into politics. Whenever he was preparing drafts of Franklin's speeches he brought them to her to talk over. He encouraged her to face the reporters. He coached her on how to speak, how to suppress her irritating nervous giggle. His confidence in her began to be returned, and before the trip was over she had come to accept him as a friend. To him she now became "Eleanor," not "Mrs. Roosevelt." "The fact that Louis had rather extraordinary eyes and a fine mind I was not to discover," she said later "and it was by the externals alone that I had judged him prior to this trip." She still thought his clothes untidy, smiled at his dinky hats, abhorred his Sweet Caporals, but came to admit that he was one of the "seven people" who had shaped her personality.

In the euphoria that envelopes a candidate, Roosevelt had expected or almost expected to win. There were times when he found his doubts mounting, but he had never anticipated the humiliation of election day. Harding swept the country, the most decisive victory in a century. Nor was it much consolation that the vote was not so much for Harding as against Wilson, against the now discredited war, against the League. In New York State Harding got twice as many votes as Cox, and even Governor Al Smith went down to defeat although he ran over a million votes ahead of the national ticket. Howe saw the Democratic reverses as merely an interlude, a detour to the great goal. His belief in Roosevelt's destiny remained unwavering. A few weeks after the election he was standing at the window of his office in the Navy Department with two admirals and a lieutenant commander looking at the White House across the street. "Boys," he said, "do you see that building over there? That's where Franklin is going some day." He paused for a moment and smiled, "Franklin and I!"

In spite of Howe's long-range optimism, he and Roosevelt after they had left the Navy Department did not seem to be going anywhere. "Thank the Lord we are still both comparatively youthful," Roosevelt told his campaign publicity agent Steve Early. He was more concerned for the moment with finding some way of making a lot of money quickly, as was Howe with far more need. In the next few years Roosevelt, with get-rich-quick zeal, was to embrace a number of fly-by-night schemes, few of which made him much and none of which made him a fortune. Vaguely he resumed the ostensible practice of law, attaching his name to the firm of Emmit, Marvin & Roosevelt. He found a sinecure position as vice-president of the Fidelity & Deposit Company of Maryland, a surety bonding house that considered his name and political connections useful to the tune of $25,000 a year. At this point he hired as his personal secretary a slender, fair-haired, blue-eyed young woman of twenty-two, Marguerite LeHand, whom he and everyone else would soon call Missy. She would become, along with Louis Howe, his most trusted associate, for the next two decades his secretary extraordinary, hostess, confidante and intimate companion. According to Elliot Roosevelt, Howe and Missy were the only two allowed to know his father totally.

Howe remained in the Navy Department after the election, staying on for several months in the new administration to assist Roosevelt's successor — ironically enough Theodore Roosevelt, Jr.

— to familiarize himself with the duties of office. On leaving the department, he was at as loose an end as he had been a decade earlier in Albany. Still for him to decide was whether to tie his fate to Roosevelt's or strike out for himself. For Howe, aging and fearful of standing alone in the world, and with his fixed belief in destiny, there was only one choice. He joined the Fidelity & Deposit Company as Roosevelt's assistant.

The summer of 1921 Roosevelt spent as usual with his family at Campobello. Howe went to Horseneck Beach for July, then with his wife traveled north in the early part of August to visit the Roosevelts. August 10 was a fateful day for both families. On that day Roosevelt jogged several miles across the island with his boys, then took a swim in the icy waters of the Bay of Fundy. That evening he went to bed tired and singularly depressed. The next day when he got up he found that his left leg dragged. On the following morning his temperature was 102 degrees and both legs were paralyzed. In two more days the paralysis had crept to his chest muscles. The local doctor diagnosed it as grippe. Howe, much distressed and fearful, wrote to Roosevelt's uncle in New York describing the symptoms minutely. Meanwhile he and Eleanor took turns as nurses, in their inexperience doing just the wrong thing by massaging their patient's feet and legs by the hour and so irreparably damaging muscle tissue. Roosevelt grew worse. His bowels and bladder ceased to function, and catheters and enemas had to be used. To get the children out of the way, Grace Howe took them on a camping trip.

Roosevelt's uncle consulted New York specialists. They at once made the diagnosis of infantile paralysis, a diagnosis that was soon confirmed by a visiting Boston specialist. For some time Howe and Eleanor managed to keep the grim fact concealed. Louis lied to reporters, forced Eleanor to put on a smiling face, and when he saw Franklin giving way to despair cursed him until the other's anger drove the black mood away. As if it were a matter of course he took charge of the Roosevelt family, even as he took over all Roosevelt's business and political correspondence. "Thank heavens he is here," Eleanor wrote, "as he has been the greatest help."

Whatever the physical facts of his illness, Roosevelt was doggedly determined to recover. On their return to New York, Howe decided to stay on as Roosevelt's personal aide, again giving up his family to live in the Roosevelt's town house, ousting the fifteen-year-old daughter Anna from her third-floor room to her great indignation. By this time Eleanor and Franklin had come to find him indispensable. But to Sara Roosevelt, living next door, he was merely "that ugly, dirty, little man," who filled her son's bedroom with vulgar political types and the house with tobacco smoke. She found his personal habits insufferable; his Sweet Caporals, his hacking cough and foul breath, the incense he insisted on burning in his littered room, his sharp tongue and crude table manners. Anna and the other children in turn viewed him as an intruder. Sara would have taken her son back to Hyde Park to round off his days as an invalid gentleman farmer. Franklin wanted no part of it. He might be under her shadow, but he refused to be eclipsed. By the next spring he was resolved to be as well as ever. Meanwhile Howe kept his interests in politics stirred up while at the same time urging the increasingly social-service-minded Eleanor to strike out on her own. Though he knew better, Howe managed to create the impression that Roosevelt's attack was mild and that he would soon be as well as ever. But when Herbert Pell of the Democratic State Committee wrote Roosevelt asking him to attend an October meeting, Howe scrawled in the letter's margin: "Mr. Pell had better wake up and hear the birdies."

Roosevelt continued to insist that he would not be crippled, yet for all his optimism he was fated to be chair-bound for the rest of his days, able at best to take a few halting steps with heavy steel braces on his lifeless legs, never able to walk alone. At least his control over his bladder and bowels returned. His jaunty manner remained as did the zest for life that overcame the inevitable moments of despair. Howe grew into an extension of Roosevelt's own personality, filling in for him at business and political and philanthropic meetings, writing his most personal letters, buying prints and antiques at auctions, running trivial errands. Even in demurring at some ultra-triviality, he would treat it as a joke. "Lord knows," he scribbled to Roosevelt, "I have acted as your alter-ego in many weird commissions, but I must positively and firmly refuse to risk my judgment on neckties, watches and pajamas."

With the ingenuity of his young Saratoga days Howe devised amusements and diversions to cheer the invalid's spirits. He joked, with the slapstick schoolboy type of jest that Roosevelt always relished, and bore up gracefully under the other's badgering adolescent humor. On Roosevelt's birthdays he organized annual parties of the Cuff Links Club, those intimates to whom Roosevelt had given gold cuff links as mementoes of the 1920 campaign. For such festivities Howe composed and staged skits and sketches.

Roosevelt, in spite of his wheelchair status, still kept his position with the Fidelity & Deposit Company. He still hoped to make a financial killing in the booming economy. For a time he and Howe were involved in a complicated scheme to get hold of German properties seized by the government during the war and held by the Alien Property Custodian.* In his more desultory moments he thought of embarking on a literary career as Cousin Theodore had done. But the few and brief political articles that he produced were ghost-written by Howe. For all his nimble mind, he was incapable of sustained intellectual effort, as he more or less admitted himself.

Howe did his utmost to keep Roosevelt's name before the public and before the politicians. He persuaded him to find jobs at the Fidelity & Deposit for sons of Tammany and Brooklyn politicians. He renewed the friendly contacts with labor leaders that he had made in his Navy Department days. Never, even in these barren months, did he lose his belief, his almost fanatic faith in Roosevelt's destiny. Roosevelt in turn did his best to insinuate Howe into various sinecure positions, finally managing to get him an undemanding job as assistant to the chairman of the Crime Commission at $4,000 a year that still left him free to work almost full-time for his old boss.

After 1926 Roosevelt's chief interest centered on Warm Springs, Georgia, the decayed winter resort with its hot mineral springs that he found, or thought he found, beneficial to his leg muscles. In 1926 with a third of a $600,000 inheritance from a half-brother, he bought up the resort with its 1,200 acres, intending to establish a permanent treatment center there for victims of infantile paralysis and, incidentally, to make a profit on his original investment. Eleanor was dubious of the whole scheme, Howe on the other hand extremely enthusiastic. When New York millionaires failed to show an expected interest in the Warm Springs Foundation, Howe worked out a successful general fund-raising

* A similar scheme would later emerge as one of the scandals of the Harding administration.

drive. Warm Springs would not bring Roosevelt his hoped-for cure but it would remain his pet project for the rest of his life, the place where he would die.

Roosevelt's physical handicap had at least the advantage of leaving him remote from Democratic failures. The year after Harding's election found him urging the national committee to reorganize and reinvigorate the party. He and Howe sent out letters to party leaders all over the country whose names, addresses, occupations and even personal characteristics the two had filed away during the 1920 campaign. Successful local Democratic candidates in the off-election year of 1921 received congratulatory notes with Howe's forged Roosevelt signature. Both Roosevelt and Howe had become convinced that Republican tenure would endure nationally until some economic reverse intervened. Howe in the depths of his conspiratorial mind thought that 1936 might be Roosevelt's *annus mirabilis.*

As the New York state election of 1922 neared, Roosevelt appealed to Al Smith, in a prearranged open letter, again to be a candidate for governor. "You represent the type of citizen the voters of the state want to vote for," he wrote, "and you can be elected." Smith delayed announcing his candidacy, maintaining an enigmatic silence until he received Roosevelt's letter. In replying to this he finally announced that if the majority of the delegates to the Democratic state convention wanted him he would "battle for them with all the energy and vigor that I possess." He was reelected by the largest plurality ever yet given a New York governor.

After the election Roosevelt wrote "Al" enthusiastically that it was the "first incentive to effective organization" in twelve years. Roosevelt and Howe both hoped that this term as governor would pave the way for Smith's nomination as Democratic presidential candidate in 1924. Howe at least, with his deeper feeling for politics, must have sensed that the chances of electing an Irish Catholic Democrat were minimal indeed, particularly after the austere atavistic Calvin Coolidge had managed to seal up the cracks in his inherited Harding administration with his laissez-faire version of prosperity. But Smith's candidacy for president might leave the governorship open for Roosevelt as perhaps the final step in that pattern set so long ago by Cousin Theodore. The way seemed clear. Roosevelt had long since buried the hatchet with the Tammany machine. When Boss Murphy died in

1924 he was even ready to extol his old enemy as New York's "most powerful and wisest leader."

Murphy died only a few weeks before the Democratic National Convention. McAdoo was again the leading candidate, backed with ferocious devotion by the West and the South, the remnants of the Bryan populists, the Protestant Bible belt, the militant prohibitionists and the revived Ku Klux Klan, then at the height of its power. Al Smith, as his chief opponent, was the candidate of the wets, the urban East, the Catholic ethnic groups. Following Murphy's death, Smith announced that Roosevelt would head the New York Citizens' Committee to promote his candidacy. But what Smith intended more as a gesture, Howe turned into a fact. With his old zeal and deftness he set up a giant pool of typists for mass production of correspondence. Eleanor was put in charge of a women's division. Smith's closest associates continued to regard Howe and Roosevelt with some suspicion, preferring to keep them at a distance. Howe tried in vain to get the governor to commit himself on national issues in a way that might appeal to the South and West. Smith kept his silence, his strategy being to make it clear to party leaders that the Democrats could not win without the East and that they could not win the East without him.

Smith had intended to have his name placed in nomination by his silver-tongued friend, Bourke Cockran. When Cockran died before the convention, Smith, with no other suitable man to turn to, then chose Roosevelt. The Protestant squire with the upper-class accent was an astute choice to help offset the southern and western caricature of Smith as a cigar-chomping pol in a brown derby and striped suit who would turn the country over to Tammany and the Pope.

That convention, held in New York's Madison Square Garden, was the longest and one of the angriest, noisiest and most intemperate that the country had ever seen. Two organizations cast sinister shadows over the echoing amphitheater: Tammany Hall, its plug-uglies packing the galleries; and the Ku Klux Klan, to which most Southern delegates bore at least a silent allegiance. When the majority of the platform committee voted to include a plank censuring the Klan, the aged Fundamentalist, William Jennings Bryan used the remnants of his golden voice to speak against it, bringing down on his head a counterpoint of vituperation from the galleries. The plank was finally defeated by four votes out of a total of 1098 delegates.

On the first ballot McAdoo received 431½ votes to Smith's 241. Though subsequently McAdoo would pick up another hundred votes, he would fall some two hundred votes short of the required two-thirds majority. The balloting continued through the heat-riven summer days for another 102 ballots in the fetid din of the Garden, a brass band playing Smith's theme song, "The Sidewalks of New York," and "The Bowery" and "Sweet Rosie O'Grady," over and over, the clenched-fist Tammanyites yelling and hooting in the galleries, the southerners on the floor hissing at any adverse mention of the Klan.

For the first time the proceedings of a convention were being broadcast. By the middle of 1924 there were already some three million radio sets in the land, and millions of listeners from coast to coast clamped their earphones on their heads to follow the turbulent proceedings. Each round of balloting began with the bellowed pronouncement that came to seem almost the trademark of the convention: "Alabama . . . votes . . . twenty-four . . . votes . . . for Oscar W. Underwood!"

When Roosevelt had stood up to nominate Smith, it marked his official reentry into politics. His steel leg-braces locked in place, grasping his son Jimmy's arm, he slowly walked the six steps from his chair to the speaker's podium. Every eye was on him. It was the most dramatic moment of the convention. Louis Howe muttered "Mein Gawd" to himself, wondering if those lifeless legs would make the distance. But Roosevelt as he gained the podium was full of genial confidence. His speech had been written by New York's Judge Joseph Proskauer, yet in Roosevelt's friendly tones it sounded as if it had come from the depths of his own heart. He concluded with the well-known lines from Wordsworth that Proskauer had hesitated on, thinking they might be too literary for an audience of politicians:

> This is the happy Warrior: this is he
> That every man in arms should wish to be.

Spoken with such mellifluous conviction, the phrase was electric. From that time on Al Smith would be the "Happy Warrior."

Although few politicians yet realized the implications, Roosevelt had a natural radio presence capable of exploiting all the resources of the new medium, a vibrant voice that seemed to radiate understanding and sympathy, that could mesmerize his hearers. He could not nominate Smith, but in his effort he made it clear to the convention and to his radio listeners that he himself was a man to be reckoned with. By contrast Al Smith had an unsympathetically harsh voice and an East Side accent that alienated those from other regions of the country.

The exhausted delegates finally picked the conservative New York lawyer, John Davis, as a compromise candidate, choosing as his running mate Bryan's bumbling brother Charles as a sop to the westerners. Davis at once urged Smith to run again for governor as the best way to help his party. Howe and Roosevelt were not wanted in the campaign that in any case was as inevitably doomed as was Cox's four years earlier. Roosevelt's image survived the election debacle. The tall crippled figure, gripping the podium so confidently despite his handicap, aroused general feelings of sympathy that went beyond politics, and the radio made his voice intimately familiar across the nation.

Smith had been opposed by the Republican Theodore Roosevelt, Jr., intent on following in his father's footsteps — for Ted had been a colonel in the World War, an assistant secretary of the navy, and he saw the next step as Albany. But the son, something of a toper and a poet manqué, had never been able to emerge from his father's shadow. In the Navy Department he had served under Harding's Secretary of the Navy Edwin Denby whose reputation had been demolished by the Teapot Dome Oil lease investigations. Though Ted was in no way implicated in that scandal, it clung to him. Whenever he went on speaking tours in upper New York State he was followed by a caravan made up of Eleanor and her friends, the lead car covered by a huge teapot that emitted live steam — another of Howe's maliciously ingenious ideas. When Ted attempted to speak, the teapot car would be driven around the crowd, steam pouring from its spout. Often the sight of it would break up a rally. Howe's teapot was merely an impish diversion without effect on the results, for in that Republican year Al was able to carry his own state by 140,000 votes even as Davis was losing it to Coolidge by 700,000.

Smith was the first New York governor in a century to be elected to a third term, one of the most able and compassionate and far-sighted that the state had ever had. Upright himself, humane and responsible, he understood from his Lower East Side background the necessary function of organizations of the Tammany ilk — for all their inevitable corruption — in a pre-welfare state. Lacking formal education, he owed much of his intellectual background to the sharp-minded New York social worker, Belle Moskowitz, a former Progressive Republican, whom he had met in his 1918 campaign and who in the years to follow became secretary of the state labor commission and his most confidential adviser. She wrote many if not most of his speeches. Before making any big decision, he invariably consulted her.

As third-term governor and with the help of Mrs. Moskowitz, Smith developed his grand plan for the reorganization of the state's government that would endure as the outstanding achievement of his public career. In 1926, at the end of his third term, he made a feint of retiring, but the New York Democratic party could not do without him. He was nominated for the fifth time by acclamation, and when he appeared before the convention the delegates cheered him as "the next president of the United States." To which he replied: "One nomination at a time, please!" His election to a fourth term as governor was inevitable. He seemed then the leading progressive Democrat in the United States. His long-range goal was to avenge his Madison Square Garden humiliation, to still those hissing southern voices, to stand in 1928 as his party's candidate for the greatest office in the land.

During Smith's last two terms as governor, Roosevelt through Howe kept in constant and growing contact with politicians all over the country. Following Davis's defeat, Howe sent out a circular letter to all the participants of the 1924 Democratic convention asking to what they attributed the electoral disaster. The replies poured in, accusations and counteraccusations, suggestions and blame. Howe tabulated the results, then arranged a program of massive correspondence such as he had prepared twenty years ago for Osborne but on a much larger scale. Carefully he fostered the belief, although he knew better, that Roosevelt's total physical recovery was only a matter of time. Roosevelt struck the pose of a selfless leader, above party rivalries, interested only in the revitalizing of his party. The pose was coldly received by professional party leaders, who saw the Howe-Roosevelt maneuver as a far from disinterested attempt to take over the party. Nevertheless Roosevelt's stature continued to grow, abetted by Howe's persistent ingenuity. When Roosevelt was asked to write an article in *Foreign Affairs* critical of Republican policy, Howe wrote the article. Roosevelt's admiration for Smith remained tinged with jealousy, but Howe saw to it that relations between the two men appeared friendly and cooperative. In

1926 Roosevelt was the keynote speaker at the Democratic state convention. A year later, after disastrous floods in the Mississippi Valley, he attracted national attention by denouncing President Coolidge's inaction and Secretary of Commerce Hoover's ineffective program. Howe urged him to make a "ringing demand in the name of humanity" for federal action. "In other words, raise hell generally." When Hoover then proposed a plan for flood relief and control similar to Roosevelt's, Howe prepared a statement complaining of "the dissipation of energy and loss of valuable time through too involved a consideration" of the problem. Roosevelt now spoke out more frequently on foreign affairs. For South America he espoused what would later be known as the Good Neighbor Policy. But, following Howe's advice, he avoided taking any part in the acrimonious debate on the current Kellogg-Briand Pact outlawing war. "The reputation you have," Howe warned him, "should not be jeopardized by backing up every day dream of the impractical theorist." His great fear was that Roosevelt might be induced to run for office prematurely, to the destruction of his political future. Howe had already managed to avoid Roosevelt's draft nomination as candidate for the United States Senate in 1926. Then as 1928 neared, Hearst's papers began spreading rumors that Roosevelt would be the next Democratic presidential candidate. Howe at once planted a counter-statement in the press from "one of Mr. Roosevelt's closest friends" that "Frank is not and will not be under any circumstances a candidate for the Presidency."

As 1928 neared, Smith as the governor of the nation's richest and most populous state, seemed the only possible Democratic presidential choice. Bryan was dead, McAdoo had declared that he was not a candidate, and party leaders were anxious to heal the schism that had led to the 1924 disaster. The more astute Southern and Western leaders were willing to let Smith have the nomination by default, rather than alienate four million urban Catholic voters, convinced in any case that no Democrat could overcome the magic Republican slogan of "Prosperity!" Howe felt that Al's enemies would nominate him, then knife him at the polls.

As a gesture of conciliation to the South the convention was held in Houston, Texas. This time there was no formal opposition to Smith and he was nominated on the first ballot. Again Roosevelt placed the governor's name in nomination, using the familiar Happy Warrior phrase that had by now come to seem part of Smith's personality. Roosevelt's speech, written primarily with the radio in mind, had a powerful and magnetic effect over the vastly expanded audience. "Limpid and unaffected in style," the *New York Times* called it, "without a trace of fustian."

Two weeks earlier the Republican National Convention in Kansas City had nominated Herbert Hoover, also on the first ballot. President Coolidge could have had the nomination for himself, but the year before he had declared that he did not choose to run — for reasons that the Vermont enigma preferred to keep to himself. The Republican Old Guard would have preferred Coolidge. They had little use for the secretary of commerce, the unpolitical food administrator under Wilson who had endorsed his League of Nations, to whom Coolidge referred sourly as "the wonder boy." But Hoover, for all his retiring manner, remained the bright star of the Republican party, and the popular demand for him was too strong, too insistent to be denied.

Smith, in exultant spirits at his Houston triumph, was confident that he would win the election. His opponent was, in his opinion, a lackluster personality. "I'm going to beat the pants off Hoover," he predicted. Roosevelt and Howe privately saw Smith's defeat as inevitable. Howe was convinced that Hoover would not only sweep the country but would be re-elected in 1932. Hoover, sunning himself in the last rays of Republican prosperity, would proclaim in his inaugural address: "I have no fears for the future of our country. It is bright with hope." Howe knew better. No prosperity, no boom ever lasted more than two decades. He remembered all too well the Panic of 1873 that had driven the Howes from Indiana, the depression during Cleveland's second administration, his own jobless months following the 1907 panic. The days of the Republican Coolidge–Hoover prosperity were also numbered. Once again Howe saw 1936 as the year of decision.

The 1928 campaign had cruel and savage overtones that Smith would discover as soon as he moved in the West. Sometimes as his train moved across the prairies he glimpsed rows of burning crosses set off by the Ku Klux Klan. Though he could not face the fact, it would take another generation for the country to reach the point of maturity, or indifference, where it would elect a Catholic president. Smith's religion was his most burdensome handicap. After he had spoken to a coldly unreceptive audience in Oklahoma City, the evangelist John Roach Stratton filled the same hall to overflowing the following night with his address "Al Smith and the Forces of Hell." Such incidents multiplied. A rumor spun wildly from state to state that the Pope had secretly bought a waterfront estate in Maryland conveniently close to Washington and planned to move in once Smith was elected. Al might be a hero to the Irish and Italians and other emergent ethnic groups who identified themselves with his rise in the world. But middle America and middle-class Americans outside New York could not see the real man for the flamboyant brown derby and the nasal whiskey-voice that said "rad-dio" with a flat A and "t'oid" for "third."

Smith had a number of eminent financial backers, chief of them John Raskob, vice-president of General Motors, a Catholic and a self-made man who had come to fancy himself in the role of president maker. At Smith's insistence Raskob was made chairman of the Democratic National Committee. Belle Moskowitz directed the Smith campaign. With Raskob and Mrs. Moskowitz in command, Howe and Roosevelt played only a nominal role. Roosevelt was named chairman of the party's Commerce and Industry Division at the Democratic Campaign Headquarters in New York's General Motors Building. He put Howe in charge of the office with its dozen stenographers while he himself relaxed at his cottage with Missy LeHand.

Smith's tour of the West taught him how strong the old Know-Nothing feeling was, what a task it would be to buck the tide of Republican prosperity. Even his own New York was coming to seem a touch-and-go state. As governor to succeed him he favored the New York banker Herbert Lehman, but Jim Farley, the secretary of the Democratic State Committee, felt that in a close election Roosevelt would be the best vote-getting personality. The only difficulty was that Franklin Roosevelt, like Calvin Coolidge, did not choose to run.

The Republican candidate for governor, Attorney General Albert Ottinger, the sole Republican to survive the Democratic sweep in Albany two years earlier, was popular and could count on New York City's large Jewish vote that had already elected him attorney general. Roosevelt might indeed be the only candidate who could beat Ottinger, and Smith urged him repeatedly to run. Each time Roosevelt refused, claiming that he needed the next two years for therapy that might at last set him free of his leg braces and put him on his feet again. Howe, fearing that

Roosevelt might weaken, bombarded him with telegrams urging him to remain firm against all pressure, insisting that his running would damage himself without helping Smith. On September 26, six days before the Democratic state convention, Howe wired Warm Springs:

> The *World* and other papers are running stories that you are being forced to run. The way things are running here, my conviction that you should not run is stronger than ever and Eleanor agrees with me in this.*

He followed this admonition with other warning telegrams: that Smith really did not need Roosevelt; that the real pressure was coming from leaders and office holders who feared for their jobs if Ottinger was elected; and he concluded: "Understand Governor trying to reach you by telephone. What I hear strongly confirms previous advice. . . . Beware of Greeks bearing gifts." Roosevelt was determined not to run. As he wrote his mother: "I have had a difficult time turning down the Governorship. . . . I only hope they don't try to stampede the Convention tomorrow and nominate me and then adjourn."

Roosevelt cagily made himself inaccessible. Not until midnight before the convention was Smith at last able to reach him by telephone. Al, Raskob and other leaders talked, argued for hours, trying to persuade the reluctant invalid. To all his objections they provided pat answers. He would not have to be an active governor. Lehman, Smith's choice as lieutenant governor, would act for him in Albany during the legislative sessions. Raskob promised to assume all the financial obligations of Warm Springs. Finally Smith asked Roosevelt pointblank if he would accept a nomination by acclamation from the convention. To this he did not reply. Smith and the others took silence for assent. Next morning New York's dapper playboy-mayor, Jimmie Walker, placed Roosevelt's name in nomination and the delegates acclaimed him unanimously. Eleanor sadly sent her regrets. Howe was furious. "Mess is no name for it," he wired Franklin and by way of congratulation suggested that Roosevelt look up the telegram Howe had sent him after Franklin's misguided entrance into the senate race in 1914.

Yet once the nomination had occurred Howe was as resolved as Roosevelt to win the election, then only a month away. His methods were his familiar ones — a pool of typists producing

* *The Man Behind Roosevelt*, p. 110.

masses of letters to politicians, with stock replies to the hundreds of letters that poured in. Each letter, however insignificant, received its answer with a cleverly forged signature. There was a vast clipping bureau as well. Howe ran two such propaganda factories: the Business and Professional Division of Smith's headquarters; and the Independent Committee for Roosevelt and Lehman, at the Biltmore Hotel. The easy-mannered back-slapping Jim Farley, who had met Howe and Roosevelt at the 1924 national convention, was in nominal charge of the Roosevelt headquarters but there was little conflict between him and Howe. As Roosevelt rose in the political world Howe grew extremely jealous of any possible rival who might insinuate himself between him and Franklin. Farley, a former Smith supporter, he did not see as a rival but as a trustworthy subordinate. "In the early days," the journalist W. E. Mullins wrote, "he [Farley] was little more than a front man for Louis Howe and he did only what the gnomelike figure in the background directed." Howe understood the minutiae of politics, but his surly manner and grotesque appearance repelled the general run of politicians. Instinctively he preferred to operate backstage. Farley, the affable Elk with the ready smile, the understanding handshake, the unfailing memory for first names, was by his Celtic nature an ideal front man, a political traveling salesman.

Louis's nervous energy as usual exceeded his physical capacities, but he refused to consider his health. His accomplishments both as publicity agent and fund raiser were extraordinary. With pride he boasted how he had raised $100,000 in less than a week, more than Smith had been able to muster for his whole 1926 campaign. Relations between the Smith and Roosevelt headquarters were less than intimate. Howe found great difficulty in getting through the barrier of aides to reach the governor, and often failed to do so. He and Mrs. Moskowitz remained wary of one another.

Commanding scores of females as typists and secretaries in his twin headquarters, Howe seemed to outward observers — and often to his girls — a petty tyrant, subject to furious bursts of temper, petulant, giving his girls "unshirted hell" for every small error, often impossibly demanding. Yet beneath all the drive and bluster, the "little boss" remained essentially kind. Felix the Cat, the girls called him behind his back, as if hunched up in his office-den, his hands clasped over one knee as he swung his foot back and forth, he were waiting to pounce on them. Some of them quit in tears at his tirades, but others endured to become devoted to him, staying with him and his Roosevelt obsession into the Washington years.

With only three weeks left before the election Howe counseled Roosevelt to "insist on limiting speeches to the four big cities with a radio hookup and generally make your campaign on the never mind me, vote for Al basis. That will have the advantage of avoiding the necessity of debating on state issues with practically no preparation." As for the day-to-day campaigning, Lehman "wants to relieve you of all routine work as Governor, and it is a good time to start now." Roosevelt had no intention of so eclipsing himself. Since his first barnstorming tour in the red Maxwell he had taken a yeasty delight in crowds, applause, movement, the friendly faces, the outstretched hands, the boisterous reception of his impromptu speeches (usually prepared by someone else). After a trip to Georgia to speak for Smith, he returned to make a ten-day whirlwind tour of upper New York State. Wearing the battered felt "good-luck" hat of his first campaign, he travelled 175 miles a day, radiating physical energy for those who had doubted his health, and ringing the charges on his three themes of public electric power (derived from Smith), reform of the criminal codes (derived from Howe) and aid to the farmers, while doing his best to dodge the wet-dry issue.

On election night Smith and his family went to New York City's 69th Regiment Armory to wait for the election returns. Roosevelt was there also with his wife and mother. Even in the earlier hours of the evening Smith's defeat became apparent, its magnitude swelling by midnight as Virginia, North Carolina and Florida of the solid South swung into the Republican column. The final humiliation for the New York governor was when he found that he had lost even his own state. It was the third Republican presidential landslide in a row. Hoover won by over six million votes, carrying five Southern states and gaining 444 electoral seats to Smith's 87.

Although Roosevelt managed to do better than Smith in New York State, by the time he left the armory in the early morning hours he was convinced of his own defeat. Not until he awoke at midday did he learn that he had won by the narrow margin of 24,500 votes out of the 4,200,000 cast. And even this margin was made possible only because of a feud between Ottinger and an upstate boss, who had swung over 20,000 Erie County Republican votes to Roosevelt.

After the initial shock of his repudiation, Smith could at least console himself that New York remained in Democratic hands. Those hands he still considered amateurish, for, as Howe remarked, he thought of Roosevelt as "a little boy who doesn't know anything about politics." The actual day-to-day business of governing, Smith expected would fall to his confidential ally, Lieutenant Governor Lehman, who could be counted on to carry out Smith policies with Smith advisers. The retiring governor intended to offer the incoming governor the full benefit of his years of experience. But in the interval between the November election and the January inaugural, he found Roosevelt singularly evasive. When he suggested that the new governor retain Robert Moses as secretary of state, Roosevelt, remembering how Big Bob had kept Howe from a sinecure job on the Taconic Parkway Commission, demurred. More important to Smith than the future of Moses was that of Belle Moskowitz, his one-man brain trust. He urged Roosevelt to appoint her his private secretary, pointing out how invaluable she had been to him. He even hinted that she would be just the person to help Roosevelt write his inaugural address. Roosevelt said he had made other arrangements. Then Smith suggested that she be appointed to some alternate office, possibly on the Public Service Commission, "where she would be close enough to the Governor to advise him." Roosevelt's reply was that he would think about it — as Smith was well aware, a politician's way of saying no. Howe was incensed at the thought of Mrs. Moskowitz serving the new administration in any capacity whatsoever and considered Smith's suggestions "a piece of effrontery."

By the time of the inauguration it was clear to insiders that relations between the outgoing and incoming governors had become tenuous. Nothing was apparent at the ceremony itself, during which the governor took the oath of office in the room that Theodore Roosevelt had taken the same oath just thirty years before. Smith and Roosevelt exchanged the conventional compliments in their addresses, with Roosevelt promising as Smith's disciple to continue the latter's program of social welfare. The new governor would not fail to note, however, that the shouts from the gallery were for Al Smith, not for him.

After the inauguration Smith stayed on for several weeks in Albany's DeWitt Clinton Hotel waiting for a call from the governor. The call never came. As Eleanor Roosevelt later explained it:

> I was not greatly surprised when after Smith's defeat it became evident that he thought he was going to retain a behind-the-scenes leadership in the state. It would not work; and he soon discovered that it would not work, and he left Albany for New York City.*

Howe put it more bluntly when he remarked that Al was dead but refused to lie down. Retreating to New York and the business world, Smith became head of the Empire State Building Corporation as well as director of two banks and an insurance company. He would not, he stated, take any further part in politics. Yet, for all such statements, politics lurked in his bloodstream, and in his deepest levels of consciousness he could never wholly dispossess himself of the thought of avenging his 1928 humiliation.

The ambivalence of the 1928 election left Louis Howe perplexed, not to say discouraged. His obsessive passion, before which everything else in his life had become secondary, was to see his Franklin in the White House. But Albany now seemed more a detour than a step forward, a premature success that might lead to a dead-end failure. For in the spring of 1929, President Hoover, the Great Engineer, the rock of Republican prosperity, looked unassailable for the next eight years. It might, as Howe saw it, be better in 1932 for someone else to win the less-than-glittering prize of the Democratic nomination. But whatever happened, he intended to build up a Roosevelt machine, to deal from a position of strength.

There was no major departmental job that Howe wanted in the new state administration nor, with his ever more precarious health, would he have been capable of extended effort as an administrator, for he could not climb a flight of stairs now without floundering and gasping for breath. He still remained Roosevelt's most intimate and confidential adviser, the only man who could talk back to the governor, but his responsibilities were limited to national politics and Roosevelt's long-range drive for the presidency. After the inauguration he set up his headquarters in New York City as the governor's Manhattan contact, occupying his old room in the Roosevelt town house and conducting his affairs

* *Al Smith: Hero of the Cities*, p. 412.

from the Crime Commission office, although by now all his time was given to Roosevelt. Letters on national politics were forwarded to him from the governor's office. Under the screening process devised by Missy he was the only one allowed to reach the governor day or night. Once a week he consulted personally with Roosevelt, traveling to Albany where a room was always kept reserved for him at the Executive Mansion. Only Howe was allowed the liberty of upbraiding Roosevelt to his face. "Can't you get anything into that thick Dutch skull of yours?" he would shout at him.

The political tasks that faced Howe and Roosevelt were formidable: to shift the allegiance of the machine Democrats from Smith to Roosevelt; to build up a nationwide network of Roosevelt supporters; to convince the nationwide public through reiterative publicity that New York's governor was the country's best Democratic hope. Again, as after the 1924 national defeat, Howe sent out letters to several thousand Democratic leaders asking what should be done for the party's future, each letter typed individually and signed with Roosevelt's forged signature. The replies were varied, but each recipient had a subtle reminder of Roosevelt's leadership. Howe took particular pains with the press, making sure that no pictures appeared of Roosevelt in his wheelchair, that no photographers caught him being carried in or out of a car, that the only photos released showed him smiling.

As governor, Roosevelt did not find his new job too demanding. From Smith he had inherited a smoothly functioning bureaucracy, and Lieutenant Governor Lehman could be trusted to handle the details. The governor needed only to pass a few months of the year at Albany, which left him pleasant months at Hyde Park, long summer vacations at Campobello. He spent much time journeying over the state on inspection tours, visiting institutions, hospitals, factories, exhilarated as ever by travel, movement, change. No governor had ever been so ubiquitous a presence. Nor had any governor managed to reach the mass of people as intimately as did Roosevelt in the persuasive fireside chats that he now initiated on the radio.

When Herbert Hoover took office in March, 1929, as the thirty-first president of the United States, it seemed even to professional economists that a new level of permanent prosperity had been attained, a new era reached. But Hoover had not been eight months in the White House when on October 25, 1929, an economic bolt struck from the serenely prosperous sky. The stock market crash marking that day was the darkest in Wall Street's checkered history. In the weeks that followed, both Hoover and Roosevelt dismissed the crash as the technical reverse of an overcharged market rather than the danger signal heralding a worldwide economic crisis. As late as December Roosevelt was still referring to it as "the little recent flurry down town," although he would grasp its implications far sooner than would Hoover.

The convulsive stock market continued jerkily downward week after week, month after month, and in the wake of bankrupt speculators, banks and businesses failed, factories closed, farmers saw their crops rot in the bins or in the fields, swelling armies of unemployed tramped the streets, and in the cruel months that followed breadlines formed in the great cities. Hoover's name, that during the World War had been a praise-worthy verb as the nation "hooverized," now became a noun of ill-repute as the tin shacks of "Hoovervilles," housing the homeless and the unemployed, sprung up on city dumps and barrens.

As the Great Depression spread from Wall Street to Main Street, Howe found in its enveloping bleakness the crisis his pessimistic soul had been waiting for. The postwar Republican tide was ebbing with astonishing rapidity. Roosevelt's election as governor in 1928, far from being premature, now appeared the luckiest of lucky strokes. In 1930, in spite of the handicap to the Democrats of Tammany's New York City scandals under Jimmy Walker, Roosevelt was re-elected governor by 725,000 votes over his dispirited Republican opponent, double the total of Smith's best record. The Democratic sweep was nationwide, the Democrats taking control of Congress with a majority in the House of Representatives and a Senate majority when combined with the remaining western Republican Progressives. On the day after the election Howe and Farley preparel a victory statement, written mostly by Howe but issued over Farley's name:

> I fully expect that the call will come to Governor Roosevelt when the first presidential primary is held, which will be late next year. The Democrats of the Nation naturally want as their candidate for President the man who has shown himself capable of carrying the most important state in the country by a record-breaking majority. I do not see how Mr. Roosevelt can escape becoming the next presidential nominee of his party, even if no one should raise a finger to bring it about.*

* *Jim Farley's Story*, p. 6.

Roosevelt issued the stereotype disclaimer that he was giving no consideration of thought or time in anything except his duties as governor, but it was obvious to all that he was the front runner intent on the 1932 nomination. It was almost as obvious after the 1930 mid-term elections that the next president would be a Democrat. Farley and Howe at once began to raise money and enlist personnel for a two-year campaign. Howe organized the Friends of Roosevelt with workers from the last two gubernatorial campaigns. From his new headquarters on Madison Avenue across the street from the Biltmore he built up a vast propaganda network. "Never in the history of politics," Farley recalled in his memoirs, "was there anything like our letter-writing and long-distance telephone campaign." No county chairman had a son married or a grandson born without receiving a congratulatory message ostensibly signed by Roosevelt. Howe's immediate goal was to dissociate Roosevelt from Smith and Raskob and to gather support from influential leaders in the West and South, to mute the prohibition issue and to appeal to the old populism-progressivism of the agrarian West. With the cooperation of Franklin and Eleanor, he primed an able journalist, Ernest Lindley, to write the New York governor's first biography, with the telling title *Roosevelt: a Career in Progressive Politics*. Earl Looker, a Republican friend of the Theodore Roosevelts, had challenged Franklin Roosevelt to submit to a physical examination to determine if he was fit to function as president. Howe used the challenge for a propaganda coup, obtaining doctors' testimony as to Roosevelt's glowing health and inviting Looker to the Executive Mansion to observe the governor's strenuous life at first hand. Looker came, saw and was conquered. He wrote a laudatory article for the national weekly magazine, *Liberty*. Howe at once ordered 50,000 reprints. He then arranged for Looker to write a four-hundred-word article for *Liberty* every other week over Roosevelt's signature using material furnished by Howe.

For all their contacts with sundry important senators, neither Farley nor Howe had had much practical experience of politics outside New York. So in the summer of 1931 Howe sent Farley, now the national president of the Benevolent and Protective Order of Elks, on what would become known as his Elks Tour, a journey to the Elks Convention at Seattle. Howe's real purpose was to have Farley sound out the more important state leaders along the way and sell Roosevelt to those who, in Howe's words, "carried the guns." In nineteen days Farley visited eighteen states. Howe had planned his itinerary and furnished him with letters of introduction to key politicians. The genial Elk, radiating goodwill, his affability highlighted by his round beaming face and bald head, found the leaders starved for patronage, eager to back a winner, and easily persuaded that Roosevelt was the man. His tour was a stunning success. Howe sent other agents to Texas and California, conferred with Southern and Western senators, accepted Farley's optimistic view that at the convention it would be Roosevelt on the first ballot. But revived Democratic hopes began to stir the presidential ambitions of favorite sons across the country as the prospect of the White House became more than a mirage. The old populist spellbinder, the florid pink-whiskered Senator J. Hamilton Lewis, felt that his belated time had come. Similar feelings were quickening in such varied leaders as Wilson's old enemy, Senator James Reed of Missouri; the patrician Governor Harry Byrd of Virginia; Wilson's War Secretary Newton Baker, the idol of the League of Nations diehards; Oklahoma's Governor Alfalfa Bill Murray of the dripping moustache and drooping socks; after forty-two years at the public trough, Speaker of the House Cactus Jack Garner, the boozy, profane, beetle-browed little congressman from Texas; Maryland's sedate Governor Albert Ritchie, who looked more like a president than anyone since Warren Harding of unblessed memory. Looming larger than all the others was the brown-derbied figure of Al Smith. Was he or was he not out of politics? Was he or was he not at this point Roosevelt's enemy? Roosevelt and Smith still addressed each other as "Al" and "Frank" in occasional perfunctory notes, but beneath this superficial goodwill lay a growing discord.

By the end of 1931 Farley's sunny prediction of an early victory in the first convention ballot had clouded over. Smith, with National Chairman Raskob behind him, was increasingly determined to block Roosevelt even if it meant the defeat of the Democratic party. Then, early in January, 1932, Hearst from his California domain unleashed an attack on Baker, Smith and Roosevelt as "international visionaries," and through his nationwide newspaper chain launched a boom for Cactus Jack. Howe was dismayed. He had counted on California and Texas. Without those votes there was the prospect of another convention deadlock like that of 1924. Hearst's attack from the right was followed shortly by a counterblow from the liberal left as Walter Lippmann in the *Herald Tribune* condemned Roosevelt as "a highly impressionable person, without a firm grasp of public affairs, and without strong convictions . . . an amiable man with many philanthropic impulses, but . . . not a dangerous enemy of anything . . . a pleasant man, who, without any important qualifications for the office, would very much like to be President." Howe on reading this wrote bleakly to Roosevelt that there was very little they could do about it.

Lippmann was no doubt convinced of the rightness of his remarks when a few weeks later Roosevelt, as a gesture to Hearst and guided by Howe, repudiated the League of Nations in a speech before the New York Grange. At once the Hearst press called off its attacks. But as the convention date neared, the New York governor found himself faced with another dilemma over Tammany, following Judge Samuel Seabury's relentless exposures of the city's vast and varied corruption in which Mayor Walker himself was shown to be deeply involved. Roosevelt's efforts to be all things to all men foundered in his attempt to placate Tammany's chief, John Curry, by questioning the good faith of the reformers. Curry, unimpressed, continued to favor a list of unpledged delegates whom he could control. Roosevelt could no longer be sure of New York. By the spring, Howe saw states that he had counted on as certainly breaking away or retreating to the neutrality of native sons. Al Smith, who had finally announced his candidacy in February, seemed secure in the Northeast. The solid South and most of the West might be for Roosevelt, but California was tightly under the control of Hearst, working with McAdoo, the adopted Californian.

Howe was preparing a large map for the convention, indicating the certain Roosevelt states in red, and the fact that there was less of this color than he had hoped for and counted on merely spurred him on. So relentlessly did he drive his emaciated body that his weight fell to less than a hundred pounds. Throughout the campaign he remained the key figure, closest to the governor, Roosevelt's most trusted subordinate. But Roosevelt's staff had expanded beyond any one man's control. It now included such seasoned and independent figures as Edward Flynn, the boss of the Bronx, who had thrown the weight of his organization behind Roosevelt in 1928, and Samuel Rosenman, the governor's aide and speech writer, who performed many of the functions that Belle Moskowitz had performed for Smith. Howe in his Crime Commission work had come to know the Columbia associate professor of history, Raymond Moley, and so impressed was he by this lithe academic that he brought him into the Roosevelt entourage. Moley recruited a group of intellectuals who would remain with Roosevelt into his White House days. In addition to constructing an intellectual foundation for Roosevelt's campaign, Moley wrote many of the Roosevelt speeches, supplying among others the unforgettable phrase "the forgotten man," for a brief but vastly influential radio address. Early in the campaign Howe had tactfully ironed out differences between Roosevelt's emissary in Kentucky and the edgy and self-important Governor Ruby Lafoon. So deftly did Howe manage to play on Lafoon's vanity that the governor in gratitude made him a Kentucky colonel. Howe delighted in his new designation. From that time on he became Colonel Howe, like those earlier men of mystery Colonel Harvey and Colonel House, the very title drawing a veil between himself and the public.

Only reluctantly had Howe and Roosevelt agreed to the choice of Chicago for the Democratic National Convention in 1932, for that city under Mayor Anton Cermak was clearly Smith territory. The delegates and leaders arriving in the latter part of June found themselves caught up in a heat wave, the humid oppressive summer weather of the Midwest. According to Howe's and Farley's calculations, Roosevelt had some six hundred delegates, a small majority, but still a tantalizing hundred short of two-thirds. Smith had two hundred or more and Garner a certain ninety. Smith, in spite of his ostensibly small number of delegates, had come to town radiating confidence, his brown derby discarded for a straw hat which he wore at a jaunty angle, announcing that he was there not to stop Roosevelt but to get himself nominated. Howe arrived in Chicago tense and suspicious, fearful of a political stab in the back. From his suite in Room 1702 of the Congress Hotel he had had a private line installed direct to the New York Executive Mansion and connected an amplifier so that Roosevelt, waiting out the results in Albany eight hundred miles away, could talk directly to delegates, "my friends from Arkansas" or "Indiana." Howe's dowdy secretary, Margaret Durand, whom he called "Rabbit" — he pinned such whimsical nicknames on all his staff — screened the visitors to 1702, assisted by Howe's son Hartley. Farley and Flynn he had quartered in widely separated suites and kept in touch with them through secret messengers. Downstairs he saw to it that his own switchboard operator managed the incoming Roosevelt calls. At the Chicago Stadium, where the convention was held, he commandeered three rooms for Farley's headquarters so that the two end rooms could be left empty as a precaution against eavesdroppers. He himself would not go to the stadium but remained in Room 1702 to map strategy and direct events from afar like a commanding general. The main Roosevelt headquarters, replete with badges and buttons and photographs, was on the ground floor of the hotel, dominated by Howe's huge map which Al Smith passed off as representing more area than votes. Roosevelt greeters were on hand to meet each incoming train. But delegates and politicians and newsmen soon became aware that the real Roosevelt headquarters, the core of the Roosevelt organization, lay in Room 1702 under the direction of the skeletal little man who hunched behind his desk there night and day, wheezing out orders, chain-smoking Sweet Caporals, angrily determined, relentless. In his files he had listed every opposition delegate and every political figure present together with weak points, on a pink card, ready to be used at some critical moment. Reporters were becoming increasingly aware of him, piercing his long-cultivated anonymity.

The convention opened on Monday, June 27. For four sweltering days the ritual preliminaries dragged themselves out, four days of ennui and festering heat in the stadium rancid with the sweat of impatient shirt-sleeved men, cloudy with billowing cigar smoke, littered with newspapers, sandwich wrappings, pop bottles, gum and cigar butts. Farley moved constantly up and down the aisles, his face in a fixed beam, pink bald head glittering with sweat drops, right hand perpetually outstretched. Under the wilted flags and banners a cacophony of music blared from the various headquarters, the theme songs of various candidates. "Anchors Aweigh" was chosen by Roosevelt, the Navy man. From the depths of the hall an organ rotated the songs in burring thirds until the amplified tones shook the rafters. The galleries, packed with Cermak's hoodlums, kept shouting for Smith and howled down any mention of Roosevelt's name.

The heat was cruel to Howe. Racked by asthmatic seizures he would retreat to a couch near his desk in spasms of coughing, his knees drawn up to his chest, a radio beside him still tuned to the convention proceedings, exhausted but never out of touch. Rabbit and some of the other girls feared he might be dying.

What he and Farley were hoping and working for was a break for Roosevelt on the first ballot, the shift of just one state delegation from its favorite son to start a stampede. They offered a succession of candidates the vice-presidential nomination — Ritchie, Byrd, Garner. But they found no takers.

The actual balloting did not begin until late Thursday, the most oppressive night yet, the air of the stadium festering, flatulent, ropy with cigar smoke, heat lightning flashing on the horizon and far-off thunder rumbling an accompaniment to the interminable seconding speeches. Over and over again the organ boomed out its theme-song medley. At each dirge-like repetition of "Anchors Aweigh" echoing tinnily from his radio, Howe groaned "Mein Gawd!" One of his girls suggested that they switch to the popular tune "Happy Days are Here Again." Howe had never heard of the song, but he called the organist and told him for God's sake to play it when Roosevelt's name was placed in nomination.

The sun had just risen by the time the first ballot was completed. Though there had been yelps and jeers from the galleries at the mention of Roosevelt's name, there had been no breakaway. Roosevelt received 661¼ votes — still 103 short of two-thirds — to 201¾ for Smith and 90¼ for Garner. A second roll call added 11½ votes to the Roosevelt total, and a third 5 more, before the convention adjourned and the bleary-eyed delegates tottered out into the morning sunshine. Farley, marshaling his forces on the convention floor, knew that he had used his last reserves, reached his peak, that in the next few ballots the Roosevelt ranks were bound to break. Then it would be the 1924 convention all over again, this time with Roosevelt and Smith pulling each other down. Already there were rumors circulating of Newton Baker as the compromise candidate.

While the convention session dragged through the night, Howe in his shirt-sleeves, sprinkled with Sweet Caporal ashes, his tie and high collar off, lay on his back on the floor of his inner room with his head on a pillow. An electric fan hummed on either side of him and the radio was close to his ear. Farley, Flynn and a few trusted leaders hurried from the convention hall after the third ballot to make their way to him. He waved limply but could not speak. While the others stood back, Farley lay down beside him to whisper that Texas was their only chance. Howe could only nod back.

During that feverish day Farley kept in touch with Texas Congressman Sam Rayburn and others close to Garner, pleading with them to avoid a repetition of 1924, again offering the vice-presidential nomination to Cactus Jack. Farley also managed to reach Hearst, warning him that his enemy Baker would be the compromise candidate if Roosevelt failed. Other Roosevelt lieutenants cornered McAdoo, the leader of the California delegation, who finally agreed to swing his state to Roosevelt if Roosevelt would take Garner as vice-president and, if he won the election, consult with McAdoo about federal patronage and appointments to the State and Treasury Departments.

Meanwhile the absent Hearst had read the signs for himself. Sometime during the morning he called his representative in Chicago, Colonel Joseph Willicombe, to relay a message to Garner in Washington that if Roosevelt's strength crumbled it would bring about either the election of Smith or Baker, a disaster to the country. The Chief (Hearst), Cactus Jack was informed at the Capitol in the speaker's private room, felt that nothing could save the country now unless Garner threw his delegates to Governor Roosevelt. The shaggy-browed little man, who had never really entertained the idea of becoming president, finally agreed. "I will carry out the Chief's suggestion," he told the Hearst man, "and release my delegates to Roosevelt." Farley, when he heard the news, raced back to the Congress Hotel's Room 1702. Kneeling beside Howe he whispered: "It's in the bag! Texas is with us!" "Jim, that is fine," Howe gasped.

All day the secret remained well-kept. When the balloting began that night the Louisiana delegation was said to be ready to desert Roosevelt, and most of the delegates and observers then thought that the New York governor had shot his bolt. As the roll was called, the Alabama, Arizona and Arkansas delegations cast their votes unchanged. But then there was a stir as McAdoo stepped forward. Grinning in triumphant malice at his Smith enemies, he announced that California's forty-four votes were now for Roosevelt. Though the furious galleries tried to drown him out, his speech set off a landslide that rapidly engulfed the convention. Roosevelt was nominated on that ballot by 945 votes. Only 190 Smith diehards refused to make it unanimous.

It had long been traditional for American presidential candidates after their nomination to remain at home in mock innocence for several weeks until formally and officially notified of their nomination by a committee. Then the candidate would make his long-prepared spontaneous acceptance speech. Roosevelt, as soon as he heard he had been nominated, drove with his family to the Albany airport where a tri-motor plane was waiting to take him to Chicago. Breaking all precedent, he set off to deliver his acceptance speech at the convention. That speech had been carefully prepared over the last few weeks by Moley with assistance from Rosenman and some supervision by Roosevelt himself. Howe had had it read to him over the telephone, then in a mixture of anger, jealousy and resentment had spent most of that night filling page after page of lined yellow paper with his impatient scrawl as he dashed off an improved speech of his own.

When Roosevelt arrived in Chicago he found that Cermak had made a quick-turn-about, sending his official white touring car with the city greeter to meet the candidate at the airport. Through the cheering pulsating streets they drove; Roosevelt in the rear seat between the smiling, expansive Farley and the shriveled Howe. As they rode, Howe took his new speech manuscript and thrust it assertively into Roosevelt's hands. "Dammit, Louie," Roosevelt protested, "I'm the nominee," but between waves and smiles he leafed through the pages, discarding all but the first page which he substituted for the first page of the Moley speech he had brought with him.

No one but Howe was aware of the transposition when Roosevelt faced the convention, smiling in triumph, his braces locked in place as he gripped the lectern to steady himself. Howe sat on the platform with Farley and the other party leaders, the first and last time in his life he would ever appear on a public platform. But his face fell when Roosevelt shifted from Howe's speech to Moley's. The speech itself was memorable, for Moley had supplied another indelible phrase that would give a label to an era. "I pledge you," said Roosevelt in as warmly convincing a voice as if he had written it himself, "I pledge myself to a *new deal* for the American people." As the applause died down, the band played "Onward Christian Soldiers."

A week before the Democrats met in Chicago, the Republicans had held their own dispirited convention in the same city. It was an assembly without banners, badges or applause, without conviction. When Hoover was inevitably named, a band struck up *America*. Even with the music, the ensuing demonstration lasted less than two minutes. A sense of doom lay over the delegates.

For Hoover had come to personify the Depression to his countrymen, an image that had been built up with cruel efficiency by the publicity director of the Democratic National Committee, Charlie Michelson. When the president rode through the streets of the big cities he found himself met with vindictive silence. Sometimes men cursed him as he passed, or dashed out of buildings to thumb their noses at him. His coming defeat loomed large. Cactus Jack told Roosevelt that all he needed to do to win was stay alive until election day. Howe agreed. Roosevelt did not. He was still intent on campaigning, an experience that had always exhilarated him; the constant movement and change of scene, the excitement of cheering crowds, the applause, the hopeful faces staring up at him, the emotional rapport that he sensed with the people. He planned a countrywide tour in September. Meanwhile he went for an extended cruise off the northern New England coast aboard the forty-four-foot yawl, *Myth II*, taking three of his sons with him, leaving Howe "to keep the shop."

While Roosevelt cruised, Howe and Farley proceeded to the enormous operation of organizing the campaign. Their job, as they saw it, was to get out the votes, leaving the ideas and issues to Moley and his assistants, whom Howe archly took to referring to as the "Brains Trust," not concerning themselves with the struggles of the conservatives and the liberal-radicals within the party. Howe collected a team of skilled ghost writers who, after studying Roosevelt's style and manner of expression, produced thousands of personal letters with forged Roosevelt signatures. Later Howe reckoned that he and Farley had sent out over 3,000,000 such letters as well as 500,000,000 buttons and 65,000,000 pamphlets. He took particular pains to see that each of the 140,000 Democratic committeemen received personal letters, telephone calls and innumerable pamphlets.

Across the street from the main Roosevelt headquarters that now took up six floors of the Biltmore, Howe dug himself in at his Friends of Roosevelt office. From there he sent out daily news reports to Roosevelt as well as summaries of the most important letters received. He prepared a list of "safe states" and of "fighting states" where the election might be won or lost, and concentrated on these latter. Eleanor Roosevelt with several of her colleagues joined him, persuaded that the campaign propaganda was far too long-winded and masculine in tone, and by way of demonstration producing the brief, clever "rainbow flyers" written by women to women. Eleanor also smoothed over the suspicions that the pathologically suspicious Howe developed from time to time about Farley.

Howe's pessimistic nature continued to be gnawed by the thought that he might not after all have read the signs right, that victory might yet slip away from him. He was particularly troubled by the expansive scandal of Tammany's Jimmy Walker, for it was by now clear that the song-and-dance mayor was more concerned with musical comedy actresses than with municipal affairs, that his administration was bogged down in corruption, and that his own $40,000 a year salary had been regularly augmented by "beneficences" from those doing business with the city. In the dozen or so hearings held before Governor Roosevelt in August in Albany's Hall of Governors, Walker's malfeasance became brazenly clear. Roosevelt's first impulse was to reprimand the "little mayor" but leave him in office. It was a political dilemma. To get rid of Walker might mean alienating the crucial states of the East with their Catholic immigrant voting blocs that saw Walker, like Al Smith, as one of their own. Toward the end of the hearings Roosevelt sat one evening with Howe and a few other intimates in the Executive Mansion. When the Walker problem came up, the governor said he did not know what to do, but it might be best to remove the little mayor. Howe, who was just lighting up a Sweet Caporal, snapped the lighted match furiously at his chief. "So you'd rather be right than president!" he shouted. "Well," said Roosevelt meditatively, "there may be something in what you say." He was spared the decision. At that moment the telephone rang to announce that Mayor Walker had resigned.

The Walker episode was ephemeral compared to Hoover's imbroglio involving the Bonus Army, the 20,000 or so unemployed World War veterans who earlier in the summer had descended on Washington to demand immediate payment of the bonus due them in 1945. Encamped in shacks and hovels on Lower Pennsylvania Avenue and the Anacostia Flats, they vowed to stay there until Congress acted. An unnerved Hoover saw their despairing gesture as a threat to the security of the government, and sent federal troops with tear gas and bayonets to rout the men from their shacks. If anything more was needed to trample Hoover's reputation into the mud, the pictures of armed soldiers — at his order — hunting down unarmed and unemployed ex-soldiers furnished it. Hoover from the beginning had no chance of being re-elected. After the Battle of Anacostia Flats he had not the ghost of a chance.

Just after Mayor Walker's resignation, Roosevelt left on his transcontinental tour aboard his special train that Howe called the "Columbus Caravel." Howe kept in touch with him by telephone at station after station, growing increasingly worried at the radicalism of some of his speeches written by the Brains Trust. Yet like most American campaigns of the past, this remained one in which personalities overshadowed issues: the buoyant, laughing Roosevelt in whose outgoing self-confidence desperate men recaptured their own, as against the morose introspective Hoover whose doctrinaire rigidity made him seem a man without a heart.

Roosevelt spent the night of the election at his Biltmore headquarters surrounded by his family, friends and staff, radiating assurance while he waited for the returns to come in. Howe sat across the street in the almost deserted Friends of Roosevelt office, with only his wife and his son Hartley — who had come on from Fall River — and Rabbit, his secretary, to keep him company. After months of driving himself beyond the point of exhaustion, he felt let down, depressed, full of gloom over the outcome. Even the early returns showing Roosevelt far in the lead failed to cheer him. "Losers always have a big spurt at the start," he told the others, hunched in his chair, the inevitable Sweet Caporal dangling from his lips. But by eleven o'clock it was clear even to his pessimistic mind that Roosevelt had won a great victory, that he himself had attained the goal he had imagined so long ago. From his desk drawer he took a bottle of sherry that he had put away in Albany twenty years before, following Roosevelt's fight against Blue-Eyed Billy Sheehan. He had vowed then he would never open it until Roosevelt became president. Now he solemnly drew the cork, filled a glass for himself and each of his guests and raised his arm in a toast, "to the next President of the United States."

When, a little after eleven o'clock, Farley and Eleanor Roosevelt crossed the street to entice Howe to the Biltmore, they found him gloating over the returns "like a miser inspecting his gold." A jubilant crowd of five hundred workers filled the Biltmore ballroom, surrounding an exultant Roosevelt, his leonine head thrown back, his infectuous laughter spreading gaiety throughout the elegant columned room. So Howe and Farley found him. The two took their places on either side of their leader. Roosevelt's words, spoken into a cluster of microphones, carried Howe's name for the first time in history across the country. "There are two people in the United States more than anybody else who are responsible for this great victory," the president-elect told his radio audience. "One is my old friend and associate, Colonel Louis McHenry Howe, and the other is that splendid American, Jim Farley."

Overnight Howe had become a celebrity, the subject of press accounts and feature articles. Reporters, photographers, job-hunters and crackpots made their way to him in such persistent swarms that he was forced to move his private office to another floor. Legends sprang up about him. Stories appeared telling what he looked like, what he read, what he wore, even what he smoked. The author of a new book on astrology devoted a whole chapter to Howe and his relationship to Roosevelt. Finally, Stanley Walker of the New York *Herald Tribune* wrote an article about him called "The Gnome Nobody Knows."

> Thus we have [Walker noted with measured irony] the fantastic creation who is to be the brains of the next administration, a perfectly amazing mixture with overtones of Colonel House, George Harvey, Harry Daugherty, Machiavelli, Frank Stearns, Mrs. Moscowitz and Talleyrand. He also reminds certain people in odd facets of his character of John the Baptist, St. Augustine, most of the Borgias and Marshal Ney. He is like Napoleon because he signs his letters "Howe."
>
> Not to make many bones about it, Louis Howe is really a simple and ordinary sort of fellow. He eats, sleeps, and occasionally visits his family at Fall River, Massachusetts. . . . All attempts to portray him as a man who conceivably could exert the same sort of influence which Colonel House exerted during the Wilson administration must fail because Howe is not that kind of person. . . . But in modern times no one, certainly no President, has had a man of Howe's background and personality, or a man who will occupy anything like the place that this smart little introvert will fill after next March 4. Presidents have had advisers, but none like Howe; they have had cronies, as Harding did, but Howe is no man's crony. His loyalty is not to himself, or to an abstract ideal of government, but solely to Franklin D. Roosevelt.*

Howe was both repelled and fascinated by his new notoriety. He had always wanted to work behind the scenes, and yet he had wanted people to be aware of him. Often now when he answered the telephone he would announce: "This is the Medieval Gnome

* *The Man Behind Roosevelt,* pp. 219–20.

speaking." But what place he would occupy in the new administration remained uncertain. "I guess I've worked myself out of a job," he said himself, although he still knew he was closer to Roosevelt than any man alive. Yet in the enlarged sphere of the presidency no one man could be what Howe had been until now, the intimate adviser above all other advisers, standing above the factional struggles of lesser politicians. Neither in temperament nor background was he suited for a cabinet or high administrative post. Roosevelt finally decided — it seemed an obvious decision — to make Howe his chief secretary. "Louis can do that job," he remarked, "and still work behind the scenes being the mysterious figure that he loves."

Howe moved into the White House with the Roosevelts, occupying the Lincoln Room with its immense Victorian-gothic bed. Ill at ease in its formidable bulk, he brought his own small bed and had it placed in the dressing room. The large room soon achieved the littered appearance of his other smaller rooms, strewn with papers and cigarette ashes, heavy with the smell of incense and Sweet Caporals, but he refused to allow the servants to tidy it up except under his direction. Once installed in the White House he immersed himself in his customary work and worry. Roosevelt brought in two members of the Cuff Links Club, Steve Early and Marvin McIntyre, old associates of the Navy Department days, to take care of the press relations and appointments that Howe had taken care of in Albany. Out of deference to Howe's vanity they were called assistant secretaries. Howe himself was secretary to the president, with a huge corner office and massive furniture. His duties were threefold: to handle the presidential correspondence; to act as liaison officer between the White House and the Capitol; to carry on as Roosevelt's adviser and political agent.

In his first six months in the White House Roosevelt received as much mail as Hoover had received in the preceding four years. More than 6,500 letters arrived daily. Howe, with his years of experience, was at his most efficient in getting this mass of correspondence sorted out, selecting the small amount that needed to come to the direct attention of the president, making extracts of letters and summaries of documents too long for Roosevelt to read and yet too important for him to pass over, providing a selection of form replies so skillfully contrived that few of the recipients would ever suspect the counterfeit. Every letter had to be answered. He impressed that on his staff of several dozen girls, many of whom he had brought to Washington with him. Form letters had to have the "Roosevelt touch" and, above all, they had to "match" the incoming correspondence. Howe had a recurrent nightmare of traveling high above the country in a plane and looking down to see the ground covered with snow that on closer inspection turned out to be a white blanket of letters flowing from every part of the United States to the White House.

The chief secretary was the last person to see Roosevelt at night, the first to see him in the morning. No one else shared his selfless intimacy. His presence filled an emotional need for Roosevelt in what the president maintained was the loneliest job in the world. While Franklin was having his bedside breakfast, Louis would wander into the room, squat on the foot of the bed, talk, argue, tell jokes. "Ludovic," the president called him in his teasing schoolboy manner. In matters of patronage and politics he usually turned to Howe for advice, and sometimes took it. "Louis has forty ideas a day," Roosevelt liked to say, "and sometimes a few good ones." If there was an obtrusive delegation to be met, Howe was sent to meet it. If Roosevelt hesitated at personally dismissing someone, Howe took on the job. He carried out odds and ends of diplomatic chores, sometimes more. Although Roosevelt warned him and the other aides not to try to interfere with cabinet appointments, he was nevertheless responsible for bringing in Cordell Hull as secretary of state. Not as powerful as he thought he was or as he would have liked, Howe was nevertheless a dangerous man to underestimate — as many found to their sorrow, for he had Roosevelt's ear as well as confidential informers in all branches of the government. Suspicious of anyone who opposed him or Roosevelt, he had a long arm. Conniving himself, he knew just how to cut through the red tape of bureaucracy. He remained trusted by the president because he contained all his own ambitions within the greater ambition of Roosevelt's career. Essentially conservative, unread in economics, he regarded the New Deal from the point of view of its effectiveness in winning votes. To its ideology he remained indifferent, privately scorning the temperamental Brain Trusters and their competing interests that he tried in vain to coordinate. Few if any final decisions were now left to him. The Colonel House of the Roosevelt years, the side-door prime minister, was Harry Hopkins. Howe could never have assumed that more encompassing role.

As presidential secretary, Howe took to being more careful of his dress, appearing often now in black coat and striped trousers. He let it be known that he preferred to be called Colonel, and he engineered press releases about his passion for anonymity. His one really expansive gesture was to buy himself a fawn-colored Lincoln roadster, the sports car of its day, although his failing health would keep him from driving it much.

When a second bonus army descended on Washington, Howe was left to handle it. At once he arranged to have a camp set up for the men across the Potomac at Fort Hunt. He talked affably with the leaders and finally drove over one afternoon with Eleanor Roosevelt, who charmed the ex-soldiers by chatting with them, drinking coffee, and joining in singing their old wartime songs. The men did not get their bonus but they were persuaded at least that the government was not hostile, that there were those who did consider them. Howe offered any of the men who wished the chance to join the Civilian Conservation Corps. Some accepted, and the rest went home.

The CCC, the Civilian Conservation Corps, was one of the first of the New Deal projects, and one close to Roosevelt's heart, combining as it did his passion for universal military service and for the land. The corps would eventually take several hundred thousand young men and put them into camps under army officers to work for a year on projects of land reclamation and reforestation — much like the National Socialist Labor Service, although no one seemed to be aware of the parallel. Howe and his wife saw the CCC as their personal crusade, something that "he and Franklin" had planned for years, a chance for the impoverished young men of the cities to see their country and to make something of themselves. In spite of his failing health he regularly inspected the CCC camps near Washington and Fall River.

His two other outside concerns were the federal drive on crime and the Subsistence Home Experiment. The latter involved him in Eleanor Roosevelt's pet project at Arthurdale, a settlement of unemployed miners in a self-sufficient model village that was intended to combine small industries with home gardening. Arthurdale, a pilot project, was a social workers' dream that like most such dreams would founder in its practical application. Prefabricated houses that Howe ordered did not fit their foundations, suitable industries failed to materialize, there were arguments about construction and plumbing, the unemployed did not take to gardening, and the cost of the homesteads ran to four or five times what a private builder would have charged. Eventually Arthurdale, and other similar settlements, broke up under the shadow of World War II.

Howe spoke on a nationwide radio network in an effort to win approval of the Subsistence Homestead Experiment. After an almost accidental beginning, he had become a radio presence, his voice effective and convincing, in odd contrast to his grotesque appearance. Soon he was receiving large fees for regular appearances on such programs as the Socony Vacuum and the Cities Service hours. On the air, in magazine articles, in speeches and interviews, he emerged as a major Roosevelt spokesman. He wrote for the *Saturday Evening Post*, the *Literary Digest*, *American Magazine*, *Cosmopolitan*, articles such as "Behind the Scenes with the President"; "The President's Mail Boy"; "Uncle Sam Starts after Crime." For the first time in his life he had more money than he could spend. He had become sought after. Even that dowager of dowagers, Sara Roosevelt — who now signed herself "Madame Mère" to her friends — grew almost friendly toward him.

Yet from the day he entered the White House, Howe's health deteriorated even as his fame grew. His breathing was more labored, his eyes more sunken, his face more wrinkled, his nights broken by fits of coughing. Always there was the danger of a heart attack. In his sixties he was already an old man. By January 1935 he was forced to spend most of his time in his room, though he tried to keep control of his office by telephoning, dictating, and holding bedside conferences. The annual Cuff Links dinner that he and Franklin set so much store on had to be canceled that year. Though he managed to hang on for another year — a "year of borrowed time" his doctor called it — he spent much of it under an oxygen tent on a diet mostly of coffee and Cream of Wheat. Grace came down from Fall River to live in the White House and be near him. In August he was so much worse that he had to be moved to the naval hospital.

In his last months he grew a scraggly beard that made him look even more wanly grotesque. Yet his spirit remained as resolute and dauntless as ever. He insisted on a private line from his room to the White House. As was his lifelong habit, he continued to place small bets on the horses, and was greatly indignant when his favorite bookie was raided by the Washington police. The approaching 1936 election excited him, and he determined to harbor his strength so that he could go to New York and take charge of Roosevelt's reelection campaign, even if it had to be from a bed in the Biltmore. He planned a Good Neighbor League that would play up Roosevelt's sympathy for racial and minority groups. He planned a more intensive use of radio. But by the spring of 1936 he realized that he would never see another election. What would the impulsive Franklin do without Louis's check rein, his cold common sense to oppose the other's hot enthusiasms? That was the question the dying man asked himself and others. He was the only one who could talk to the president openly and fearlessly, who could if necessary tell him to go to hell. His main value, he knew, was "to sit on Franklin's toes." His last words to Garner were "Hold Franklin down."

Eleanor Roosevelt, with the kindness that came so naturally to her, visited Howe every day she was in Washington. The president managed to see him only every ten days or so. Imperceptively and relentlessly, time had divided the two friends. Franklin had outgrown and grown beyond Louis far more than the dying man could comprehend. Two days after Howe's death Roosevelt told Farley how badly he felt, but added:

> In view of the circumstances it must be considered a blessing in disguise, because Louis had been getting to the point where he gave a lot of orders that were annoying and likely to cause a lot of trouble. He indicated that he was going to headquarters in the Biltmore and run the campaign and if he did that, of course, he would cause a lot of confusion.*

As a young man Howe had considered Carlyle his favorite author. Carlyle's theory of the great man in history he had found embodied in Franklin Delano Roosevelt. "I have been as close to Franklin as a valet," he said when he was close to the end, "and he is still a hero to me." To young John Keller, who had been hired to read to him each day during those final weeks, he spoke wistfully of the autumn presidential campaign and how he would love to be there to run it. "But you will be," Keller told him. "They can't run it without you."

"No, I shall not be there," said Howe finally. "Franklin is on his own now."

* *Jim Farley's Story*, p. 61.

*A rare cartoon of Joseph Kennedy and his unloved father-in-law, Honey Fitz. Throughout his career, Kennedy generally managed to avoid the cartoonist's pen.*

CHAPTER EIGHT

# The Dynast from East Boston: Joseph Patrick Kennedy

HE MIGHT HAVE been one of Balzac's relentless characters, destined to batter his way up under any circumstances and condition in a world he would take as he found it and bend to his will. In Nazi Germany he could have been a gauleiter; in Soviet Russia a commissar; in England an international financial manipulator, ending up with a knighthood or in the peerage; in Sweden a more careful Kreuger. But fate made Joseph Patrick Kennedy an American, antecedently Irish, son of a minor Boston politician. He was born on September 6, 1888, in East Boston, just across the channel from the real Boston, and if he was not born to wealth, he was at least born to a sufficiency that would have seemed more than wealth to his immigrant grandfather and to most of the Boston Irish of his own day. For his father was Patrick Joseph Kennedy, "P.J.," "the Spalpeen," one of a handful of iron-fisted ward bosses who controlled Boston's political destiny.

The first Kennedy, Joseph's grandfather, a cooper from Wexford and also a Patrick, fled Ireland in the Famine years, sailing from Cork and landing in East Boston merely because it was the western terminus of the Cunard Line's Liverpool run. East Boston had been Noddle's Island until in the eighteen-thirties it was developed by the East Boston Company, whose backers planned it as part commercial, part a favored residential community. Tentatively they built several rows of brick swell-front town houses on the high ground overlooking the harbor, until the mass waves of Famine immigration eroded such embryonic hopes of elegance. The twenty-five-year-old Patrick Kennedy stayed where he landed, in the Irish shantytown near the Cunard pier sheds, and worked at his hereditary trade. Two years after his arrival he married a Cork girl, Bridget Murphy. Bridget bore him three daughters and then a son, Patrick Joseph, before he died of cholera at the age of thirty-five, a worn-out old man with little more money than when he had landed ten years before. His children survived, even though in the Boston slum rookeries sixty per cent of all children died before their fifth birthday. Bridget kept her little brood together by running a notions and stationery shop near the ferry, and when that proved too slim a means of support took a job as hairdresser in the Jordan Marsh department store in downtown Boston. The boy Pat, along with all the other children of East Boston, went to the Assumption School, run by the Sisters of Notre Dame. At twelve, solid and heavy-fisted, he quit school to work as a longshoreman on the local docks. Unlike the other dockers he neither drank nor roistered, but kept a cold blue eye out for the main chance, any main chance. As he grew older he sometimes worked nights as a swamper in one of the many dockside saloons. Even after paying his mother a share of his shoestring wages, he always managed to save a little. Through such scrimping he was able by the time he came of age to make a down payment on a seedy saloon in Boston's ramshackle Haymarket Square just across the channel. Old in appearance and manner beyond his years, he knew that this was his beginning. No careless conviviality would divert him from his drive for recognition and power, and this drive he would pass on to his descendants. He saved his profits — a slum Boston saloon could not lose money — and in a short time became part owner of two other bars, one near the docks, the other in the Maverick House, the politicians' hangout that survived from the day when East Boston still hoped to rival the Back Bay's elegance. Each evening found him behind the counter in his white apron, solid, affable, his blue eyes masked to geniality by rimless spectacles, a walrus moustache concealing his pugnacious mouth. Not until he was twenty-eight did he feel secure enough to marry. His wife, Mary Hickey, was several steps above him — but marrying up would become a Kennedy characteristic. The following year their first child, Joseph Patrick, was born. In the days when the saloon was the political as well as the social center of an Irish immigrant community, P. J. gradually acquired influence. A nod from him came to be worth votes. Before he had reached his thirties he had become boss of Ward Two and most of East Boston's Ward One — where a recalcitrant Yankee minority still persisted — duly recognized at City Hall as controller of East Boston patronage and regulator of liquor licenses. On election day the dead were known to rise from their graves to vote for P. J. Kennedy's candidate. On one such day, when he was election commissioner, he beamed approval at two of his "boys" who announced with raucous virtuousness that they had just voted one hundred and twenty-eight times. Those in Ward Two who were in need, sorrow, sickness or any other adversity turned to P. J. Like the "Mahatma" of Boston's Ward Eight, Martin Lomasney, whom he in many ways resembled, he shepherded his flock, running what in those pre-welfare days was in fact a private welfare bureau. Lomasney himself liked to say that the great mass of people were interested in only three things, "food, clothing and shelter." And Pat had grasped the Lomasney axiom instinctively. As his son's journalist-biographer, Bill Duncliffe wrote in the Boston *Record American*:

> Because he was lord of the fiefdom of Noddle's Island, it was part of Pat Kennedy's job to take care of those who needed his unique talents, to make sure that a bag of coal was delivered to an unheated cold-water flat, to put food on the table for a hungry family, to set things right for a belligerent voter in trouble with the cops, to do any number of favors, both great and small.
>
> In turn, Kennedy's vassals had an implicit duty toward him — to back with their ballots the candidates who had won his favor. Theirs was not to reason why, theirs was but to do.

The running cost of such welfare was high. Those who received jobs from P. J. were expected to pay back a percentage, a finder's fee. Saloon keepers all contributed, for P. J. had come to have the final say in East Boston's saloon traffic. So did firms doing business in East Boston. Such money did not stick to his fingers. His private capital he accumulated through his own saloons and through a wholesale liquor business. Like Lomasney, he managed to profit by foreknowledge of real estate takings. Within the limitations of a ward boss he was an upright man, personally and publicly. He never raised his voice, though his arm had always been ready enough in throwing any disorderly drunk out of his bar. Not for him the japes and caperings of a "Honey Fitz" Fitzgerald whom he considered a venereous clown; the boozy booming oratory and stiletto thrusts of a Jim Curley; the blackmailing insolences of a Dan Coakley. He was uncomfortable on a public platform, lacking both the knack and the will to be an effective speaker. His chief political concern was to funnel patronage to his ward, and to further this he had himself elected from East Boston to five annual terms in the Massachusetts House of Representatives. In 1891 he served two terms in the state senate. Under the gilt State House dome he remained inconspicuous, mute, attentive, making contacts and observing how deals were made on Beacon Hill. He continued to control his East Boston fief, and that was all he aspired to control. In 1895, seeing no reason why the minute savings of the Irish should breed interest for the Yankees, he helped organize the Columbia Trust Company. He also acquired an interest in a savings bank and a local coal company. Mayor Patrick Collins appointed him wire commissioner — duties unknown, but salary high. Like Lomasney he could, when a close election required it, produce more votes in his ward than there were residents. The aldermen then, rather than the mayor, controlled the city, and the ward bosses controlled the aldermen.

Boston, in the rise to power of the Irish Democrats, never produced an all-controlling boss like New York's Croker. The closest approach was what Lomasney labelled the "Strategy Board," four regional bosses known variously as the Big Four and the Mayor Makers, but lacking the preponderant strength they might have had combined with the Mahatma of Ward Eight who, they feared, would dominate them all if they included him. Leader of the Strategy Board was "Smiling Jim" Donovan of the South End, a butcher's boy who had climbed the political ladder to become chairman of the Democratic City Committee. Smiling Jim, a dapper, flamboyant man, liked to throw his weight and his money round by walking into hotel bars and ordering drinks for everyone. P. J. was a member of this board, as was Joe Corbett of Charlestown, its legal brains, later to become a land court judge. Ward Six's Honey Fitz — so-called from his mellifluous rendering of "Sweet Adeline"— made the fourth member. The board met with discreet regularity in the Quincy House on the fringe of Honey Fitz's North End — one of the few hotels to accept city vouchers for meals — to parcel out patronage and dictate Democratic nominations throughout the city.

Though P. J. and Honey Fitz might meet amicably at the Quincy House or on summer strategy sessions aboard P. J.'s sixty-foot cabin cruiser, the *Eleanor*, there was not much affection between them. In 1894, after a year as a state senator, Honey Fitz announced that he would contest the seat of Congressman Joseph "Tip" O'Neill, who had served three terms from Massachusetts's only Democratic Congressional district. The remaining Big Four — Kennedy, Donovan and Corbett, nevertheless supported O'Neill. That Fitzgerald won in spite of such formidable opposition was due chiefly to his "bull-pushers," hulkers from the cattle ships whom he paid to bar most of the polling places to all but Fitzgerald voters. Honey Fitz — the "Napoleon of Ward Six" — did not, however, carry East Boston. Once nominated and elected, he served three terms in Congress, although the Big Three managed to block his fourth term.

In 1905 Kennedy again opposed Fitzgerald after the dapper Honey Fitz announced his candidacy for mayor. Earlier that year the respected and highly respectable Mayor Patrick Collins had died in an office he had come to detest. P. J., Smiling Jim and the Mahatma then decided on City Clerk Edward Donovan as their candidate, an inconspicuous figure further obscured by Honey Fitz's flamboyant personality. Never had Boston seen such a political campaign as that primary of Democrat against Democrat. In the city's first motorcade, Honey Fitz toured the wards in a bright red car followed by flying squads of what the press described as "Napoleon's lancers," making ten speeches a night, and on the final night before the primaries speaking thirty times. He even invaded sacrosanct Ward Eight where one of his lancers pulled a pistol on several of the Mahatma's henchmen. Young for a Boston politician — he had just touched forty — dynamic, irrepressible, the embodiment of the Irish instinct for ethnic revenge on proper Boston, he formed alliances with other younger insurgent Democrats, even with his later archenemy James Michael Curley. The wave of the future — however muddy it might be — was with him.

P. J. did his best to hold the line for Donovan, escorting that uninspiring candidate to the public platform in both wards of his island bailiwick. Yet even in his own Ward Two there was disaffection, and Donovan carried the ward by a mere thirty-five votes. Under the Mahatma's iron grip, however, Ward Eight produced so many votes for Donovan — phantom and otherwise — that it took Fitzgerald half the city's remaining wards to beat him by a hair. The election brought two Republican candidates into the field, one of them secretly encouraged and supported by Honey Fitz. In spite of disaffected Democrats like Lomasney and unenthusiastic ones like the Boss of East Boston, Fitzgerald carried the election, though with only a minority of the votes cast.

"Burglars in the House!" John Cutler entitled his chapter on Fitzgerald's first mayoralty term in his Honey Fitz biography, the most bizarre and gaily corrupt administration that Boston had yet seen. With Fitzgerald's brassy arrival in City Hall, ethnic revenge had triumphed over such upright earlier assimilationists as Patrick Collins, Boston's first Irish mayor Hugh O'Brien, and the poet and editor of *The Pilot,* John Boyle O'Reilly. New categories of jobs were invented to circumvent the vestigial civil service — City Dermatologist, Tea Warmers, Tree Climbers, Wipers, watchmen to watch watchmen. Boston found itself paying for four sides of each granite paving brick, giving sixty cents more than the going price for a barrel of cement, purchasing property for three times what anyone had imagined it could be worth. As the austere assistant city clerk and Irishman of the old school, Wilfred Doyle, noted disapprovingly, "when Fitzgerald was mayor everybody in City Hall had to pay, from the scrub-women to the elevator man." During his two-year term the mayor is said to have attended 1200 dinners, 1500 dances, 200 picnics and 1000 meetings, made 3000 speeches and danced with 5000 girls. Convivial, brimming with animal spirits, he liked to drop in for a sudden meal with his entourage at the larger city hotels and watch the deferential bustle of the staff. His more intimate moments of social revelry were reserved for the South End's naughtily Edwardian Woodcock Hotel where the brass-bed blonde, Toodles Ryan, reigned as queen of the revels. Contemporary doggerel had it that

A whiskey glass
And Toodle's ass
Made a horse's ass
Of Honey Fitz.

Though the reaction against Honey Fitz was sharp enough to deny him reelection in 1907, he was able to take office again in

1909, this time for four years under the terms of a new city charter that greatly enhanced the mayor's power and reduced that of the ward bosses. The Big One — the mayor himself — now replaced the Big Four.

After Fitzgerald's nomination, Kennedy had shaken tentative hands and made his peace with him, but he remained apart from the shenanigans of Fitzgerald's administration. Although he would live on another twenty years, he would play only a minor role in future city politics, endorsing city and state candidates at elections but contenting himself with solid second rank.

Such a limitation of power would come to seem intolerable to P. J.'s son. "Always be first!" Joseph Kennedy liked to admonish his own children, meaning by "first" not academic or intellectual or artistic distinction but first in the struggle for power. When Joe was born, his father still lived in the dingy upstairs flat over a block of stores at 151 Meridian Street where P. J. had started his married life, but by the time the boy's memories had become cohesive the family had moved halfway up the hill to a square white house of bourgeois respectability on Webster Street. "P. J.'s boy Joe" with his red hair and bustling manner became even at an early age a recognized figure in East Boston, sheltered by his father's shadow, guided by his father's protective hand. From his bedroom window young Joe could look out over the masts and spars and funnels of the docked ships below him, across the rancid channel to Boston on its hill. Through his boyhood and adolescence, on his later daily ferry crossings to the Boston Latin School, that would be his prospect until he was twenty — the clutter of shipping at the piers, the obelisk of the Custom House towering above the grey city, the steep straight line of State Street rising up the crest of Beacon Hill with its gilt-domed State House. The city was the world, a throbbing honey-heavy hive, and he the Celtic Rastignac, determined to conquer it, to plunder its store of sweetness. Sometime during his Latin School days that knowledge and that cold resolution must have come to him. But even before then, he showed signs of a more than childish calculation, of what the world called "enterprise."

Although, unlike most East Boston urchins, he did not lack money, the thought of it stirred him at an early age. Money and athletics would become his engrossing interests. As a young boy he sold papers, he clerked part-time in a haberdashery, he ran errands for his father's bank. For a time, after a nod from his father, he sold peanuts and candy on the excursion ship *Excelsior*. Legend would have him getting tips from Orthodox Jews for lighting their stoves on high holy days, though this was probably not true since the Jewish community was then centered in Chelsea and there were few if any Jews in East Boston. More probable is the tale of his joining with a friend to smuggle a pair of tame pigeons under their coats across the channel to Boston. Released on the Common, the birds returned home, usually followed by two or three other stray Common pigeons that the boys captured and sold for squab.

Leaving the Xavieran Brothers school at thirteen, he entered Sixth Class of the Boston Latin School. The school, founded in 1635 — the oldest in the country, private or public — was city-run, with a stern six-year course in which Latin was compulsory and Greek only recently elective. To those who could survive its somewhat unimaginative rigors it practically guaranteed admission to any college. In the past it had been *the* school of the Massachusetts Yankees, a way station on the road to Harvard. Franklin, Hancock, Samuel and Charles Francis and Charles F. Adams, Jr., had all gone there as had Emerson, Sumner, Charles W. Eliot and Santayana. But in the period after the Civil War the Boston Yankees, in their retreat before the massed Irish, abandoned their public scholastic redoubt for hastily-founded private day schools or the plush imitations of Rugby and Harrow that were now springing up in the alien New England landscape. By the time Joe Kennedy entered Boston Latin, the school still kept to its high academic tradition but its social standing was nil.

Studies were for Joe handicaps that had been set for him rather than challenges or matters of interest. He did poorly. Athletics brought out his combative eagerness and his organizing skill. He managed the football team, he was a fair basketball player, but his first love was baseball, even to his nursing the vague idea of becoming a professional. At Boston Latin he played on the team for four years, and in his last two years was captain. In 1908 Mayor Honey Fitz awarded him the Mayor's Cup for the highest batting average, .667, in the Boston high school league. Power and prestige within the schoolboy world were what he strove for and what he achieved — president of his class, twice captain of the baseball team, colonel of the schoolboy cadet regiment. His studies continued to fare less well; indeed, he was forced to spend an extra year at them before he could enter college. Yet the mark of success was on him. His yearbook predicted that he would make his fortune "in a very roundabout way."

An ordinary Irish Catholic bartender's son from East Boston might have gone on to Jesuit Boston College or to Worcester's Holy Cross, if he had gone anywhere in a day when only five percent of those who finished high school went to college at all. But Joe was not ordinary. Brash and greenly confident, he determined to go to Harvard, to make the same name and place for himself in that elitist world that he had at Boston Latin. Only, at Harvard, he would learn with a certain corrosion of his driving ego, most of the names had already been made — or rather inherited — before a freshman ever entered. The red-haired bartender's son would achieve a measure of success at college, but it would fall far short of his inner image of himself. In his later years he came almost to hate Harvard. "I guess I have the old Boston Irish prejudice against it," he admitted ruefully some decades afterward.

The Latin School baseball captain and cadet colonel had no such surly premonitions as he took the East Boston ferry on his way to Cambridge in September 1908 to enroll in Harvard's Class of 1912. As at Boston Latin, any pattern of academic success was a matter of indifference to him. In later years he would never read a book. According to his unwelcomed biographer Richard Whalen, "his main interest was in making the grade socially." Deliberately he cultivated the varsity athletes and his more popular classmates. And even in Cambridge he sensed P. J.'s protective hand, for the boss of East Boston had past favors to call in as well as future favors to confer.

In the first week or so of the academic year Joe asked Tom Campbell of his German A section if he knew Bob Fisher, whom Joe's father had instructed him to look up. Campbell did, and arranged a meeting with Joe. Robert Fisher, a football star at Andover, was marked before he entered Harvard; destined to be the outstanding man of his class — captain of the football team, picked by Walter Camp for two years as All-American; class president; chairman of the Committee on Athletics; member of the governing board of the Harvard Union; second marshal at Commencement; and various lesser honors. No Brahmin, he came from a solid, properly Protestant middle-class family in the solid unfashionable Boston suburb of Dorchester. He had gone to Dorchester High School. But unlike Joe, who arrived with all his crudities intact, he then spent two years at Andover polishing off the roughnesses of the Boston public school system. Fisher was soft-spoken. Joe spoke in the hard Irish-American accent that had somehow evolved in Boston from the undulant and easy speech of the motherland. His insecurity he masked with assertiveness. "Fisher gave him a model of self-respecting behavior in the company of young Brahmins," Whalen wrote. "He reminded Kennedy, who was not always comfortable, that he was always being watched for any lapse that would justify the anti-Irish prejudice of snobbish classmates." Shortly after their meeting Joe and Fisher became roommates. They were to share rooms for the next four years. One classmate remarked long afterward that when he saw Kennedy rooming with Fisher he knew then how ambitious Joe was.

The Boston Latin star failed to fulfill his earlier promise on the playing fields of Harvard. He did make his freshmen baseball team as first baseman* but showed himself slow, with his batting eye not what it had been at Latin School. His confidence remained undiminished. As a sophomore, while walking over to the Briggs Cage for the first day of varsity baseball tryouts with his friend Arthur Kelly, Joe remarked loudly that "we're the two best damn ballplayers on the team." The prediction fell short of the mark. Kelly made the team, but Joe to his open resentment lost out at first base to a junior, Charles "Chick" McLaughlin, later captain. Joe, still sulking the following year, did not even go out for practice. Consequently, those who knew him were more than surprised to see him suddenly in uniform on the Harvard bench during the final Yale game. To win an "H," it is not enough simply to be on a Harvard varsity team; one has to play against Yale, if only for a fraction of a game. In this game Harvard was leading 4-1 in the ninth inning with two out. Suddenly Captain McLaughlin stopped the play and told the coach to send in Kennedy at first. Joe scampered from the bench, a letterman even as he reached

* Another freshman, Ralph Lowell — a Lowell of Lowells — also nursed the ambition of becoming first baseman, although already manager of the freshman crew. Again one senses P. J.'s shadow, for when Lowell first went out for practice an assistant coach took him aside and, according to Duncliffe, told him: "Look, we've already got a first baseman, named Kennedy, and he is pretty good. Why . . . uh . . . why don't you stick with the crew?" Lowell got the message."

his base. The next batter hit an easy grounder, which was thrown to Joe for the put-out and the game's end. He stuffed the ball in his pocket. When McLaughlin as captain asked for it, Joe refused to hand it over. He had made the put-out, he told the indignant McLaughlin; the ball was his.

How Joe got into the game in the first place was a mystery that the Harvard captain shamefacedly explained a year later to a team-mate who asked him about it. McLaughlin said he had been planning to open a moving picture theater after graduation. A few days before the Yale game some friends of Joe's father took him aside and told him that if he wanted a theater operator's license he had better see that Joe won his letter. "Perhaps I did wrong," McLaughlin admitted. To the team-mate, Joe seemed "the kind of guy who, if he wanted something bad enough, would get it, and he didn't much care how he got it. He'd run right over anybody."

There were 622 freshmen in that class of 1912, of whom 498 would graduate. One in four would in the sophomore year be picked by the Institute of 1770; the following year the same names would appear on the roster of the Hasty Pudding Club.* These large twin clubs were a threshold, a selection ground for the small final clubs. A number of years before, the Institute of 1770 had absorbed the DKE fraternity. Its vestige remained in the "Dickey," the club within a club composed of the first eighty members of the Institute taken in lots of ten. Social status and, after that, athletic ability were the criteria. Bob Fisher would almost automatically be found "running for the Dickey." In ordinary circumstances Joe would have been passed over, but somehow Fisher carried him in his wake. Joe not only became a member of the Institute of 1770 but even attained the more elite level of the Dickey. He would get no farther than the threshold, however. The doors of the final clubs remained closed to him. Even Bob Fisher only made one of the lesser final clubs. In his senior year Joe did join the D. U. fraternity, one of the several that still survived at Harvard although most had long since transformed themselves into clubs.† Though they provided convivial associa-

* In 1926 the two clubs would combine in the Hasty Pudding-Institute of 1770.

† The Harvard chapter of DU would later take the step the other Harvard fraternities had taken of disaffiliating from the national organization and transforming itself into a final club. In time, DU would work its ticket. Cleveland Amory rated it eighth socially among the ten Harvard final clubs.

tion for their members, the fraternities had no social standing at all.

Joe's interest in his studies — he majored in economics and history — remained negligible. In a course in accounting he did so poorly that he dropped out rather than risk taking the final examination. Yet he continued his sharp practical interest in money matters. One of his classmates recalled how he used to retire to the toilet each morning with the financial section of the New York *Times*.

According to Whalen, Joe and a Boston Latin-Harvard classmate, Joe Donovan, as undergraduates bought an old bus for a few hundred dollars and through Pat Kennedy's string-pulling were able to get a license and share the touring concession previously granted to the Colonial Auto-Sightseeing Company. During several summers of running tours Kennedy and Donovan each managed to make $5000 — in a day when Harvard's tuition was only $125. According to Drew Pearson, most of the windfall came about when the sightseeing company suddenly found its license fee raised from two dollars to three thousand dollars a year. "The fee had been upped by Mayor John F. Fitzgerald. Once a month a dapper Harvard student would come round to pick up the check." The student was Joe Kennedy.

Joe may not have garnered much from the Harvard curriculum but he had learned a great deal in Cambridge about the ways of the world and he had determined to become a millionaire before he was thirty-five. Surveying the predatory financial jungle, he would prepare himself for it with feline cunning, for it was not a world of production that drew him on but a world of prey. Already the young Harvard graduate had determined on his future wife, none other than Mayor Fitzgerald's daughter Rose, a young woman whose beauty was an inheritance from her mother rather than from the obstreperous Honey Fitz. When Rose Fitzgerald graduated from Dorchester High School in 1906 at fifteen, she was voted the prettiest senior by her classmates. The following year she studied at the Sacred Heart Convent in Boston, with an exotic additional year in the Convent of the Sacred Heart in Blumenthal, Germany, near the Dutch border. Then she spent a year at Manhattanville College of the Sacred Heart, returning to make her debut in Irish Boston. The Social Register world of the Back Bay debutantes, of the Junior League and the Vincent Club would be triply barred to her by her religion, her ethnic background and her attendance at Dorchester High. But the emergent Irish, the daughters of rising politicians and expanding contractors, had their own Catholic equivalent of the Junior League in the Cecilian Guild, of which Rose became an enthusiastic member. She also founded a social club of her own, the Ace of Clubs, for Catholic girls who "belonged," as well as the Travel Club for those who had been to Europe. On January 2, 1911, she had her own coming-out party in Honey Fitz's huge mansard-roofed house in Dorchester, a wooden chateau in the beer-baronial style with a stained glass window on the landing emblazoned with the Fitzgerald coat of arms and the Gaelic motto *Shawn a Boo (John the Bold)*. The Boston City Council postponed its meeting that day so that all members could attend.

A little over three and a half years later Rose and Joe Kennedy were married. So little had he been Rose's father's choice that Joe had had to slip the engagement ring on her finger on a Boston sidewalk. As head of one of what James Michael Curley had mockingly called the First Irish Families, Honey Fitz took a poor view of an East Boston saloon keeper-politician's son, preferring a young man like the more assimilated offspring of the contractor Harry Nawn who had gone to small, private Yankee Roxbury Latin School before Harvard and who was on the way to becoming indistinguishable in manner and accent from his Back Bay contemporaries. But Joe had long been Rose's choice, and Rose was a strong-willed young woman. Honey Fitz at last gave his somewhat reluctant consent. Joe had as little use for his flamboyant father-in-law. Years later he told Franklin Roosevelt: "I can't help it that I married into a son-of-a-bitch of a family." On graduation from Harvard Joe's first determination had been to become a banker. His approach was indirect. After passing a qualifying examination, and with his father's influence, he became a state bank examiner. The salary was only $29 a week but the job gave him unexampled insight into the banking world. As his Harvard classmate, the banker Ralph Lowell, wrote: "That bank examiner's job laid bare to Joe the condition of every bank he visited, and what he learned about the structure and securities of state banks was valuable to himself — and to others."

One of the things he learned was that the Columbia Trust Company was about to be taken over by the First Ward National Bank.

Joe rallied proxies throughout East Boston and borrowed from his father and relatives to buy up Columbia Trust stock. He still needed $45,000 when he approached another Harvard alumnus, Eugene Thayer, the president of the Merchants National Bank. As Fisher's roommate, Joe had often been able to accommodate Thayer and others with scarce Yale-game football tickets. Such foresight now paid off. Thayer agreed to lend Joe the money, and Kennedy was able to control or buy up enough Columbia Trust stock not only to thwart the merger but to have himself elected president.

At twenty-five Joe Kennedy was the youngest bank president in the country. Acquiring the Columbia Trust had, however, left him with little ready cash. After his marriage he had to borrow $2,000 for a down payment on the $6,500 house that he now bought on Beale Street in suburban Brookline. A plain square seven-room house (with two extra rooms in the attic) in a respectable middle- to upper-middle class Protestant neighborhood, it was several removes from East Boston and one at least from Dorchester. It was also the last modest house that Joe and his family would ever live in. While the East Boston bank president was taking stock, both his father and his father-in-law suffered political eclipse with the emergence of Curley as candidate for mayor in 1913. Eleven years younger than Honey Fitz, relentless, gifted and unscrupulous, Curley the loner was the most ruthless politician that Irish Boston had yet produced, the orator with the knife beneath the frock coat. When Mayor Fitzgerald announced that he would be a candidate to succeed himself, Curley moved against him with such exploitive skill that within a few weeks Honey Fitz withdrew. And when Fitzgerald and Pat Kennedy backed an opposition candidate, Curley after his election remained implacably vengeful. Honey Fitz would never again hold public office; Pat Kennedy would vegetate within his island fief.

Fitzgerald's term expired with the year 1913. During his last city hall months, hoping to make his son-in-law better known in banking circles, he appointed him city director of the Collatoral Loan Company, a large semi-public pawnshop founded ostensibly to protect the city's poor against loan sharks. The gesture backfired, for Kennedy's arrival coincided with the discovery that $26,000 of the company's funds had been embezzled, and after a few turbulent fruitless months he resigned. Meanwhile he ran his bank with a tight rein, quite as quick as any Yankee in calling a loan or foreclosing a mortgage. Bringing every influence he could, he finally obtained a seat on the board of trustees of the moribund Massachusetts Electric Company, and when a friend asked him why he took so much trouble for so little, he asked in return: "Do you know a better way to meet people like the Saltonstalls?"

"Joe was born mature," a Harvard classmate said of him. "He would meet powerful, socially prominent men in passing, and later they would say to each other, 'That young fellow has something.' " One of those men whom the young bank president went out of his way to meet was the most powerful lobbyist in Massachusetts, the Yankee Democrat Guy Currier. A man of jungle ethics and low visibility, suave spokesman for insurance, utility and railroad interests, Currier was linked by golden threads of interest to politicians of both parties. His shadow moved legislators. He could be a friend of Jim Curley's and at the same time a friend of Calvin Coolidge's. Among his many lobbyist concerns was that of the Bethlehem Steel Corporation which, after the United States entry into the war in 1917, launched a ship-building subsidiary at the Fore River Shipyard in Quincy about ten miles south of Boston. Currier offered Kennedy the job of assistant manager of Fore River.

Like his earlier capitalist counterparts of the Civil War, Kennedy showed no inclination to let the call of country interfere with his upward career. While most of his Harvard classmates took pride in volunteering for military service before the draft, he felt no such emotional urgency. His first task at Fore River was to build houses for the hordes of workers swarming there, for with the arrival of some 22,000 newcomers that section of Quincy had become a boom town. His talent for getting things done was at once apparent. On his own he built a huge cafeteria, the Victory Lunchroom, that fed thousands daily and that swelled his salary of $20,000 a year, further increased by the fat bonuses with which Charles Schwab, the chairman of Bethlehem Steel, rewarded his efficient executives. With the 1918 armistice, the ship-building boom collapsed overnight. Months before, Kennedy had been trying to conjure up civilian orders, but none appeared. In his persistence he managed to make a fifteen-minute appointment to see Galen Stone, the chairman of the Atlantic, Gulf & West Indian Steamship Line and also the senior partner of the brokerage firm of Hayden, Stone. When he arrived for his interview, he found that Stone had been called unexpectedly to New York. On learning that the train had not yet gone, Joe took a taxi to the station and maneuvered himself into a seat next to Stone for the four-hour journey. Stone was not interested in ships, but he did show interest in the young-man-on-the-make beside him. It was an interest soon reinforced by the intercession of the financial buccaneer Frederick Dumaine, then treasurer of New Hampshire's huge Amoskeag cotton mills, who happened to be under considerable if devious obligations to Honey Fitz. Not long after the impromptu train ride, Kennedy was appointed manager of the stock department of Hayden, Stone. Kennedy stood in awe of the elderly Stone, director of several dozen companies and one of the shrewdest speculators in Boston. His own first ventures into the stock market on a hunch and tip basis turned out badly, but from them he learned his lesson. To make real money on the market, he concluded, one needed to be part of an inner circle such as the one the Stones and the Curriers and the Dumaines were in. Noting Joe's initial missteps, Stone charitably let him know that he was selling his interest in the Pond Creek Coal Company to Henry Ford, who was then buying up companies to piece out and integrate his industrial empire. Borrowing every cent he could, Kennedy bought 15,000 shares of Pond Creek at $16 a share and sold them not long afterward for $45 — a profit of almost half a million.

Kennedy's keen amalgamative eye had noted the small moving picture theaters springing up across New England in the wake of that mushrooming industry. With Currier he now formed a group to buy up thirty-one such small theaters. For them he acquired the regional franchise of Universal Pictures. These theaters would remain the longest-term investment that Kennedy would ever make.

By his tenth Harvard class reunion Joe Kennedy had reached the million-dollar goal he had set for himself a decade earlier. At that reunion he played the genial host, providing prize-fight films — then illegal — for his classmates of the Jack Dempsey-Jess Willard and the Dempsey-George Carpentier bouts. He also arranged to have an ample supply of Scotch furnished by his agents who landed it at a beach near Plymouth from ships beyond the three-mile limit. Watching the flow of booze, a classmate mused that "Joe was our chief bootlegger."

When Stone retired at the end of 1922, Joe branched off on his own. East Boston was for him now nothing more than a view in reverse across the channel. In the same Milk Street building as Hayden, Stone, he opened his own office. There, behind a door lettered *Joseph P. Kennedy, Banker,* he set himself up as a stock market speculator. The months at Hayden, Stone had been for him a seminar in the moves and countermoves of market manipulation, the rigging of stock pools, the hidden interpretation of the figures on the financial pages of the daily press. Still relatively unknown, still relatively limited in his operations, he applied a coldly analytical mind to his trading, undistorted (a rare quality, even in the financial world) by wishful thinking. Shrewd, close-mouthed, always the loner, he considered himself a speculator rather than a gambler, subtly defining the difference:

> While gamblers naturally want to win, the majority of them derive pleasure even if they lose. The desire to win, rather than the excitement involved, seems to me to be the compelling force behind speculation.*

A business acquaintance considered that Kennedy had the ideal temperament for speculation: "a passion for facts, a complete lack of sentiment, a marvelous sense of timing."

During the twenties he remained a man of mystery on Wall Street, buying and selling on the stock market through straw men. "He moved in the intense, secretive circles of operators in the wildest stock market in history," according to *Fortune Magazine,* "with routine plots and pools, inside information and wild guesses." Together with partners like Harry Sinclair and "Sell 'Em Ben" Smith he would inflate cheap stocks through rumors and well-publicized buying and selling; then when the price had been inflated and the gullible were rushing in to buy, his pool would sell short for huge profits.

Within those inner circles that had for so long been his goal, Kennedy's reputation was growing. When John Hertz, the former newspaperman and prize-fighter manager turned taxi-fleet owner, found that the stock of his Yellow Cab Company was being beaten

* *The Founding Father,* p. 66.

down by a group of raiding New York brokers, he turned to Kennedy for help. Kennedy came to New York, set himself up in a suite at the Waldorf with telephones and a ticker and prepared to fight the phantom battle of figures. For seven weeks he lived in that suite, never venturing outside, having his meals brought in, plotting, planning. He had told Hertz that he would need five million dollars "to play around with" and Hertz borrowed the sum from his friend William Wrigley, the chewing-gum magnate. With that five million he bought and sold Yellow Cab stock through brokers all over the country in his efforts to wrest control of the stock from the raiders and stabilize it at the best possible price. The price vacillated between forty-six and sixty-two before Kennedy finally succeeded in beating off the raiders and stabilizing it, while ending up with the five million intact. There was an aftermath. Months later Yellow Cab stock plummeted, and Hertz always suspected Kennedy of pulling out the props he had previously erected and selling short. So convinced was he, that he threatened to punch Kennedy in the nose if ever the two should meet.

Kennedy's family was growing with his income, and he had moved from Beale Street to a twelve-room house on Naples Road. By 1926 there were seven children — Joseph, Jr., John Fitzgerald, Rosemary, Kathleen, Eunice, Patricia and Robert. For Joe, his children were an extension of himself, a continuity, the ultimate reason for his passion for wealth. The knowledge that they would never be really accepted or acceptable to the Proper Bostonians of the Back Bay rankled increasingly in his mind. The Kennedys, for all their house in upper-middle-class Brookline, their Rolls-Royce and chauffeur and servants, their children in private schools, would still be ignored by the Boston *Social Register*. Joe's daughters would never find their names on the season's list of debutantes or be asked to join the Junior League or the Vincent Club — "not that our girls would have joined anyway," Kennedy later told a reporter, "they never gave two cents for that society stuff. But the point is they wouldn't have been asked in Boston." Joe's last straw was his rejection for membership in the Cohasset Country Club, to which his secretary Eddie Moore already belonged.

In their early years the Kennedy family had spent vacations in Hull, the high-hilled peninsula jutting beyond Nantasket Beach where the First Irish Families of Boston had their summer houses. But the Kennedys with their rise in the world had moved upward to Cohasset, the summer home of many Back Bay families. In that ancestor-conscious community where the society and genealogical pages of the *Transcript* provided tea-time reading, such new-rich intruders were not made welcome. "It was petty and cruel," Ralph Lowell remarked in an interview decades afterward. "The women in Cohasset looked down on the daughter of 'Honey Fitz'; and who was Joe Kennedy but the son of Pat, the barkeeper?"

In the spring of 1926, Kennedy bade adieu to Boston in the grand manner, hiring a private railroad car to move his family and servants to an estate in Riverdale, an upper-class New York suburb. Yet for him and his wife the old sense of alienation and rejection remained, the smouldering bitterness at Boston hauteur. Even a dozen years later, when Jack Kennedy was a Harvard undergraduate, Rose was still unable to forget. Mother and son were driving back from Cambridge to New York one afternoon with a Harvard classmate "well entrenched in Boston's formidable high society." As George Herman, a CBS White House correspondent, recorded the incident:

> During the course of the ride, Mrs. Rose Kennedy turned to the friend and, with a sort of desperation, said: "Tell me, when are the nice people of Boston going to accept us?" History does not record what must have been the polite and fumbling answer, but the import of the question is clear. Throughout Kennedy's youth his family felt itself to be on the outside; wealthy and powerful though his father had grown, they were still struggling to get in.
>
> The "nice" golf club at Palm Beach would not accept Joseph P. Kennedy for membership. The "nice" people of Boston would not have the self-made millionaire and his wife, the daughter of Mayor Fitzgerald, in their homes. The Kennedy children were thus brought up with the feeling that they were almost "in," that the goal was in sight, that they needed only that extra bit of effort to make the difference.

About the time that Kennedy was shaking the Boston dust from his feet, and almost by chance, he impelled himself into the moving picture industry where he would in a few years pyramid his already sizable fortune. For some time he had been buying American rights to British pictures for his theater chain and in doing so had gradually built up an association with English film makers, sometimes even acting as their agent. When he learned that the British owners of Film Booking Offices (FBO), an American film-producing company, were in financial straits, he hurried to London to try to buy them out. "From the theater side of the business," an associate later observed, "Kennedy learned Hollywood could wring you dry. He wanted to get where the wringing was done." In London the lawyers proved elusive, and he found himself at a dead end when he happened to read in the paper that Edward, Prince of Wales, was staying briefly in Paris. That was enough to set the boy from East Boston on his feet. Dashing across the Channel, he reached Paris, ferreted out the Prince's favorite restaurant and times of eating, and bribed a waiter to reserve a table near him. When Edward appeared, Kennedy stood up and walked toward him smiling with outstretched hand. After introducing himself, he explained that he had met the Prince at Bayard Tuckerman's reception in Massachusetts the year before. Bayard (he pronounced his name Byr'd) was a socially prominent North Shore sportsman who had entertained the prince briefly on the latter's American visit. Hundreds of figures had flitted past Edward in the reception line on that North Shore evening, although by no stretch of the social imagination would Kennedy have been included. Yet, for all the prince knew, the smiling stranger might well have been there. By way of conversation he asked the American what brought him to Europe, and when Kennedy explained his difficulties with the evasive lawyers he promised to write a letter of introduction that would take care of the matter. That letter, arriving next day, did indeed open all the necessary doors in London.

Only after Kennedy had returned to the United States was the deal finally completed, his biggest coup to date. Even though he had bought out the British owners for a fraction of their original investment, it was still too large a deal for him to handle alone, and he turned to Currier for help in forming a syndicate. He now found himself president and chairman of the board of the Film Booking Office of America. Once he had organized the company efficiently and staffed it with loyal henchmen, he headed for Hollywood, the gilt kingdom where he knew the real gold lay.

FBO's studio was a minor affair compared to Paramount, Metro-Goldwyn-Mayer or First National. Nevertheless the new company produced fifty films that first year, low-budget second-features, for the most part trashy Westerns and lurid adventure pictures — *A Poor Girl's Romance, Red Hot Hoofs, Rose of the Tenements,* and the like — but all money-makers. For Loew, Mayer and Goldwyn, the Hollywood moguls, Kennedy nursed a basic Celtic contempt. "Pants-pressers," he called them, in refence to their origins.

Kennedy's arrival in Hollywood almost coincided with the arrival of sound in moving pictures. That innovation, though it rocked the foundations of the larger companies, gave him his long-sought opportunity. Heading syndicates, engineering mergers, consolidating companies, pyramiding multiple stock options, he seemed after two-and-a-half hectic years about to emerge as the super-capitalist, the financial ruler of the film capital; and when his ultimate deal fell through, he returned East some five million dollars the richer.* During that Hollywood period he formed an intimate relationship with the most regal of film stars, Gloria Swanson, acting as her adviser, banker, friend and all but constant companion. Their degree of intimacy as well as the reasons for their parting would furnish reams of copy for gossip writers for decades afterward. After he left Hollywood their friendship ended abruptly, but Kennedy's friendships had a way of so ending.†

In their upward mobility the Kennedys soon found a more permanent base than the rented Riverdale house in a neo-Georgian mansion in Bronxville that Eddie Moore had ferreted out and purchased for his chief for a quarter of a million dollars. The family now summered on Cape Cod at Hyannis Port — a long distance from Cohasset — in a house that Joe first rented then bought, expanding it and remodeling it to form the nucleus of what would later come to be known as the Kennedy Compound.

The great bull market that would end so ignominiously a year later was hitting its stride when Kennedy returned to New York. But his calculating and wary nature was far more capable than most of standing apart from the prevailing time-spirit. He saw a

* According to Hedda Hopper, "Joe Kennedy's father-in-law, the legendary Honey Fitz, ordered Joe to wind up his film affairs and get out of Hollywood by a given date or certain secrets — still secret except to a few — would burst out into the open."

† Currier, his FBO partner, parted from Joe permanently with cold distrust after their Hollywood partnership.

financial shipwreck ahead. In after years he liked to tell the implausible story that in the summer of 1929 as he was heading for a broker's office he stopped at a shoeshine parlor on Wall Street:

> The kid who shined my shoes didn't know me. He wasn't looking for a tip on the market or anything like that. . . . All the time he was snapping the polishing cloth over my shoes, he kept telling me what was going to happen that day, what stocks would rise and what the market would do.
>
> I just listened to him, and when I left the place I thought: "When the time comes that a shoeshine boy knows as much as I do about the stock market, tells me so and is entirely correct, there's something wrong either with me or with the market, and it's time for me to get out."*

It *was* time for him to get out, but a cold and detached process of reasoning brought him to that conclusion, whether or not the vaporings of the shoeshine boy took place in fact or in his imagination. His stock-market profits before the crash are estimated at $15 million. Even shipwrecks can be of immense profit to salvagers, and Kennedy made more by selling stocks short during the market's four-year decline than he did selling out just short of the peak. With uncanny intuition, aided by a naturally pessimistic nature, he had read the future correctly. Once early in 1929, with his customary brashness, he had gone to call on J. P. Morgan only to be told that the remote financier was too busy to see him. Now, inoculated against the spreading gangrene of the Great Depression, he could laugh at the Morgans.

Nevertheless his basic pessimism found the relentless advance of the Depression unnerving with its all-too-visible accompaniment of closed factories, foreclosed farms, breadlines and the drained, bewildered faces of the unemployed. Although he turned his pessimism to account by selling short and doubling and tripling his fortune while others were losing theirs, he could not get over the numb feeling that in the threatening social convulsions even he might not be able to hold on to his possessions. He later wrote that he would willingly part with half of what he had if he could be sure, under law and order, of keeping the other half.

As sensitive to political trends as he was to the vagaries of the stock market, Kennedy early sensed that Franklin Roosevelt would be the Democratic presidential candidate in 1932. In spite

* *The Kennedy Family*, p. 35.

of his own Democratic inheritance he respected and admired Hoover, but he knew in 1932 that Hoover's reelection was impossible. In the Republican landslide of 1928 Massachusetts Democrats had carried their state for Al Smith — the only northern Smith state except Rhode Island — and they still clung to him with tribal loyalty. Kennedy reasoned coldly that the East Side boy had had his day, and he saw Roosevelt as the magnetic alternative destined to take over and reshape the Democratic party. As he later told a political writer: "Long before the stock market crash, back at the peak of the boom, when Jack was nine or ten years old, I had established million dollar trust funds for each of our children. After the Crash, I began to wonder if those trust funds were going to be worth a damn. I was really worried. I knew that big, drastic changes had to be made in our economic system and I felt that Roosevelt was the one who could make those changes. I wanted him in the White House for my own security, and for the security of our kids, and I was ready to do anything to help elect him."

Early in 1931 Kennedy visited Roosevelt's Madison Avenue headquarters, striding with his overextended smile into Louis Howe's office. Howe, hunched over his desk feigning sleep as he often did, opened one eye and fixed it balefully on his visitor, making clear that he wanted no part of a man he considered a notorious stock market plunger and pool operator. Nevertheless, Kennedy was as determined to enter the inner Roosevelt circle as he had been years before to win his Harvard "H." Disregarding Howe's rebuff, he contributed $25,000 to the Roosevelt nomination campaign, lent $50,000 more and raised an additional $100,000 from his Wall Street acquaintances, through his fund-raising zeal forcing his way into the small group of wealthy Roosevelt backers. With his usual abundant energy he continued making himself useful, even — he hoped — indispensable, touring the country to extract money with the canny knowledge of where money was.

William Randolph Hearst, controlling the delegates of California and Texas, held the balance of power in the 1932 Democratic National Convention, and Kennedy had been friendly with Hearst through the latter's mistress, Marion Davies. Roosevelt despatched Kennedy shortly before the convention to California to see if he could win over the publisher whose loathing of "internationalism" was notorious. Kennedy let him know that Roosevelt's heart was no longer with the League of Nations, that in this and many other respects he was far more amenable than Smith. Hearst warmed to the other's isolationist assurances, and hinted that in certain circumstances he might indeed consider releasing his delegates to Roosevelt. At least he would not release them to Smith. So much Kennedy was able to report back to the Roosevelt headquarters. A week before the convention he arrived in Chicago, set up his own private headquarters and began working with the feverish underhanded zeal he was able to summon up when he had an end in view. With Howe's arrival, however, he faded discreetly into the background. Before the balloting began, he called Hearst several times at San Simeon to warn him that unless he acted quickly the choice might fall on the arch-internationalist Newton Baker. Hearst replied that he would wait and see what happened in the first few ballots. During the first ballot the Roosevelt managers tried desperately to reach Hearst by telephone. His secretaries replied that he had gone to bed. Kennedy was finally able to get through to Hearst's chief legal counsel, John Neylan, telling him bluntly that "if you don't want Baker you'd better take Roosevelt because if Roosevelt breaks on the next ballot, it'll be Baker." Neylan repeated what Kennedy said to Hearst who was standing beside him. Arthur Krock, in the room with Kennedy at the time, recalled the conversation afterward: "Kennedy was an operator," he wrote. "Hearst didn't make a move until Kennedy said that he was going to get Newton D. Baker. . . . When Kennedy quit talking to Neylan, Hearst made his move."

Many men had a hand in the switching of the California and Texas votes to Roosevelt, but Kennedy always felt that he was primarily responsible and that Roosevelt owed his nomination to him. He liked to boast that his telephone call finally brought Hearst round, but he added sourly, "you don't find any mention of it in history books."

Through the summer Kennedy continued to persuade wealthy Democrats to give money for the Roosevelt cause, even extracting $30,000 from Hearst. Roosevelt was grateful to Kennedy and in September invited him to ride on the campaign train. It was a new road for Kennedy and one he welcomed. As a boy he had seen money as power, and he had made his fortune in the jungle world of finance. Now, as a middle-aged man of wealth, he saw power more nakedly revealed in politics, not the petty politics of the Boston wards, but on the national level as the ultimate power, carrying with it the status that Harvard and Boston had denied him. In the two months Kennedy spent on the Roosevelt train he became known as one of Roosevelt's "Silent Six," his half-dozen most intimate councillors. When the train made one of its periodic stops he would go off on his own to talk with local bankers and businessmen, impress on them the ominous slogan "Roosevelt or ruin!" By choice a background figure, he was not often personally identified even in his old state of Massachusetts. Just before the election the Boston *Globe* reported:

> Unrecognized in his home town and his presence here known only to a few close friends and relations, Joseph P. Kennedy, New York financier, former motion picture magnate, and one of Gov. Roosevelt's confidential advisers in the presidential campaign, slipped into Boston on the eve of Al Smith's local appearance and departed Tuesday after the Roosevelt speech. . . . On his Boston visit of almost a week he lived up to his reputation as "a man of mystery."

Roosevelt's victory over President Hoover was more overwhelming even than Kennedy had anticipated, and as one of Roosevelt's political field marshals Kennedy expected his baton. "He moved in close to those in power," his actor friend Eddie Dowling recalled years later. "He knew what he wanted and he fought for it, because he felt he had as much right to it as anyone else." He told his friends confidentially that he expected to be the next secretary of the treasury. Yet after the inauguration his reward failed to materialize. Other members of the inner circle became cabinet officers and ambassadors. Kennedy received nothing but a polite letter of thanks from the White House with a vague invitation to "be sure to let us know when you are going through Washington and stop off and see us." Hurt and affronted, he cursed Roosevelt's ingratitude privately in the argot of East Boston, and demanded repayment of his $50,000 loan to the Democratic Party. For a time he even threatened court action. His friends finally calmed him down to the point where he suppressed his anger enough to write a flattering letter to Roosevelt. Then he went to Washington to see him. At that initially awkward meeting the president turned on all his high-powered charm. "Hello,

Joe," he said. "Where have you been all these months? I thought you'd got lost." Warmed by that charm, Kennedy left the White House convinced that he need only wait to receive his due.

He was to wait a considerable time, for Howe and the New Dealers were still implacably opposed to giving him anything. But while his right hand was idle, his left hand was occupied as usual. Using Eddie Moore as a straw, he formed a pool with a Wall Street broker, Henry Mason Day, Harry Sinclair's right-hand man at the time of the Teapot Dome oil leases, to run up the stock of the Libby-Owens-Ford and the Owens Illinois Glass Company, the latter being a bottle manufacturer and as such a genuine "repeal stock." Kennedy's profits in phantom bottles were modest compared to what he would now make with the help of James Roosevelt through his liquor importing company, Somerset Distillers. He had got to know the president's son during the 1932 campaign and had cultivated him extensively afterward. Jimmy was much like Kennedy in temperament though much less astute. After failing at Harvard Law School and then Boston University School of Law, he had set himself up in Boston as an insurance broker and by adroit use of his father's name had gathered in such profitable clients as the Boston Port Authority, National Distillers, Hayden Stone, and the National Shawmut and First National banks. Jimmy's two-fold ambition was to make as much money as fast as possible and to become governor of Massachusetts. With Repeal only months away, he and Kennedy made a quick trip to England in September, 1933, a trip on which Kennedy managed to corner the American franchise of Haig & Haig, King William and John Dewar whiskies, and Gordon's gin. "The British didn't select their agents haphazardly," a knowledgeable American liquor dealer told Richard Whalen. "They felt Jimmy Roosevelt was a good connection so they gave their lines to Kennedy." Through licenses "for medicinal purposes" issued in Washington, to which Kennedy seemed to have easy access, Somerset Importers was able to bring in thousands of cases of bonded liquor. Months before Prohibition ended, Kennedy's warehouses were bulging. So huge were his liquor imports that Roosevelt's federal liquor controller finally ordered the Somerset Importers' quotas reduced, although he took care to announce there was no impropriety in the way the licenses had been issued. When Prohibition did end on December 5, 1933, Kennedy was ready to flood the country with his Scotch and gin. Joe McCarthy, the author of *The Remarkable Kennedys,* wrote that "maybe Jimmy thought he and Joe were going to be partners. If so, he soon found out that when Joe Kennedy is starting a business he doesn't have partners." Kennedy managed to fob Jimmy off with the excuse that such a partnership at such a time would embarrass the president, while keeping Jimmy's friendship by assuring him of future favors. Meanwhile the months passed with no word from the White House. The ailing and inconsequent Woodin's days as secretary of the treasury were obviously numbered, and Kennedy still nursed the hope of eventually succeeding him. When, however, Woodin resigned in January, 1934, the president, to Kennedy's blasphemous fury, turned to his Dutchess County neighbor, Henry Morgenthau.

Nevertheless Roosevelt had not forgotten his "Secret Six" counselor. In 1934, over the violent objections of Wall Street, Congress passed the Securities Exchange Act aimed at regulating the more blatant malpractices of the stock exchange. Then in mid-June, fifteen months after the inauguration, on the analogy that it takes a thief to catch a thief, Roosevelt appointed Kennedy to the chairmanship of the newly-formed Securities and Exchange Commission. When Kennedy met with Roosevelt to have his appointment confirmed, Raymond Moley was also present and asked Kennedy bluntly if there was anything specific in his business past that might injure the president if it became known. Kennedy flared up with East Boston anger, telling Roosevelt he had nothing to worry about. "What was more," Moley recorded, "he would give his critics — and here the profanity flowed freely — an administration of the SEC that would be a credit to the country, the President, himself, and his family — clear down to the ninth child."

New Deal liberals could not at first believe their eyes when they read of the appointment of the stock-market wolf, the man who in the depth year of the Depression could describe himself in his Harvard class report as a "capitalist," to head the acronymous SEC. The *New Republic* found the appointment grotesque, exceeding the expectations of Roosevelt's more ardent ill-wishers. Kennedy saw the chairmanship of the Securities and Exchange Commission as his longed-for opportunity to attain stature. He was rich, and what he wanted now was to put the seal of respectability on his wealth. His goal was power and continuity. Where the Honey Fitzes and the Jim Curleys and other Boston Irish politicians would fade quickly into oblivion, he wanted to establish the Kennedy name as something beyond himself to equal those old impervious Boston Yankee names.

Roosevelt's impish assistant, the accordian-playing "Tommy the Cork" Corcoran, watched Kennedy with amused detachment and wrote:

> Joe analyzed the increments of power and cut away the fuzz on the edge until the bare bones showed. He had the sense to recognize the opportunity offered by the SEC. While the Secretary of the Treasury *symbolized* power and prestige, here, in the new SEC was the *real* power. The treasury was the tent, hung with trappings, but the SEC was the sword of command, the power to purge. Joe could tell the moneymen in New York what they would do, and they damned well better do it, or he could sweep them into the sea.*

Under Kennedy the commission rapidly expanded to seven hundred employees, many of them experienced professionals whom he had enticed from banks, brokerage houses and law firms. He rented an estate in Maryland and there with Eddie Moore set up a bachelor establishment as he had in Hollywood. He worked prodigiously. Unlike many of the New Dealers, his approach was conciliatory. He was not out to challenge an already ruffled Wall Street. What he aimed for was to obtain the cooperation of the more responsible brokers and to persuade the stock exchanges to regulate themselves. At the same time he wanted to restore business confidence sufficiently to bring about the resumption of new financing. Within a year the hostility of the business and financial community to the Securities and Exchange Commission had turned to an extraordinary degree of acceptance. Kennedy had taken a law that seemed unworkable and had administered it so that business was reassured, corporate borrowing simplified and investor confidence renewed. Under his astute chairmanship the commission came to be regarded by earlier critics as the New Deal's most constructive reform.

During these months his intimacy with the president grew. Roosevelt seemed to enjoy his company. Often the president liked to slip away to the Maryland retreat on an evening, relax,

* *Record American*, Jan. 16, 1964.

and drink an old-fashioned while watching the latest Hollywood film in Kennedy's private theater.

After a year, when Kennedy felt he had completed his task of organizing the commission as an effective agency, he resigned. In that year he had indeed attained the prestige that his nature demanded. No longer was he the parvenu operator whom a Morgan could turn away from his office door but a man of standing, much sought-after now as a corporate consultant. Once he had left the commission, such ailing giants as Radio Corporation of America and Paramount turned to him for guidance in reorganization. For Roosevelt's 1936 election campaign he published *I'm for Roosevelt,* a book ghost-written for him by *New York Times* columnist Arthur Krock, in which out of loyalty to the president he seemed to have back-tracked on his own capitalist convictions by advocating — without defining — a planned economy and efficient social controls. But in the back of his mind there lurked the vague but persistent notion of himself as a presidential candidate in 1940. Some time in the thirties a Boston paper had referred to him as an Irish-American. The term had stirred up all his old resentments. "I was born here," he shouted angrily. "My children were born here. What the hell do I have to do to be an American?" The White House might provide the answer.

After Roosevelt's re-election he persuaded Kennedy to take over the recently established Maritime Commission in an effort to create an efficient merchant marine out of the inefficient, strike-plagued shipping industry. "Such is the penalty of having once performed a miracle," Arthur Krock remarked on hearing of Kennedy's appointment. Kennedy knew that neither he nor anyone else could perform a miracle against the dedicated intransigency of the shippers and the maritime unions. He did his quick-tempered best, at one point ordering striking American seamen put in irons, on another occasion throwing a punch at the maritime union leader Harry Bridges when he met him in a hotel. When after almost a year of unremitting if vain efforts, he resigned from "the toughest job I ever handled in my life," he left the president deeply indebted to him for taking on such a thankless task. His hoped-for reward was to replace Morgenthau as secretary of the treasury. But Roosevelt remained obdurate. "I couldn't put Joe Kennedy in his [Morgenthau's] place," he told a friend in confidence, "because Joe would want to run the treasury in his own way, contrary to my plans and views."

Jimmy Roosevelt — at Kennedy's prompting — first suggested to his father that Kennedy replace the ailing ambassador to Great Britain, Robert Bingham. In spite of the failed liquor partnership, Joe and Jimmy had remained wary friends. After Louis Howe's death Jimmy had to a great extent assumed the gnomish little man's confidential role, moving into the White House to act as a "clearing house" for his father with independent government agencies. "Jimmy has his father's ear at all times," the irascible Secretary of the Interior Harold Ickes noted in his diary of March, 1938. "When the President is tired or discouraged, Jimmy is at hand to say what may be influential."

To Kennedy the ambassadorship to the Court of St. James's was as glittering a goal as the Treasury Department and one within easier reach. For ever since Wilson's secretary of state, William Jennings Bryan, had shattered the professionalism of the State Department by his ruthless application of the spoils system, it had been customary for wealthy party contributors to claim their reward by occupying the embassies of London or Paris or Rome or Berlin. The president seemed at first to consider the London appointment an adequate way of paying off Kennedy but then developed second thoughts, suggesting that Kennedy might be better off as secretary of commerce. Kennedy refused to consider it. He held out for the post that would make him the most important American in Europe. There was a certain vengefulness in his importunity. For the Irish-Catholic parvenu, unacceptable to Boston's *Social Register*, would occupy a position that to anglophile Old Boston would seem more desirable than the presidency. Roosevelt finally agreed, hinting that if his new ambassador performed well he might later even swap jobs with Morgenthau.

Kennedy's arrival in England in the spring of 1938 with his nine children aged from six to twenty-two was a week's wonder. The popular press seized on the novelty of the photogenic Kennedys, writing them up with the maudlin reportage usually reserved for the royal family. Fresh, young and vital, the Kennedy tribe, if not individually handsome, managed to convey such a collective impression.

That crisis year, culminating in Hitler's confrontation with Prime Minister Chamberlain at Munich, sent ominous shadows across Europe but failed to dim the brightness of the London social season. The Kennedys, as recorded in the press, seemed omnipresent, the daughters presented at court, Kennedy and his wife entertained by the king and queen and the prime minister. The stock-jobber turned ambassador felt very much at ease with the Birmingham businessman turned politician. "I'm just like that with Chamberlain," he told a friend not long after his arrival in London. "Why, Franklin himself isn't as confidential with me." For Kennedy that first year was an inner triumph. He was dazzled, charmed, delighted by his acceptance in that greater city of which Back Bay Boston was such a provincial imitation.

Buoyed up by his extensive if superficial popularity, Kennedy could see nothing esoteric in diplomacy and considered that, unlike himself, the "career boys" in the State Department did not really know what was going on in Europe.

No American ambassador of the twentieth century had been more cordially received in England. Yet there were Englishmen detached from social London who took a less rosy view of the brash new envoy. After receiving a long critical letter from the Liberal member of parliament, Colonel Josiah Wedgewood, Ickes noted in his diary: "At the time when we should be sending the best that we have to Great Britain, we have not done so. We have sent a rich man, untrained in diplomacy, unlearned in history and politics, who is a great publicity seeker and who is apparently ambitious to be the first Catholic President of the United States." A military attaché, Colonel Raymond Lee, the quiet-spoken grandson of Robert E. Lee, looked on the parvenu ambassador with patrician disdain, considering him "crude, blatant and ignorant in everything he did or said." Kennedy, he concluded, "has the speculator's smartness but also his *sharpshooting* and *facile* insensibility to the great forces which are now playing like heat lightning over the map of the world."

Chamberlain's appeasement aims had Kennedy's solid support. To Kennedy, who flattered himself on his "practicality," Hitler was a fact of life, brutal but fixed, and sensible men would in the end have to be prepared to do business with him. Like Chamberlain he hoped privately that Hitler would exhaust his new military machine in an attack on Russia, just as Stalin in the Kremlin nursed the idea that Hitler might be induced to spend his strength against the West.

When in September, 1938, Chamberlain returned from the

Munich conference bringing back his forlorn "Peace in Our Time," the momentary public enthusiasm (Roosevelt sent him a cable of congratulation) soon turned to doubt. But while Hitler's belligerency increased, Kennedy remained firm in his support of Chamberlain. The thought of war horrified him, with its threat to all he had accumulated and to the very life of his four sons. Two months after Munich when the National Socialists unleashed their anti-Jewish frenzy of looting and burning and killing that, from the litter of broken glass in the cities, became known as the Crystal Night, Kennedy came up with an impromptu plan for resettling German Jews in the more sparsely populated regions of Africa and North and South America. Though in its practical aspects as incapable of being fulfilled as a Boston politician's pre-election promise, it brought Kennedy a wave of approval from influential sections of American opinion and revived for him an old dream. *Life* commented: "Kennedy is rated the most influential U. S. Ambassador to England in many years. If this plan for settling the German Jews, already widely known as the Kennedy Plan succeeds, it will add new luster to a reputation that may well carry Joseph Patrick Kennedy into the White House."

Hitler's occupation of Czechoslovakia just two months after the Munich agreement did not change Kennedy's belief that England and America must somehow come to terms with the German dictator. He still could not bring himself to believe in the inevitability of the inevitable war. Up until the very last moments of August, 1939, he did not feel that England would honor the pledge given to Poland. The British war declaration on September 3, brought out all his innate pessimism. "It's the end of the world," he told friends, "the end of everything." On a brief visit to the United States in December, 1939, he kept insisting that there was no place in the war for America, that "this is not our fight." Harold Nicolson noted in his diary of February 29, 1940, his worry at the return of Joseph Kennedy "who has been spreading it abroad in the U. S. A. that we shall certainly be beaten and he will use his influence here to press for a negotiated peace."

The fall of France the following June only confirmed Kennedy's pessimism. He was sure that England would go down fighting but would still go down. For a time he thought Roosevelt might act as a mediator between England and Germany. "To anyone who comes within hailing distance," the columnist Joseph Alsop wrote, "our Ambassador to England freely predicts the collapse of capitalism, the destruction of democracy and the onset of the dark ages. He says that only an early peace, at almost any price, can save the world."

The defiance of the English was in buoyant contrast to the American ambassador's voluble pessimism. His popularity in England faded rapidly. While Roosevelt thought England's survival essential for America's security, Kennedy doubted the possibility of survival. He much resented being by-passed by Roosevelt's special envoys, and he was undiplomatically explicit about what he considered the pro-war liberal clique surrounding the president. Churchill, when he replaced Chamberlain in May, 1940, had little patience with Kennedy and his bleak dispatches to Washington. Six weeks later Chamberlain, now a dying man, noted in his diary: "Saw Joe Kennedy who says everyone in the U. S. A. thinks we shall be beaten before the end of the month."

Though his family had long since returned to America, Kennedy remained in England, living that autumn through the better part of the blitz that he had predicted in advance Britain could not survive. He left on October 27, 1940, after two years and nine months in England, ostensibly to be on hand at the American presidential election in November, although it was clear to him and to the English that he would not return. A. J. Cummings of the London *News Chronicle* wrote the epitaph of Kennedy's departure:

> While he was here his suave monotonous style, his nine over-photographed children and his hail-fellow-well-met manner concealed a hard-boiled business man's eagerness to do a profitable business deal with the dictators, and deceived many decent English people.

So close to the isolationists was Kennedy on his return to the United States that it was thought by some that he might publicly turn against Roosevelt and endorse the Republican candidate, Wendell Willkie. Those who thought so did not understand Kennedy's opportunist nature, his cold calculation of odds. The odds were on Roosevelt. More than aware of Kennedy's indiscretions and anti-Roosevelt remarks, the president was still not wholly sure of his election to the unprecedented third term and he was anxious to mollify his envoy. Whenever the latter appeared at the

White House, Roosevelt exerted all his considerable charm. Kennedy left, according to Alsop, convinced that he had been promised the Democratic nomination in 1944. Two evenings later he made a radio address endorsing Roosevelt, paying for the time himself and speaking over a hook-up of 114 CBS stations. He told his nationwide audience that "this country must and will stay out of war," and that in "this, probably the most critical election year of our existence," there was no truth that the president was trying to take the country into war. After defending the president at length, he concluded:

> My wife and I have given nine hostages to fortune. Our children and your children are more important than anything else in the world. The kind of America that they and their children will inherit is of grave concern to us all. In the light of these considerations I believe that Franklin D. Roosevelt should be re-elected President of the United States.

That endorsement by a known isolationist was one of the most effective of the campaign, reassuring still dubious Americans that Roosevelt would not take this country into war. The next evening Roosevelt himself spoke at the Boston Garden, welcoming back "that Boston boy, beloved by all of Boston and a lot of other places, my ambassador to the Court of St. James's, Joe Kennedy." And he concluded with his ringing promise: "I have said this before, but I shall say it again and again and again. 'Your boys are not going to be sent into any foreign wars.' "

For expediency's sake Kennedy had succeeded in masking his pessimism, but the week after the election he dropped the mask while talking informally with three newsmen who had dropped in on him at his suite in the Ritz Carlton on his brief visit to Boston. Whether he had intended to speak off the record, or whether he was merely carried away by the sound of his own voice, he let himself go. One of the newsmen, Louis Lyons of the Boston *Globe,* assumed that Kennedy had no objection to being quoted and wrote his interview up accordingly. Sitting in his shirt sleeves, Kennedy told them he was willing to spend all he had to keep the country out of war. "There's no sense in our getting in," he said in his flat bitter voice. "We'd just be holding the bag." Democracy, in his view, was finished in England, and it might be here. "People call me a pessimist," he concluded. "I say 'What is there to be gay about?' Democracy is all done."

That interview, spread across the pages of American and English newspapers, marked the end of Kennedy as a political figure. The man without faith, without belief was finished. Two days later he announced his resignation as ambassador as of November 6. Never again would he or could he move in the circles of political power.

Beyond the mere accumulation of wealth, whatever future there now was for the Kennedy family lay with Joe's sons. Joe had managed somehow to shape them to his purpose, impose his views on them. Curiously enough they never resented him. Although they later would follow their own thought patterns, their own paths, they would never in adolescence or after feel the need of rebelling against the father-figure.

Catholicism was of course a Boston Irish trademark. Yet Kennedy's Catholicism was Latin rather than Celtic — to accede to the Church, accept it, but not to let it interfere too much with one's private habits or one's daily life. The pieties were for women. So it was only natural that the Kennedy girls would be educated by nuns whereas the boys would go to upper-middle-class and basically Protestant preparatory schools.

Kennedy's eldest son, Joseph Kennedy, Jr., was most like his father in temper and temperament, what Kennedy himself might have been, brought up in an easier environment. He sent Joe to Choate where the boy, though no born student, managed to win the Harvard Trophy as the football player best combining scholarship and sportsmanship. Even as an adolescent Joe announced that he was going into politics and that he would become the first Roman Catholic president of the United States. Graduating from Choate in 1933, the eighteen-year-old was sent by his father to study for a year at the London School of Economics under Harold Laski. Laski found the young American engaging, invited him to the famous "Laski Sunday teas" and even took him on a trip to Russia. "His mind was only just beginning to discover the enchantment of thought," Laski wrote afterward. "He had his heart set on a political career. He had often sat in my study and submitted with that smile that was pure magic to relentless teasing about his determination to be nothing less than President of the United States."

Joe's years at Harvard were not unlike those of his father. His chief interests were sports and social life, but he did not have his father's need to force his way ahead. Like his father, he regarded his courses as hurdles in an accepted obstacle course. Yet he learned easily and in the end he managed to win a *cum laude* degree with his thesis *Intervention in Spain* in which he took issue with prevailing academic opinion in its support of the Madrid government.

In his sophomore year he had been taken into the Hasty Pudding Club, now combined with the Institute of 1770. Indicative of his social naivety, he also joined Pi Eta, an imitative Hasty Pudding for those who could not make the original. Where Joe, Sr., however, had had to settle for the D. U. fraternity, Joe, Jr., was asked to join Iroquois, last socially of Harvard's ten final clubs. Still it *was* a final club, marking a great gap between the minority who belonged and the majority who did not.

Joe's early athletic promise never fully developed. He made the freshman football squad but not the team. In his sophomore year, he was again on the squad, a third-string substitute end, big enough but not quite hard-hitting enough, fast but not quite fast enough, prone to injuries. His junior year he did not go out for the team at all. Quick-tempered, quick-fisted, he was nevertheless popular as an undergraduate, being elected to the Winthrop House Committee, the Student Council and in his senior year chairman of the Class Day Committee. That same year he again went out for football, again making the squad though not the team but this time determined to win his varsity "H." The father was as determined as the son. On the night before the Yale game the Harvard coach, Dick Harlow, received a telephone call from a man close to Kennedy asking if Joe was going to get his letter next day. "Nobody's going to high-pressure me!" Harlow angrily told his line coach after repeating the conversation. That same evening Kennedy himself called Harlow, but the coach refused to come to the phone. In that long-forgotten game Harvard managed to break out of a tie and score a touchdown a few minutes before the game's end. Harlow sent in few substitutes, and young Kennedy to his white-faced chagrin was not one of them. The father, watching from the stands, then scrambled down furiously to the field and fought his way through the crowd until he reached Harlow to curse him out in his most vivid East Bostonese.

It was not Kennedy's first grudge against Harvard. The year

before he had been one of a dozen graduates nominated to the Harvard Board of Overseers from which the alumni would elect five. In spite of much undercover canvasing, to his humiliation, he came in tenth. This and the affront on Soldiers Field were compounded a year later after Kennedy had been appointed ambassador to England. On his return to the United States in the spring of 1938 for his son Joe's graduation, he had hoped and expected to be awarded an honorary Harvard doctorate. The degree committee, however, rejected him as insufficiently distinguished. Kennedy never forgave Harvard, never contributed another dollar to the university as long as he lived.

After graduation Joe spent the year abroad, several months in the Paris embassy followed by a short visit to Germany where he observed: "They are really a marvelous people and it is going to be an awful tough time to keep them from getting what they want." Later in his *Wanderjahr* he visited Republican Spain, passing some weeks in beleaguered Madrid and arriving back in London to meet his father and family just after the German army had marched into Poland.

That first autumn of the war found him in Cambridge, Massachusetts, at the Harvard Law School where he would spend the next two years. Law in itself interested him only minimally. He regarded it chiefly as preparation for a political career. His father later wrote nostalgically "Joe used to talk about being President someday and a lot of smart people thought he would make it. He was altogether different from Jack, more dynamic, more sociable and easygoing." Whatever his interests, Joe managed to stay in the upper fifth of his law class. A classmate recalled him as "good looking, articulate, attractive, energetic. A very tough guy. Just a little bit unfeeling; he wouldn't have been elected the most popular man in the class."

His father's isolationist views he took as his own, expressing them with voluble belligerency. He maintained that Germany could not invade America; that if England went under, the United States could and if necessary would do business with Hitler; that for America to convoy British ships would mean war. With his classmates Robert Taft, Jr., and Theodore Roosevelt's grandson Quentin he formed the Harvard Committee Against Military Intervention in Europe in opposition to the Committee for Militant Aid to Britain. Yet he was no pacifist. He believed in aid to Britain short of war and he believed in American preparedness. The key phrase was, as with his father, "short of war."

In May, 1941, when the American draft law passed the year before was beginning to induct larger and larger numbers of American young men into the forces, Joe signed up for the Naval Cadet program. A month later at the end of the semester he was sworn in as a seaman second class, U.S. Naval Reserve. "Wouldn't you know?" his father complained in a mixture of anguish and pride. "*Naval aviation,* the most dangerous thing there is!"

The Japanese attack on Pearl Harbor found Joe a cadet at the naval air station at Jacksonville, Florida. His brother Jack, two years his junior, was by then also a naval cadet. In the spring Jack had tried to join the army and then the navy, being rejected by both services because of a back injury sustained in a football scrimmage three years before. But after five months of corrective exercises he had at last been able to pass the navy fitness test.

Father Joe's reaction to the Pearl Harbor disaster was both emotional and theatrical. At once he telegraphed President Roosevelt: "In this great crisis all Americans are with you. Name the battle front. I am yours to command." The command never came. A letter that he arranged to have personally delivered to the president received a cordially noncommittal reply. The most that could be offered him was to supervise two shipyards in Portland, Maine!

Kennedy's divergence from Roosevelt had been a gradual process, the more so because Kennedy felt a prudent hesitancy at making a complete break. He had sympathized with but never given his full backing to the isolationist America Firsters. But now as any possibility of an appointment or future political career dissolved, he became more and more outspoken in his criticism of Roosevelt's conduct of the war. He took no further part in the war effort, nor was he asked to.

While Kennedy waited for a war opportunity that never came, his two older sons moved on from training to active service. Tied at first to a desk in Washington, Jack appealed to his father. Though Kennedy's friendship with Under Secretary of the Navy James Forrestal, Jack was finally accepted for sea duty with a squadron of PT's, motor torpedo boats, and after six months of training was shipped out to the South Pacific. In March, 1943, as lieutenant junior grade he took command of the PT-109 in the Solomon Islands. On the night of August 2 the PT-109, while cruising west of New Georgia in the dark waters of Blackett Strait, was rammed and sunk by a Japanese destroyer. Though the sinking was a palpable error of navigation by the skipper of such a speedy, highly maneuverable craft, Jack behaved afterward with coolness and courage. In spite of further injuries to his back he escaped from the flaming hull with ten others, towed a wounded man to safety and after fifteen hours in the water managed to reach a tiny island near a Japanese base. There he repeatedly risked his life swimming into dangerous waters trying to signal a rescue ship. After three days he and his crew were finally found.

Kennedy on receiving word from the Navy Department that Jack was missing in action kept the news from his family. The key word was "missing," and in spite of his anxiety he held tenaciously to his belief in his luck, his destiny. Four days later he learned that his son Jack was saved. Jack returned undermined in health but a hero, to be awarded the Navy and Marine Corps Medal. While the press of America was enlarging on his deeds, his older brother was disgustedly engaged in ferrying Liberator bombers from San Diego to the East Coast. Not until September, 1943, would he finally get to England as a pilot in the U. S. Fairwing Seven Squadron, attached to the RAF. From the Dunkeswell Airdrome in Devon he then flew a radar-equipped Liberator on antisubmarine patrols over the Channel and the North Sea. It was arduous and at times dangerous duty, frustrating in its monotony, demanding and essential but scarcely glamorous.

In mid-June the German V-1's, the flying bombs, began falling on London. One of the hastily planned countermeasures was to send pilotless radio-controlled bombers loaded with explosives against the V-1 sites just across the channel. Such a drone plane could climb, bank and dive, but it could not take off by itself. For that it required a crew of three who would then parachute to earth. When naval volunteers were requested for such a mission, Joe was among the first to step forward, and one of the first to be accepted. On the morning of August 12 he took off from Fersfield Airdrome in East Anglia with two other volunteers in a

Liberator containing ten tons of explosives and accompanied by fighters and pilot planes. Forty-five minutes after takeoff the three crewmen were to bail out near Dover and let the unmanned drone continue to its target. After twenty-eight minutes in the air the Liberator suddenly exploded. Not even a trace of Joe's body could be found.

For Kennedy, his son's death was an inconceivable turn of fate. Rose could find a stern consolation in her religion. He could not. Avoiding friends and acquaintances, he retired within his emptied self. In young Joe he had seen a continuity extending beyond himself to goals he could not attain. As his son Jack later wrote of the dead brother: "It is the realization that the future held the promise of great accomplishments for Joe that has made his death so particularly hard for those who knew him. His worldly success was so assured and inevitable that his death seems to have cut into the natural order of things."

Kennedy remained a recluse for over half a year, but he was not out of touch enough to lose his business touch. A year before Joe's death, and more or less by chance, he had begun to move his wealth into land and buildings. With that luck that he felt was his birthright he had moved in just before real estate inflation began. Through private holding companies he bought and sold properties in New York and elsewhere, always in a rising market. His most spectacular and profitable acquisition was Chicago's Merchandise Mart, the world's largest commercial building.

In 1945 Kennedy told the Economic Club of Chicago: "I wish I hadn't acquired respectability. I'd be out selling the market short." With his ingrained pessimism, he saw economic dislocations after the war and a break in the stock market like that of 1920 or even 1929. If he had followed his instinct then he would have lost most of his substance, but his luck again held. As a result of his real estate ventures he moved from the level of the rich to the super-rich, his fortune not valued in millions but in hundreds of millions. In 1957 *Fortune* listed him among the dozen wealthiest Americans and noted that he owned more valuable real estate than anyone else in the United States. Always he remained the pure capitalist, indifferent to what he owned, how it functioned, and what it produced so long as it made money. He did, however, at this time — and at a vast profit — sell out his liquor interests, as incompatible with the Morgan image he was striving to create for himself and with his long-range goal that he had put aside after Joe's death but not forgotten. His eldest son was now Jack.

"I got Jack into politics, I was the one," Kennedy wrote after his son had become United States senator. "I told him Joe was dead and that it was his responsibility to run for Congress. He didn't want to. He felt he didn't have the ability. But I told him he had to." Jack Kennedy said later that it was like being drafted. "My father wanted his eldest son in politics. 'Wanted' isn't the right word. He demanded it. You know my father."

Two years younger than his brother, Jack had lived in the shadow of the more gregarious Joe. Perhaps that was why he entered Princeton instead of Harvard, although before he had completed his freshman year his health gave way — possibly the first onslaught of Addison's disease, an infection of the adrenal glands that would distress him all his life. Once his health had improved he transferred to Harvard where Joe was now a junior, entering as a freshman in September of 1936. Unlike his back-slapping older brother he was shy and, as the master of Winthrop House described him, "reasonably inconspicuous." One of his tutors, his later associate John Kenneth Galbraith, found him "gay, charming, irreverent, good-looking, and far from diligent." Too slight to be an athlete, he tried nevertheless and managed to make the junior varsity football squad until he sustained his back injury. For a time he was on the swimming team. His grades were mediocre, he showed no particular interest in politics or political causes, yet of all the Kennedys he liked Harvard and Cambridge best. As an indication of the rising Kennedy status he made the Spee Club, the fourth ranking final club in Harvard's social hierarchy. In his junior year his father, now ambassador, suggested that he take an extended tour of Europe to see whether he might be interested in a diplomatic career. Jack then left Harvard for a semester to spend six weeks in Paris, a month in Warsaw, and briefer periods in Germany, the Balkans, Russia and Palestine. Returning to college in the war autumn of 1939, he admitted afterward that he had had to "work like hell" to make up the lost semester. Up until then relatively indifferent to his studies, he now determined to write a thesis and graduate with honors in political science. At first he planned a study of "English Foreign Policy since 1731" but at his father's suggestion soon put this far too ambitious project aside for "Appeasement at Munich." In his thesis he repeated his father's defense of the Munich agreement as being both necessary and desirable in giving Britain time to re-arm. He blamed British opinion and the failure of England earlier to re-arm, rather than Baldwin and Chamberlain, for making the Munich surrender inevitable. Perhaps the most distinguishing feature of this essay was its detachment. It was, according to Kennedy's biographer James MacGregor Burns, "a typical undergraduate effort — solemn and pedantic in tone, bristling with statistics and footnotes, a little weak in spelling and sentence structure." Brother Joe thought it represented a lot of work "but did not prove anything." It did bring Jack a *magna cum laude*, however. For the ambassador it was a "swell job" and he quickly determined to promote it to a full-time book. Much edited, much rewritten, with editorial assistance by Arthur Krock and a foreword by Henry Luce, it was published under the title *Why England Slept*, recalling Churchill's earlier *While England Slept*. Appearing during the blitz, it was an immediate best-seller, a Book of the Month Club selection, praised by the *New York Times*, the *Herald Tribune* and more modestly by the London *Times Literary Supplement*. Kennedy in his pride sent copies to Laski, Churchill and Queen Elizabeth. "You would really be surprised," he wrote to his son, "how a book that really makes the grade with high-class people stands you in good stead for years to come." But it was Laski's wife Frida long after, who spoke the last word on *Why England Slept*. "If you have a rich daddy," she told a Kennedy biographer, "you can get a book published."

After a disk operation on his back, Jack Kennedy was discharged from the navy in January, 1945. He was thin, almost wasted from the after-effects of malaria, with the incision in his back still unhealed. His Addison's disease was controlled but not cured by cortisone. He would continue to be troubled by his back injury, though only at times incapacitated. Through his father's friend Hearst he was able to join the International News Service. Billed as the "PT hero" who could explain the "GI viewpoint" he covered such varied spectacular events as the founding of the United Nations and Churchill's 1945 election defeat. In spite of such glamorous assignments, he found he was not a born reporter. Such a life seemed to him too "passive" and his attitude was reflected in his flat and uninspired copy. None of his brother's political ambitions had yet filtered down to him. Years later he reflected that he would probably have gone to law school if Joe had lived. "Beyond that," he concluded, "I can't say. I was at loose ends. I was interested in ideas and I might have gone into journalism. The exchange of ideas that goes with teaching attracted me, but scholarship requires a special type of discipline; it wouldn't be my strength." In his sixth-year Harvard report he described himself as a journalist and added that he was pessimistic about the future of his country. To his navy friend Paul "Red" Fay he wrote confidingly early in 1945: "I'll be back here with Dad trying to parlay a lost PT boat and bad back into a political advantage. I tell you Dad is ready right now and can't understand why Johnny boy isn't 'all engines ahead full.' "

Just before the war's end Ambassador Kennedy had returned briefly to public life in his native state when he accepted Governor Maurice Tobin's invitation to serve as chairman of a commission to study the establishment of a state department of commerce. Touring the Bay State fitted in with his long-range plans, and he began to see his dynastic goal in more specific terms. It was a year when Boston's off-and-on mayor, James Michael Curley, had resigned from Congress to run for a fourth mayoralty term. Under indictment for using the mails to defraud, he found this no handicap to his re-election. But he left the 11th Congressional District vacant — the most securely Democratic district in the state — and to Joseph Kennedy it was a made-to-order opportunity. Comprising the slums of East Boston, the North and South Ends, Charlestown and Somerville, with Harvard and Cambridge thrown in for good measure, the 11th district had spawned both Honey Fitz and Pat Kennedy. Now part Italian where it had once been all Irish, it had many petty ward bosses but no real leader. Yet the Kennedy roots were there. As Curley remarked when he heard that John Fitzgerald Kennedy would be a candidate for Curley's renounced congressional seat: "With those two names, how could he lose?"

Jack had been born in Brookline, brought up in Bronxville and Palm Beach, educated in Connecticut and in Cambridge, and had never lived in Boston. Nor was he even a registered Democrat. For tax purposes the Kennedys were all legal residents of

Palm Beach. These were obstacles that could be easily overcome. First of all Jack had to establish residence in Massachusetts. His father installed him in the Hotel Bellevue, a politician's eyrie, known as "the political nineteenth hole, hiring hall and auction block" across the street from the State House where Honey Fitz himself was living out his old age. Not long after that, Jack rented a small apartment in a plain and faded building at 122 Bowdoin Street on top of Beacon Hill, and this would be his legal residence for the rest of his life. His campaign headquarters remained at the Bellevue.

In spite of Curley's dictum, father Kennedy believed in leaving nothing to chance. The year before the nomination he set up his own headquarters in a suite at the Ritz-Carlton. "I just called people," Kennedy explained in later years. "I got in touch with people I knew. I have a lot of contacts."

> The telephone [Whalen noted] was the instrument and symbol of Kennedy's power. That a man with his enormous wealth enjoyed influence was not unusual; but the scope of his influence was extraordinary. He knew precisely whom to call to move the levers of local political power.*

Kennedy laid out a plan of campaign as exact as a blueprint. As Jack's manager he brought in the seasoned politician Francis X. Morrissey, Tobin's former secretary and a well-known funeral-home proprietor. He also brought his cousin Joe Kane to teach Jack the political facts of life. "Pickles" Kane had once served a term on the Boston Common Council but a hare lip thwarted his ambitions for higher office. Forty years of rough-and-tumble Boston politics had taught him much. Three things, he maintained, were necessary to succeed in political life: money, money, and lastly money. Although scorned by Jack's Harvard friends, he gave the young candidate a slogan: "The New Generation Offers a Leader." Ironically, Pickles had had an under hand in unseating Honey Fitz from Congress in 1919 after Fitzgerald had nosed out Congressman "Weeping Peter" Tague in an election in which "mattress" voting and suffed ballot boxes had been too blatant even for Boston.

Jack's campaign was two-sided. On one side and very obvious in the Bellevue were the clean-cut amateurs, his college and navy

* *The Founding Father,* p. 633.

friends, volunteers eager to help, new-look Democrats and some of them not even Democrats. On the other side, vitally inconspicuous, were the hard-faced, beady-eyed pros his father had gathered together, profanely contemptuous of the amateurs and their innocent ways.

From his command post at the Ritz-Carlton the senior Kennedy passed the word and the money along. There were nine other candidates for the 11th District's Democratic nomination, but by the time they were ready to start campaigning, Jack Kennedy, the early unknown, had preempted the field. A Boston advertising agency was called in to put its best brains into the campaign. Kennedy's name was blazoned throughout the district as reiteratively as a cigarette advertisement: on billboards, on streetcar and bus placards, on bumper stickers, on walls, wherever there was an empty space. Kennedy "spots" echoed from every Boston radio station. One worker recalled that the people of the district "saw Kennedy, heard Kennedy, ate Kennedy, drank Kennedy, slept Kennedy, and Kennedy talked and we talked Kennedy all day long. . . . He was well advertised." The campaign issue, if it could be called that, was Jack's war record. John Hersey had written the story of the PT-109 for the *New Yorker* and Father Joe saw to it that it was reprinted in the *Reader's Digest*. Copies of that reprint were distributed to every family in the 11th district. Pickles took care of the opposition. He paid one candidate $7,500 "to stay in or get out," whichever Kane decided might be more useful. When a Joseph Russo threatened to monopolize the North End's Italian vote, Pickles produced a second Joseph Russo to run against him. Kane and others took Jack on tours of his unfamiliar district, through mean streets and fetid back alleys the like of which he had scarcely been aware. Between five and six in the afternoon they climbed the back stairs of innumerable three-deckers rank with the smell of cooking to "catch them in the kitchen." They walked with set smiles into barrooms, fruit stores and tiny delicatessens. At first Jack was awkward and diffident, repeating that he would never have gone into politics if his brother Joe had lived. But under Kane's watchful eye he began to find it easier to speak, to meet people, to approach casual strangers with fixed smile and extended hand. Joseph Kennedy, standing one morning on a street corner near East Boston's Maverick

Square and watching his son waylay prospective voters to ask for their support, marveled at Jack's adaptability. "Hell," he told Morrissey, "I never thought he had it in him!"

Young volunteers might flock to the Bellevue to give a new direction to local politics but Kennedy at the Ritz-Carlton kept undisputed control. Workers engaged by his son were engaged subject to his approval. Not a dollar was spent without his authorization. Several times a week he called the Bellevue headquarters to demand a detailed account of every aspect of the campaign. All plans and arrangements had to be submitted to him. To win would be as easy as Curley had predicted. What Kennedy wanted was a spectacular win that would make his son's name familiar all over the state. The whole Kennedy family pitched in, even the women. Sisters Eunice, Pat and Jean rang doorbells throughout the district. Mother Rose inaugurated a "social campaign," she and her daughters persuading volunteer hostesses throughout the district to give teas to meet the young candidate and his mother and sisters. For such informal festivities the Kennedy organization provided silver, china, flowers and food. Sometimes Jack would attend as many as six of these in the course of an evening. Housewives were enchanted by his tousled forelock and boyish manner, just as they were overcome by the high-powered charm of the Kennedy ladies. The social campaign culminated in a huge evening reception at the Hotel Commander in Cambridge for which formally engraved hand-addressed envelopes were sent out to every name in the Kennedy files. The line of guests, several thousand of them, extended through the hotel lobby, across the street and into a nearby park. Ambassador Kennedy, in white tie and tails, had emerged from the Ritz-Carlton to join his son and his women folk for the last grand gesture before the balloting. For many of the women guests, dressed in their somewhat frowsy best, it would be the glamorous evening of their lives. "That reception was the clincher," one of Jack's disconcerted rivals remarked. "Everybody wanted to be in Society."

Much derided at first by the pols, Rose's tea-party technique turned out to be a brilliant innovation. The whole campaign, as master-minded by Kennedy, was a virtuoso performance. No detail was neglected. When the voters finally went to the polls, the men at each precinct passing out Kennedy cards were wearing Eisenhower jackets. The results topped even the earlier opinion polls which had seemed for a time to Kennedy too good to be true. Jack defeated his nearest opponent by two to one, in a ten-man field taking over 40 percent of all ballots cast. As soon as the good news reached the Hotel Bellevue Honey Fitz clambered creakily onto a table, danced a jig, and sang "Sweet Adeline." In that moment of victory Pickles Kane couldn't help reflecting on the "staggering sum" that Kennedy had spent. "It wasn't necessary," he told a friend. "Jack could have gone to congress for ten cents!"

Two years later Jack was renominated and re-elected without opposition, and in 1950 he defeated a hapless Republican opponent five to one. Nevertheless he found Congress itself boring in the six years he spent there, although as one of the capital's more eligible young bachelors he enjoyed the social life of Washington and Georgetown. Sailing, swimming, playing golf and that Kennedy game-of-games touch football, he found far more attractive than sitting through long-drawn-out debates, and he was much addicted to movies and the company of pretty women. But if he took his legislative duties lightly, he never neglected the interests of his predominantly Catholic and piously anti-Communist constituency. He voted for the liberal Fair Deal measures that appealed to the interests of the 11th District voters and the conservative foreign issues that appealed to their prejudices. Later when he needed a more liberal image to match his extending ambitions, he would explain that as a freshman congressman he had "just come out of my father's house at the time, and these were the things I knew." Theodore Sorensen, who was to become one of his closest advisers and his chief speech writer, wrote of those six congressional years:

> The intellectual journals of opinion had doubts about his credentials as a liberal, about his religion and, above all, about his father. . . .
>
> His performance in the House of Representatives had been considered by most observers to be largely undistinguished — except for a record of absenteeism which had been heightened by indifference as well as ill health and by unofficial as well as official travels.*

Every Thursday evening he flew from Washington to Boston, to be met at the airport by Frank Morrissey, now his permanent Massachusetts manager. Together they would set off across Massa-

* *Kennedy*, pp. 11–12.

chusetts with "Muggsy" O'Leary, Jack's chauffeur, for a long weekend of speech making and public appearances. Dozens of times they crisscrossed the state, visiting all the 351 cities and towns, with the aim of making Jack's name and face and personality so familiar that it would be taken for granted. On Monday evening Jack would fly back to Washington.

Congress was at best only a way station. At one point the governorship of Massachusetts seemed the next station, but only briefly, for a far more intriguing prospect was emerging, that of the seat in the United States Senate held by Henry Cabot Lodge. Grandson and namesake of the waspish aristocrat who in 1916 defeated Honey Fitz for the same seat, young Lodge had the common touch that his grandfather lacked. A notable vote-getter, appealing to the emergent middle-class Irish, he had at the age of thirty-six overcome the battle-scarred Curley in a 1936 contest for the United States Senate. After his re-election he had resigned in 1944 for combat duty with the army and had returned after the war to beat the supposedly unbeatable Senator David I. Walsh. His election for a fourth term in 1952 he had come to take for granted. When he first heard that he might be opposed by young Jack, he sent indirect word to father Joe not to waste his money because he, Lodge, would win by at least 300,000 votes.

Kennedy's careful private surveys had led him to think otherwise. Four years before the 1952 senatorial election, he began to organize his political machine, to oil the wheels before setting them in motion. Lodge was the best, he kept insisting to his son, and to beat him was to beat the best. At the very beginning of the campaign he told Jack and Morrissey that it would be the toughest fight imaginable, but there was no question that Lodge would lose. If that came to pass, he maintained that Jack's nomination and election to the presidency would follow. "I will work out the plans to elect you President," he told his son. "It will not be more difficult for you to be elected President than it will to win the Lodge fight. . . . You will need to get about twenty key men in the country to get the nomination, for it is these men who will control the convention."

No Democrat appeared brash enough to oppose Jack for the 1952 Democratic senatorial nomination. The campaign that followed was not one of issues but of personalities, and the personalities were much alike. Senator Lodge and Congressman Kennedy were both millionaires, Harvard graduates, young, personable, moderately liberal, and with distinguished war records. Both had to a degree acquired an easy manner not wholly natural to them. Lodge might be of the entrenched Yankee caste but Kennedy was in D. W. Brogan's words, an Irish "eupatrid."

"We're going to sell Jack like soap flakes," Kennedy announced to his associates. In contrast to his highly visible family, he chose to remain in the shadows of his Ritz-Carlton command post, consulting his hand-picked brains trust, setting up his filing systems, planning the future advertisements and TV coverage. Although he did not seem to be running things, they happened according to his plans. Bobby Kennedy, fresh from the University of Virginia Law School, was the ostensible campaign manager, but the real manager was father Joe. When the pols and the professionals and the volunteers gathered for a conference, whether at the Ritz-Carlton or at the Hyannis Port house, he dominated the room, even telling the others where to sit. Time, money and effort he was ready to expend without limit. His organization expanded to corporate size. Soon there were almost three hundred Kennedy secretaries at work, over twenty thousand volunteers. Kennedy headquarters distributed about a million copies of an eight-page tabloid with comic-strip drawings of Jack rescuing his shipmates of the PT-109. The facing page showed a photograph of Joe, Jr. in uniform, with the heading JOHN FULFILLS DREAM OF BROTHER JOE WHO MET DEATH IN THE SKY OVER THE ENGLISH CHANNEL. Enclosed in the tabloid was the reprint of the old *Reader's Digest* article. In the bitter Taft-Eisenhower fight at the Republican convention in June, Lodge had supported Eisenhower. There were many disgruntled and unreconciled Taft Republicans in Massachusetts, and Kennedy made a bid for their support by organizing the Independents for Kennedy headquarters at the Sheraton Plaza. Though Taft loyally if reluctantly endorsed Lodge, a number of his embittered supporters deserted to Kennedy.

At this time Senator Joseph McCarthy of Wisconsin was at the height of his vituperative power. He was and would remain a good friend of the Kennedy family, and a particular friend of Joe Kennedy's, whom he occasionally visited at Hyannis Port. Jack contributed to his campaign fund. Bobby Kennedy would later work for his Permanent Investigations Subcommittee. Anathema to liberal intellectuals, McCarthy — the hard-voiced tribune of the people — though a Republican, held the belligerent and deeply emotional allegiance of Massachusetts's piously Catholic and vehemently anti-Communist Democrats. If McCarthy should come to the state to speak for Lodge he might sway enough voters to make Jack's election all but impossible. McCarthy's party allegiance was balanced by his dislike for Lodge. The Wisconsin senator, always hard up for funds, was indebted to Kennedy as well for the contribution Joe had made to his primary campaign. So when Joe asked him as a favor to stay out of Massachusetts during the Lodge-Kennedy contest, McCarthy acquiesced. McCarthyism, so-called, was an issue the Kennedys preferred to ignore. When the old New Dealer, Pat Jackson, whose reflex liberalism dated back to the Sacco-Vanzetti case, tried to get Jack's commitment to the banner cause of anti-McCarthyism, he came up against the stone wall that was father Joe. Jackson had managed to persuade the initially dubious Americans for Democratic Action and the labor unions to support Kennedy as a promising if not proven liberal, and in turn he demanded that Jack take a stand against McCarthyism. He had even prepared a newspaper manifesto for Jack to endorse with the heading COMMUNISM AND McCARTHY: BOTH WRONG. Jack tentatively agreed to sign it if his fellow Boston congressman, House Majority Leader John McCormack, would also sign. Such an endorsement by Jack Kennedy might well have alienated enough Massachusetts voters to have destroyed his election chances. Jackson, viewing the matter through his own ultra-liberal spectacles, arrived happily at Jack's Bowdoin Street apartment the following morning to tell him that McCormack had agreed to sign. "The place was a hubbub of activity," he later recalled. A grim-faced father Joe sat at a card table in the center of the room with three of his son's speech-writers. Jack had his coat on and was preparing to leave. He looked embarrassed. Just before he dashed out, he asked Jackson to read the advertisement to his father. "I hadn't gone two sentences," Jackson related afterward "when Joe jumped to his feet with such force that he tilted the table against the others." For a moment Jackson thought that the red-faced Kennedy was going to attack him. Instead, and to the embarassment of the others, he cursed him out in the lingo of his youth. "You and your sheeny friends are trying to ruin my son's career," he shouted, telling Jackson hoarsely that he liked Joe McCarthy, and that the liberals and the labor people and the Jews were out to hurt his son. "I can't estimate how long he poured it on me," Jackson recalled. "It was just a stream of stuff — always referring to 'you and your sheeny friends!' "

That was the end of the McCarthy advertisement. Next day an aggrieved Jackson met a placatory Jack. "How do you explain your father?" he asked the younger man. "I guess there isn't a motive in it which I think you'd respect," Jack said, "except love of family." Then he paused for a moment. "And more often than not, I think that's just pride."

As crucial for Jack Kennedy's election as McCarthy's failure to support Lodge was the Boston *Post's* turnabout Kennedy endorsement. In its heyday the *Post* had been the Democratic family paper of New England, the unofficial spokesman for the Catholic Archdiocese. Outmoded, sagging in circulation after World War II and steadily losing money, the paper had been bought in 1951 by a quick-shot speculator, John Fox. Like the senior Kennedy, Fox was an old Boston Latin boy, though of two decades later, Irish-American, a Harvard graduate who had become a sudden millionaire through New York real estate and oil and gas speculations, a predator who operated through loans and mortgages, making one dollar do the work of three or four. Unlike Kennedy, he was a Republican. Early in 1952 Fox with his *Post* supported Eisenhower and favored Lodge. But after Eisenhower's defeat of Taft in the convention with Lodge's able assistance, disgruntled Taft supporters urged the publisher-financier to repudiate the Massachusetts senator. Meanwhile the *Post* was on the verge of bankruptcy.

Whatever his reasons, however involved his later explanations, Fox after backing Lodge decided to switch to Kennedy and wrote a front page editorial announcing his reversal. The night before the editorial appeared he arranged to meet Joe Kennedy in a night club he owned. Unaware of Fox's decision, Kennedy approached him warily, but when he learned that the *Post* was going to endorse his son his eyes filled with tears and he told Fox that if there was anything in the world he needed, all he had to do was ask for it. Fox suggested that a half million dollar loan would help him greatly with the *Post*. Kennedy agreed to let him have it. When the matter came to light long afterward, Kennedy maintained that the loan was "purely a commercial transaction, for sixty days only" and had no connection with Jack's endorsement. Whether it did or not, the fact remains that the *Post* even in its decline carried weight, particularly among the more pious Catholic women, possibly weight enough to swing the election either way.

Meanwhile Rose and her daughters intensified the social campaign of six years earlier, enlarging and amplifying it. They held thirty-three formal receptions, attended by 75,000 entranced women. "It was all they could do to keep those old gals who came to the affairs from curtsying," a veteran reporter observed. "They had every tendency to drop to one knee." Sometimes Jack seemed to have more women than men working for him. There was even a television program put on by Rose and her girls called "Coffee with the Kennedys." It is estimated that members of the Kennedy family shook some two million hands in Massachusetts, rang a hundred thousand doorbells. To the sordid slough of political Massachusetts, this sparkling and self-confident family brought glamor, wealth by association, ethnic pride. "What is there about Jack Kennedy," an out-of-state Republican asked, "that makes every Catholic girl in Boston between eighteen and twenty-eight think it's a holy crusade to get him elected?" John Mallan tried to answer that question in the *New Republic*:

> While the liberal may have reservations about Kennedy [he wrote] the average Democrat seems to have none; when the altogether handsome and charming Kennedy — still a bachelor — makes an appearance anywhere in Massachusetts, the effect is overwhelming. Kennedy is, for one thing, an Irishman of family — and breeding — rare in a state where almost all Democratic leaders are self-made, one-generation and often crude in manner and appearance. He is wealthy enough to be honest without question, in a state where many vote Democratic but feel a little guilty about it. . . . His family has long been active in Catholic charities, and has been officially decorated by the Pope; this again, plus Kennedy's appearance over the years at Communion breakfasts across the state, brings him a kind of personal support which few of the more "secular" Irish politicians could hope to equal.

Jack, with his family, was ubiquitous, on the well-tried advertising principle that repetition brings acceptance, whether of soap, stomach powders or politicians. "Holy hell," one frustrated

Republican remarked. "Every place you look there's a Kennedy." Jack later admitted that he had been campaigning for four and a half years. His official campaign expenses came to $350,000. What the real cost was only father Joe knew. Lodge, engrossed in his campaign for Eisenhower and taking his re-election for granted, did not realize what was happening in his own home state until two months before the election. By the time the alarm signals reached him and he started campaigning, it was too late, as Joe Kennedy from his Ritz-Carlton command post could have told him. Eisenhower swept normally Democratic Massachusetts, with a half-million vote majority, carrying in his wake all the Republican state candidates — except Henry Cabot Lodge. Jack Kennedy, the neophyte, had breasted the Republican tide, winning his election by 70,000 votes. "It was those damned tea parties," Lodge said sourly when he heard the result. A friend tried to cheer him by remarking that he had really lost "by 9,500,000 cups of tea!" But it was Rose Kennedy who had the last word. "At last," she said, "the Fitzgeralds have evened the score with the Lodges."

Massachusetts' waddling, boozy Governor Dever was scarcely an intuitive man, but he did have a flash of intuition when he labelled Jack Kennedy the first Irish Brahmin. Joe Kennedy's relentless instinctive thrust for power that had now culminated in his son's election to the United States Senate was a sociological phenomenon the significance of which he only vaguely sensed. What the Kennedys had come to represent in and to Massachusetts was that periodic phenomenon of history, the emergence of a new class.

When young Jack Kennedy appeared without forewarning on the Boston political scene in 1946, the newly arrived middle-class Irish hailed him with joy and relief. After half a century of oafish politicians, this attractive, well-spoken, graceful, witty, Celtic, Harvard-bred and very rich young man was what every suburban Catholic matron in Milton and West Roxbury would have liked her son to be. In fact, many came to see Jack as their son.

Jack's election may have been the wish-fulfillment of Democratic mothers in Massachusetts. But it was very much resented by the old-line pols who had come up the ladder rung by rung, often by knocking the feet from under the man just above them. Not the slow way for Jack, through the wards, into the legislature, to the state senate, with all the little wheels and deals along the way.

This was, in the now banal term, "instant politics." Privately the pols expressed their outrage at being outflanked by a young whippersnapper who pronounced his *A*'s broad, and there was envenomed backroom talk of old scandals; Honey Fitz's caperings, and father Joe's romantic diversions. Through the corridors of the State House and the dingier corridors of Boston's City Hall there were derisive and derogatory references to "those Kennedys," gossip about Joe's private life, scatological recollections of Honey Fitz. But as the Kennedy star (or stars) continued to rise, the talk faded away, the corridors grew ominously quiet. Back-room talk died too. The last outburst was in 1962 when Eddie McCormack, nephew of the speaker, had the temerity to oppose the untried Ted Kennedy in the Democratic state convention for Jack's vacant senate seat. "Don't let them twist your arm!" was his slogan, but the twist was on. The doomed Eddie was certainly the more experienced and possibly the better man. But even beyond the twist there was the legend. As one political worker then explained it: "When they [the Boston Irish)] hear Eddie McCormack speak, they think of South Boston and their parents' lives. When they see Ted Kennedy they think of Palm Beach, Beacon Hill, the Virginia fox-hunting country and their children's future." To a degree all of us live by legends. And it is within this Kennedy legend that the descendants of the Famine immigrants achieved respectability, assurance, acceptance of themselves, their ancestors and their religion.

Ralph Lowell, a constant if wary observer of his Harvard classmate's meteoric rise, remarked after Jack Kennedy's election to the Senate: "Joe knew he was controversial, so he stayed out of the way. He's sort of like a caterpillar; he wouldn't quite become a butterfly, but his boys were going to fly no matter what." Astute opportunist that he was, Joe realized that in the future he could best help his son by becoming inconspicuous, by minimizing his own role in Jack's career. He would continue to give advice, his Fortunatus purse would remain open, but he would keep his distance. Politically he and his son were bound to diverge, for Jack was feeling his way toward an acceptable liberalism while Joe's views had scarcely altered from the time when he was ambassador to England. Early after World War II he had sensed the Soviet threat but his isolationist response was to call for a retreat to a Fortress America, a withdrawal from Asia and from Europe, letting the Communist counterforce take over where it would and could. He considered the United Nations a "hopeless instrumentality" for preserving peace and doubted that the Marshall Plan would save Europe from Moscow's domination. Obviously such views could never elect anyone president of the United States, and Senator Kennedy's office took pains to publicize the divergent views of Kennedy and his father. By 1960 Jack the candidate was saying flatly that his disagreement with his father was "total" and he added: "We never discuss it. There is no use because we can't agree." As Whalen explained:

> Answering the needs of his ambition, Jack Kennedy adopted the attitudes and acquired the techniques of established liberalism.
>
> There was no fundamental clash between his compassionate liberalism and his father's temperamental conservatism. Each was a political pragmatist, alert to the moment's opportunity, heedless of the philosophical inconsistency between one action and the next.*

Kennedy's legislative assistant, speech-writer and alter ego, Theodore Sorensen, summed up Kennedy's eight senatorial years in a paragraph:

> John Kennedy was not one of the Senate's great leaders. Few laws of national importance bear his name. And after he graduated in November, 1958, from the traditionally inactive freshman class, his opportunities for major contributions to the Senate — except for his battle for fair labor reforms and against rackets — were increasingly eroded by the demands of his Presidential campaign.†

Harsher critics would maintain that he was an absentee senator with no laws of national importance to his merit. The most noteworthy quality of the new Massachusetts senator was his youthful and persuasive charm. Zealous for New England's regional interests, he never made a name for himself in the Senate on any wider issues. But he was the youngest senator, among the handsomest and most sportive, the most appealing to women. When, with his smile and tousled forelock, he said "Ladies, I need you!" he was irresistible. A *Saturday Evening Post* article called him "The Senate's Gay Young Bachelor." His brother Bobby remarked more earthily that it was not true that Jack "made out"

* *The Founding Father*, p. 425.
† *Kennedy*, p. 43.

with all the girls in the District of Columbia. "There wasn't time enough!"

The reputation of a man-about town, tolerable for a young bachelor senator, could be damaging for a serious presidential candidate, as father Joe was well aware. Even in Boston, Jack's casual affairs had been far too conspicuous. In September, 1953, he finally "settled down" by marrying Jacqueline Bouvier. Undoubtedly his father had been urging him to take such a step for some time. One cannot probe the secrets of the human heart or measure the affections, but on the surface at least the match was, as Dr. Joseph Brusch of Cambridge's Brusch Clinic* described it, "a eugenic marriage." A blueprint for Jack's prospective bride would have specified that she must be Catholic but not of Irish descent, and of a more assured social position than the Kennedys. Jacqueline Bouvier was all of these things, of a Long Island Catholic family with European overtones, originally French, and firmly entrenched in the *Social Register*, a former pupil of Miss Porter's School, a Vassar student who had studied at the Sorbonne and at George Washington University, and one of the most glittering debutantes of the year. She moved gracefully in the world of hunt meets, country estates and assured inherited wealth, a world Joe Kennedy knew from the outside looking in. Her interest in politics was negligible.

Marriage, even if, as some asserted, it was not more than a marriage of convenience, gave Jack a more mature and settled image, but the Kennedy long-range plans were shadowed by his precarious health. His old back injury that at times had forced him to take to crutches in his political campaigns now threatened to incapacitate him completely. Only surgery could help him. But doctors warned that with Addison's disease the chances of his surviving a spinal operation would be slim. Pounding his crutches Jack told them he would rather die than spend the rest of his life hobbling about as a semi-invalid. In October, 1954, he underwent an operation for double fusion of the spinal disks at Manhattan's Hospital for Special Surgery. As the doctors had predicted, it was even odds whether he would live. Twice he received the last

*The Brusch Clinic, modelled after that of the Laheys, has functioned as a medical center for Massachusetts Democratic politicians. As senator, Jack Kennedy often dropped in there for minor remedies. Speaker of the House McCormack, anxious to conceal a heart condition, came there evenings by the back entrance and was known as "Mr. Hush-Hush."

rites of his church. Even when, after several weeks, it became clear that he would recover, he was faced with a second operation and then with five bedridden months of painful convalescence. It was during this time, in Florida, that he assembled the materials for his book, *Profiles in Courage*. "All it was ever meant to be," he said later with disarming accuracy, "was a treatment of an interesting idea, the pressures that are put on a politician." Most of the research work was done by others. Professor Jules Davids of George Washington University and Arthur Schlesinger, Jr., rewrote and correlated much of the historical material. Jack had boxes of reference books shipped in from the Library of Congress for what became a joint enterprise. Sorenson wrote drafts of several chapters and kept up a constant flow of research suggestions. Nevertheless the final dictated version was Jack's own.* Joe Kennedy devoted all the efforts of his massive organization to give this second "high class" book its maximum publicity. *Profiles in Courage* became a best-seller, a Book of the Month Selection that the following year won the Pulitzer prize. As a "high class" book it brought Jack into the public eye as few senatorial efforts could have done. There were a few sour notes sounded, not so much because of the book as because of its author. Some liberals tartly observed that Senator Kennedy had more profile than courage. "McCarthyism" had become the acid test for them, and by liberal standards Kennedy had failed that test. When, in December, 1954, the McCarthy issue came to a head as the Senate voted on the motion to censure the Wisconsin senator for conduct unbecoming a United States senator, Jack Kennedy was in the hospital. From there he could have gone on record either for or against the motion, by pairing his vote with that of another colleague. This, he alone of the absent senators failed to do. Gardner Jackson wrote reprovingly that "though Kennedy was suffering a serious illness involving operative procedures, he was not in so grave a condition that he could not have let his position be known on so grave a political-social question as censure of fellow-Senator McCarthy."

This Kennedy preferred not to do. It was an issue he would continue to hedge on, refusing even to state how he might have

* Drew Pearson in a television broadcast in 1957 charged that *Profiles in Courage* was ghost-written. Later he was forced to retract. Although the book as regards the material was a collective effort, Kennedy had given it its final shape.

voted if he had been in the Senate at the time of the censure motion. Liberals like Mrs. Roosevelt could not forgive him. But, as he admitted privately, he was in a dilemma. McCarthy was his father's friend, his sister Eunice's friend, and his brother Bobby had worked for McCarthy's subcommittee. What else could he do, he asked, but keep quiet?

However painful and slow his recovery, Jack knew by the time *Profiles in Courage* was in the press that he would be able to lead a normal life, to walk and run and swim and play touch football again with his family. His back would always trouble him, but he could live with it. With this knowledge came a revived buoyancy of spirits, a renewed interest in the goal that had obsessed his father for so long — somewhat precipitately it turned out.

The presidential year 1956 had a flat certainty about it. President Eisenhower, however limited he might appear to those who knew him, had become a fixed father-figurehead to the great majority of his countrymen. His reelection was inevitable. Adlai Stevenson would again be the Democratic candidate, and with equal inevitability he would again lose. Nevertheless, to share the ticket with the urbane Stevenson as vice-presidential candidate would be a glittering prize for a freshman senator, or so it seemed to Jack Kennedy and the somewhat academic young men who now surrounded him. In the spring of 1956 Jack's brother-in-law, Sargent Shriver, who was helping manage the Merchandise Mart, wrote to the elder Kennedy about the enticing vice-presidential prospects. Kennedy was not enticed. He warned his son against what he considered an act of political suicide. "I knew Adlai Stevenson was going to take a licking," he explained after Eisenhower's reelection, "and I was afraid Jack might be blamed because he was a Catholic. That would have made it much more difficult for another Catholic in years to come." Nineteen fifty-six was not the year, and the vice-presidency was not the office. Four years later, there would be an interregnum after the senescent Eisenhower had stepped down. That would be the time to move. Joe's speculative instinct still knew when to buy, when to sell, when to stay out of the market.

Father Joe had left for his villa at Cap d' Antibes by the time the Democratic National Convention opened in Chicago. Heedless of his father's warning, led on — in Sorensen's opinion — more by a sense of competition than conviction, Jack made his bid for the vice-presidential nomination so forcefully, with such eclat, that he almost succeeded in defeating Senator Estes Kefauver for the substanceless position. Though in the immediate disillusioning moment he did not realize it, he was far luckier than Kefauver. None of the onus of the coming defeat would cling to him. What is more, the televised convention proceedings had made the country increasingly conscious of his engaging youthful presence. Millions of viewers saw and heard him place Stevenson's name in nomination. He was also the narrator of the "Keynote" motion picture, "the Pursuit of Happiness." Time and again during the long-winded convention proceedings, as if he were a magnet, the roving television cameras focussed in on him.

After his defeat Jack, like a chastened small boy, telephoned the news to the Riviera villa. "We did our best," he excused himself contritely. "I had fun, I didn't make a fool of myself." A few weeks later he crossed the ocean to consult with his father. "I told him that God was still with him," Joe recalled, "and that he would be President if he wanted to and worked hard."

Jack returned to campaign for Stevenson, knowing well that Stevenson was doomed. He traveled 30,000 miles, visiting twenty-six states and speaking over 150 times. He took care to be highly visible. When someone suggested that he would certainly be the favorite vice-presidential candidate in 1960, he replied coldly: "I'm not running for vice-president any more. I'm now running for president."

Following Stevenson's overwhelming and humiliating defeat in November, Jack realized with renewed clarity how lucky he had been not to have prevailed over Kefauver in June. As he told a Hearst reporter:

> Joe was the star of our family. He did everything better than the rest of us. If he had lived, he would have gone on in politics and he would have been elected to the House and Senate as I was. And, like me, he would have gone for the vice-presidential nomination at the 1956 convention, but, unlike me, he wouldn't have been beaten. Joe would have won the nomination. And then he and Stevenson would have been beaten by Eisenhower and today Joe's political career would be in shambles and he would be trying to pick up the pieces.

A month after the election, Jack Kennedy and Sorensen began a methodical preparation for the national convention still almost four years away. That year saw the beginning of a Kennedy build-up the like of which in long-range planning had not been seen since Mark Hanna had pushed McKinley forward. Though a junior senator and relatively unimportant, Kennedy outside the Senate was becoming increasingly publicized, the most conspicuous post-World War II figure to emerge from the Democratic ranks, handsome, urbane, with a beautiful wife and colorful family, a political celebrity akin to a glamorous film star. Just in his appearance he was newsworthy. Father Joe did his best to see to it that every last inch of such publicity was fully exploited. In most cases the publicity came of itself; the *Life* report of Jack's wedding; feature stories about Jacqueline in *McCall's* and *Redbook,* and a rash of similar articles. "Jack is the greatest attraction in the country today," Joe said after his son's reelection to the Senate in 1958. "I'll tell you how to sell more copies of a book. Put his picture on the cover. Why is it that when his picture is on the cover of *Life* or *Redbook* that they sell a record number of copies? You advertise the fact that he will be at a dinner and you will break all records for attendance. He can draw more people to a fund-raising dinner than Cary Grant or Jimmy Stewart. Why is that? He has more universal appeal. That is why the Democratic party is going to nominate him. The party leaders around the country realize that to win they have to nominate him."

Jack's re-election to the Senate was so assured that for a time Massachusetts Republicans considered letting him run unopposed, then finally produced an obscure sacrificial candidate, Vincent Celeste, who received little financial support and little else. By this time the Kennedy mythos was so fixed in Massachusetts that to be against Jack was like being against Mother's Day. There was no question about defeating Celeste, the only question was by how much. For Joe the election seemed the last stepping-stone to the White House. "If we can get a plurality of half a million," he told a Harvard classmate, "they can't stop us for the presidency."

In the era of mass media Joe understood, as Hanna had understood in a simpler era, how to put his choice across. He went out of his way to entertain publishers and editors, or rather entertaining them was part of his way. It was a matter of emphasizing personality through the media of a streamlined electronics age, of creating images rather than issues. Joe's role had now become by necessity an almost invisible one. No longer would he occupy the command post at the Ritz-Carlton and deliver his staccato decisions. He would retain essential contacts with the old-line professionals, but his chief function from now on was to furnish the means for his son's ever-expanding organization. At the time of the Depression he had said he would part with half of his possessions to preserve the other half. Now, to elect his son president, he would part with half the much larger fortune he had since acquired. Or even more!

Jack Kennedy would never revolt against his father; rather, he would absorb and obscure him. For this self-confident young man, as he approached his forties, was evolving into an astute, cold, highly integrated politician, as if he had inherited in his genes the instincts of Honey Fitz and the more prudently calculating Pat Kennedy. His presidential rival, Senator Hubert Humphrey, and many others would sense the basic coldness beneath the genial, gracious exterior, sunny smile and easy manner. Around him as organizers and tacticians he gathered a group of relentlessly determined younger men. Like himself they were the post-World War II breed of politicians, urbane, ivy-educated, and in enough cases third-generation Irish to provide the journalistic cliché-label of "Irish Mafia." Many of the figures came and went during Jack's transition from freshman congressman to presidential candidate, but the organization persisted, grew, over and above father Joe's directives. By the spring of 1958 Jack was receiving more than a hundred speaking invitations a week and was becoming generally recognized as the frontrunner among the undeclared Democratic presidential candidates for 1960. Joe scoffed at suggestions that Jack was starting too early, might "peak" too soon. "The only way we can win this is to wrap it up very, very early," he said. "In our position, that's the risk we're most willing to take, and it's the least of our worries. When you start from scratch, you've got to run like hell all the way."

Although he still referred to a political "us," to "our position," he kept out of sight. In the months before the 1958 senatorial election he hid himself away in a rented Beacon Street apartment. Even without him, the Kennedy vote-collecting machine functioned with clockwork precision. The hoped-for half million plurality turned out to be 874,608, with Jack winning 73.6 percent of the votes cast, the highest percentage total of any senator in the country and the most overwhelming victory in Massachusetts since the state's direct election of senators.

Yet even this victory did not bring the older party leaders round nor impress the Americans-for-Democratic-Action liberals. "I like Jack. He is a nice person," ex-President Truman remarked. "But I don't like his daddy and never did." Not long after the election, Mrs. Roosevelt saw fit to warn that Joe was "spending oodles of money all over the country" to advance his son and "probably has paid representatives in every state by now." Remembering the Kennedy ambivalence about McCarthy, she observed that Jack was "someone who understands what courage is and admires it, but has not quite the independence to have it."

To the professional politicians in the waning months of 1958, the convention prospect of 1960 seemed that of a deadlock. Other senators with presidential aspirations, Humphrey, Stuart Symington of Missouri and Lyndon Johnson of Texas, could still muster enough strength to keep Senator Kennedy with his photogenic face and all his familial resources from gaining a majority of the delegates, to say nothing of the required two-thirds. As Joe Kennedy kept repeating, "we" would have to start early and run late. To those who asked where he himself fitted in his son's organization, he replied that he didn't fit at all. "I just call people to explain. You call people that you know and ask them to help in any way they can. . . . That's all." Among those he asked, even before the senatorial election, was the wizened, hard-faced boss of the Bronx, Charles Buckley, whose help would be vital in capturing New York's big bloc of convention delegates. Nor did he neglect Chicago's Richard Daley, where his Merchandise Mart was located. Quietly, with unobtrusive insistence, Joe kept his contacts with other New York leaders in this crucial state, and he took pains to see that the key bosses in Pennsylvania, Illinois and New Jersey were for Jack. He kept in touch with the old, but was out of touch with the new. In earlier campaigns he had told his son what to do. Now he asked him. Sometimes his advice was taken. Sometimes it was not. The Kennedy machine, streamlined, computerized, electronic, financially unlimited, was the envy and admiration of all the other candidates. When a primary seemed crucial, the full weight of the Kennedy money and talent was thrown into the balance. In impoverished, fundamentalist West

Virginia, a bellwether state, sheriffs — who wielded the political muscle in the counties — were bought up wholesale at a thousand dollars a head. Truman in his sharp-tongued retirement still kept his sense of outrage at such Merchandise Mart tactics. "Joe thought of everything. Joe paid for everything," he told Merle Miller in 1962. "Old Joe Kennedy is as big a crook as we've got anywhere in this country." Humphrey, campaigning on a shoe-string against that massed wealth, complained: "I don't have any daddy who can pay the bills for me. I can't run around with a little black bag and a checkbook." After Kennedy's overwhelming West Virginia triumph, his candidacy seemed to be gaining an irresistible momentum. So indeed it appeared to Joe, who told a friend confidentially: "For the Kennedys it's either the shit-house or the White House — no in-between."

By the time the Democratic convention met in the Los Angeles Sports Arena in the first week of July, Kennedy had lined up more than 600 of the necessary 761 delegates. When Joe arrived by plane from the East, reporters swarmed round him. "There's only one candidate," he snapped at them, "and I'm his old man." He and his wife did not stay in the city but eleven miles away at the villa of Marion Davies. There he remained out of sight, though connected by a battery of telephones to Jack's head-quarters. Mrs. Roosevelt was at the convention, vainly backing Adlai Stevenson. Lyndon Johnson, still hoping to emerge as a compromise candidate, attacked Kennedy's mediocre legislative record, his wealth and his family, and referring to Father Joe he remarked sarcastically to the Washington state delegation: "I wasn't any Chamberlain umbrella man. I never thought Hitler was right." Jack Kennedy himself he considered "a little scrawny fellow with rickets."

Whatever the hopes and doubts of the others, the Kennedy revolution had already seized control of the Democratic party. It was a revolution periodic in any party; the emergence of the young men, elbowing the old guard aside. As the Kennedy guard had foreseen and the old guard had not, Jack was nominated on the first ballot. When the exhausted but triumphant Bobby telephoned the results to his father, Joe told him elatedly that it was the best organization job he had ever seen in politics. Johnson remained unforgiven, yet it was Joe, the old strategist, who first proposed that the Texan be given the vice-presidential nomination as a way of insuring the election support of the South. It was the smartest move the Kennedys made.

Except for differences about the platform, the Republican convention was a cut and dried affair. Vice-President Nixon, with Eisenhower's offhand blessing and the regulars behind him, had an unbreakable grip on the nominating process months before the convention opened. The delegates were not there to choose but to ratify. Obviously the ensuing election was going to be close. Nixon had the prestige of the vice-presidency behind him and the avuncular presence of Eisenhower; Kennedy had style, charm, wit and the ease of manner lacking in Nixon for all his striving. Kennedy drew out the enthusiasm of crowds as Nixon could not. Yet both candidates seemed curiously artifact, neither one a genuine and spontaneous popular choice but superimposed by the machinery of politics. And to many the Kennedy machine was too streamlined, too efficient. Outside Massachusetts, beyond the rim of those shifting crowds drawn to gape at any presidential candidate, most Americans remained unenthusiastic, whatever their final choice. Occasional bumper stickers appeared reading: *Neither One.* In the light of Kennedy's tragic death and subsequent apotheosis, one tends to forget that there was very little public demand for either candidate. The editor of the *Progressive* saw Kennedy and Nixon as "men who are cool and calculating. Men of measured movement . . . and of measured tears."

Murray Kempton thought that neither candidate seemed to be a man at whose funeral strangers would cry. "No *charisma* in this cool and calculating man. . . ." Milton Mayer wrote of candidate Kennedy a decade after his death. "No identification with what we were and are. No adoration, no madly-for-Adlai following. No magic and no mystique beyond the mystique of competent power. Here was the Boss with his hand on the tiller, and the methodologist with his eye on the computer he used to be elected." Truman thought that the whole Kennedy family was merely interested in *getting* power. 'They don't care a hoot in hell about using it. They're afraid to use it for fear it might not be *popular*."

There was a wry saying in circulation during the election campaign that Jack was running, Bobby was Jack's manager, and Ted had been assigned the job of keeping the old man out of sight. For the young men around Jack who with remorseless efficiency were remodeling the Democratic party in their image, Joe remained an embarrassment, an encumbrance, a counter-image. So, although his wife and daughters played their customary social role on a national stage, he stayed out of the way, a subterranean influence though at moments more essential than was generally realized. "Joseph P. Kennedy had labored hard in his privacy and through his purposeful channels," Theodore White wrote in his study of the 1960 election. "It was he who had master-minded the coup of delegates in New York City; he who had organized the north New Jersey delegates out from under Governor Robert Meyner . . . ; he who had been most influential in bringing Dick Daley of Chicago into camp and thus the votes of Illinois." No detail was too small for him. Just before the election he sent out henchmen with a quarter of a million dollars to wager in barrooms, clubs and public places so that the press would note the odds tilting in favor of Kennedy.

It has been generally agreed that Nixon lost the election through his four television debates with his opponent. In fact it was the initial debate that doomed him. He arrived at the studio fatigued, insufficiently prepared and still suffering from the aftereffects of blood-poisoning that had kept him a week in the hospital. A light coating of "Lazy shave" pancake make-up did little to conceal the heavy beard-shadow beneath his too transparent skin. The television lights, too, were unkind, emphasizing his stubble, the darkness of his eye wells, the sharpness of his nose, giving his face a slightly sinister expression. He appeared nervous. Kennedy by contrast was casually self-possessed, skillfully made up and thoroughly rehearsed. What the two men said in their brief minutes of debate was irrelevant. Kennedy looked better, spoke better. As White remarked, it was not a campaign of issues but of personalities, and on this television screen encounter Jack Kennedy had projected himself as the winner.

The election was destined to be close, the closest in American history. Of the almost 69 million votes cast, Kennedy's popular majority was only 112,881, a tenth of one percent. His electoral college total was 303 votes to 219 for Nixon. If only 5,000 voters in Illinois and 28,000 in Texas had changed their minds, Nixon would have carried these states for an electoral majority of two. Privately he always maintained that he had been cheated out of the election. Politicians are convinced that an honest count would have given him Illinois, where Daley's Cook County bailiwick had long been suspected of manipulating the returns with only occasional reference to the ballot boxes. There were similar gross irregularities in the Texas returns, and again an honest count might have given Nixon the state. But an honest count in both cases would have been difficult if not impossible to come by, and neither Nixon nor Kennedy wanted a repetition of the disputed Hayes-Tilden election of 1876 that remained undecided until forty-eight hours before Hayes's inauguration.

Delighted though father Joe was at the Kennedy triumph, he was disappointed at the thin margin of victory. "I was wrong on two things," he said. "First, I thought he [Jack] would gather a bigger Catholic vote than he did. Second, I did not think that so many would vote against him because of his religion." The father was regarded, in Arthur Schlesinger's words, as "a hot potato." So resolutely had he been kept out of sight that he had not been allowed to appear with the rest of his family when Jack made his acceptance speech in Los Angeles. Now that the campaign was over he suddenly let himself be photographed everywhere with Jack. A reporter asked him if this was just a coincidence. "There are no accidents in politics," Joe snapped back. "I can appear with him any time I want to now." To a friend who asked him how it felt to be father of a president, he replied: "Hell, I don't know how it feels. Of course I'm proud, but I don't feel any different. I don't know how I feel."

He knew better how he felt on the chill January morning of Inauguration Day when, with a pride that welled up into tears, he watched his son being sworn in as the 35th president of the United States before the thronged notables in the Capitol Plaza. As a boy he had looked out across the gap of water to Beacon Hill and the gilt-domed State House, symbols of a world he was determined to conquer. Now the much vaster dome behind him was the focal point of a whole nation, the symbol of his triumphant house, the sudden coruscant house of Kennedy. Before him, coatless in the clear, ice-edged air, his son stood with hand upraised, handsome, youthful-seeming, flanked by his svelte wife and the grey, assembled elders of the nation. John Fitzgerald Kennedy, the youngest man ever to be elected president, was Joe's second self, the continuation of the boy who died. It was a long way from East Boston.

A palmist had once told the elder Kennedy that his hand was a hand of destiny, and this he had always believed, heart and mind. Here was the truth of it, in this moment before the Capitol. He was untroubled by the dark and inexorable side of destiny, the relentless Greek triad of fulfillment — pride — disaster. Rose had more of the sense of the ineluctable as on election day she sat, rosary in hand, under the dryer at the world-famous hairdresser's, Alexandre, praying for her son's victory.

That bright day of days seemed for Joseph Kennedy not so much a peak as a plateau. "Well, this is the pay-off!" he announced to Jacqueline. His son Jack was president, his son Bobby would become the next attorney general, and Jack had given Bobby a silver cigarette box inscribed: "When I'm Through, How About You?" On Kennedy orders, Massachusetts's Governor Furcolo had appointed one of Jack's college roommates to occupy Jack's vacant senate seat until the 1962 election. By that time Ted Kennedy would be thirty, the statutory minimum age for senators, and Joe had begun to groom him for the post. Bobby and Jack objected that there might be too many Kennedys, too much Kennedy visibility in Washington. Joe overruled them. "You have what you want now," he told his elder sons, "and everyone else helped you work to get it. Now it's Ted's turn. Whatever he wants, I'm going to see he gets it. . . . I spent a lot of money for that senate seat. It belongs in the family!" A story circulated in Massachusetts about this time that Jack would be reelected in 1964. Bobby would take his place in the White House in 1968. After two terms in office Bobby would be succeeded by Ted in 1976. After two terms of Ted, it would be 1984!

Ted was to be overwhelmingly elected to the Senate, as Joe had planned. But eleven months before that, destiny, fate, chance, whatever it may be called, at last overtook the father in his 74th year. He had started off on a warm December day in 1961 for a round of golf at the Palm Beach Country Club. At the 16th hole, he complained that he felt weak, sat down and then left the course to have his niece drive him home. After climbing the stairs to his bedroom he collapsed. For a time he seemed to be dying, and the president hurried to his bedside. His right side was paralyzed. He could not speak. Though after some months he had recovered sufficiently to shuffle about, he never really regained his speech, never progressed beyond a yammering babble. To communicate he could do no more than raise his eyebrows or shake his left forefinger. He could recognize people. He could understand what they said, but no one knew how well. He could read headlines, but no one knew if he could put words together. He could watch television by the hour, but no one knew how much he could comprehend. Sometimes he would have a fit of giggling, sometimes of crying. He lived, not under but within a cloud that outlined him yet was impenetrable. Within this cloud he would linger for eight dragging years until 1969.

When on that belatedly sunny Friday afternoon of November 22, 1963, a maid in the house at Hyannis Port heard the news on the radio and came screaming up the stairs to stammer out to Rose that President Kennedy had been shot down in Dallas, Joseph Kennedy was taking his nap. He was not told. When he woke up he was wheeled downstairs to the basement theater to see a moving picture. After a short time watching the film he grew restive and gestured that he wanted to leave. On the first floor he beckoned to have the television set turned on. It and all the other sets in the house had been disconnected. When he grasped that it did not work he beat his left hand on the chair in anger.

By evening he was already in bed before his daughter Eunice at last came to tell him. As he listened to her strained deliberate voice his eyes darted back and forth. Otherwise his withered sunken face remained immobile. Next morning he had his orange juice. A paper was brought to his bedside and he looked glassily at the front page edged in black with his son's picture. Then he had breakfast. Once a tear ran down his cheek, once he seemed to cry out Jack's name. Later in the day, sitting in his wheelchair and still in his dressing gown, he pointed and jabbed with his finger to indicate that he wanted to go on his usual afternoon ride.

This time his son Ted drove, while he sat in the back seat wrapped in a blanket next to his nurse, a beret perched on his head. They drove along the shore road beyond Hyannis Port with its white houses and long lawns and fake windmills to the grubbier outskirts of Hyannis, then back down the wide main shopping street, garish and crowded in summer, but by November shabbily forlorn. At the brick post office and all along the street the flags were at half-staff. Kennedy may or may not have noticed as he passed, may or may not have wondered why.

# Bibliography

CHAPTER ONE

There has been no modern life of Mark Hanna, and in the light of his fading image it seems unlikely that there will be one. Herbert Croly's biography of two generations ago is still the standard source of information about Hanna and his political development. Thomas Beer's engaging study written seventeen years later is too impressionistic to stand up. John Flynn's article in *Scribner's* is the most adequate postscript to Croly. There are a number of useful Hanna references in the Harding Collection of the Ohio Historical Society.


Alderfer, H. K. "The Personality and Politics of Warren G. Harding." Ph.D. dissertation, Syracuse University: 1928.

Beer, Thomas. *Hanna*. N.Y.: 1929.

Crissey, Forrest. *Theodore Burton—American Statesman*. N.Y.: 1956.

Croly, Herbert. *Marcus Alonzo Hanna*. N.Y.: 1912.

Flynn, John T. "Mark Hanna: Big Business in Politics." *Scribner's*, August, 1933.

Foraker, Joseph B. *Notes of a Busy Life*. Cincinnati: 1916.

Harbaugh, William. *Power and Responsibility*. N.Y.: 1961.

Howe, F. C., *Confessions of a Reformer*. N.Y.: 1925.

Ickes, Harold L. *The Autobiography of a Curmudgeon*. N.Y.: 1943.

Jordan, Philip D. *Ohio Comes of Age*. Columbus: 1943.

Josephson, Matthew. *The Politicos 1865–1896*. N.Y.: 1938.

———. *The President Makers*. N.Y.: 1940.

Leech, Margaret. *In the Days of McKinley*. N.Y.: 1959.

Morgan, Wayne. *William McKinley and his America*. Syracuse: 1963.

Rienow, Robert and Leona T. *Of Snuff, Sin and the Senate*. Chicago: 1965.

White, William Allen. *Masks in a Pageant*. N.Y.: 1928.

Williams, Wayne C. *William Jennings Bryan*. N.Y.: 1936.


Books used in subsequent chapters are not listed again.

CHAPTER TWO

Thomas Collier Platt was by preference a man of the shadows, and no one book brings him wholly into the light. Harold Gosnell's study of Platt and his machine comes closest but is overweighted with the ephemera of history, and somehow the man himself escapes. Platt's own autobiography, "compiled and edited" by Louis Lang, is an untrustworthy apologia with many entertaining sidelights. The Albany *Argus* of July 1 and 2, 1881, contains the only detailed account of Platt's misadventures in Room 113 of the Delavan House, although the story is hinted at in the New York *World*. William Allen White in his *Masks in a Pageant* devotes two impressionistic chapters to Platt whom he sees as "the Blind Earthworm in Politics." Roosevelt's own autobiography is, in contrast to Platt's, extremely accurate if somewhat muted when he deals with the Easy Boss. By far the best account of Roosevelt's efforts *not* to be vice president is in G. Wallace Chessman's article, "Theodore Roosevelt's Campaign Against the Vice-Presidency."

Bloom, John Morton. *The Republican Roosevelt.* Cambridge: 1954.
Chessman, G. Wallace. *Governor Theodore Roosevelt.* Cambridge: 1965.
———. "Theodore Roosevelt's Campaign against the Vice-Presidency." *The Historian*, Spring, 1953.
Churchill, Allen. *The Roosevelts: American Aristocrats.* N.Y.: 1965.
Depew, Chauncey M. *My Memories of Eighty Years.* N.Y.: 1922.
Gosnell, Harold F. *Boss Platt and his New York Machine.* Chicago: 1924.
Harbaugh, William H. *Power and Responsibility: The Life and Times of Theodore Roosevelt.* N.Y.: 1961.
*The Autobiography of Thomas Collier Platt.* N.Y.: 1910.
Pringle, Henry F. *Theodore Roosevelt, A Biography.* N.Y.: 1931.
Putnam, Carleton. *Theodore Roosevelt, Vol. I. The Formative Years.* N.Y.: 1958.
Sullivan, Mark. *Our Times.* Six volumes. N.Y.: 1926–35.
Thayer, William Roscoe. *Theodore Roosevelt.* Boston: 1919.
*Theodore Roosevelt: An Autobiography.* N.Y.: 1912.

The Albany *Argus.* July, 1881.

CHAPTER THREE

Two recent books have shed new light on the Roosevelt-Taft feud of 1912: William Manners's *TR and Will: A Friendship That Split the Republican Party,* and Frank Kelly's *The Fight for the White*

*House.* Henry Pringle's massive *Life and Times of William Howard Taft,* a superior work to his Roosevelt biography, says all that needs to be and probably will be said about Taft. For an intimate glimpse of the Roosevelt and Taft household years, however, there is nothing like the letters of the military aide and gossipy bachelor Archie Butt to his niece. Butt's death on the *Titanic* in April 1912 just before the beginning of the Bull Moose campaign is a still-felt loss to history.

Bishop, Joseph B. *Theodore Roosevelt and His Time.* N.Y.: 1920.
*Taft and Roosevelt: The Intimate Letters of Archie Butt.* N.Y.: 1930.
Kelly, Frank K. *The Fight for the White House: The Story of 1912.* N.Y.: 1961.
Longworth, Alice Roosevelt. *Crowded Hours.* N.Y.: 1933.
Lorant, Stefan. *The Presidency.* N.Y.: 1951.
Mann, Alpheus T. *William Howard Taft: Chief Justice.* N.Y.: 1965.
Manners, William. *TR and Will: A Friendship That Split the Republican Party.* N.Y.: 1969.
Mowry, George E. *Theodore Roosevelt and the Progressive Movement.* N.Y.: 1938.
Pringle, Henry F. *The Life and Times of William Howard Taft.* N.Y.: 1939.
Ross, Ishbel. *An American Family.* Cleveland: 1964.
Taft, Helen H. *Recollections of Full Years.* N.Y.: 1914.
Thompson, Charles Willis. *Presidents I've Known.* Indianapolis: 1929.
Warner, Hoyt L. *Progressivism in Ohio.* Columbus: 1964.

## CHAPTER FOUR

Willis Johnson's *George Harvey—A Passionate American,* is as indicated by the subtitle, conscious of few flaws in this flawed character. Written the year after Harvey's death, it is still the only source available for the details of his early life. Arthur Link's *Wilson: The Road to the White House,* is a matured and measured corrective to Johnson's overblown enthusiasms. Harvey's lieutenant, William Inglis, who took a strategic part in Wilson's nomination both for governor and president, wrote an accurately detailed account of the inside maneuverings that appeared just before Wilson was elected to his second presidential term.

Baker, Ray Stannard. *Woodrow Wilson: Life and Letters.* Vols. I–V. N.Y.: 1927–1937.
Daniels, Josephus. *The Wilson Era; Years of Peace, 1910–1917.* Chapel Hill: 1946.
Dodd, William. *Woodrow Wilson and His Work.* Garden City: 1920.
Freud, Sigmund and William C. Bullitt. *Thomas Woodrow Wilson—A Psychological Study.* Boston: 1966.

Inglis, William. "Helping to Make a President." *Collier's,* October 7, 14, 21, 1916.
Johnson, Willis Fletcher. *George Harvey: A Passionate Patriot.* Boston: 1929.
Link, Arthur S. *Wilson: The Road to the White House.* Princeton: 1947.
McCombs, William. *Making Woodrow Wilson President.* Fairview Publishing Co., 1920.

## CHAPTER FIVE

There has never been a serious biography of Harry Daugherty, although if all the facts could be unearthed — which seems improbable — it would provide more interesting reading than the standard biographies of his fellow Ohioans, Foraker and Burton. Daugherty himself, stung by Hoover's barbed references to him at the dedication of the Harding mausoleum in 1931, hired the Rev. Thomas Dixon to ghost-write his autobiography-apologia. Dixon was the author of *The Klansman,* from which D. W. Griffith derived the first film epic, *The Birth of a Nation.* The Dixon-Daugherty *Inside Story of the Harding Tragedy* is as interesting for what it omits as for what it includes. The best that can be said is that it is unreliably enlightening. In his own defense Daugherty boasts that he was never convicted of any wrongdoing in any court, but fails to mention that this was due to hung juries. Harding, he concludes, was another Lincoln, but he fails to say how or why.

Wesley Bagby in *The Road to Normalcy* deftly disposes of the myth of the Smoke-Filled Room where the decisions of the 1920 Republican National Convention were reputed to have been made. Documentary sources for Daugherty himself are scanty. He took care of that. The largest collection of material is in the possession of the Ohio Historical Society, letters that Daugherty in his retirement wrote to Ray Baker Harris and Cyril Clemens. The most encompassing, if scarcely the liveliest, biography of Harding is that of Randolph Downes whose 734 pages take Harding only to the threshold of the White House. There is little of Harding's personal life in this enormous book and nothing of his double life. Downes, a professor of history at Toledo University, was forced by his publisher, the Ohio State University Press, to submit his manuscript for censorship to Dr. George Harding, nephew of the late president.

Adams, Samuel Hopkins. *The Incredible Era.* Boston: 1939.
Bagby, Wesley M. *The Road to Normalcy: The Presidential Campaign and the Election of 1920.* Baltimore: 1962.
Cox, James M. *Journey Through My Years.* N.Y.: 1946.

Downes, Randolph. *The Rise of Warren Gamaliel Harding: 1865–1920.* Columbus, Ohio: 1970.
Garraty, John A. *Henry Cabot Lodge.* N.Y.: 1943.
Giglio, James N. "The Political Career of Harry M. Daugherty." Ph.D. dissertation, Ohio State University: 1968.
Hard, Charles E. "The Man Who Did Not Want to Become President." *Northwest Ohio Quarterly* XXXI, No. 3. 1959.
Harris, Ray Baker. *Warren G. Harding: An Account of His Nomination for the Presidency by the Republican Convention of 1920.* Washington, D.C.: 1957.
Hutchinson, William T. *Lowden of Illinois: The Life of Frank O. Lowden.* Chicago: 1957.
Kohlsaat, H. H. *From McKinley to Harding.* N.Y.: 1923.
Murray, Robert K. *The Harding Era: Warren G. Harding and His Administration.* Minneapolis: 1969.
Russell, Francis. *The Shadow of Blooming Grove.* N.Y.: 1968.
Sinclair, Andrew. *The Available Man.* N.Y.: 1965.

Manuscript collections of the Ohio Historical Society: Cyril Clemens, Harry M. Daugherty, Warren G. Harding, Ray Baker Harris, Malcolm Jennings, Frank E. Scobey.

### CHAPTER SIX

Claude Fuess, Coolidge's authorized biographer, once planned to write Stearn's biography but found the life of the Boston merchant so devoid of interest, except for his doglike devotion to Coolidge, that he gave up the project. No one is ever likely to resume it. What little material there is about Stearns is in the libraries of Holy Cross and Amherst Colleges and the Calvin Coolidge Collection of the Northampton Public Library. Cleveland Amory has some snide references to him in *The Proper Bostonians.* At his death the Boston papers, the *Transcript,* the *Herald* and the *Globe,* gave the customary fulsome accounts of his career. It was never his ambition to make his mark in history, and indeed he did not except by proxy.

Ables, Jules. *In the Time of Silent Cal.* N.Y.: 1969.
Amory, Cleveland. *The Proper Bostonians.* N.Y.: 1947.
*The Autobiography of Calvin Coolidge.* Boston: 1929.
Coolidge, Calvin. *Have Faith in Massachusetts.* Boston: 1919.
Fuess, Claude M. *Calvin Coolidge, The Man from Vermont.* Boston: 1940.
Hennessey, Michael. *Four Decades of Massachusetts Politics: 1890–1935.* Norwood, Mass.: 1935.
Lathem, Edward C. (editor). *Your Son, Calvin Coolidge. A Selection of Letters from Calvin Coolidge to His Father.* Montpelier, Vermont: 1968.

McCoy, Donald R. *Calvin Coolidge, The Quiet President.* N.Y.: 1967.
Russell, Francis. *A City in Terror. 1919—The Boston Police Strike.* N.Y.: 1975.
———. *The Great Interlude.* N.Y.: 1964.
White, William Allen. *A Puritan in Babylon. The Story of Calvin Coolidge.* N.Y.: 1938.
Manuscript collections: Amherst College Library, Holy Cross Library, Northhampton Public Library.

## CHAPTER SEVEN

The key account of Louis Howe, one that was years in the making, is that of Professor Alfred Rollins's *Roosevelt and Howe.* So intricate in detail is it, however, that much will be of concern only to close students of the period. Lela Stiles, who went to work as one of Howe's secretaries in 1928 and stayed with him until his death, gives the most personal account of Howe during the 1928 campaign and afterward in the White House years. There is also much insight in John Keller's *Saturday Evening Post* article of 1940. Keller, a young Dartmouth graduate, was hired to read to Howe in his last illness. References to Howe are also enlightening in the first volume of Joseph Lash's biography of Eleanor Roosevelt. Passing references to Howe elsewhere are too numerous to mention in detail.

Burns, James MacGregor. *Roosevelt: The Lion and the Fox.* N.Y.: 1956.
Busch, Noel F. *What Manner of Man.* N.Y.: 1944.
Daniels, Jonathan. *The End of Innocence.* Philadelphia: 1954.
Farley, James A. *Jim Farley's Story.* N.Y.: 1948.
Farr, Finis. *FDR.* New Rochelle, N.Y.: 1972.
Flynn, Edward J. *You're the Boss.* N.Y.: 1947.
Freidel, Frank. *Franklin D. Roosevelt.* Vols. 1–4. Boston: 1952–1973.
Gunther, John. *Roosevelt in Retrospect, A Profile in History.* N.Y.: 1950.
Josephson, Matthew and Hannah. *Al Smith: Hero of the Cities.* Boston: 1969.
Keller, John, with Joe Boldt. "Franklin's On His Own Now." *Saturday Evening Post,* Oct. 12, 1940.
Lash, Joseph P. *Eleanor and Franklin.* N.Y.: 1971.
Moley, Raymond. *27 Makers of Politics in Perspective.* N.Y.: 1949.
Perkins, Frances. *The Roosevelt I Knew.* N.Y.: 1946.
Rollins, Alfred B., Jr. *Roosevelt and Howe.* N.Y.: 1962.
*The Autobiography of Eleanor Roosevelt.* N.Y.: 1961.
Roosevelt, Elliott, and Brough, James. *An Untold Story: The Roosevelts of Hyde Park.* N.Y.: 1973.

———. "The Most Unforgettable Character I've Met." *Reader's Digest.* Feb., 1953.
Schlesinger, Arthur M., Jr. *The Crisis of the Old Order.* Boston: 1957.
———. *The Coming of the New Deal.* Boston: 1958.
Smith, Gene. *The Shattered Dream.* N.Y.: 1970.
Stiles, Lela. *The Man Behind Roosevelt: The Story of Louis McHenry Howe.* N.Y.: 1954.
Tugwell, Rexford G. *The Brains Trust.* N.Y.: 1968.

## CHAPTER EIGHT

Of the making of books on the Kennedys there seems to be no end. Over two hundred have already been published, ranging from the adulatory to the defamatory, the latter representing a very minor percentage. Richard Whalen's was the first full-length biography of the senior Joseph Kennedy. An encompassing book, it is limited to a degree by what cannot be told within our generation about this devious, dominant man. David Koskoff's later biography tells somewhat more but still hesitates. Bill Duncliffe's earlier biography appeared as a series of articles in the Boston *Record American* and was not reprinted. It has neither the ampltiude nor the accuracy of Whalen's and Koskoff's books, but does contain some facts that the others missed. *The Fruitful Bough,* a series of brief recollections by many friends and acquaintances of Joseph Kennedy, privately printed by the Kennedy family, gives him a set of wings with which he is not wholly comfortable. There will undoubtedly be additional mention of him as further facts are released or emerge.

Burns, James MacGregor. *John Kennedy: A Political Profile.* N.Y.: 1961.
Cameron, Gail. *Rose: A Biography of Rose Kennedy.* N.Y.: 1971.
Carbozi, George, Jr. *The Hidden Sides of Jacqueline Kennedy.* N.Y.: 1968.
Cutler, John Henry. *"Honey Fitz." Three Steps to the White House.* N.Y.: 1962.
Dallas, Rita with Jeanry Ratcliffe. *The Kennedy Case.* N.Y.: 1973.
Damore, Leo. *The Cape Cod Years of John Fitzgerald Kennedy.* N.Y.: 1967.
Dinneen, Joseph F. *The Kennedy Family.* Boston: 1959.
Fay, Paul B., Jr. *The Pleasure of His Company.* N.Y.: 1973.
Gallagher, Mary B. *My Life with Jacqueline Kennedy.* N.Y.: 1969.
Healey, P. F. "The Senate's Gay Young Bachelor." *Saturday Evening Post,* June 13, 1953.
Kennedy, Rose. *Times to Remember.* N.Y.: 1974.
Koskoff, David E. *Joseph P. Kennedy—A Life and Times.* N.Y.: 1974.

Lee, Raymond E. *The London Journal of General Raymond E. Lee.* Ed. James Leutze. Boston: 1971.
Lincoln, Evelyn. *My Twelve Years with Kennedy.* N.Y.: 1965.
McCarthy, Joe. *The Remarkable Kennedys.* N.Y.: 1960.
Manchester, William. *The Death of a President.* N.Y.: 1967.
———. *Portrait of a President.* Boston: 1962.
Martin, Ralph G. and Plant, Ed. *Front Runner, Dark Horse.* N.Y.: 1960.
Nicolson, Harold. *The War Years 1939–1945.* N.Y.: 1967.
Schlesinger, Arthur M., Jr. *A Thousand Days: John F. Kennedy in the White House.* Boston: 1965.
Searle, Hank. *The Lost Prince: Young Joe, the Forgotten Kennedy.* N.Y.: 1969.
Sorenson, Theodore C. *Kennedy.* N.Y.: 1965.
Sparks, Fred. *The $20,000,000 Honeymoon.* N.Y.: 1970.
Thayer, Mary Van Rensselaer. *Jacqueline Bouvier Kennedy.* N.Y.: 1961.
de Toledano, Ralph. *RFK: The Man Who Would Be President.* N.Y.: 1967.
Vidal, Gore. "The Holy Family." *Esquire,* April, 1967.
Whalen, Richard. *The Founding Father: The Story of Joseph P. Kennedy.* N.Y.: 1964.
White, Theodore. *The Making of a President.* N.Y.: 1960.
*The Fruitful Bough.* Privately printed. Boston: 1955.
Boston *Record American.* Series of articles by Bill Duncliffe. January, 1964.
*The Progressive,* December, 1964.

# Index

# Picture Credits

*Page*

viii Originally published by De Witt, 1898. Courtesy of the New York Public Library Branch Libraries Picture Collection.

42 From *The Verdict*, April 16, 1900. Reprinted from *Boss Platt and His New York Machine* by Harold Gosnell by permission of The University of Chicago Press. Copyright 1924 by the University of Chicago.

86 Bernard Partridge in *Punch*, June 17, 1903.

130 F. G. Cooper in *Colliers*, February 3, 1912.

186 By permission © 1922 old *Life* magazine.

226 Walter "Norman" Ritchie in *The Boston Post*. Courtesy of the Calvin Coolidge Memorial Room of Forbes Library, Northampton, Mass.

266 S. Robles in *The New York Review of Reviews*, April 1, 1935. Courtesy of The Franklin D. Roosevelt Library.

324 Goldsmith in *The Boston Post*. Courtesy of the John F. Kennedy Library.